A FADE OF LIGHT

BY NATE FAKES

WEST
MARGIN
PRESS

Library of Congress Cataloging-in-Publication Data

Names: Fakes, Nate, author, artist.
Title: A fade of light / Nate Fakes.
Description: Berkeley, CA : West Margin Press, 2022. | Summary: "A memoir of a cartoonist's formative experiences in life and his close relationship with his stepdad, who is later diagnosed with FTD" —Provided by publisher.
Identifiers: LCCN 2022009837 (print) | LCCN 2022009838 (ebook) | ISBN 9781513134994 (paperback) | ISBN 9781513135007 (hardback) | ISBN 9781513135014 (ebook)
Subjects: LCSH: Fakes, Nate. | Cartoonists--United States--Biography. | Stepfathers--United States--Biography. | Frontotemporal dementia--Patients--Biography.
Classification: LCC PN6727.F29 F33 2022 (print) | LCC PN6727.F29 (ebook) | DDC 741.5/973092 [B]--dc23/eng/20220311
LC record available at https://lccn.loc.gov/2022009837
LC ebook record available at https://lccn.loc.gov/2022009838

Printed in China
26 25 24 23 22 1 2 3 4 5

Published by West Margin Press®

WEST
MARGIN
PRESS
WestMarginPress.com

Proudly distributed by Ingram Publisher Services

WEST MARGIN PRESS
Publishing Director: Jennifer Newens
Marketing Manager: Alice Wertheimer
Project Specialist: Micaela Clark
Editor: Olivia Ngai
Design & Production: Rachel Lopez Metzger

FOR RON

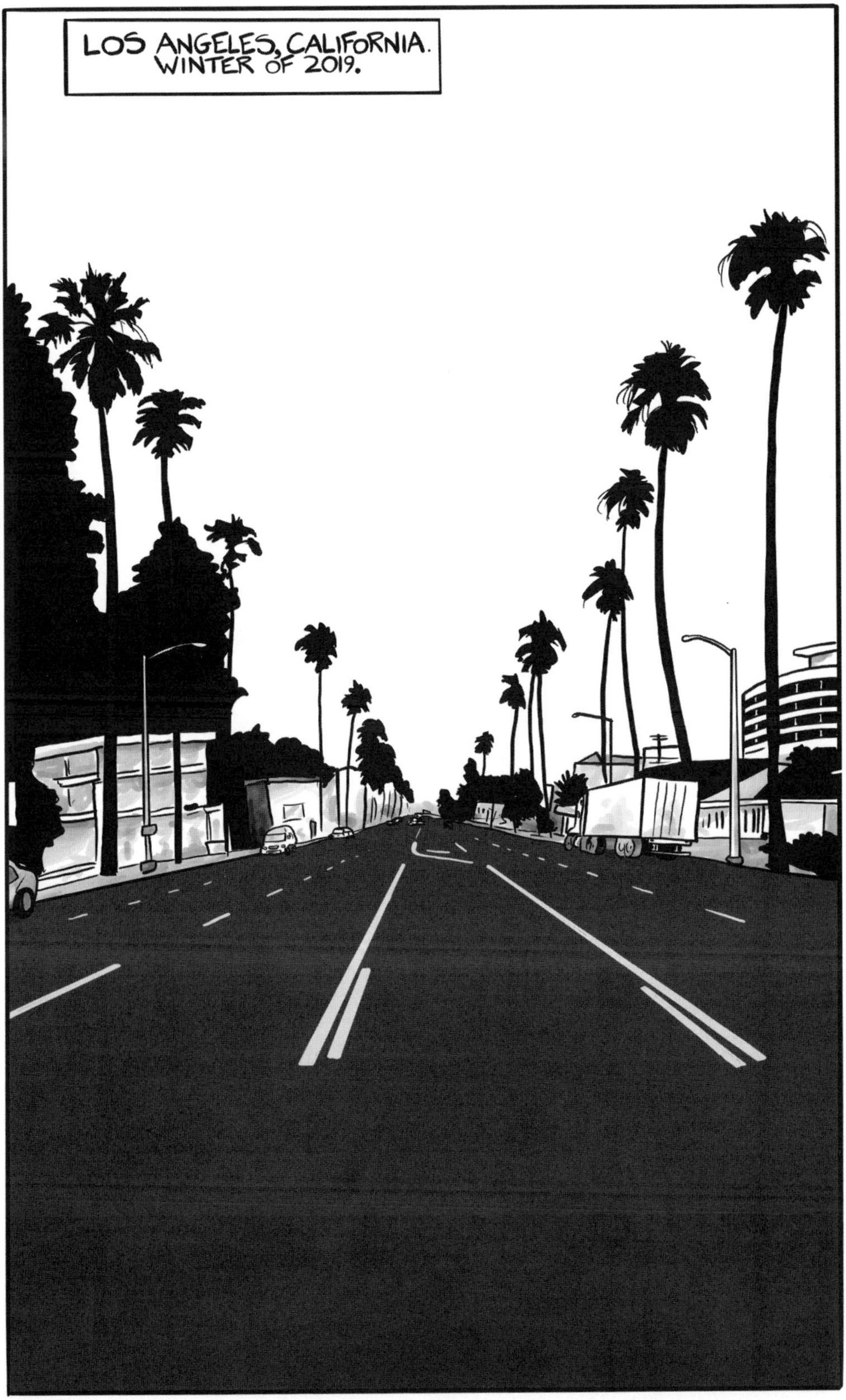
LOS ANGELES, CALIFORNIA.
WINTER OF 2019.

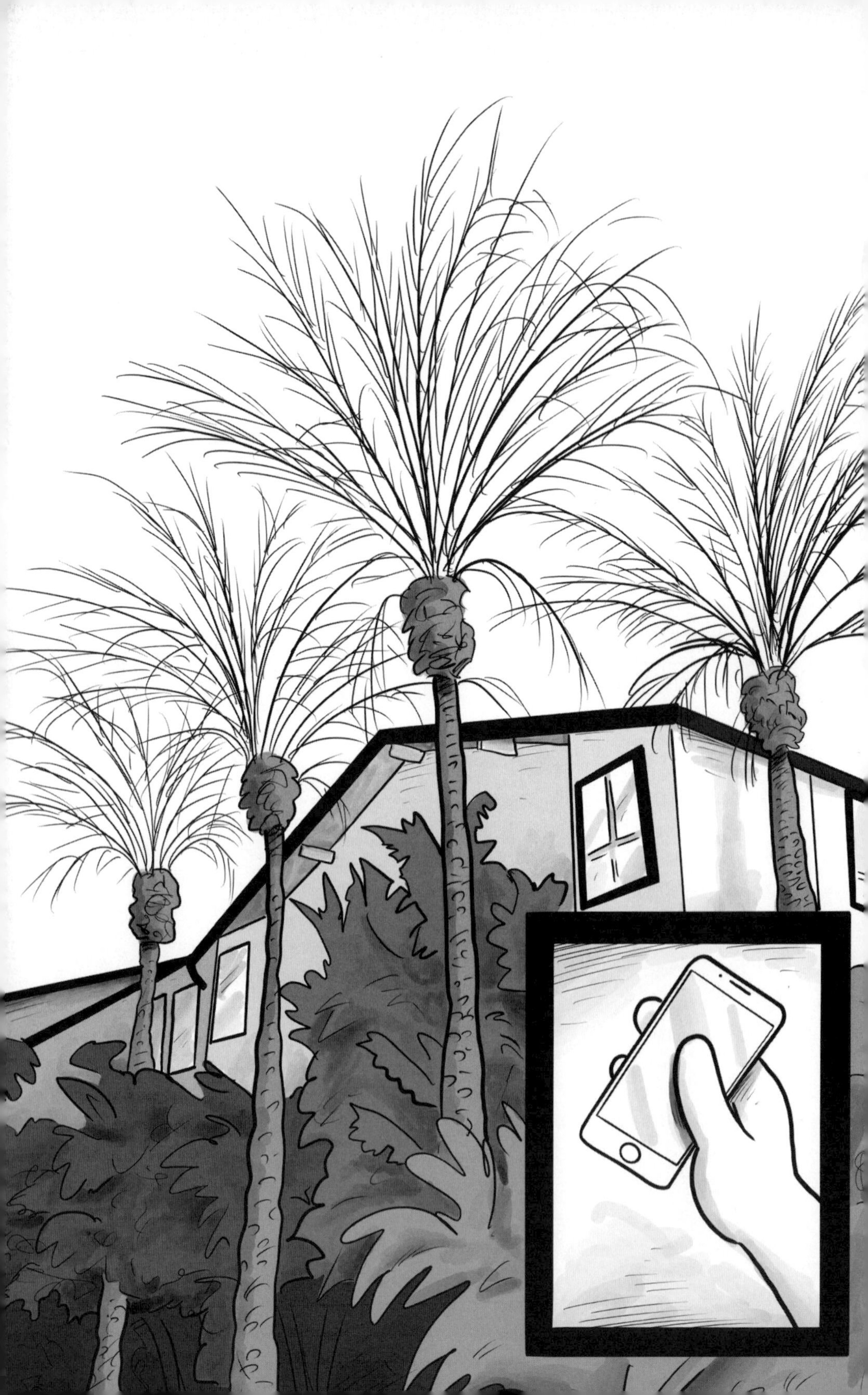

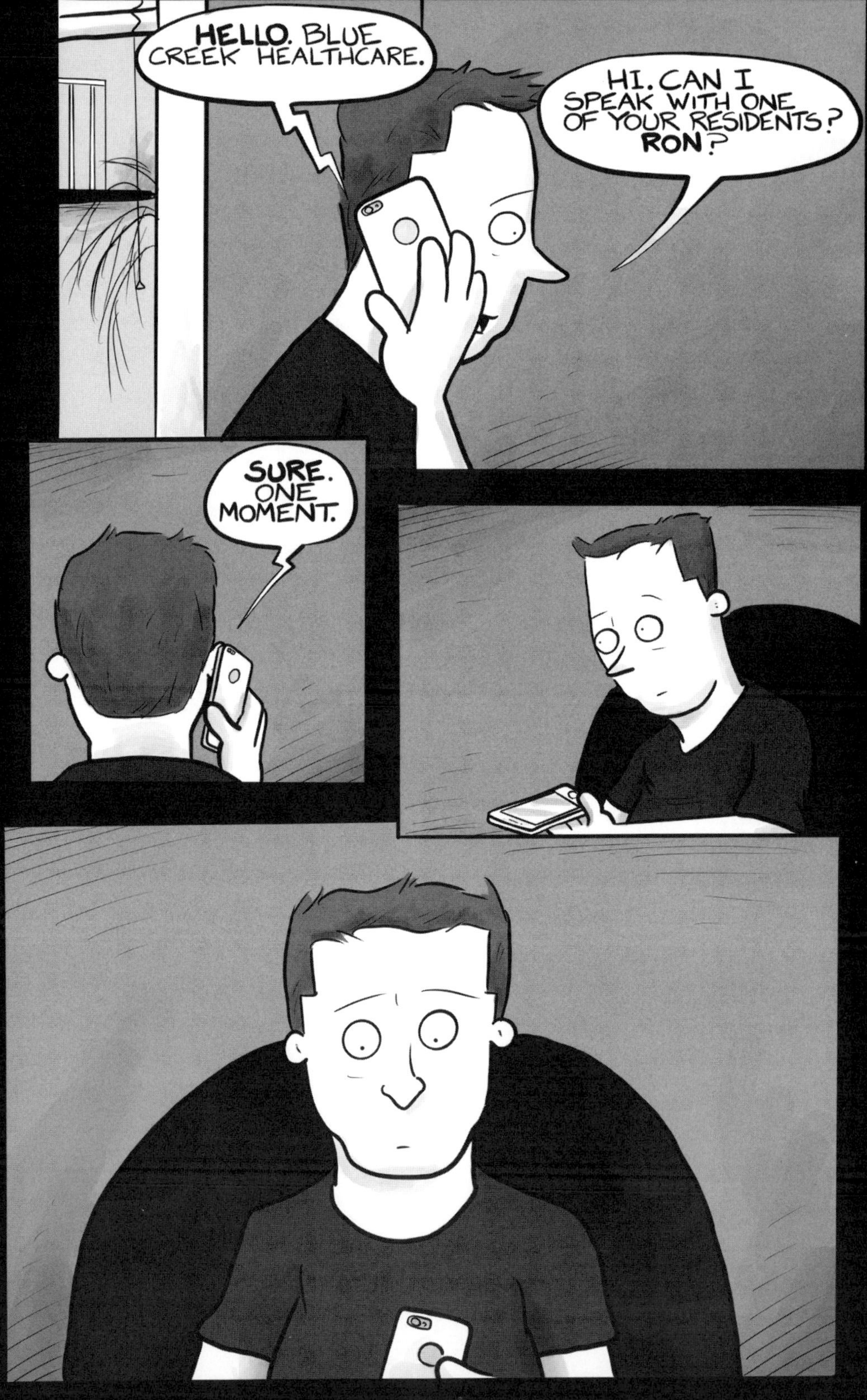
HELLO. BLUE CREEK HEALTHCARE.
HI. CAN I SPEAK WITH ONE OF YOUR RESIDENTS? RON?
SURE. ONE MOMENT.

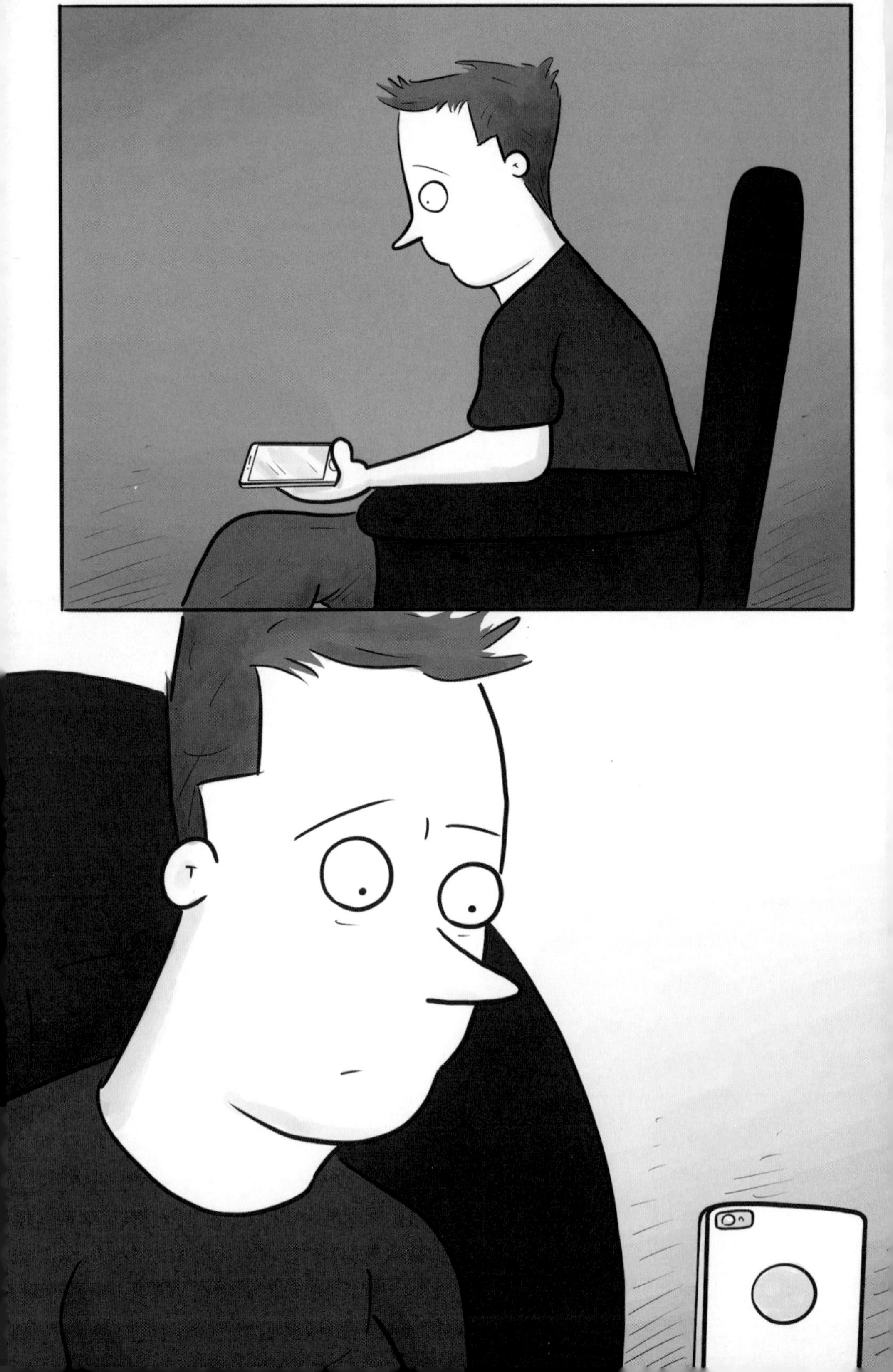

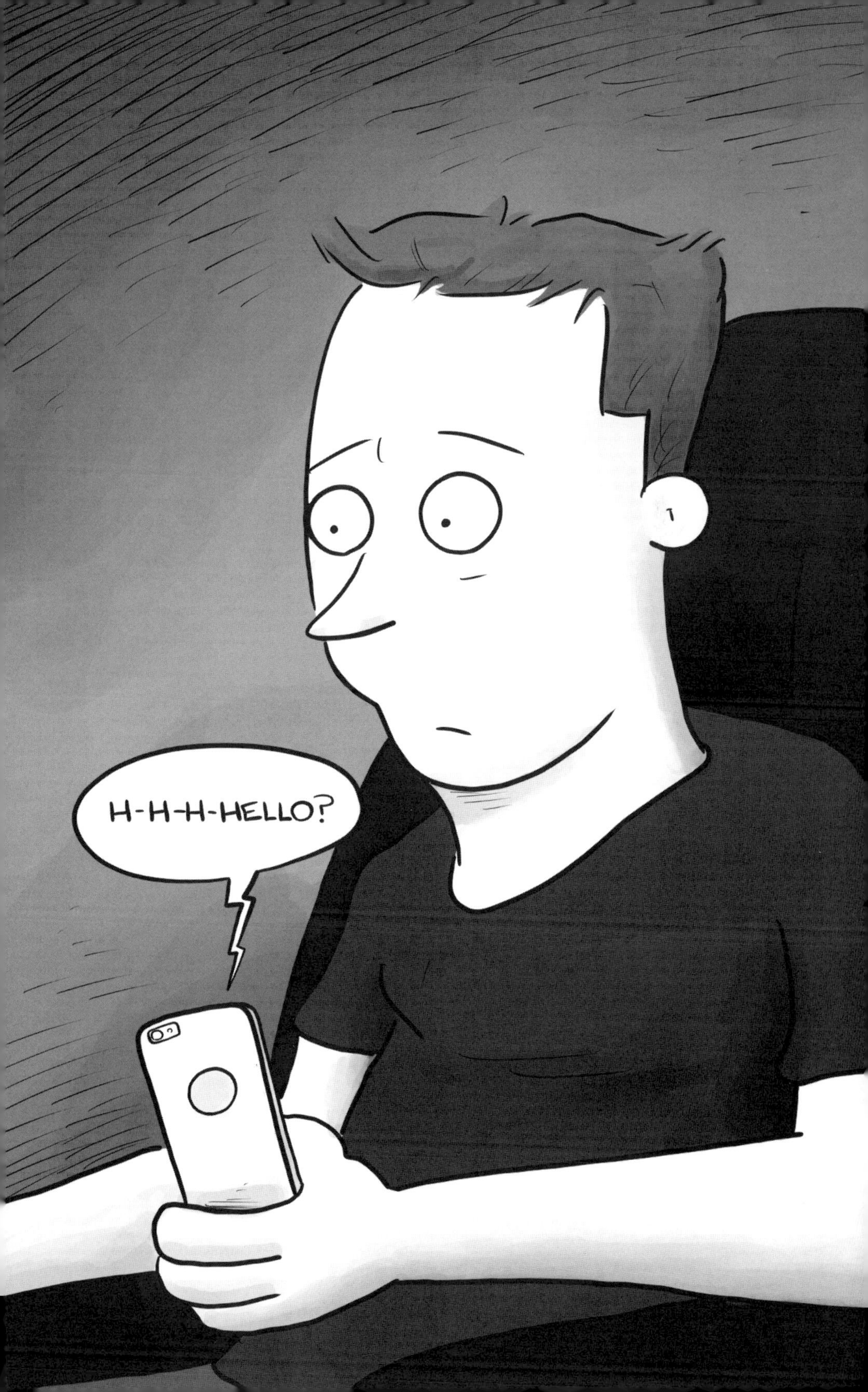
H-H-H-HELLO?

PART ONE
MEET RON

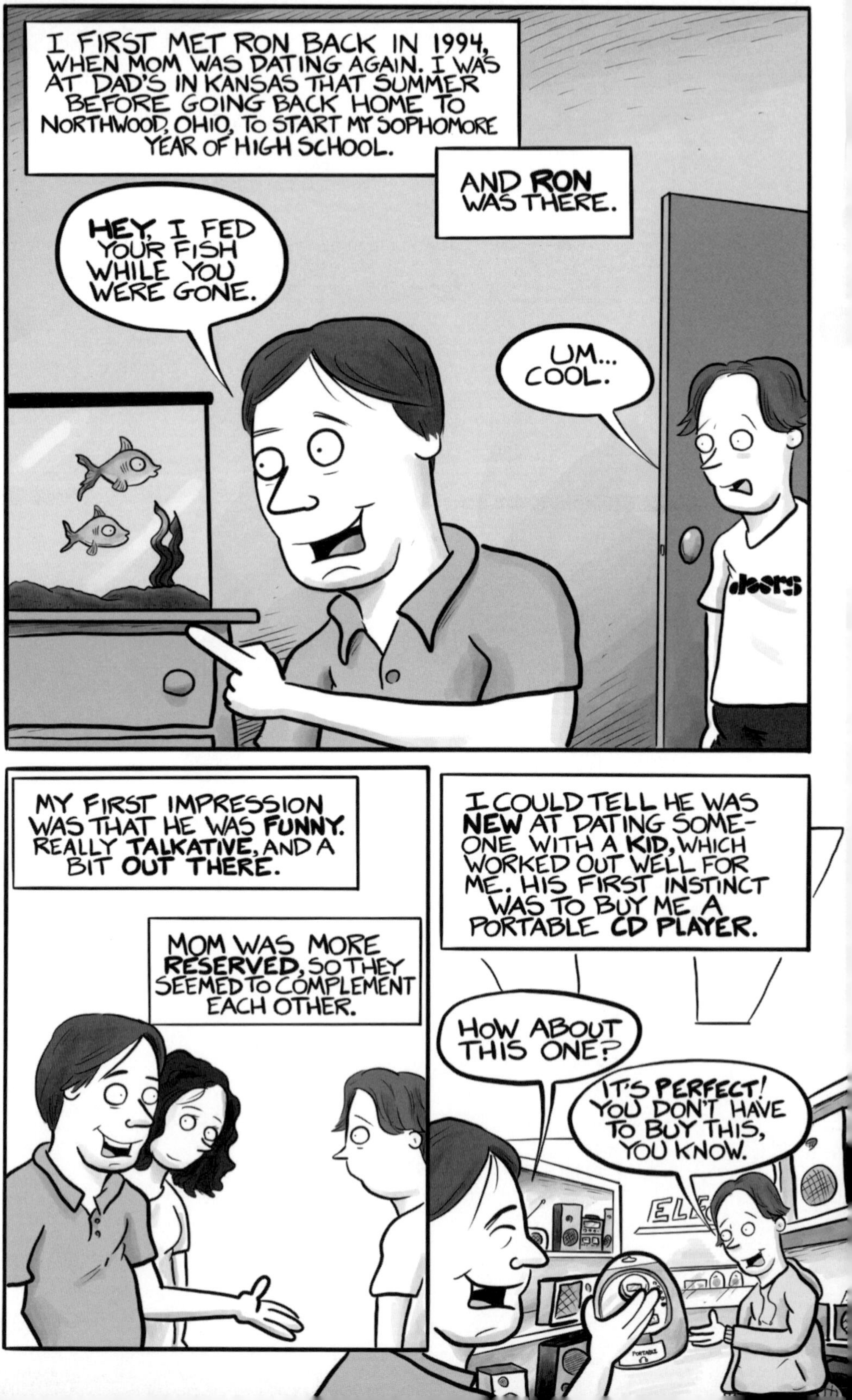
I FIRST MET RON BACK IN 1994, WHEN MOM WAS DATING AGAIN. I WAS AT DAD'S IN KANSAS THAT SUMMER BEFORE GOING BACK HOME TO NORTHWOOD, OHIO, TO START MY SOPHOMORE YEAR OF HIGH SCHOOL.
AND RON WAS THERE.
HEY, I FED YOUR FISH WHILE YOU WERE GONE.
UM... COOL.
MY FIRST IMPRESSION WAS THAT HE WAS FUNNY. REALLY TALKATIVE, AND A BIT OUT THERE.
MOM WAS MORE RESERVED, SO THEY SEEMED TO COMPLEMENT EACH OTHER.
I COULD TELL HE WAS NEW AT DATING SOME-ONE WITH A KID, WHICH WORKED OUT WELL FOR ME. HIS FIRST INSTINCT WAS TO BUY ME A PORTABLE CD PLAYER.
HOW ABOUT THIS ONE?
IT'S PERFECT! YOU DON'T HAVE TO BUY THIS, YOU KNOW.

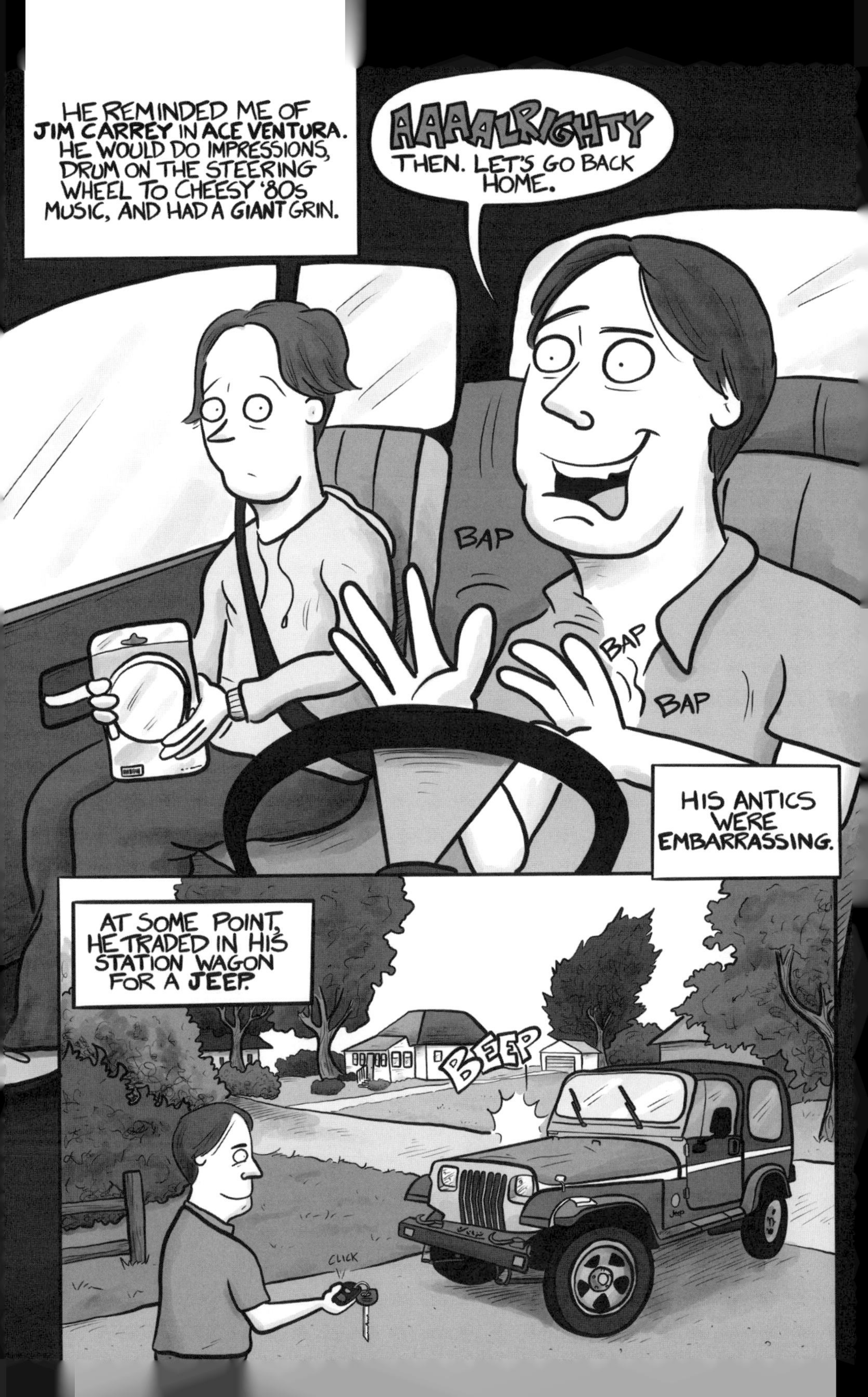
HE REMINDED ME OF JIM CARREY IN ACE VENTURA. HE WOULD DO IMPRESSIONS, DRUM ON THE STEERING WHEEL TO CHEESY '80s MUSIC, AND HAD A GIANT GRIN.
AAAALRIGHTY THEN. LET'S GO BACK HOME.
BAP
BAP
BAP
HIS ANTICS WERE EMBARRASSING.
AT SOME POINT, HE TRADED IN HIS STATION WAGON FOR A JEEP.
BEEP
CLICK

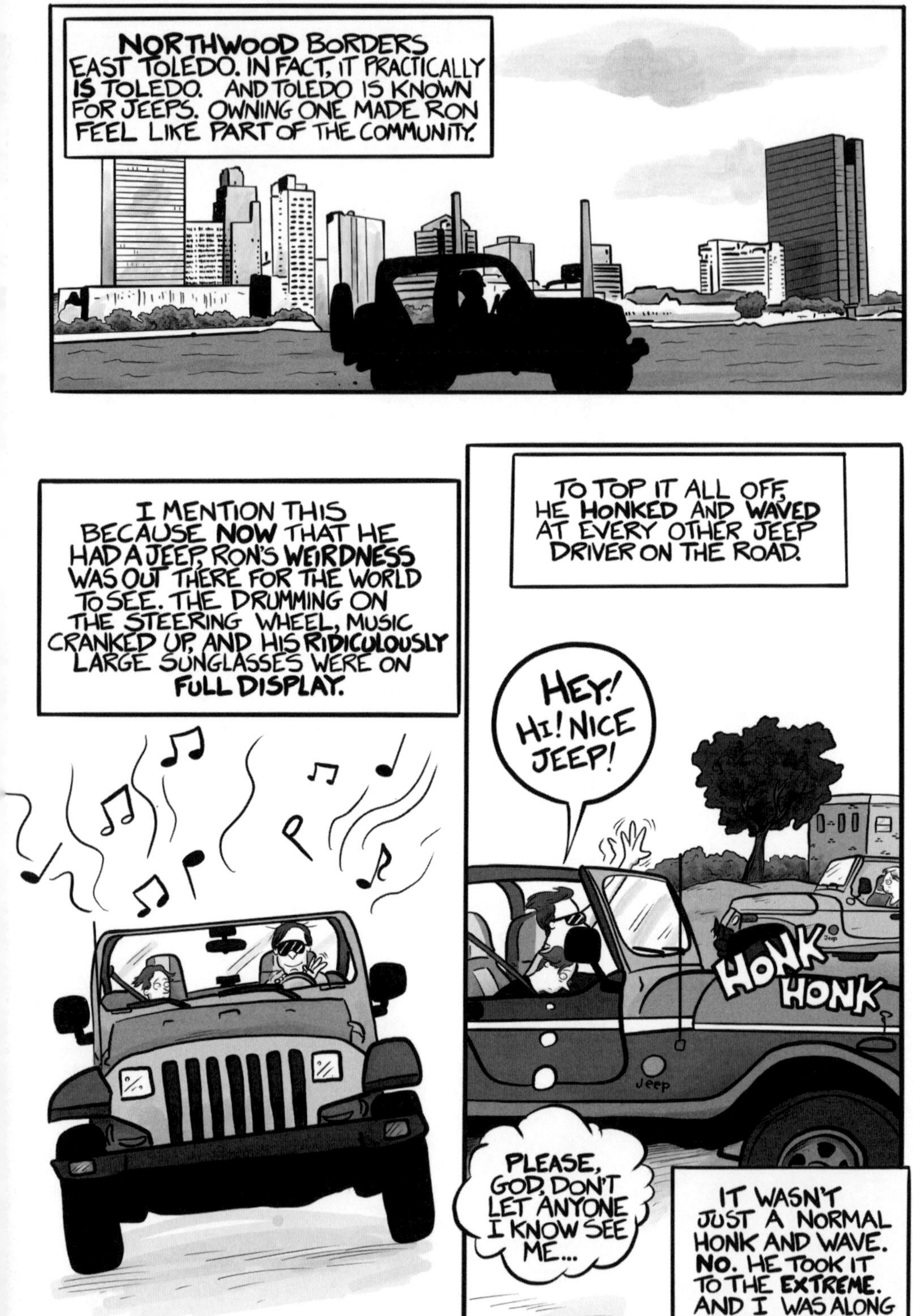
NORTHWOOD BORDERS EAST TOLEDO. IN FACT, IT PRACTICALLY IS TOLEDO. AND TOLEDO IS KNOWN FOR JEEPS. OWNING ONE MADE RON FEEL LIKE PART OF THE COMMUNITY.
I MENTION THIS BECAUSE NOW THAT HE HAD A JEEP, RON'S WEIRDNESS WAS OUT THERE FOR THE WORLD TO SEE. THE DRUMMING ON THE STEERING WHEEL, MUSIC CRANKED UP, AND HIS RIDICULOUSLY LARGE SUNGLASSES WERE ON FULL DISPLAY.
TO TOP IT ALL OFF, HE HONKED AND WAVED AT EVERY OTHER JEEP DRIVER ON THE ROAD.
HEY! HI! NICE JEEP!
HONK HONK
Jeep
PLEASE, GOD, DON'T LET ANYONE I KNOW SEE ME...
IT WASN'T JUST A NORMAL HONK AND WAVE. NO. HE TOOK IT TO THE EXTREME. AND I WAS ALONG FOR THE RIDE.

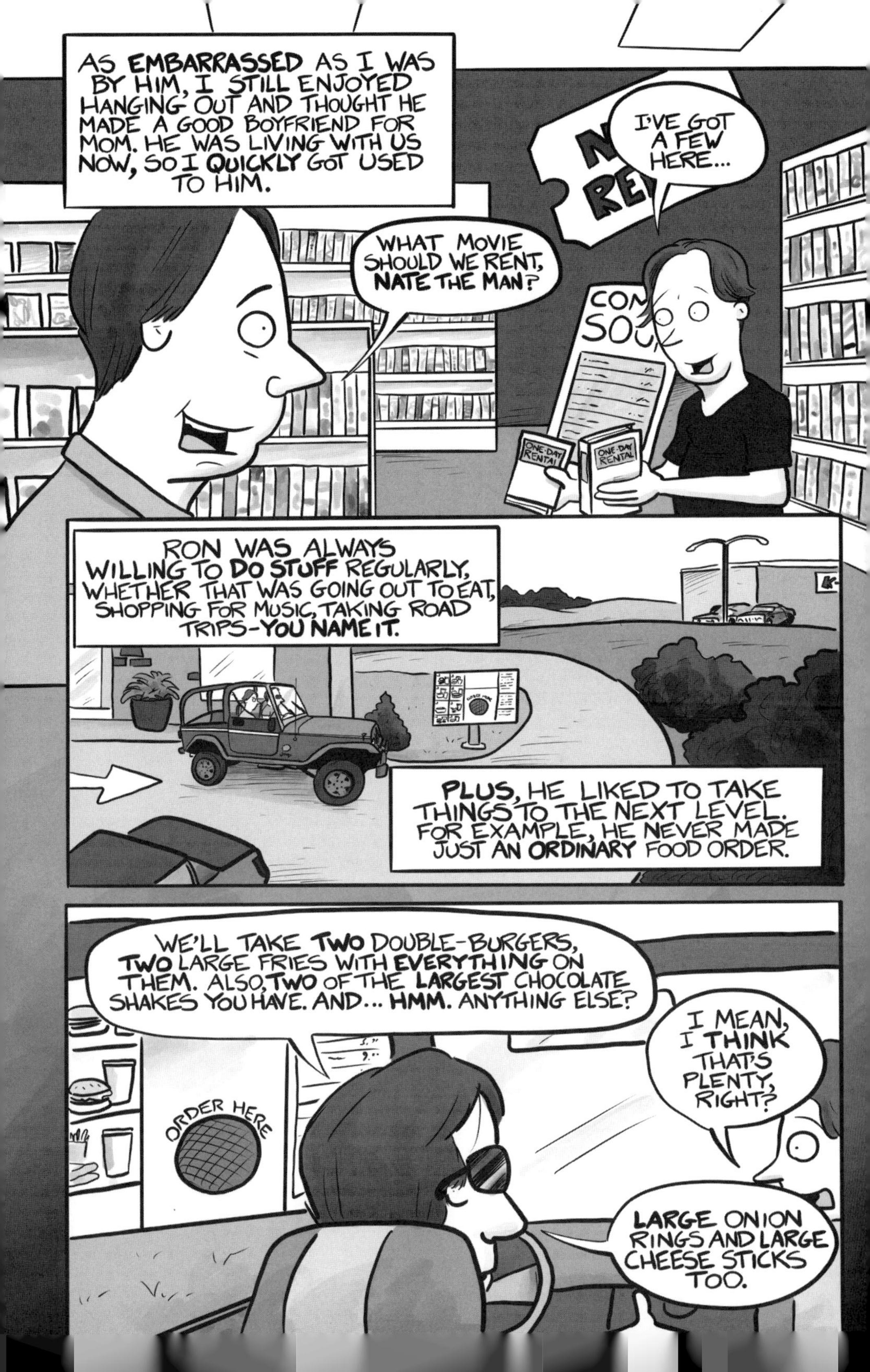
AS EMBARRASSED AS I WAS BY HIM, I STILL ENJOYED HANGING OUT AND THOUGHT HE MADE A GOOD BOYFRIEND FOR MOM. HE WAS LIVING WITH US NOW, SO I QUICKLY GOT USED TO HIM.
I'VE GOT A FEW HERE...
WHAT MOVIE SHOULD WE RENT, NATE THE MAN?
ONE-DAY RENTAL
ONE-DAY RENTAL
RON WAS ALWAYS WILLING TO DO STUFF REGULARLY, WHETHER THAT WAS GOING OUT TO EAT, SHOPPING FOR MUSIC, TAKING ROAD TRIPS–YOU NAME IT.
PLUS, HE LIKED TO TAKE THINGS TO THE NEXT LEVEL. FOR EXAMPLE, HE NEVER MADE JUST AN ORDINARY FOOD ORDER.
WE'LL TAKE TWO DOUBLE-BURGERS, TWO LARGE FRIES WITH EVERYTHING ON THEM. ALSO, TWO OF THE LARGEST CHOCOLATE SHAKES YOU HAVE. AND... HMM. ANYTHING ELSE?
I MEAN, I THINK THAT'S PLENTY, RIGHT?
ORDER HERE
LARGE ONION RINGS AND LARGE CHEESE STICKS TOO.

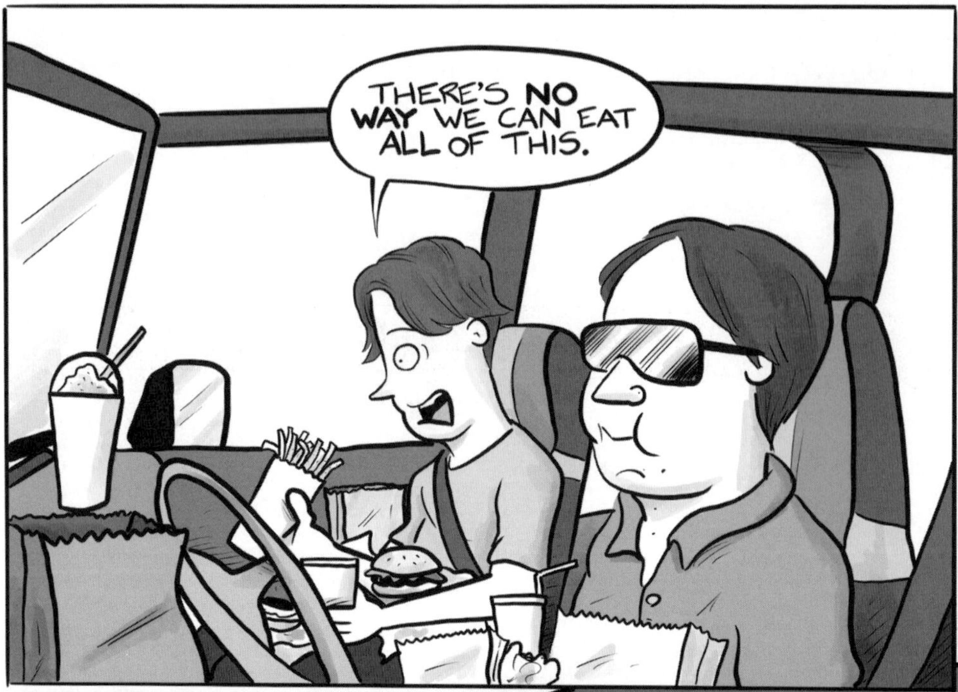
THERE'S NO WAY WE CAN EAT ALL OF THIS.

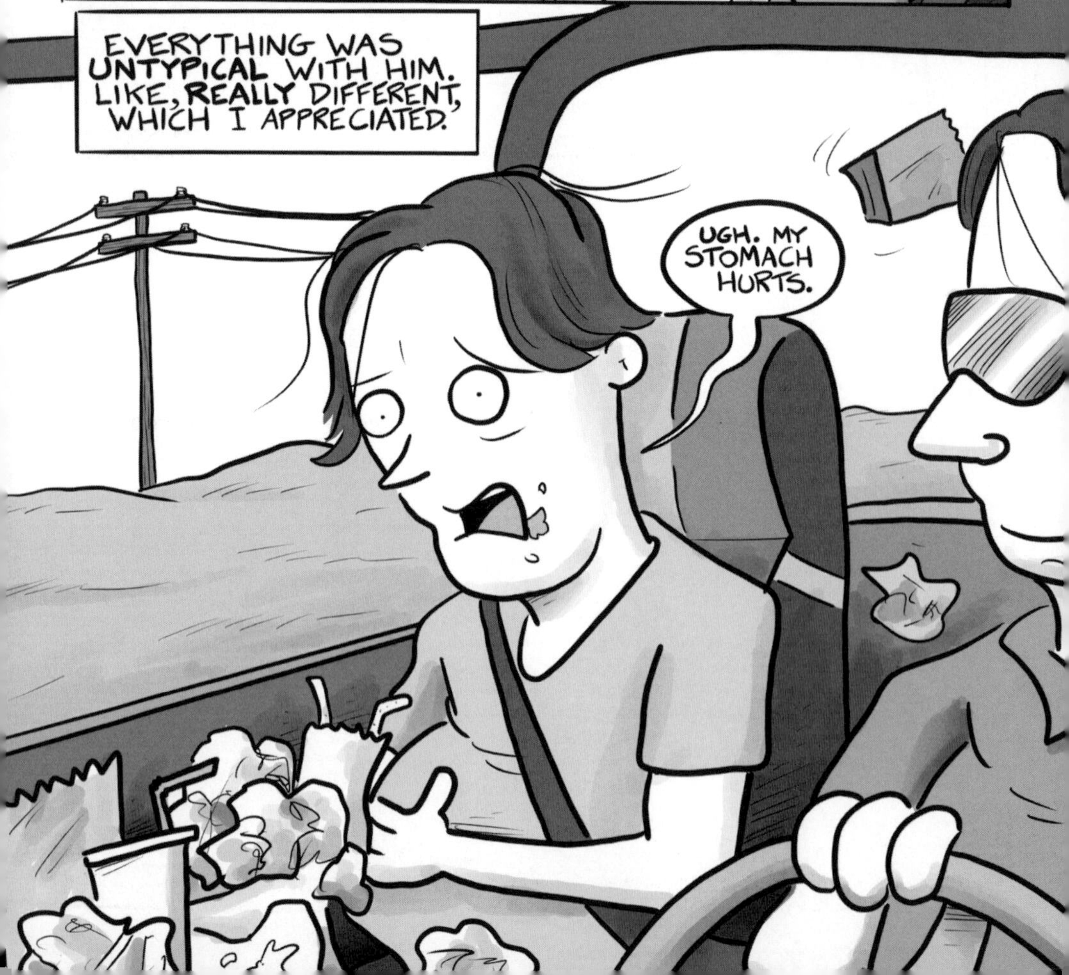
EVERYTHING WAS UNTYPICAL WITH HIM. LIKE, REALLY DIFFERENT, WHICH I APPRECIATED.
UGH. MY STOMACH HURTS.

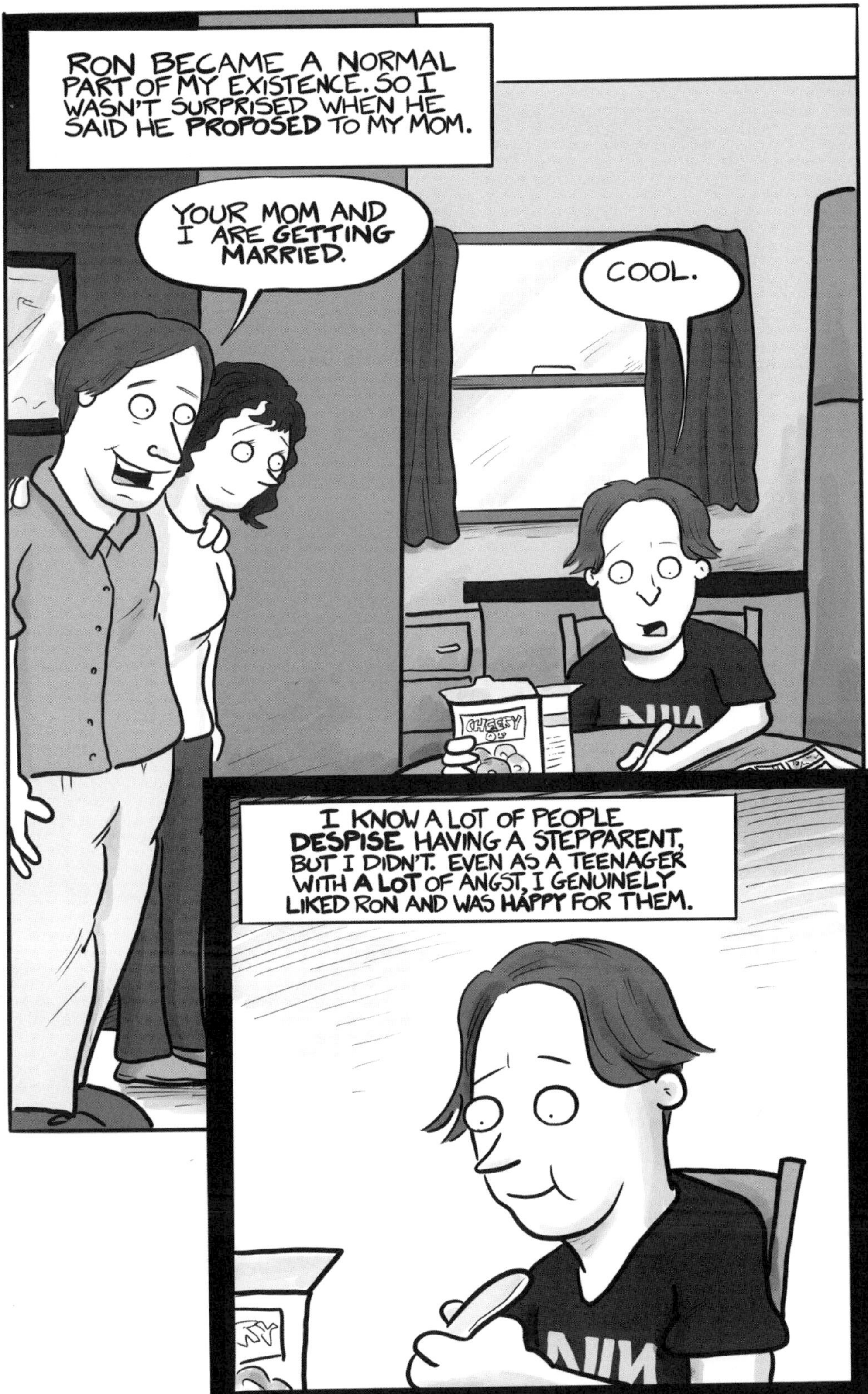
RON BECAME A NORMAL PART OF MY EXISTENCE. SO I WASN'T SURPRISED WHEN HE SAID HE PROPOSED TO MY MOM.
YOUR MOM AND I ARE GETTING MARRIED.
COOL.
CHEERY O'S
I KNOW A LOT OF PEOPLE DESPISE HAVING A STEPPARENT, BUT I DIDN'T. EVEN AS A TEENAGER WITH A LOT OF ANGST, I GENUINELY LIKED RON AND WAS HAPPY FOR THEM.

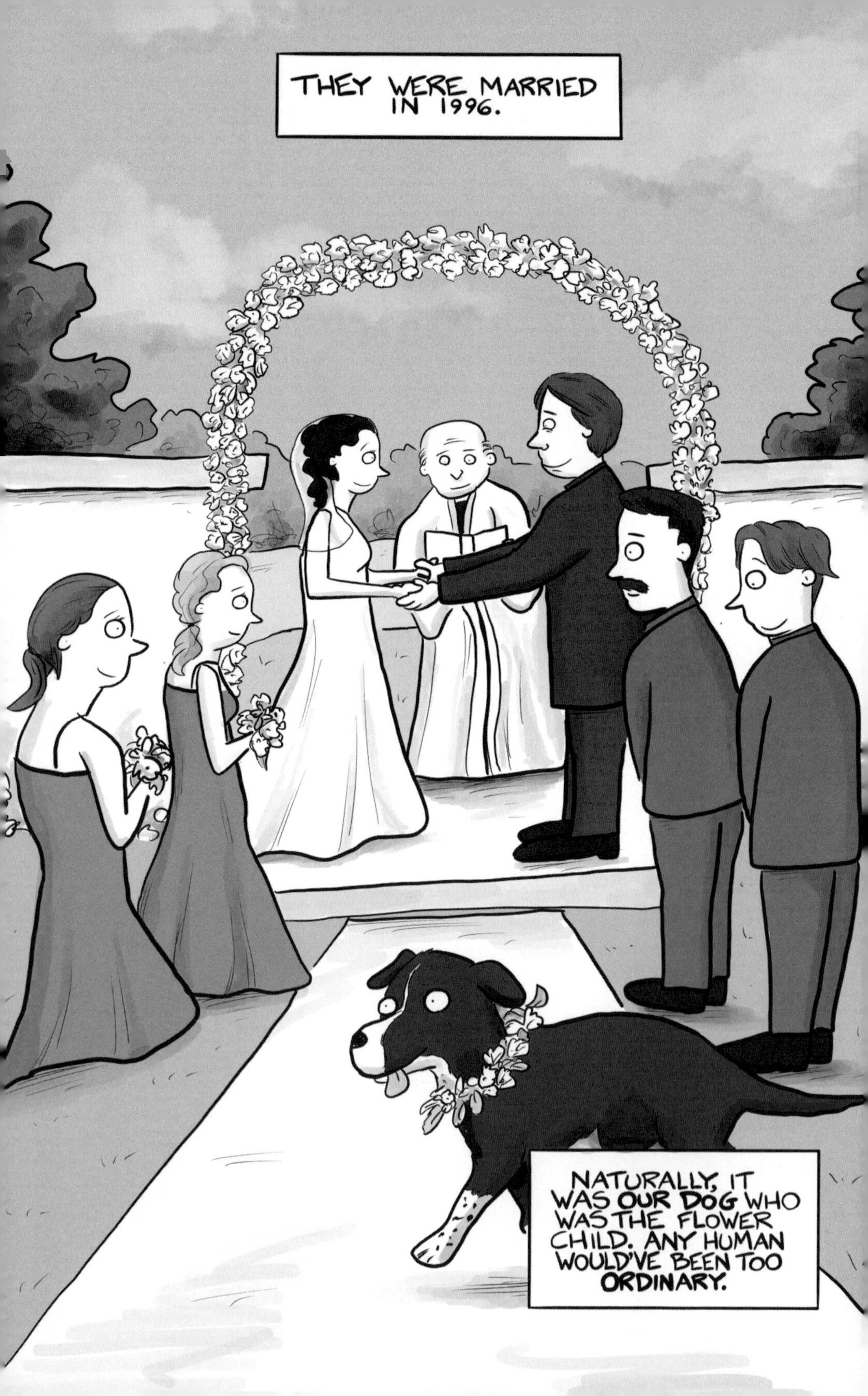
THEY WERE MARRIED IN 1996.
NATURALLY, IT WAS **OUR DOG** WHO WAS THE FLOWER CHILD. ANY HUMAN WOULD'VE BEEN TOO **ORDINARY**.

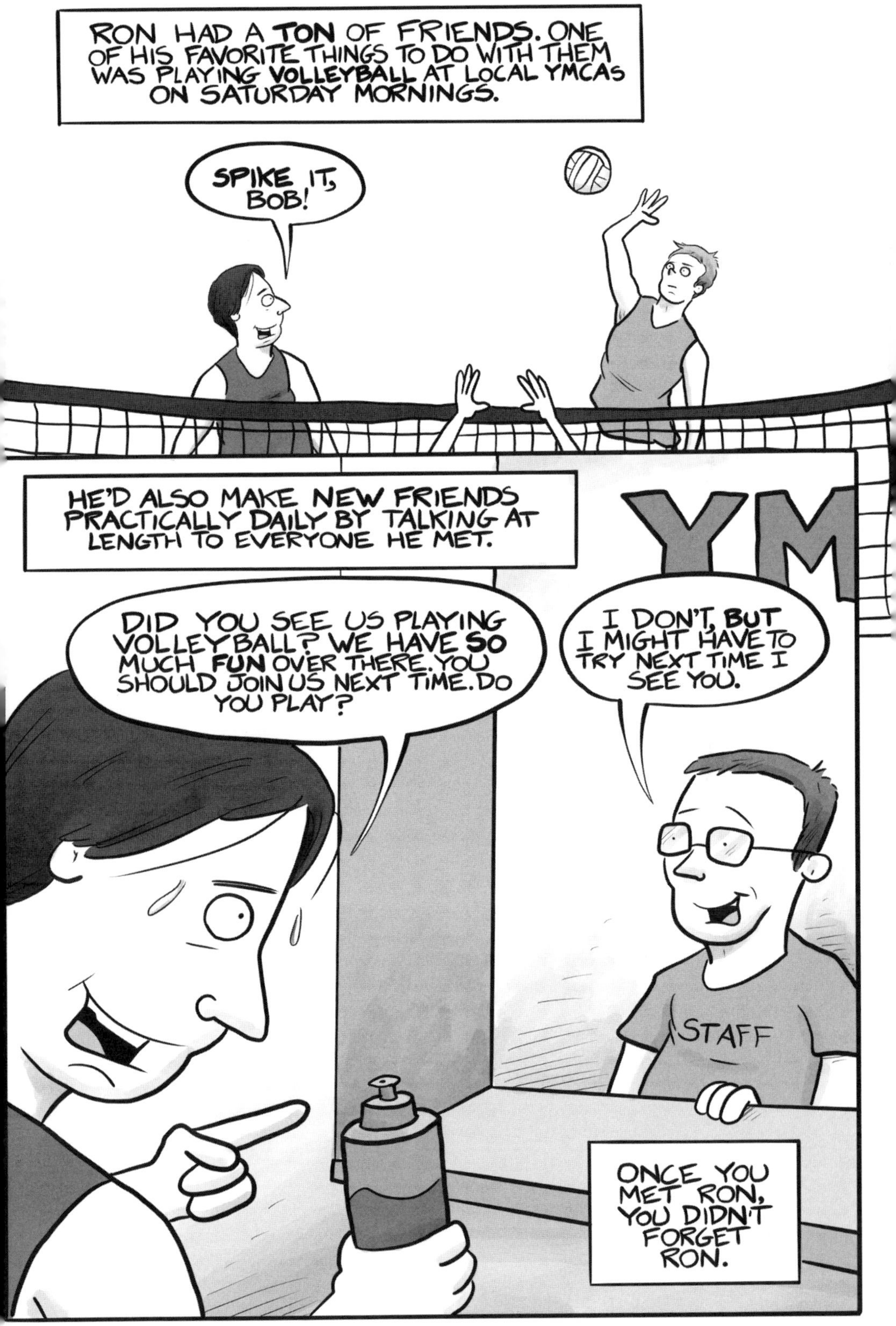
RON HAD A TON OF FRIENDS. ONE OF HIS FAVORITE THINGS TO DO WITH THEM WAS PLAYING VOLLEYBALL AT LOCAL YMCAS ON SATURDAY MORNINGS.
SPIKE IT, BOB!
HE'D ALSO MAKE NEW FRIENDS PRACTICALLY DAILY BY TALKING AT LENGTH TO EVERYONE HE MET.
YM
DID YOU SEE US PLAYING VOLLEYBALL? WE HAVE SO MUCH FUN OVER THERE. YOU SHOULD JOIN US NEXT TIME. DO YOU PLAY?
I DON'T, BUT I MIGHT HAVE TO TRY NEXT TIME I SEE YOU.
STAFF
ONCE YOU MET RON, YOU DIDN'T FORGET RON.

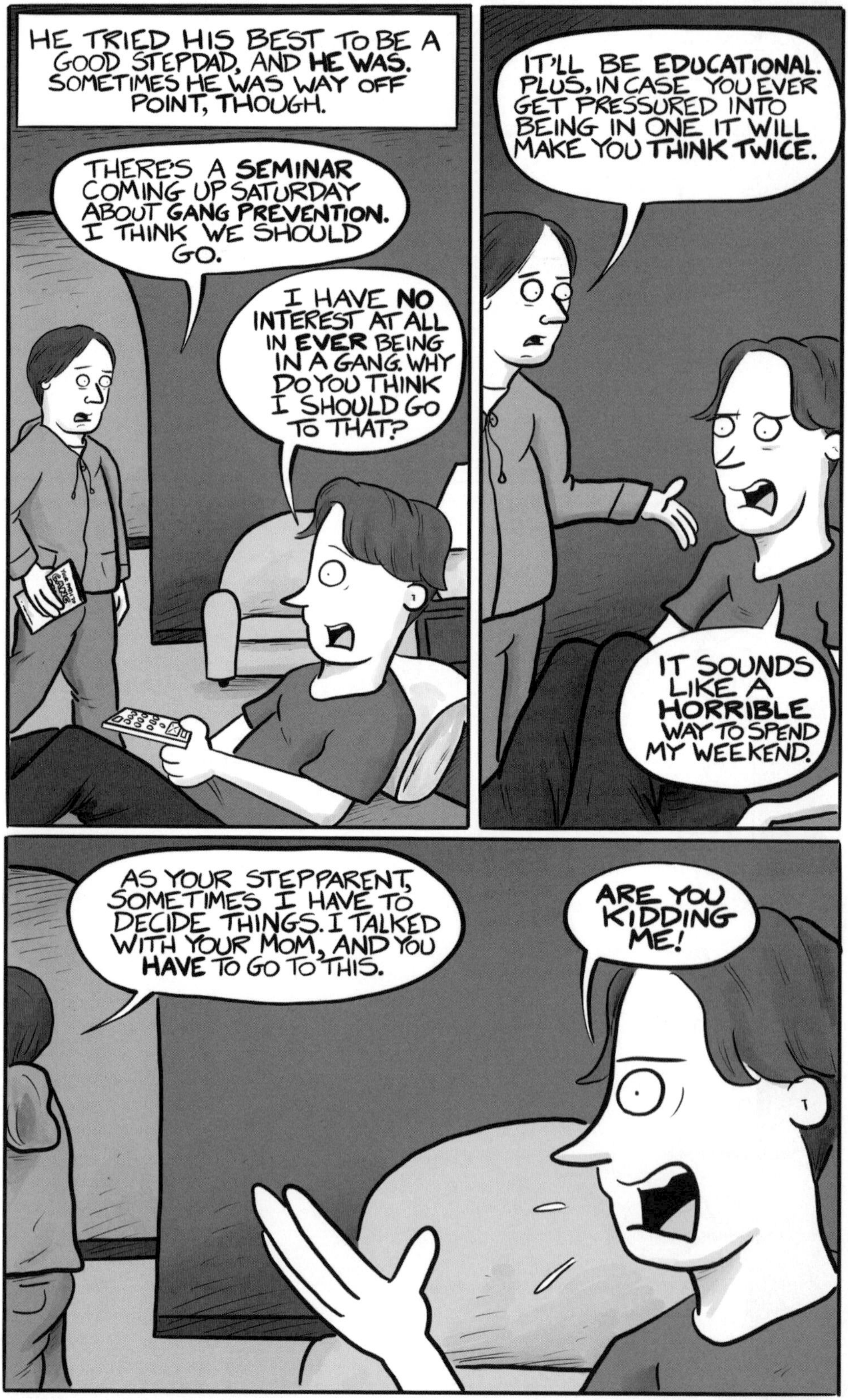
HE TRIED HIS BEST TO BE A GOOD STEPDAD, AND **HE WAS.** SOMETIMES HE WAS WAY OFF POINT, THOUGH.
THERE'S A **SEMINAR** COMING UP SATURDAY ABOUT **GANG PREVENTION.** I THINK WE SHOULD GO.
I HAVE **NO** INTEREST AT **ALL** IN **EVER** BEING IN A GANG. WHY DO YOU THINK I SHOULD GO TO THAT?
IT'LL BE **EDUCATIONAL. PLUS,** IN CASE YOU EVER GET PRESSURED INTO BEING IN ONE IT WILL MAKE YOU **THINK TWICE.**
IT SOUNDS LIKE A **HORRIBLE** WAY TO SPEND MY WEEKEND.
AS YOUR STEPPARENT, SOMETIMES I HAVE TO DECIDE THINGS. I TALKED WITH YOUR MOM, AND YOU **HAVE** TO GO TO THIS.
ARE YOU KIDDING ME!

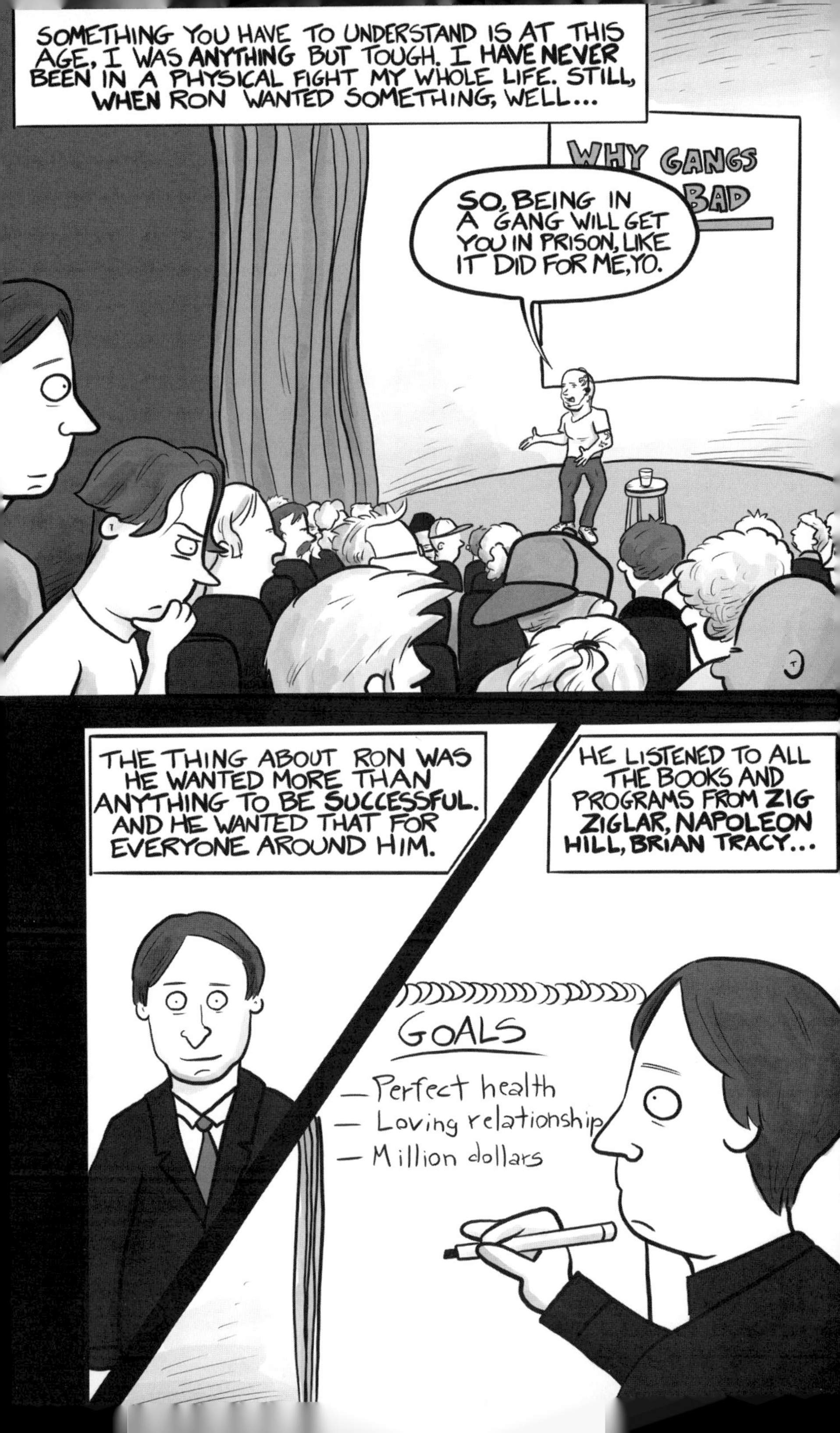
SOMETHING YOU HAVE TO UNDERSTAND IS AT THIS AGE, I WAS ANYTHING BUT TOUGH. I HAVE NEVER BEEN IN A PHYSICAL FIGHT MY WHOLE LIFE. STILL, WHEN RON WANTED SOMETHING, WELL...
WHY GANGS
BAD
SO, BEING IN A GANG WILL GET YOU IN PRISON, LIKE IT DID FOR ME, YO.
THE THING ABOUT RON WAS HE WANTED MORE THAN ANYTHING TO BE SUCCESSFUL. AND HE WANTED THAT FOR EVERYONE AROUND HIM.
HE LISTENED TO ALL THE BOOKS AND PROGRAMS FROM ZIG ZIGLAR, NAPOLEON HILL, BRIAN TRACY...
GOALS
— Perfect health
— Loving relationship
— Million dollars

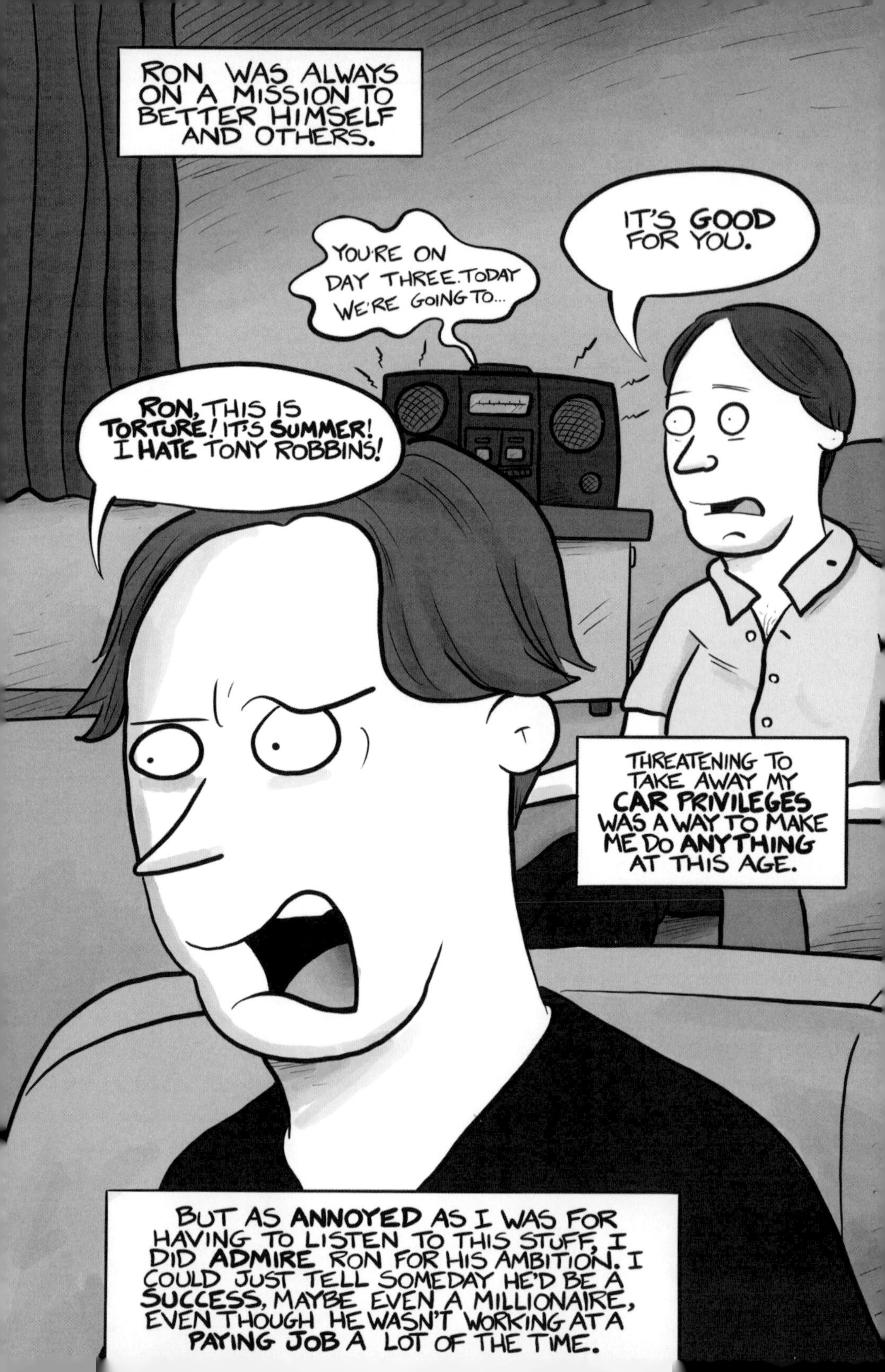
RON WAS ALWAYS ON A MISSION TO BETTER HIMSELF AND OTHERS.
YOU'RE ON DAY THREE. TODAY WE'RE GOING TO...
IT'S **GOOD** FOR YOU.
RON, THIS IS **TORTURE!** IT'S **SUMMER!** I **HATE** TONY ROBBINS!
THREATENING TO TAKE AWAY MY **CAR PRIVILEGES** WAS A WAY TO MAKE ME DO **ANYTHING** AT THIS AGE.
BUT AS **ANNOYED** AS I WAS FOR HAVING TO LISTEN TO THIS STUFF, I DID **ADMIRE** RON FOR HIS AMBITION. I COULD JUST TELL SOMEDAY HE'D BE A **SUCCESS,** MAYBE EVEN A MILLIONAIRE, EVEN THOUGH HE WASN'T WORKING AT A **PAYING JOB** A LOT OF THE TIME.

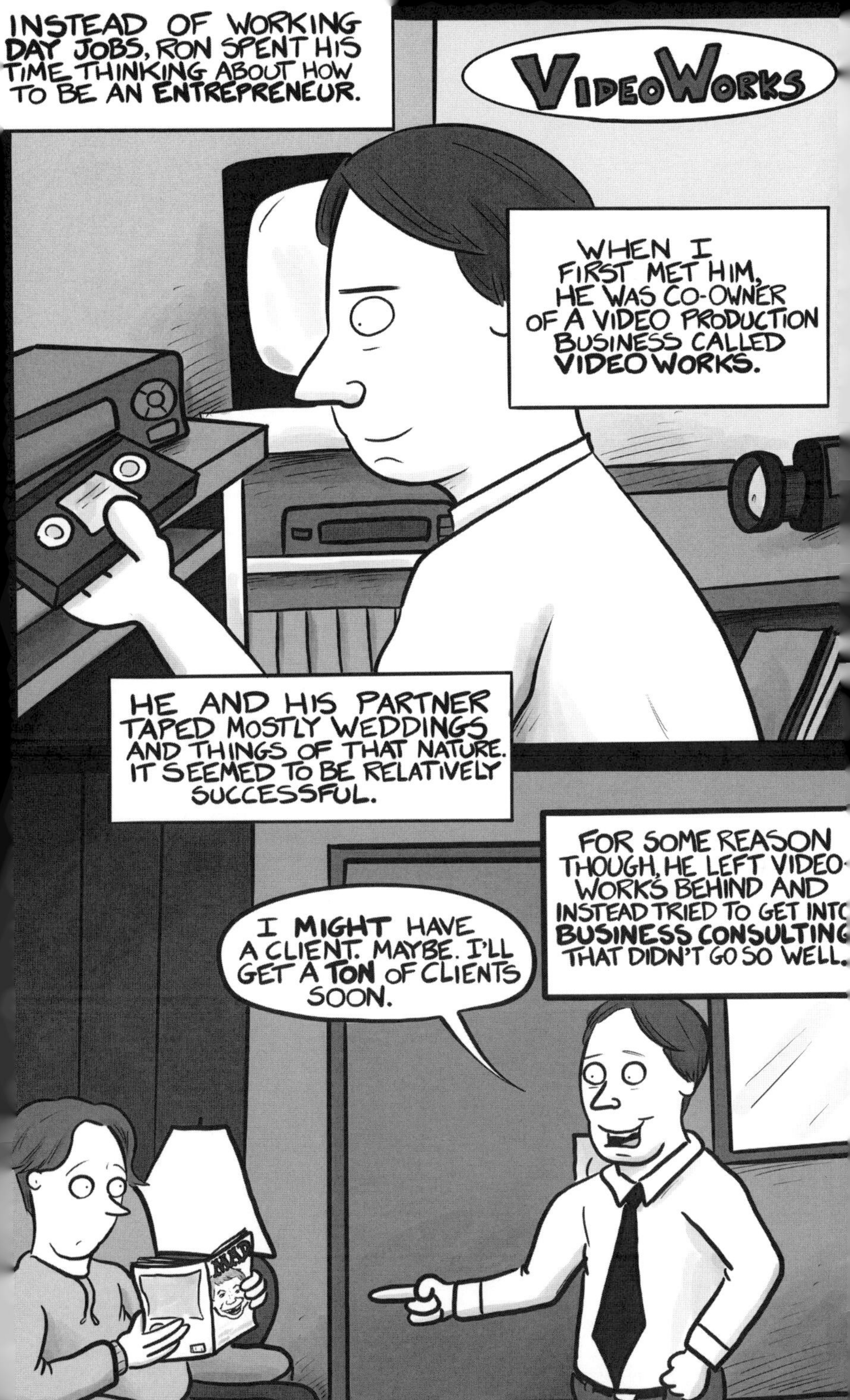

INSTEAD OF WORKING DAY JOBS, RON SPENT HIS TIME THINKING ABOUT HOW TO BE AN ENTREPRENEUR.
VIDEOWORKS
WHEN I FIRST MET HIM, HE WAS CO-OWNER OF A VIDEO PRODUCTION BUSINESS CALLED VIDEOWORKS.
HE AND HIS PARTNER TAPED MOSTLY WEDDINGS AND THINGS OF THAT NATURE. IT SEEMED TO BE RELATIVELY SUCCESSFUL.
FOR SOME REASON THOUGH, HE LEFT VIDEO-WORKS BEHIND AND INSTEAD TRIED TO GET INTO BUSINESS CONSULTING. THAT DIDN'T GO SO WELL.
I MIGHT HAVE A CLIENT. MAYBE. I'LL GET A TON OF CLIENTS SOON.
MAD

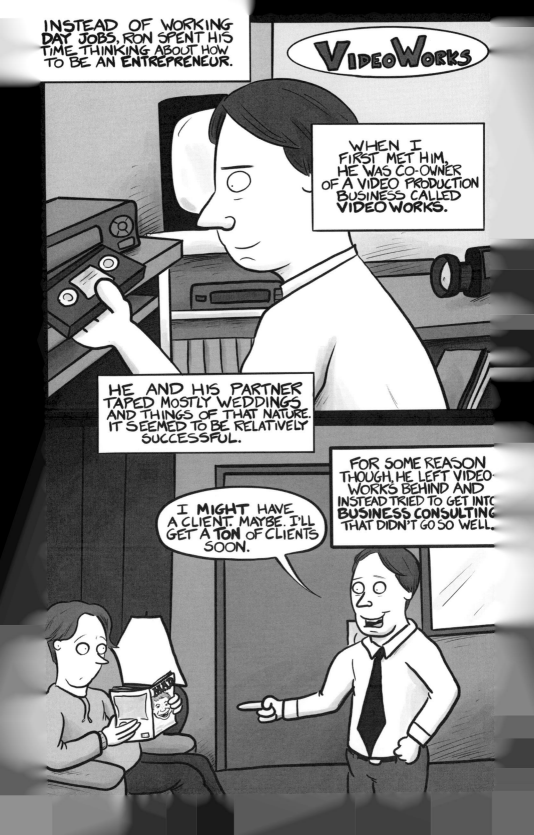

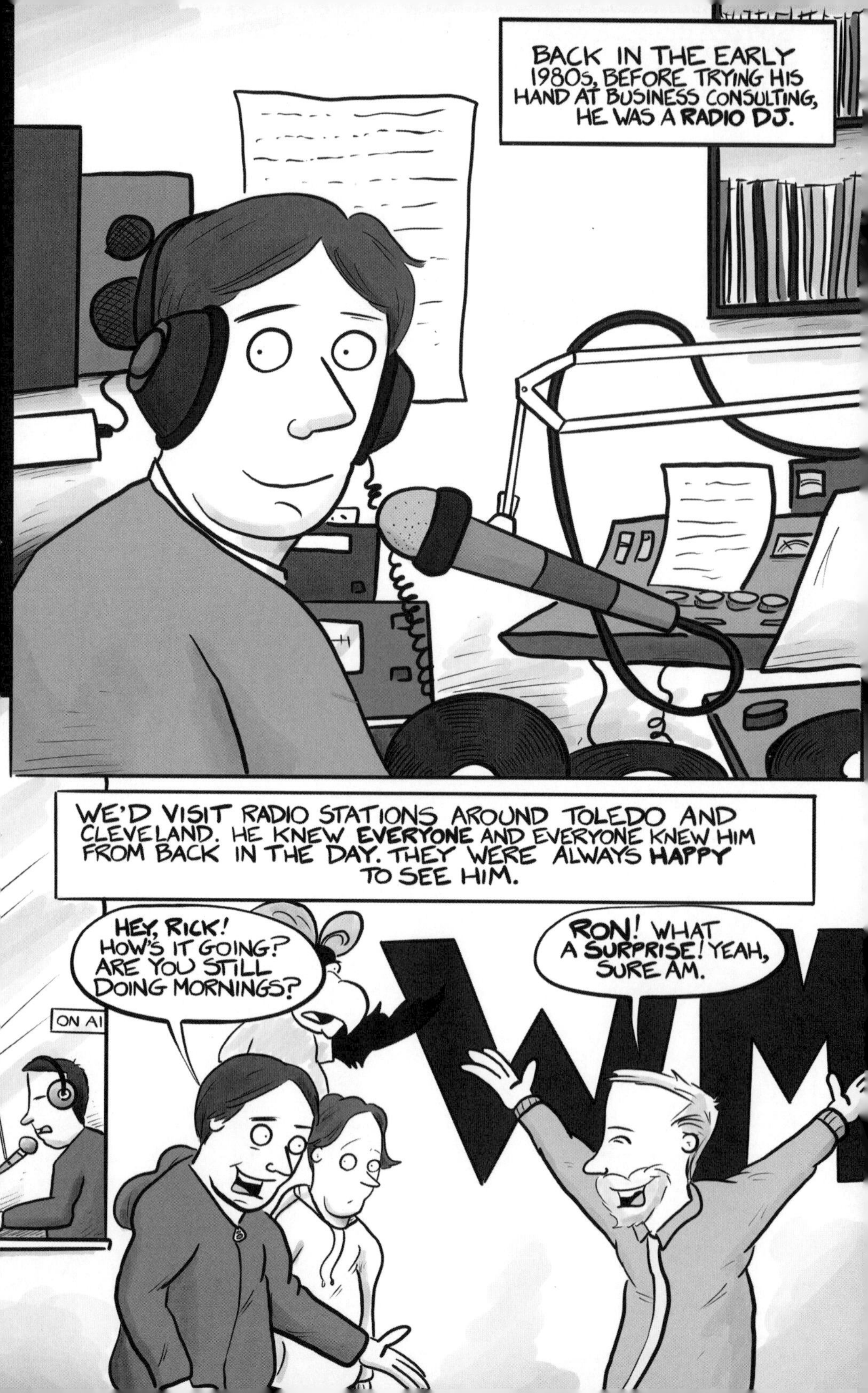
BACK IN THE EARLY 1980s, BEFORE TRYING HIS HAND AT BUSINESS CONSULTING, HE WAS A **RADIO DJ**.
WE'D VISIT RADIO STATIONS AROUND TOLEDO AND CLEVELAND. HE KNEW **EVERYONE** AND EVERYONE KNEW HIM FROM BACK IN THE DAY. THEY WERE ALWAYS **HAPPY** TO SEE HIM.
HEY, RICK! HOW'S IT GOING? ARE YOU STILL DOING MORNINGS?
RON! WHAT A **SURPRISE**! YEAH, SURE AM.

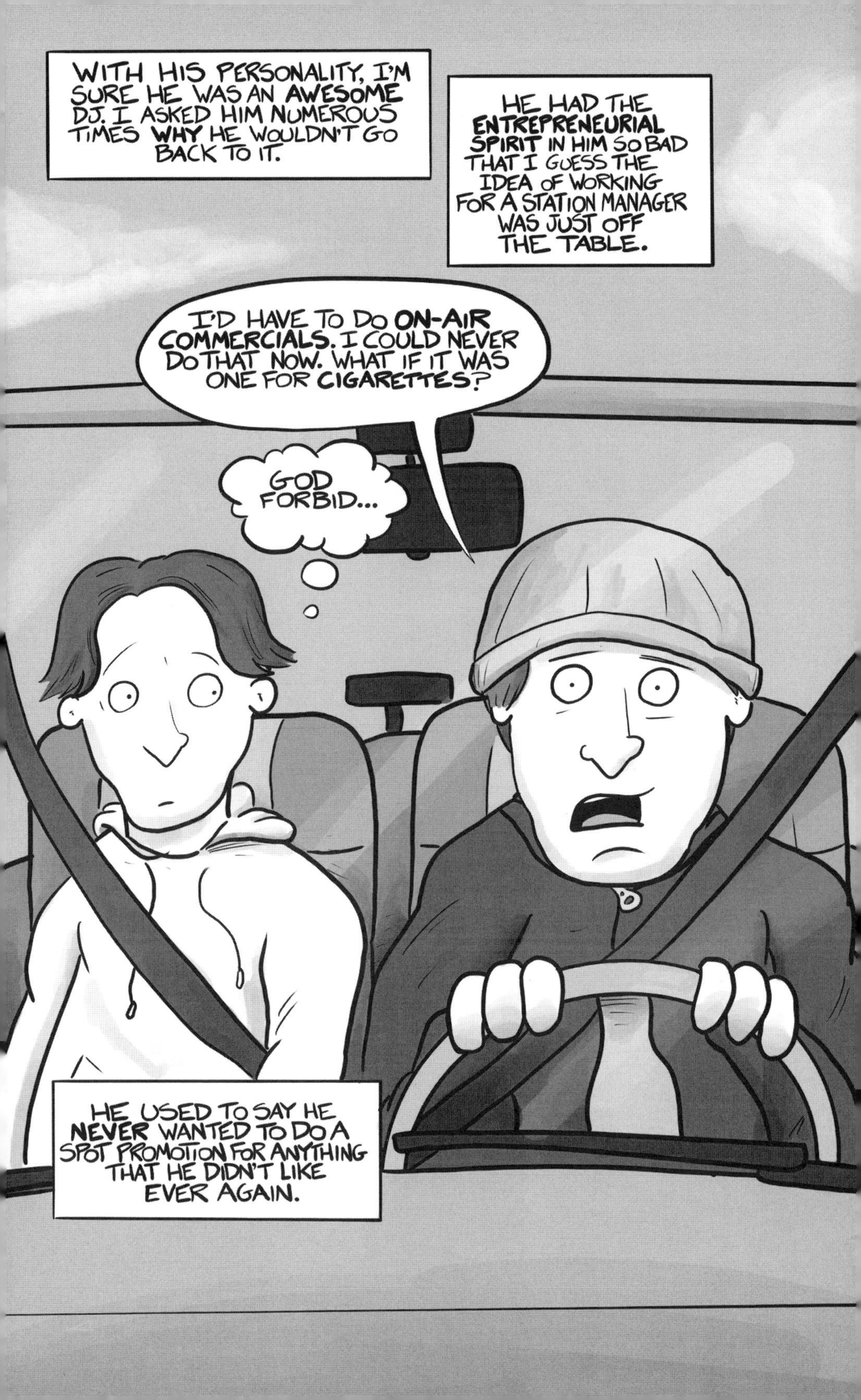

WITH HIS PERSONALITY, I'M SURE HE WAS AN **AWESOME** DJ. I ASKED HIM NUMEROUS TIMES **WHY** HE WOULDN'T GO BACK TO IT.
HE HAD THE **ENTREPRENEURIAL SPIRIT** IN HIM SO BAD THAT I GUESS THE IDEA OF WORKING FOR A STATION MANAGER WAS JUST OFF THE TABLE.
I'D HAVE TO DO **ON-AIR COMMERCIALS**. I COULD NEVER DO THAT NOW. WHAT IF IT WAS ONE FOR **CIGARETTES**?
GOD FORBID...
HE USED TO SAY HE **NEVER** WANTED TO DO A SPOT PROMOTION FOR ANYTHING THAT HE DIDN'T LIKE EVER AGAIN.

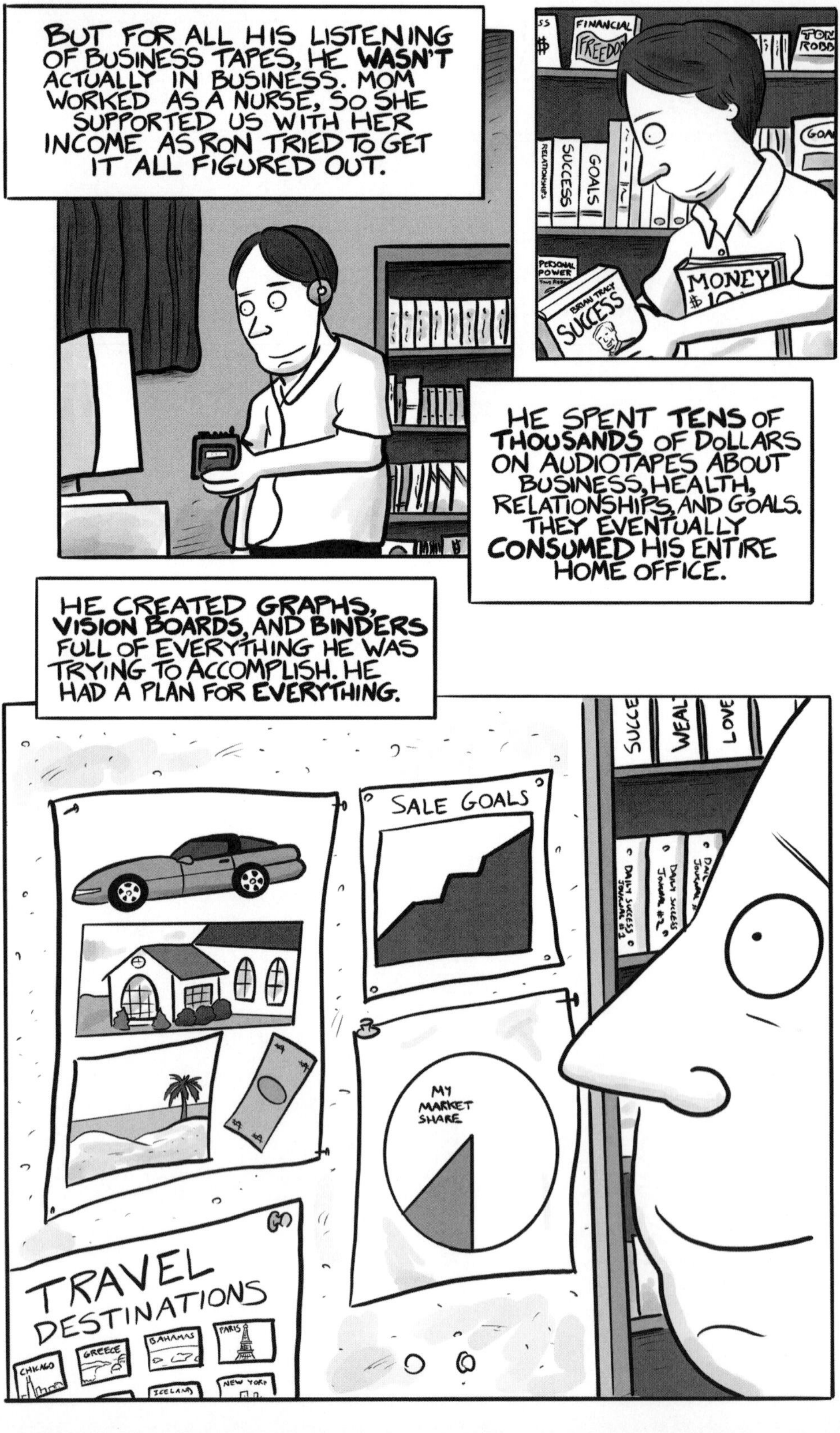
BUT FOR ALL HIS LISTENING OF BUSINESS TAPES, HE WASN'T ACTUALLY IN BUSINESS. MOM WORKED AS A NURSE, SO SHE SUPPORTED US WITH HER INCOME AS RON TRIED TO GET IT ALL FIGURED OUT.
FINANCIAL
RELATIONSHIPS
SUCCESS
GOALS
PERSONAL POWER
BRIAN TRACY
SUCCESS
MONEY
HE SPENT TENS OF THOUSANDS OF DOLLARS ON AUDIOTAPES ABOUT BUSINESS, HEALTH, RELATIONSHIPS, AND GOALS. THEY EVENTUALLY CONSUMED HIS ENTIRE HOME OFFICE.
HE CREATED GRAPHS, VISION BOARDS, AND BINDERS FULL OF EVERYTHING HE WAS TRYING TO ACCOMPLISH. HE HAD A PLAN FOR EVERYTHING.
SALE GOALS
MY MARKET SHARE
TRAVEL DESTINATIONS
CHICAGO
GREECE
BAHAMAS
PARIS
ICELAND
NEW YORK
LOVE
DAILY SUCCESS JOURNAL #1
DAILY SUCCESS JOURNAL #2

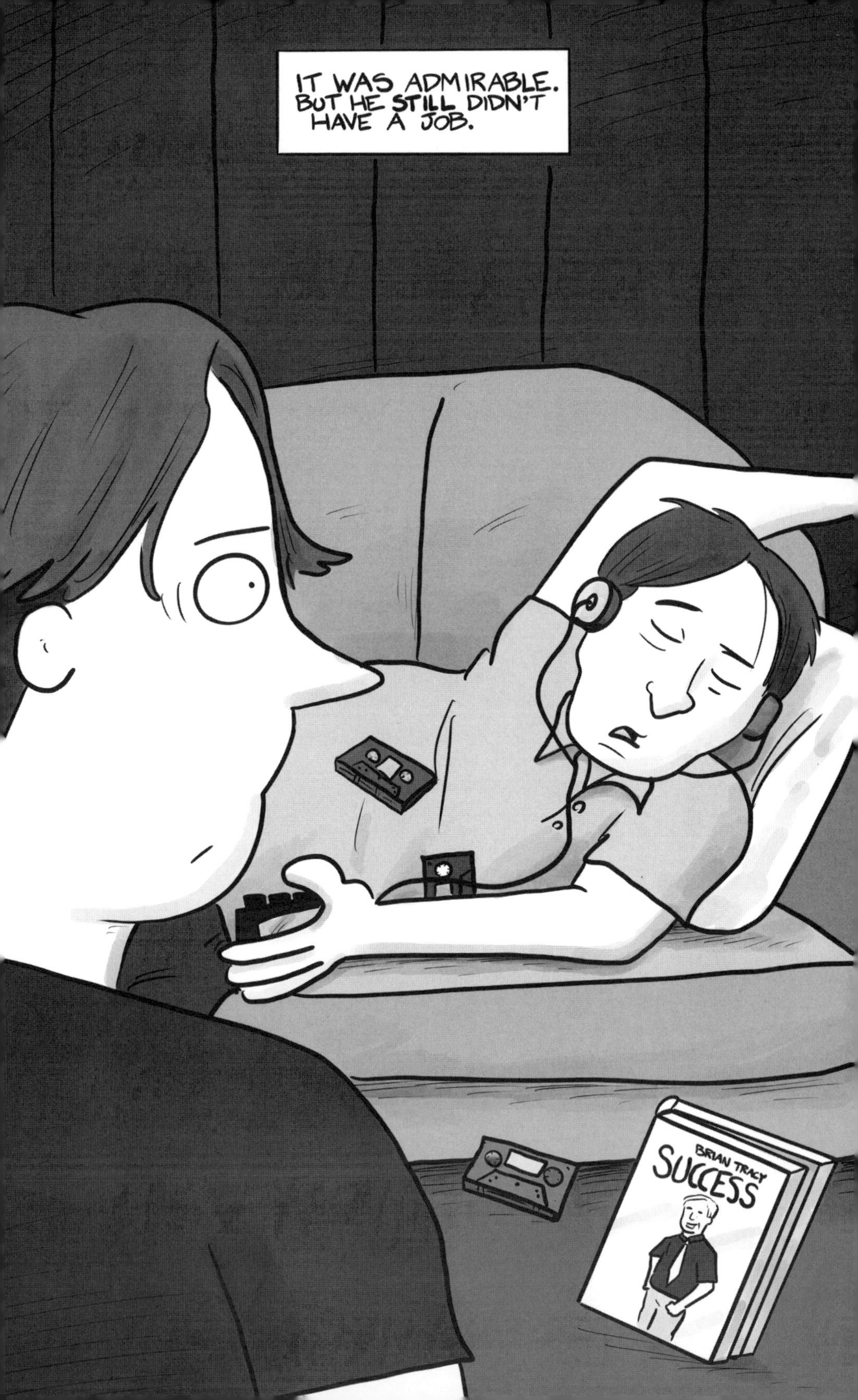
IT WAS ADMIRABLE. BUT HE STILL DIDN'T HAVE A JOB.
BRIAN TRACY
SUCCESS

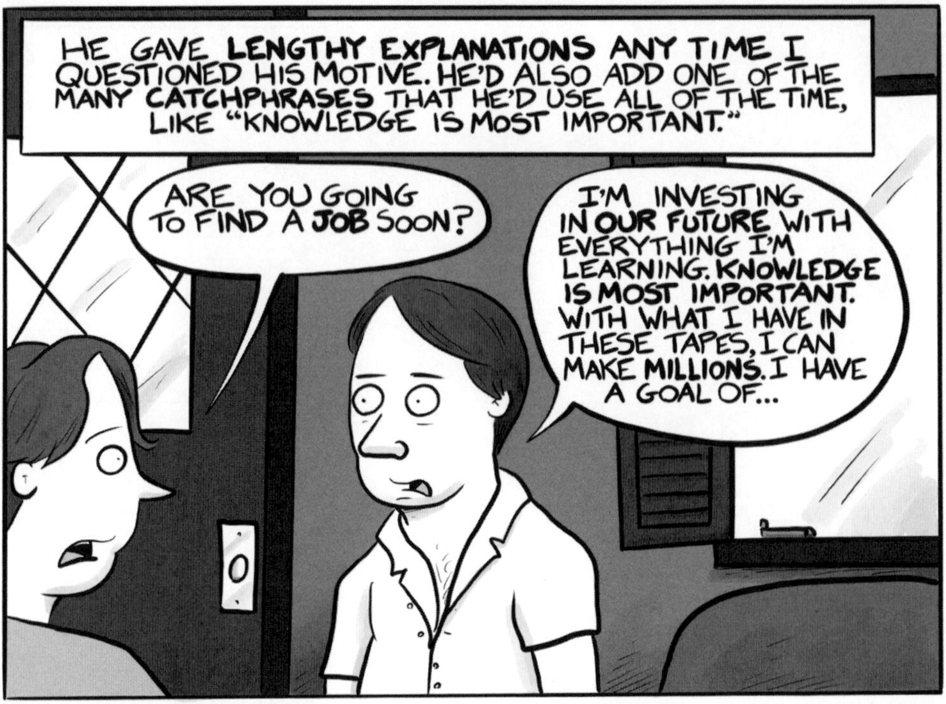
HE GAVE LENGTHY EXPLANATIONS ANY TIME I QUESTIONED HIS MOTIVE. HE'D ALSO ADD ONE OF THE MANY CATCHPHRASES THAT HE'D USE ALL OF THE TIME, LIKE "KNOWLEDGE IS MOST IMPORTANT."
ARE YOU GOING TO FIND A JOB SOON?
I'M INVESTING IN OUR FUTURE WITH EVERYTHING I'M LEARNING. KNOWLEDGE IS MOST IMPORTANT. WITH WHAT I HAVE IN THESE TAPES, I CAN MAKE MILLIONS. I HAVE A GOAL OF...

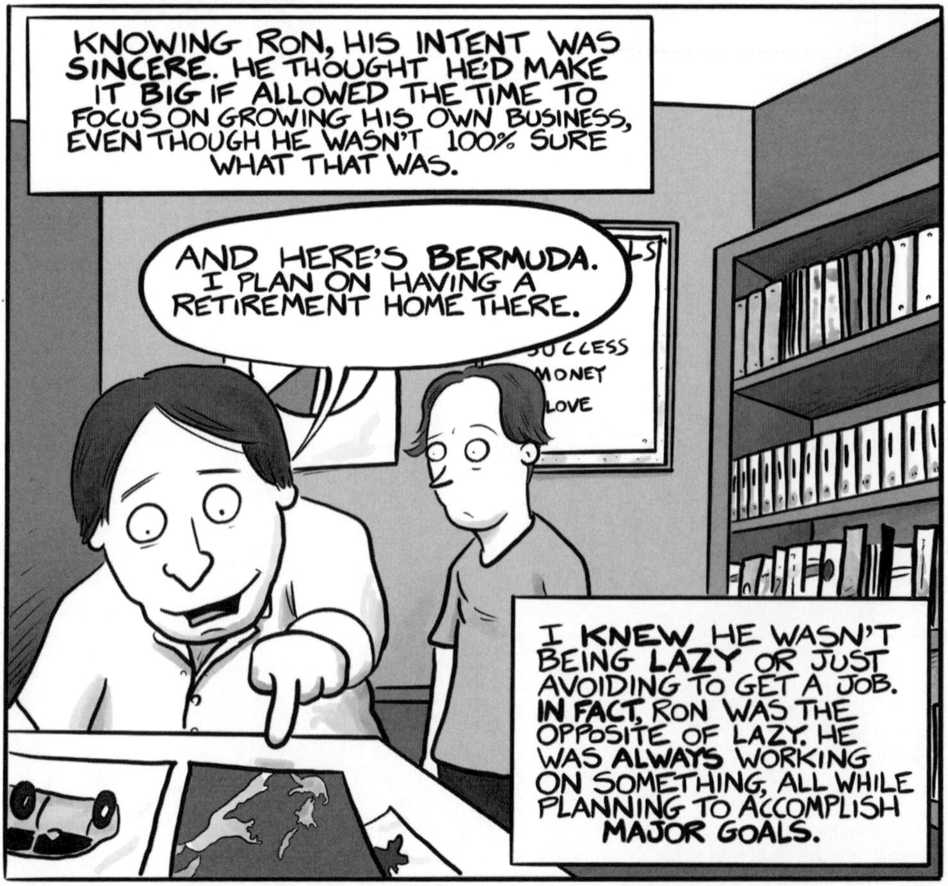
KNOWING RON, HIS INTENT WAS SINCERE. HE THOUGHT HE'D MAKE IT BIG IF ALLOWED THE TIME TO FOCUS ON GROWING HIS OWN BUSINESS, EVEN THOUGH HE WASN'T 100% SURE WHAT THAT WAS.
AND HERE'S BERMUDA. I PLAN ON HAVING A RETIREMENT HOME THERE.
MONEY
LOVE
I KNEW HE WASN'T BEING LAZY OR JUST AVOIDING TO GET A JOB. IN FACT, RON WAS THE OPPOSITE OF LAZY. HE WAS ALWAYS WORKING ON SOMETHING, ALL WHILE PLANNING TO ACCOMPLISH MAJOR GOALS.

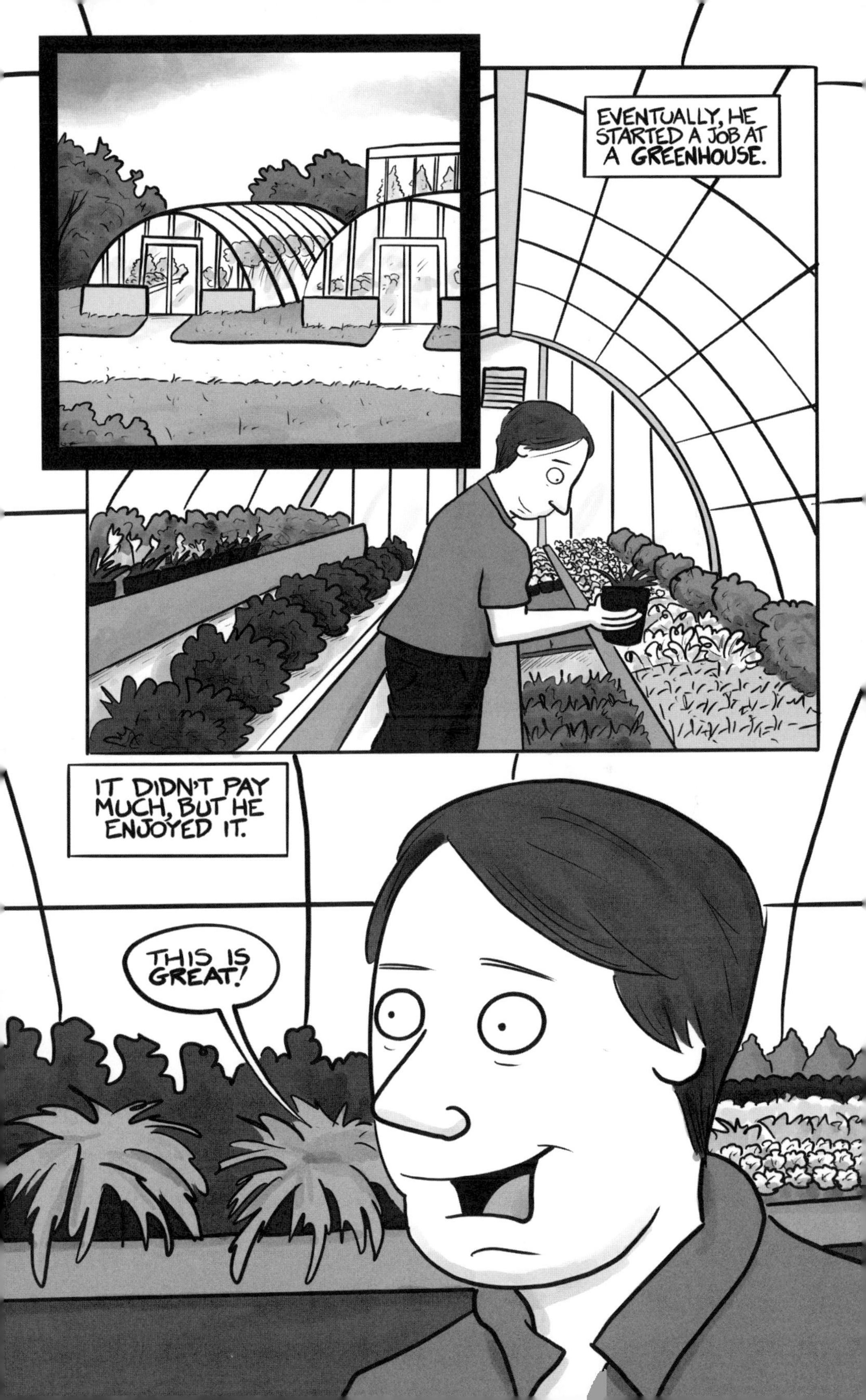
EVENTUALLY, HE STARTED A JOB AT A GREENHOUSE.
IT DIDN'T PAY MUCH, BUT HE ENJOYED IT.
THIS IS GREAT!

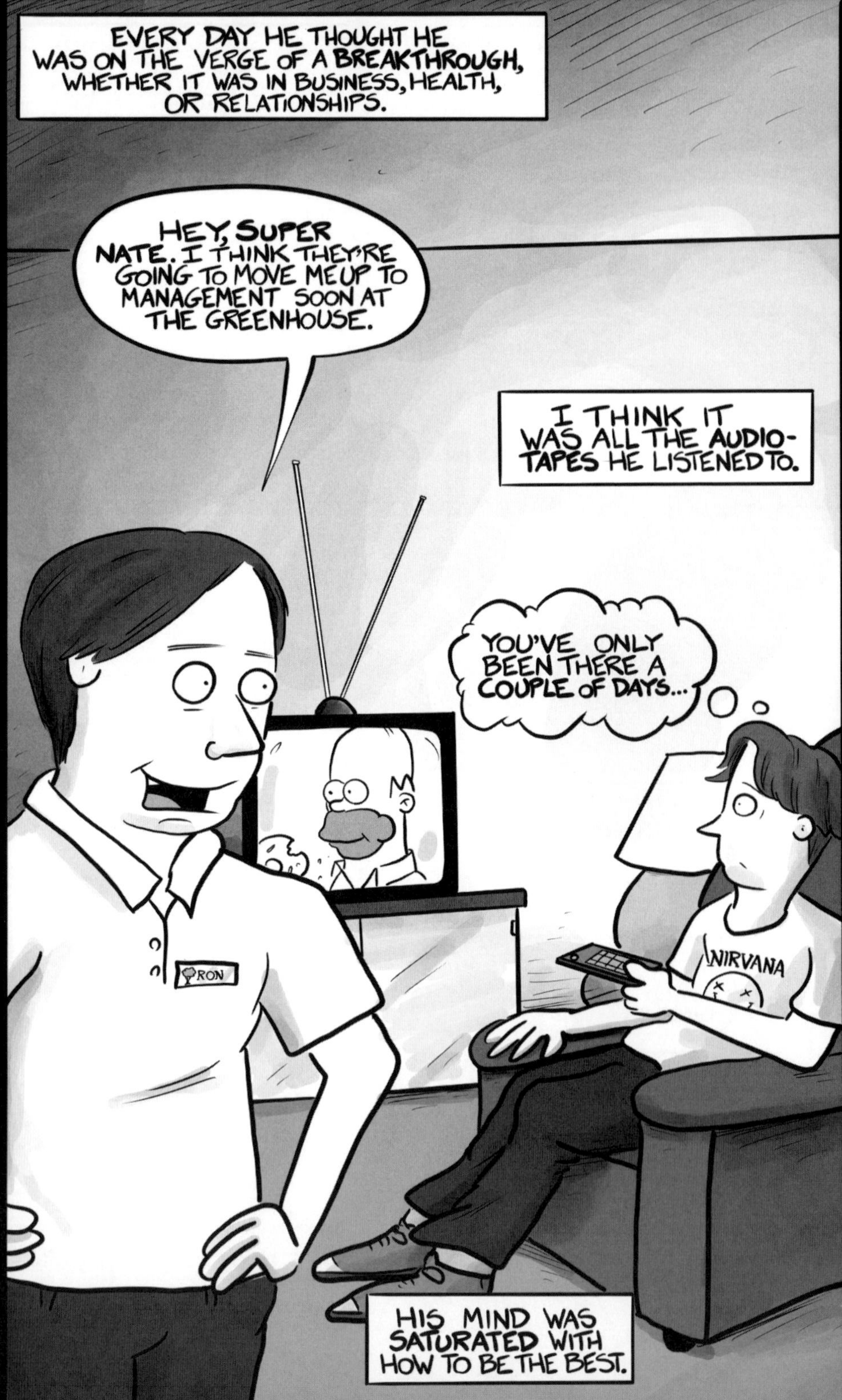
EVERY DAY HE THOUGHT HE WAS ON THE VERGE OF A BREAKTHROUGH, WHETHER IT WAS IN BUSINESS, HEALTH, OR RELATIONSHIPS.
HEY, SUPER NATE. I THINK THEY'RE GOING TO MOVE ME UP TO MANAGEMENT SOON AT THE GREENHOUSE.
I THINK IT WAS ALL THE AUDIO-TAPES HE LISTENED TO.
YOU'VE ONLY BEEN THERE A COUPLE OF DAYS...
RON
NIRVANA
HIS MIND WAS SATURATED WITH HOW TO BE THE BEST.

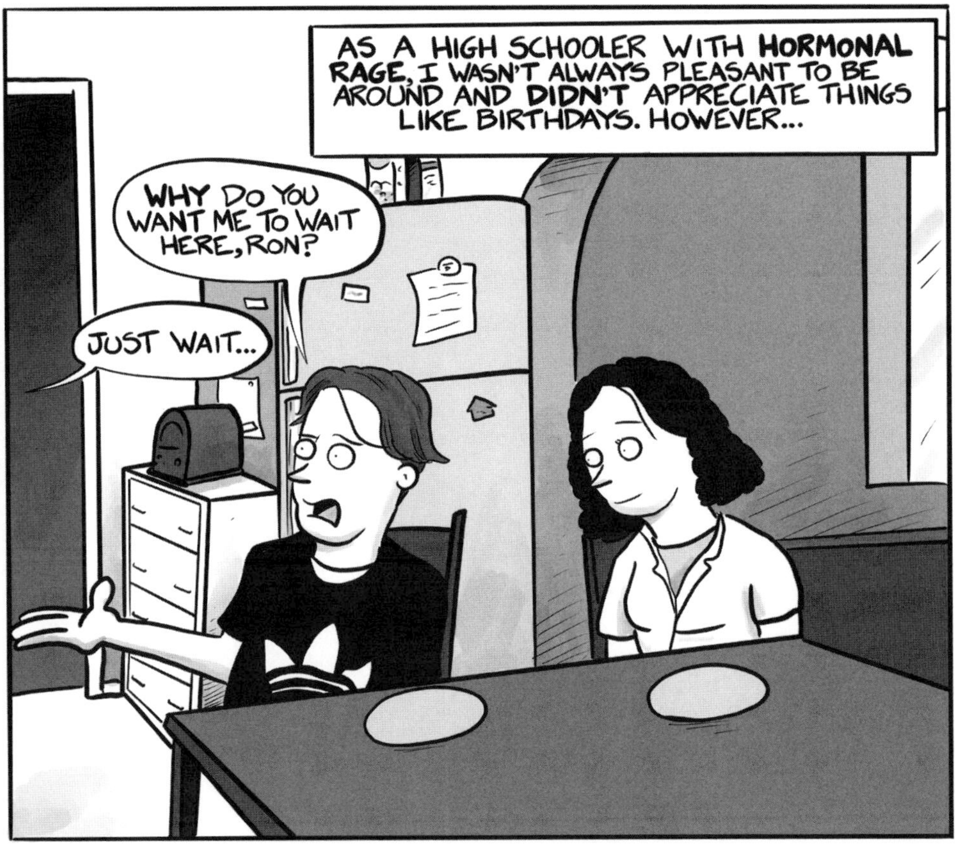
AS A HIGH SCHOOLER WITH **HORMONAL RAGE**, I WASN'T ALWAYS PLEASANT TO BE AROUND AND **DIDN'T** APPRECIATE THINGS LIKE BIRTHDAYS. HOWEVER...
WHY DO YOU WANT ME TO WAIT HERE, RON?
JUST WAIT...

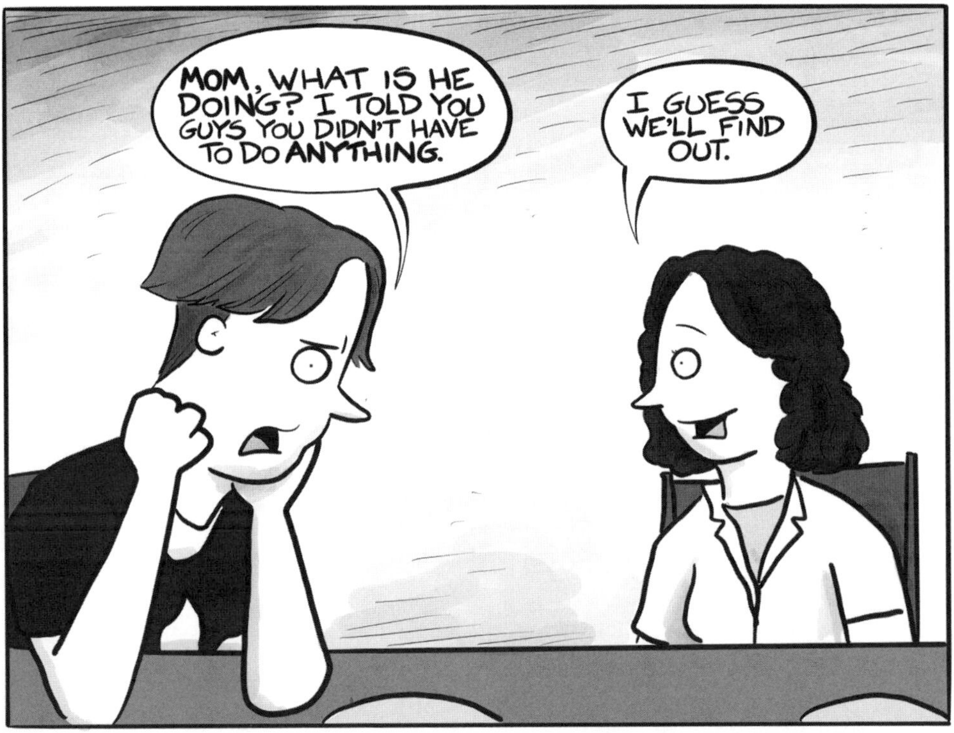
MOM, WHAT IS HE DOING? I TOLD YOU GUYS YOU DIDN'T HAVE TO DO **ANYTHING**.
I GUESS WE'LL FIND OUT.

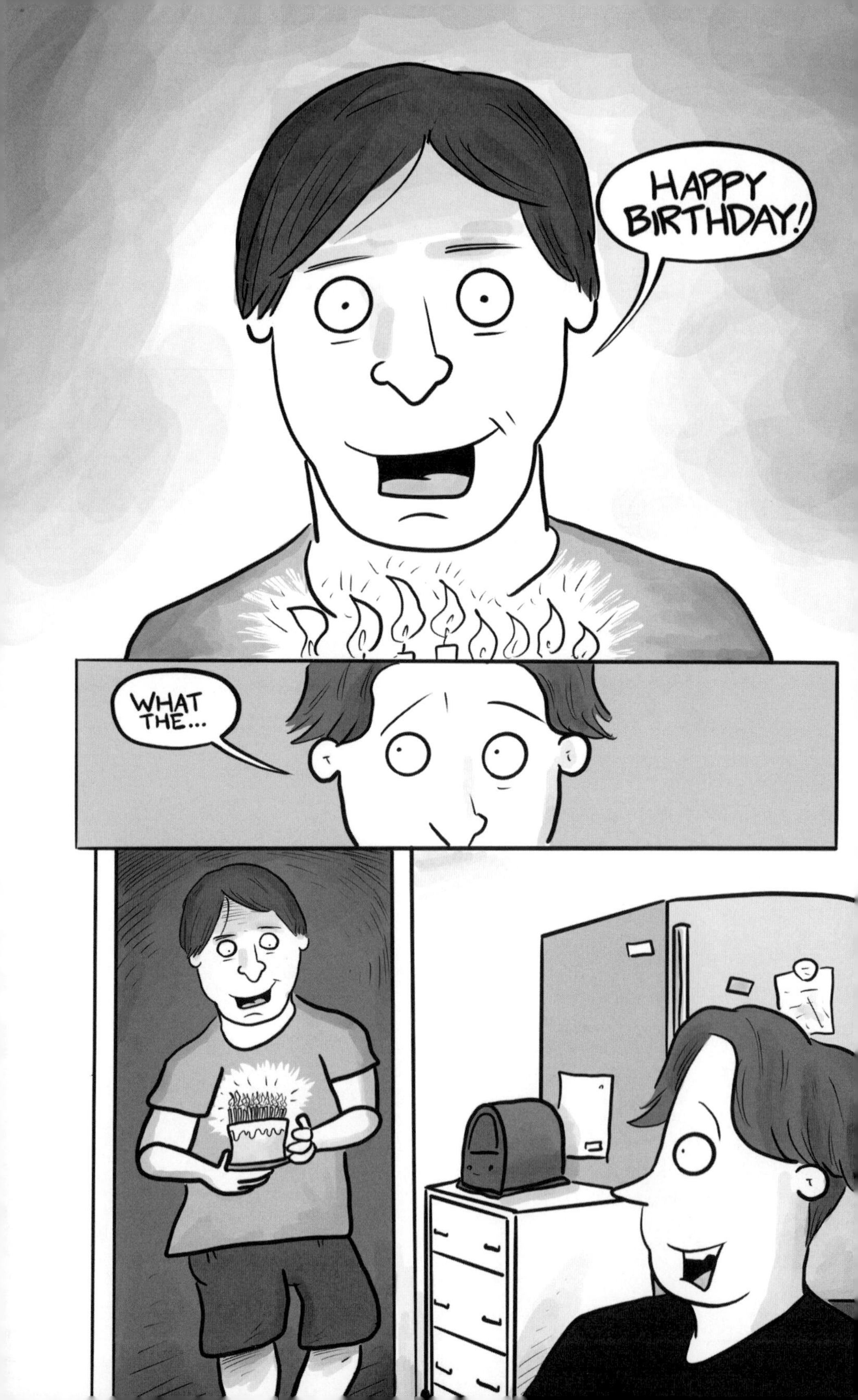
HAPPY BIRTHDAY!
WHAT THE...

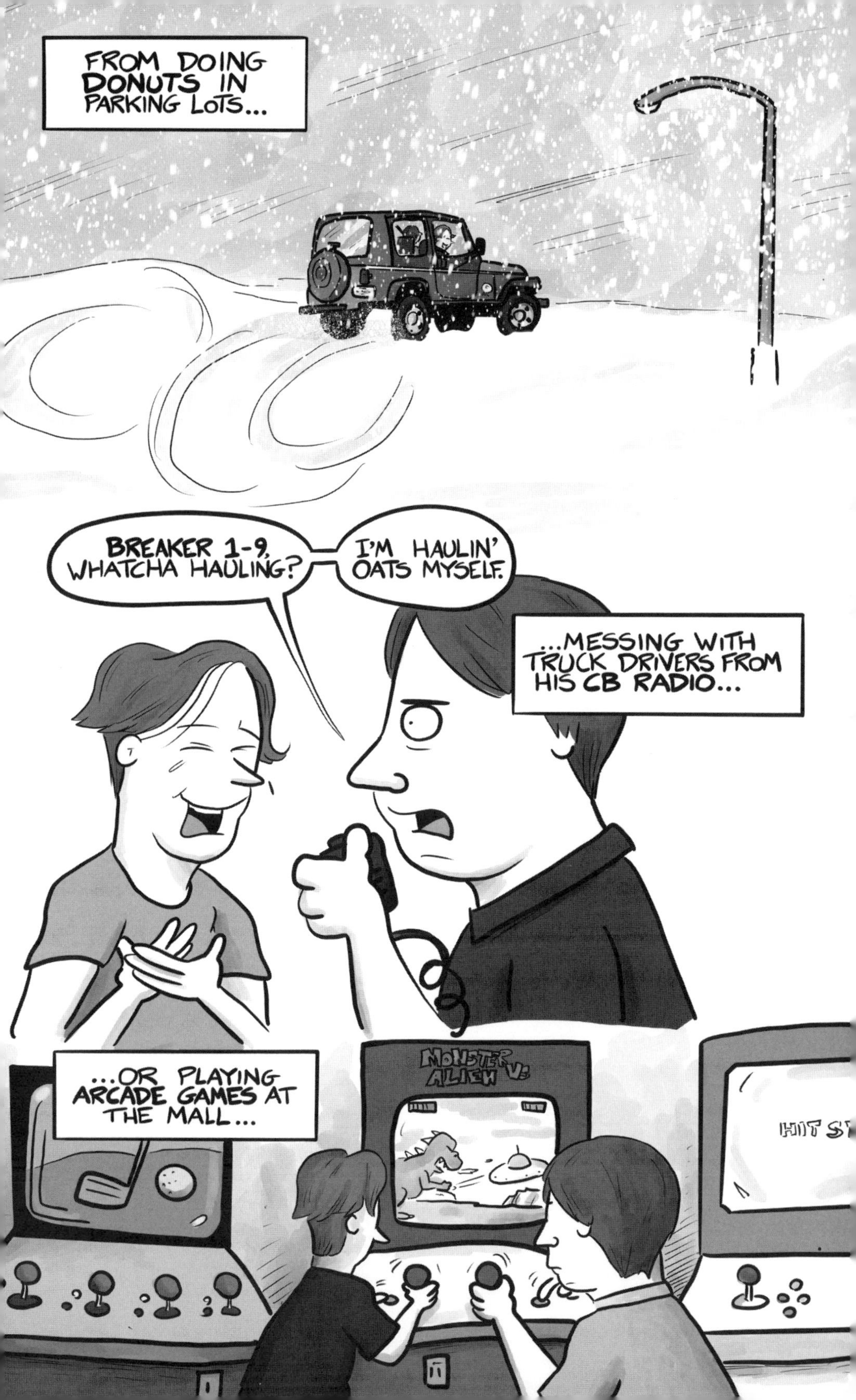
FROM DOING DONUTS IN PARKING LOTS...
BREAKER 1-9, WHATCHA HAULING?
I'M HAULIN' OATS MYSELF.
...MESSING WITH TRUCK DRIVERS FROM HIS CB RADIO...
...OR PLAYING ARCADE GAMES AT THE MALL...
MONSTER VS ALIEN

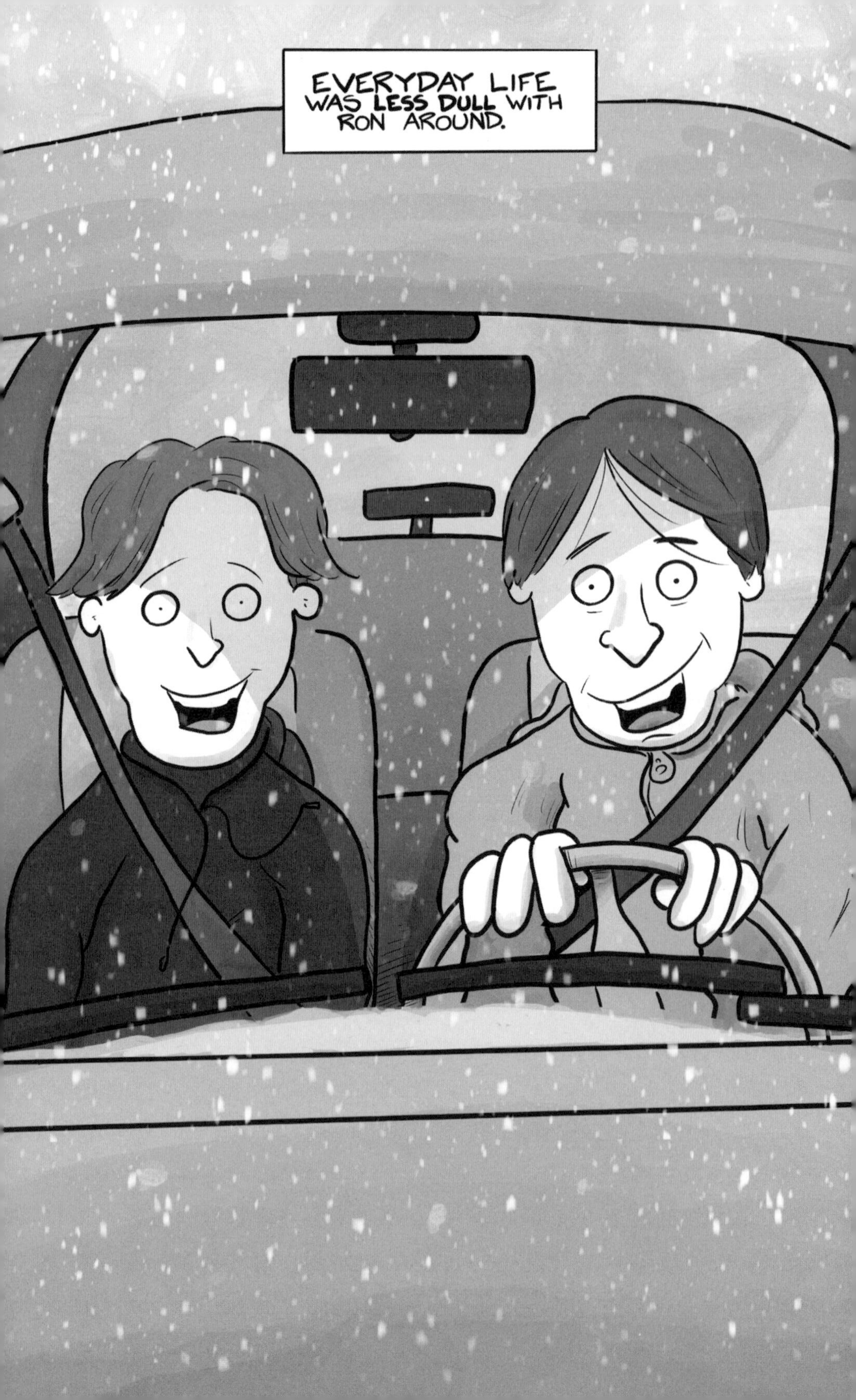
EVERYDAY LIFE WAS LESS DULL WITH RON AROUND.

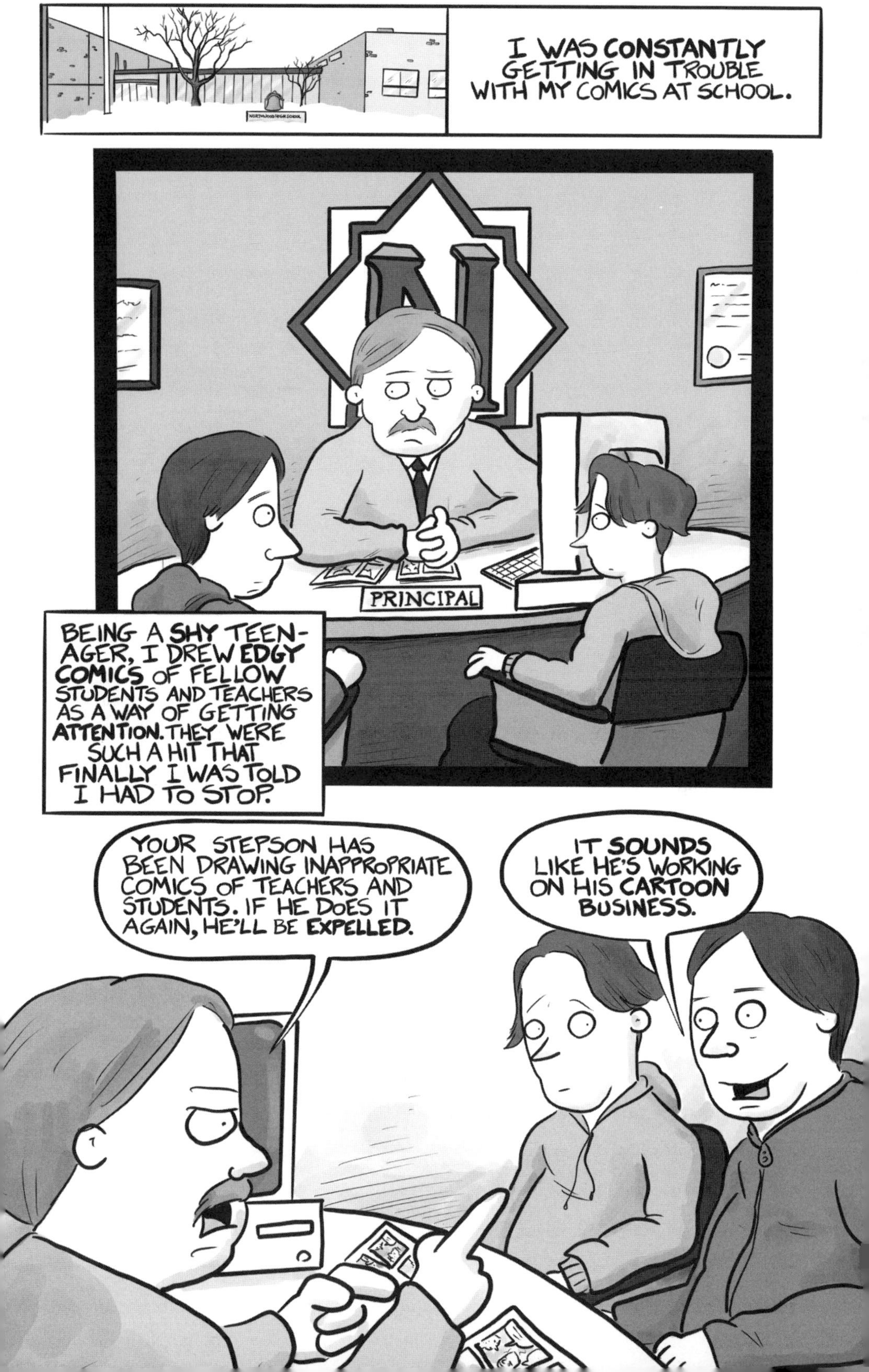
I WAS CONSTANTLY GETTING IN TROUBLE WITH MY COMICS AT SCHOOL.
PRINCIPAL
BEING A SHY TEEN-AGER, I DREW EDGY COMICS OF FELLOW STUDENTS AND TEACHERS AS A WAY OF GETTING ATTENTION. THEY WERE SUCH A HIT THAT FINALLY I WAS TOLD I HAD TO STOP.
YOUR STEPSON HAS BEEN DRAWING INAPPROPRIATE COMICS OF TEACHERS AND STUDENTS. IF HE DOES IT AGAIN, HE'LL BE EXPELLED.
IT SOUNDS LIKE HE'S WORKING ON HIS CARTOON BUSINESS.

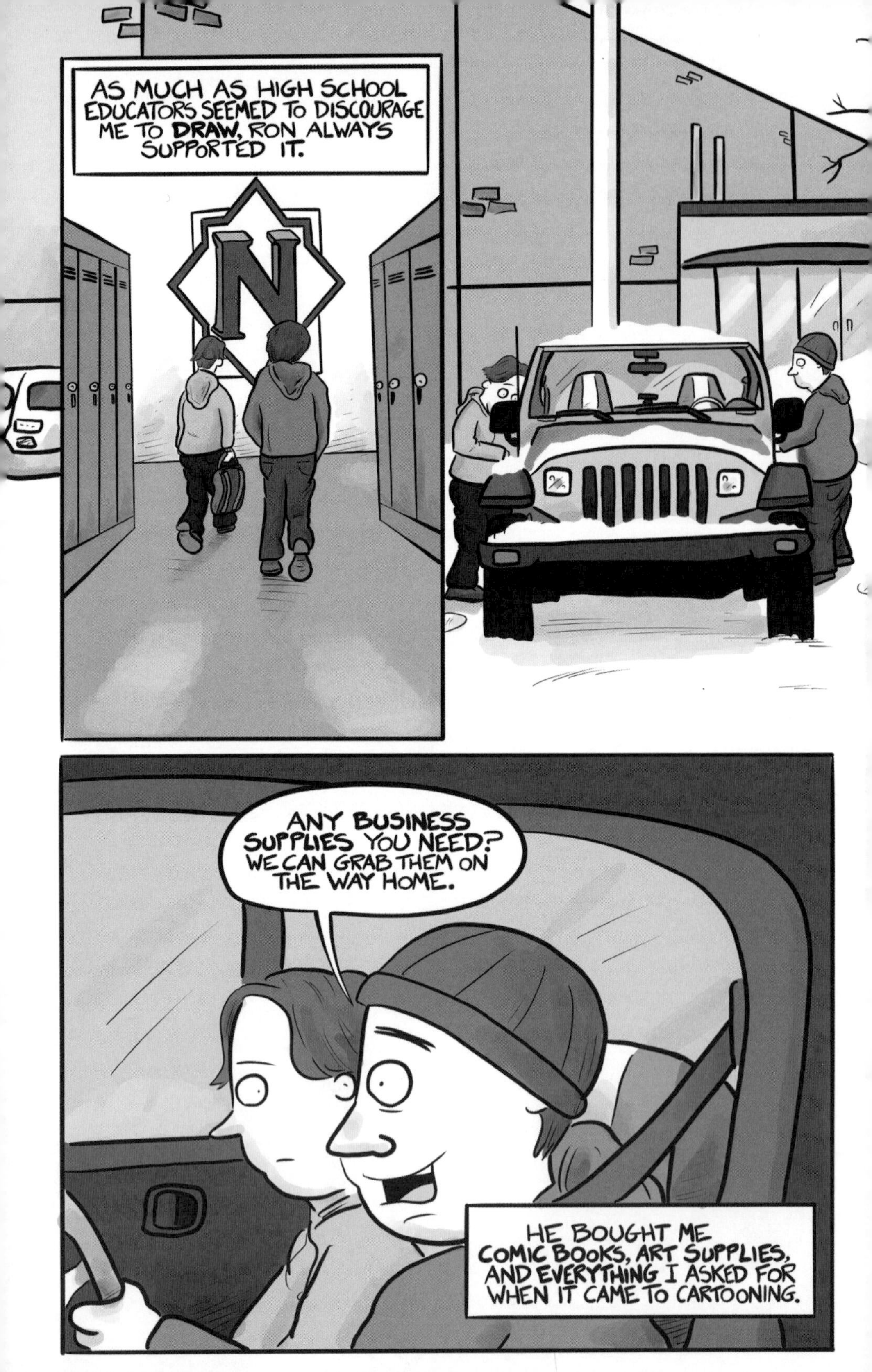
AS MUCH AS HIGH SCHOOL EDUCATORS SEEMED TO DISCOURAGE ME TO **DRAW**, RON ALWAYS SUPPORTED IT.
N
ANY BUSINESS SUPPLIES YOU NEED? WE CAN GRAB THEM ON THE WAY HOME.
HE BOUGHT ME COMIC BOOKS, ART SUPPLIES, AND EVERYTHING I ASKED FOR WHEN IT CAME TO CARTOONING.

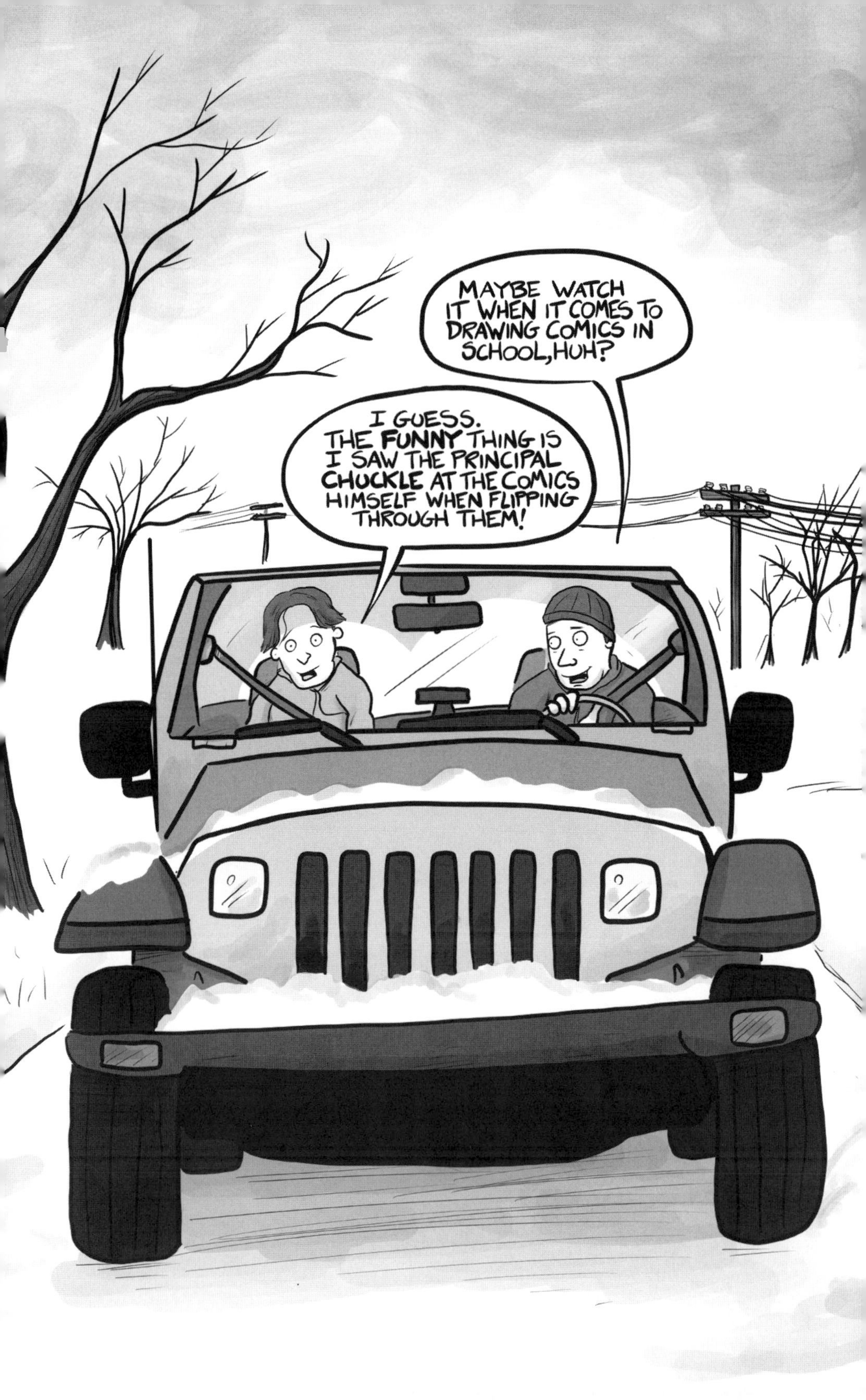
I GUESS. THE FUNNY THING IS I SAW THE PRINCIPAL CHUCKLE AT THE COMICS HIMSELF WHEN FLIPPING THROUGH THEM!
MAYBE WATCH IT WHEN IT COMES TO DRAWING COMICS IN SCHOOL, HUH?

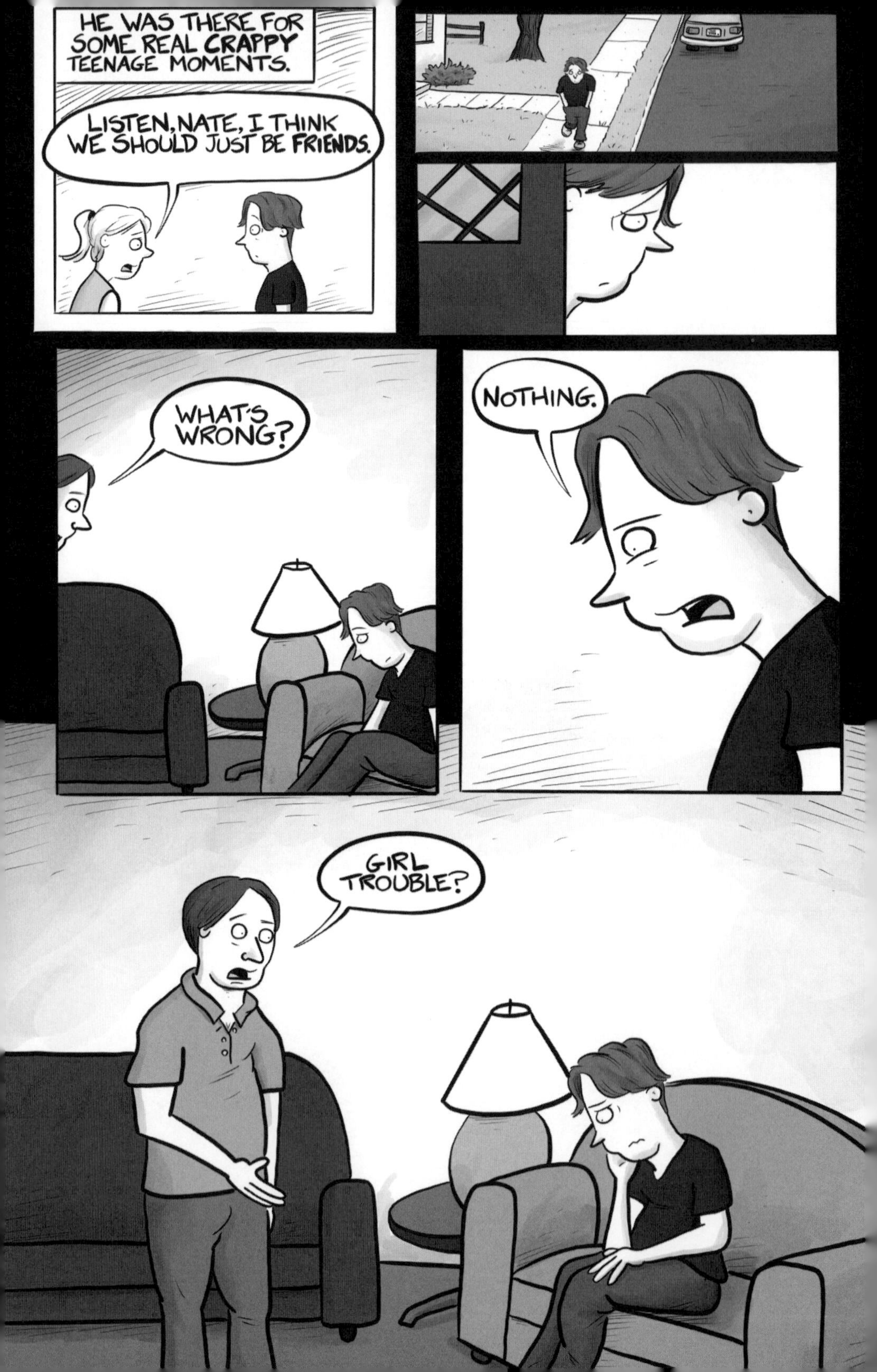
HE WAS THERE FOR SOME REAL CRAPPY TEENAGE MOMENTS.
LISTEN, NATE, I THINK WE SHOULD JUST BE FRIENDS.
WHAT'S WRONG?
NOTHING.
GIRL TROUBLE?

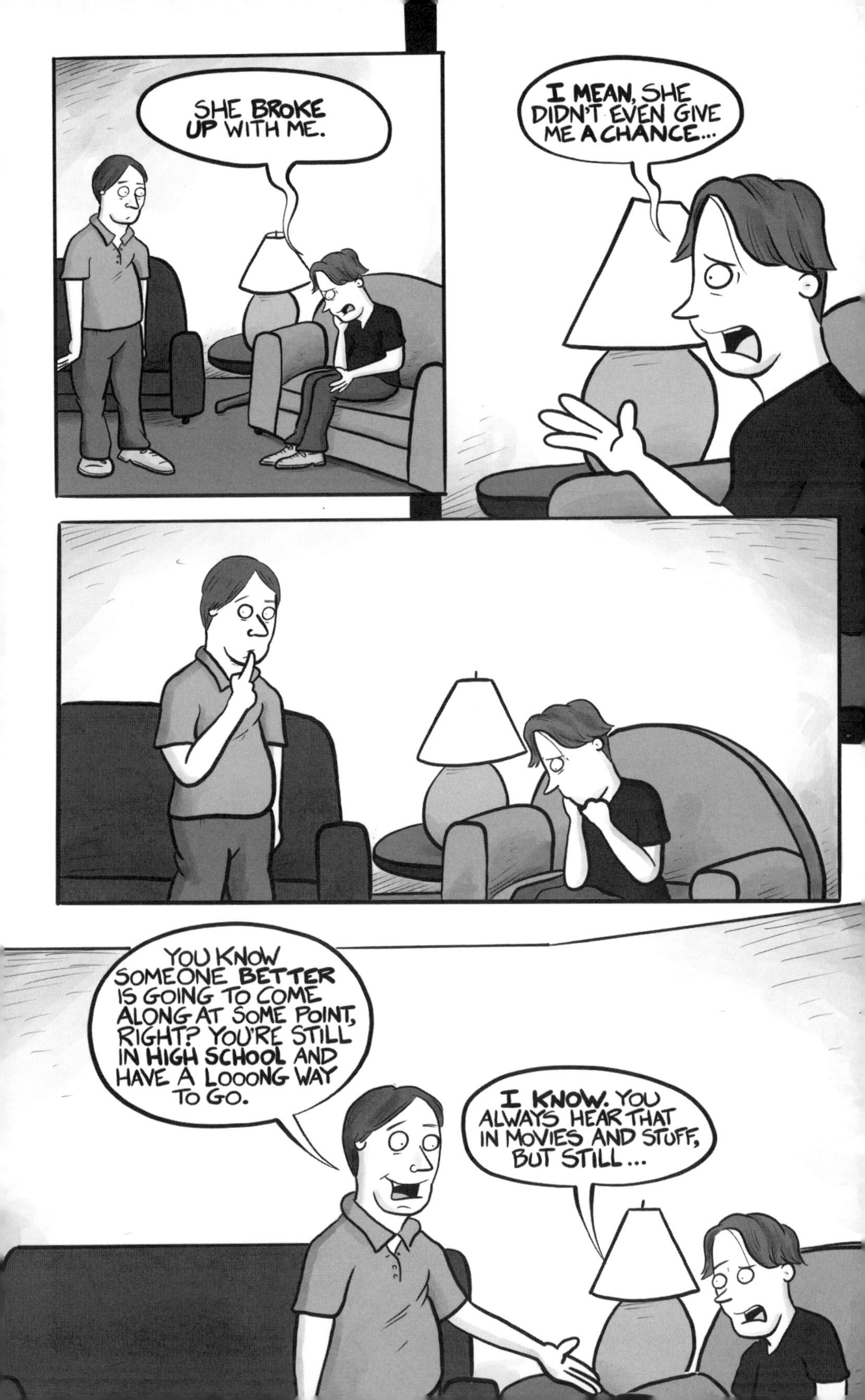
SHE BROKE UP WITH ME.
I MEAN, SHE DIDN'T EVEN GIVE ME A CHANCE...
YOU KNOW SOMEONE BETTER IS GOING TO COME ALONG AT SOME POINT, RIGHT? YOU'RE STILL IN HIGH SCHOOL AND HAVE A LOOONG WAY TO GO.
I KNOW. YOU ALWAYS HEAR THAT IN MOVIES AND STUFF, BUT STILL...

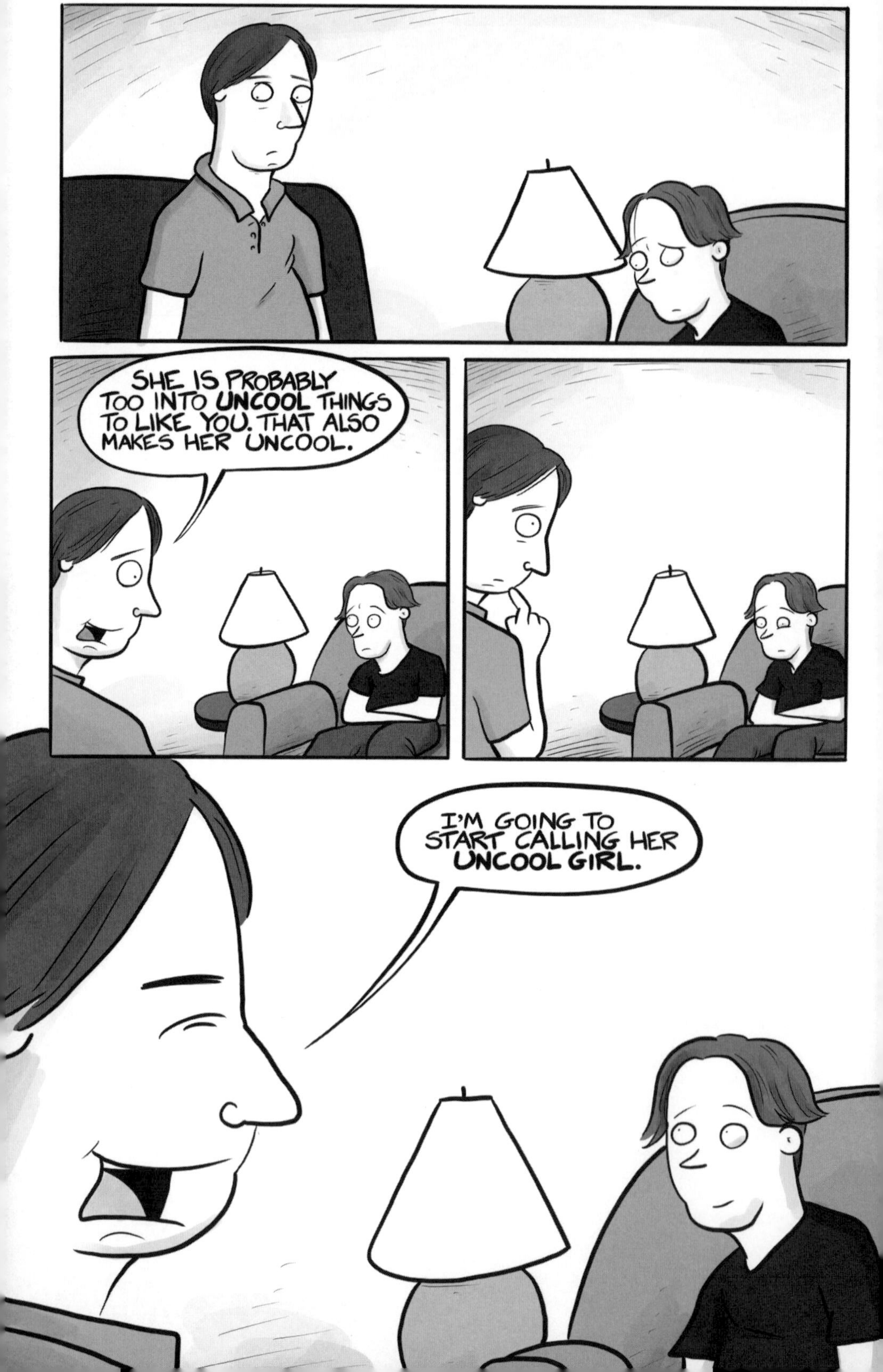
SHE IS PROBABLY TOO INTO UNCOOL THINGS TO LIKE YOU. THAT ALSO MAKES HER UNCOOL.
I'M GOING TO START CALLING HER UNCOOL GIRL.

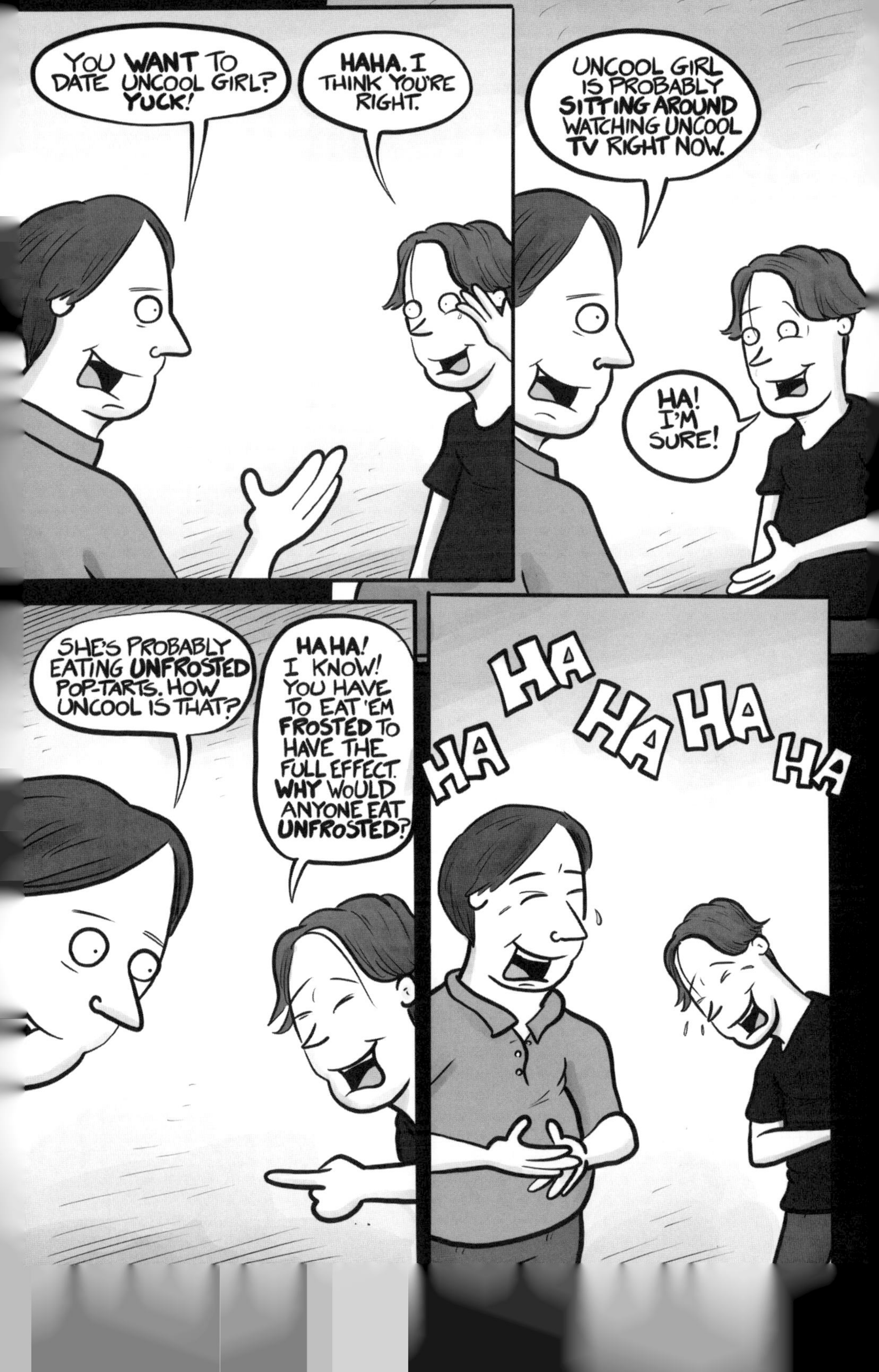

YOU **WANT** TO DATE UNCOOL GIRL? **YUCK!**
HAHA. I THINK YOU'RE RIGHT.
UNCOOL GIRL IS PROBABLY **SITTING AROUND** WATCHING UNCOOL **TV** RIGHT NOW.
HA! I'M SURE!
SHE'S PROBABLY EATING **UNFROSTED** POP-TARTS. HOW UNCOOL IS THAT?
HAHA! I KNOW! YOU HAVE TO EAT 'EM **FROSTED** TO HAVE THE FULL EFFECT. **WHY** WOULD ANYONE EAT **UNFROSTED?**
HA HA HA HA HA HA

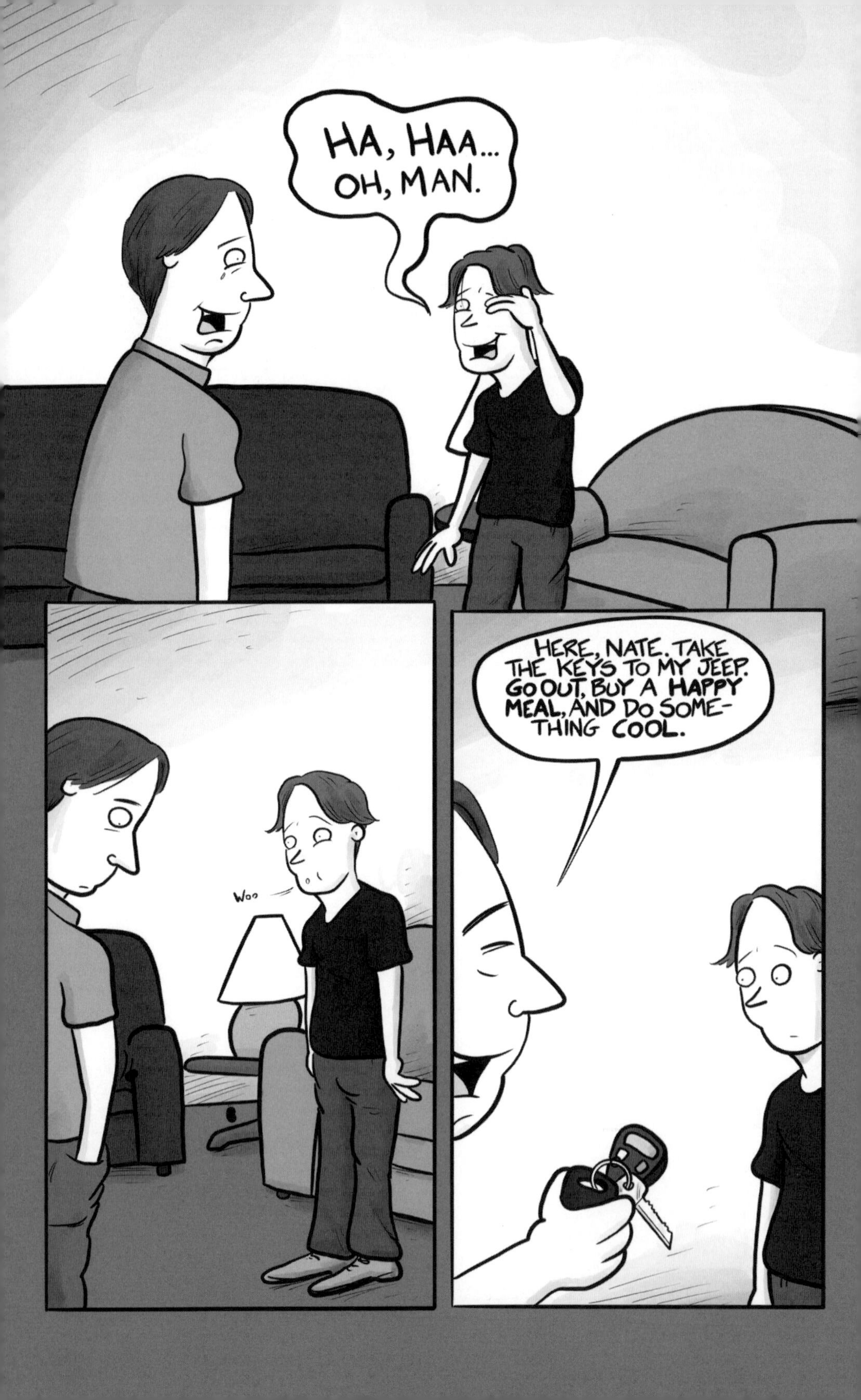
HA, HAA...
OH, MAN.
Woo
HERE, NATE. TAKE THE KEYS TO MY JEEP. GO OUT, BUY A HAPPY MEAL, AND DO SOMETHING COOL.

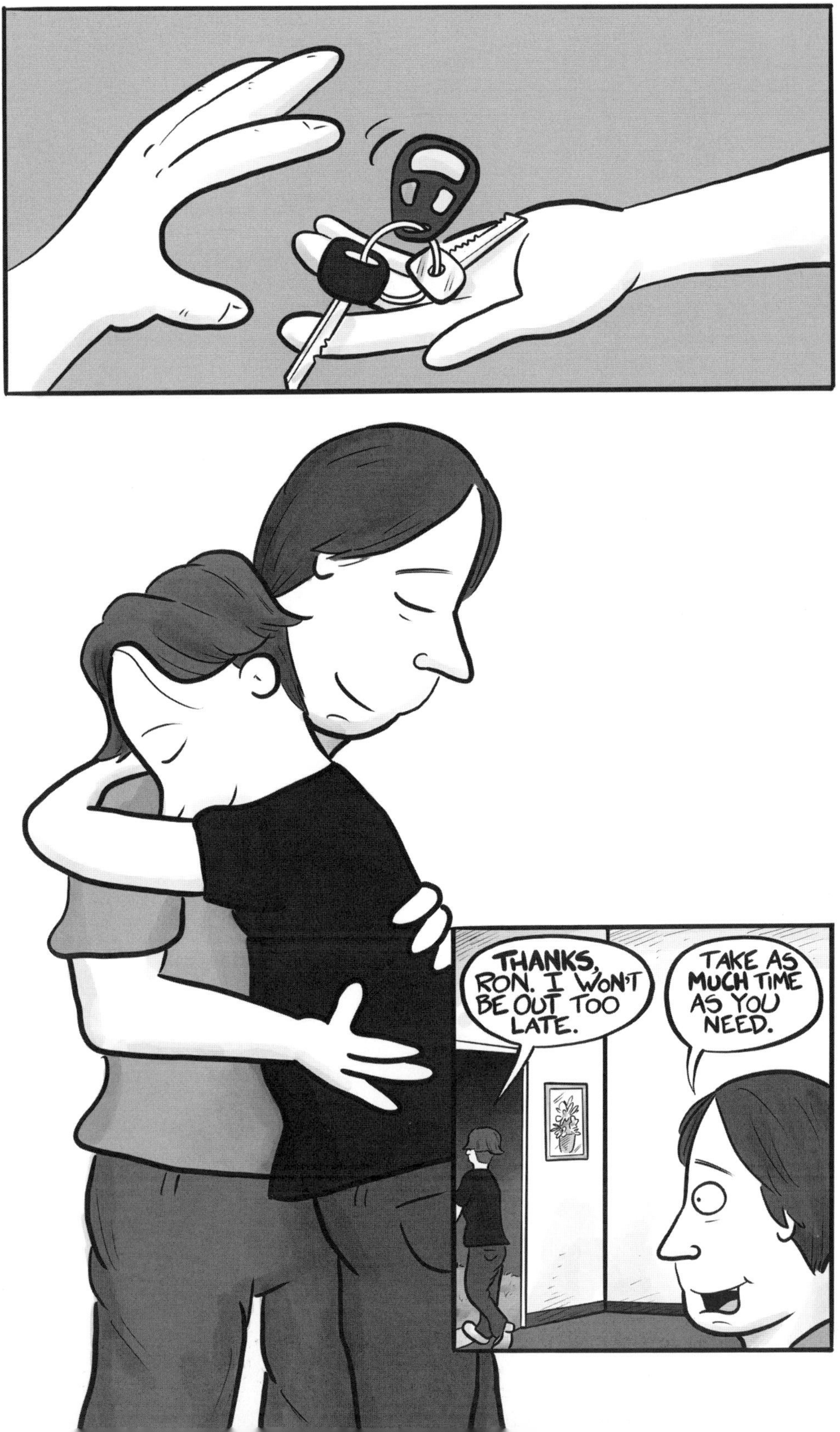
THANKS, RON. I WON'T BE OUT TOO LATE.
TAKE AS MUCH TIME AS YOU NEED.

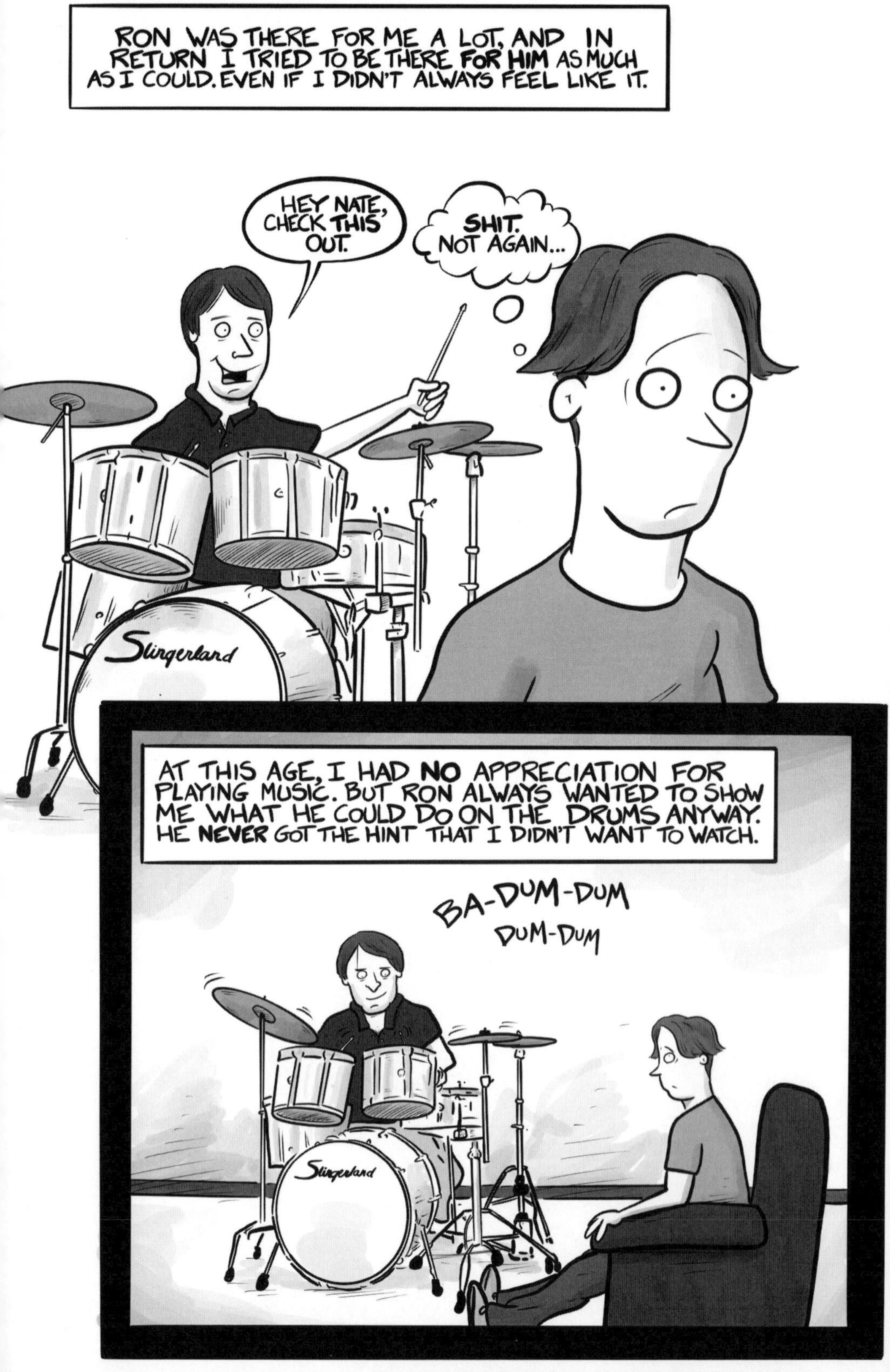
RON WAS THERE FOR ME A LOT, AND IN RETURN I TRIED TO BE THERE FOR HIM AS MUCH AS I COULD. EVEN IF I DIDN'T ALWAYS FEEL LIKE IT.
HEY NATE, CHECK THIS OUT.
SHIT. NOT AGAIN...
Slingerland
AT THIS AGE, I HAD NO APPRECIATION FOR PLAYING MUSIC. BUT RON ALWAYS WANTED TO SHOW ME WHAT HE COULD DO ON THE DRUMS ANYWAY. HE NEVER GOT THE HINT THAT I DIDN'T WANT TO WATCH.
BA-DUM-DUM
DUM-DUM
Slingerland

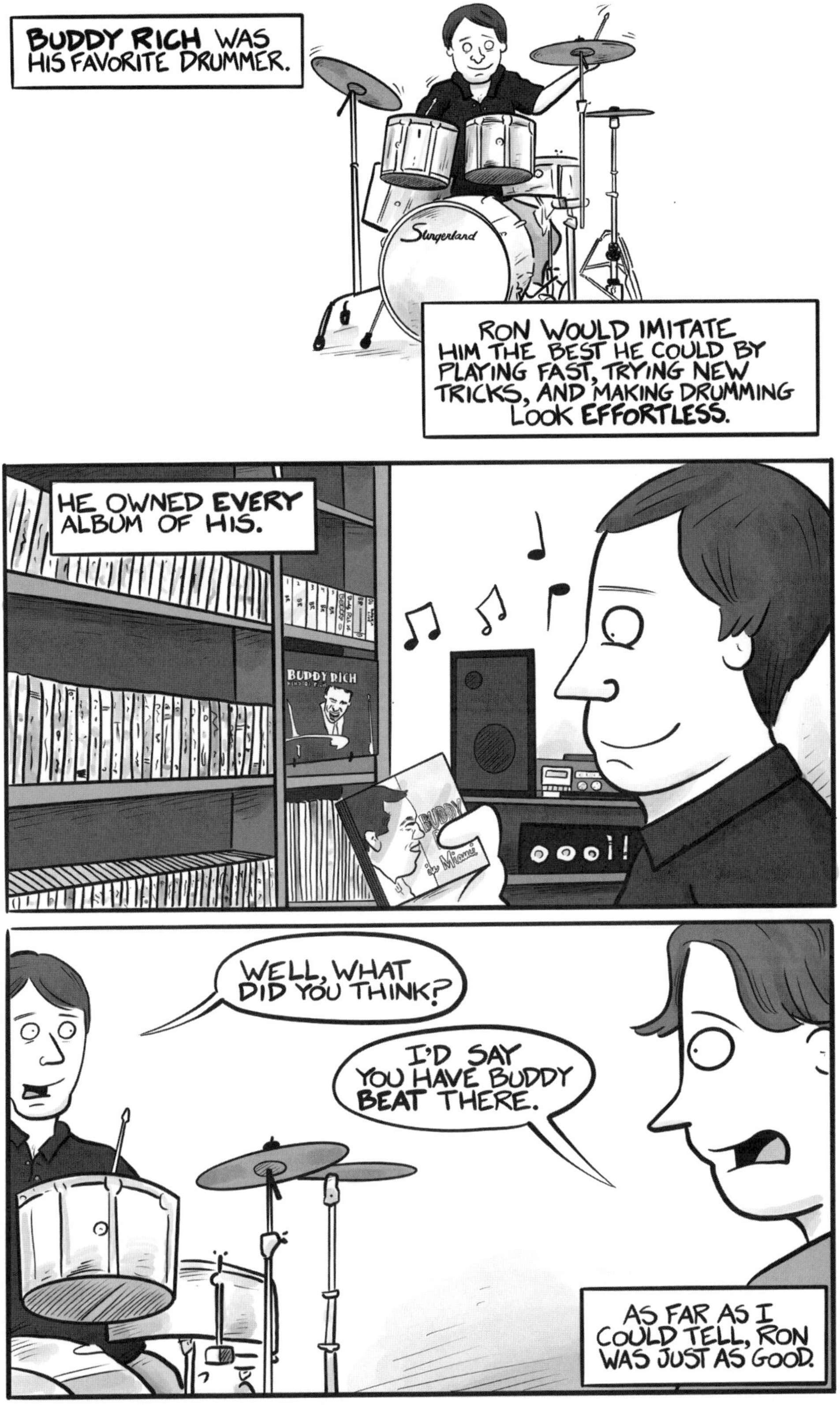
BUDDY RICH WAS HIS FAVORITE DRUMMER.
Slingerland
RON WOULD IMITATE HIM THE BEST HE COULD BY PLAYING FAST, TRYING NEW TRICKS, AND MAKING DRUMMING LOOK EFFORTLESS.
HE OWNED EVERY ALBUM OF HIS.
BUDDY RICH
WELL, WHAT DID YOU THINK?
I'D SAY YOU HAVE BUDDY BEAT THERE.
AS FAR AS I COULD TELL, RON WAS JUST AS GOOD.

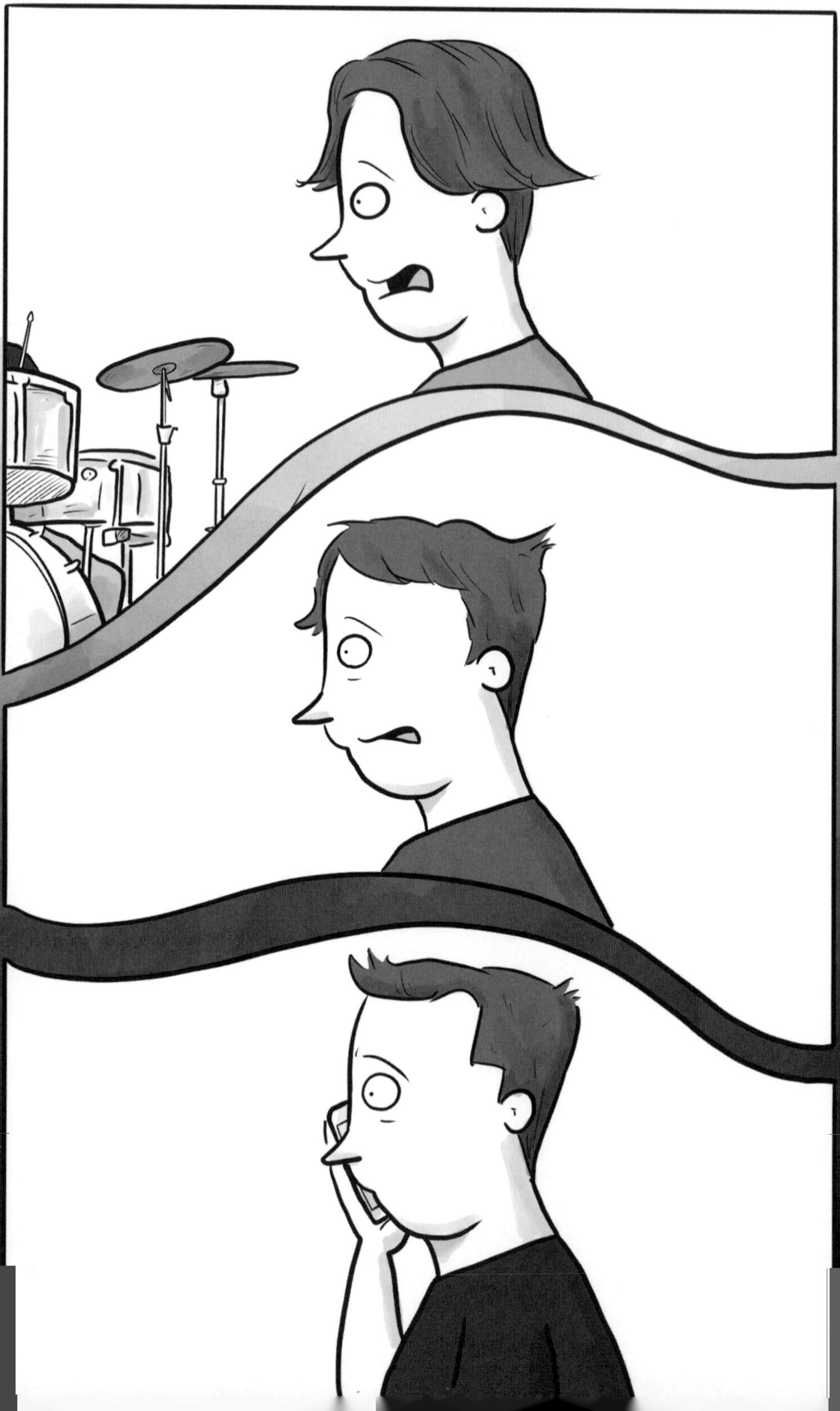

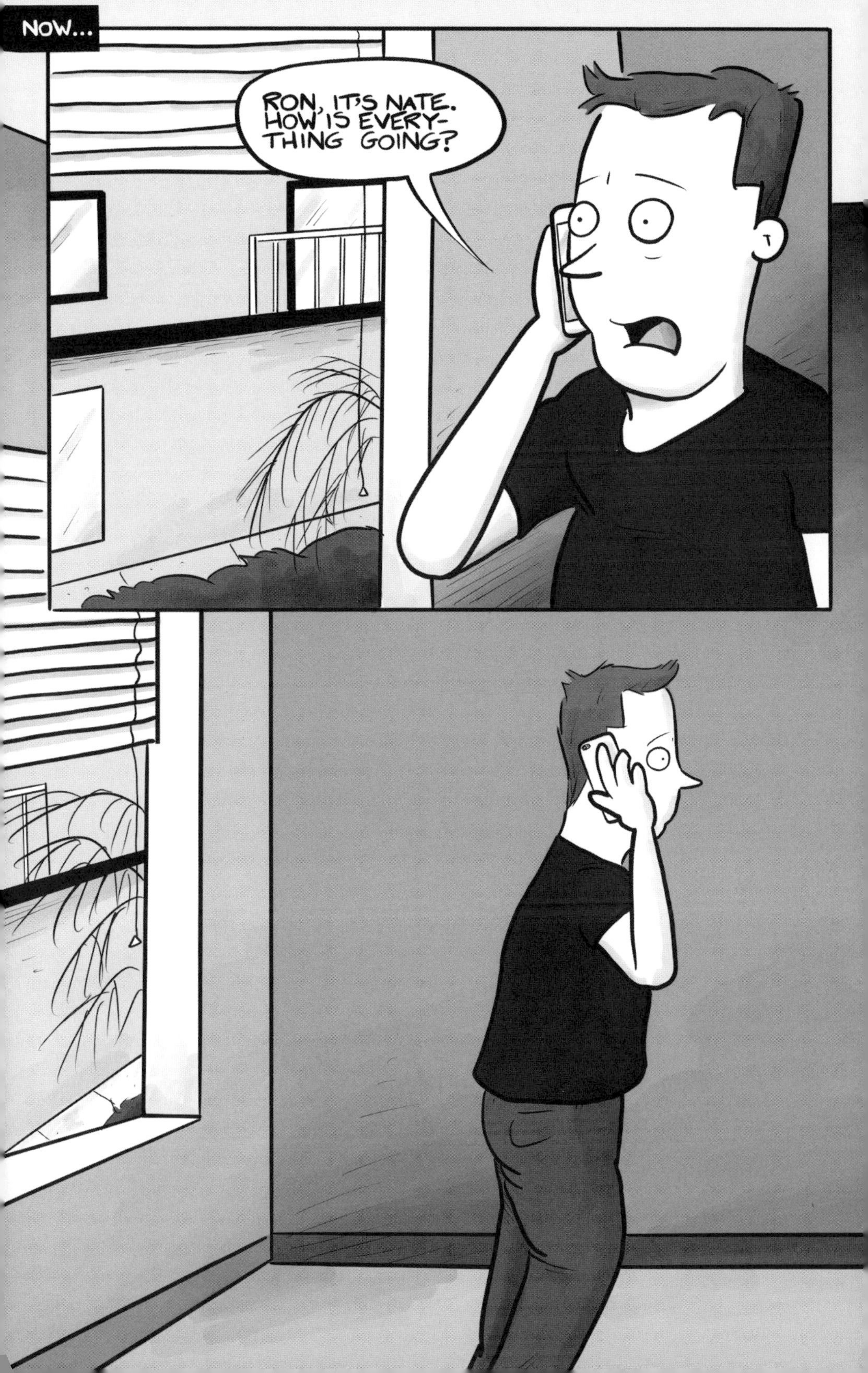
NOW...
RON, IT'S NATE. HOW IS EVERY-THING GOING?

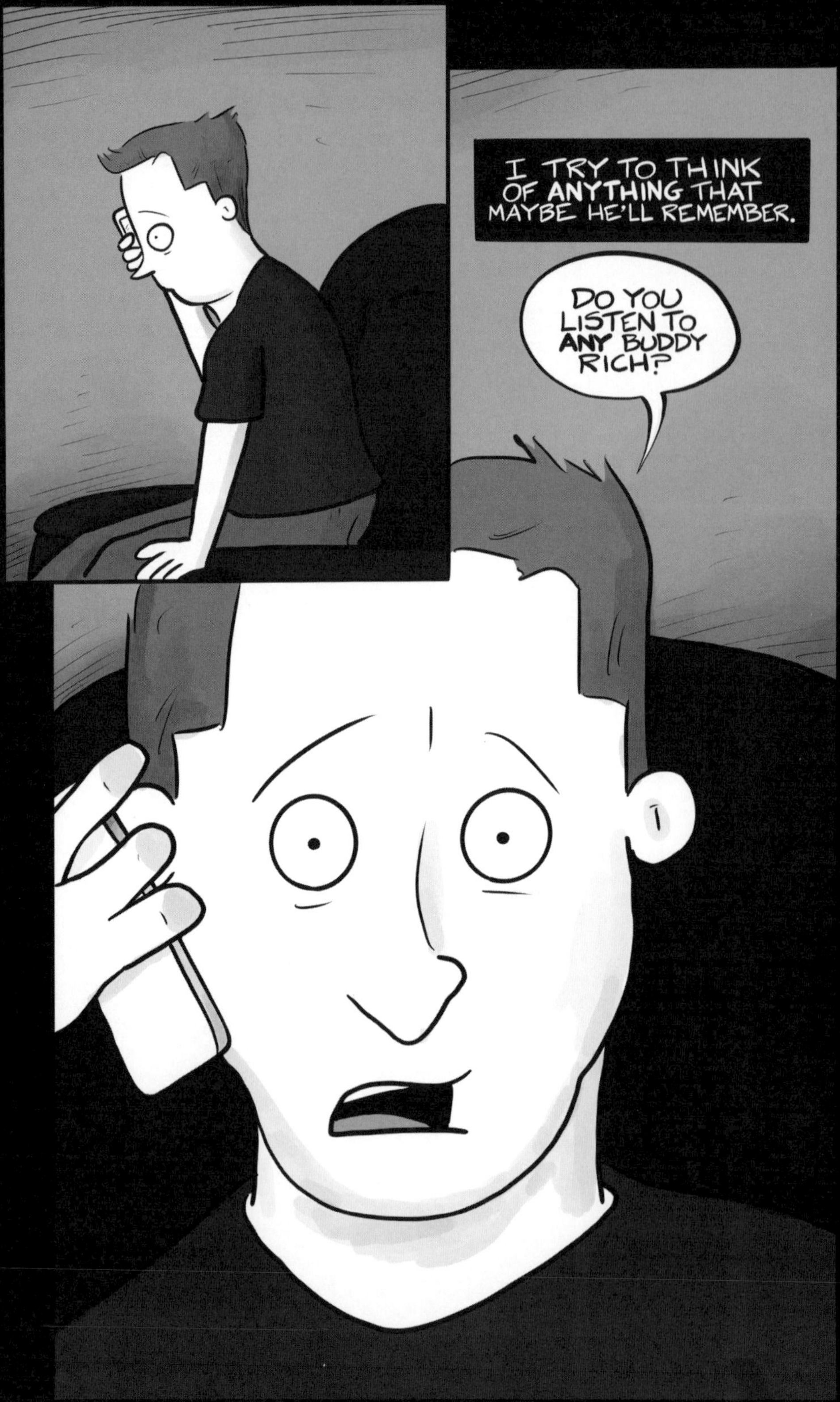
I TRY TO THINK OF ANYTHING THAT MAYBE HE'LL REMEMBER.
DO YOU LISTEN TO ANY BUDDY RICH?

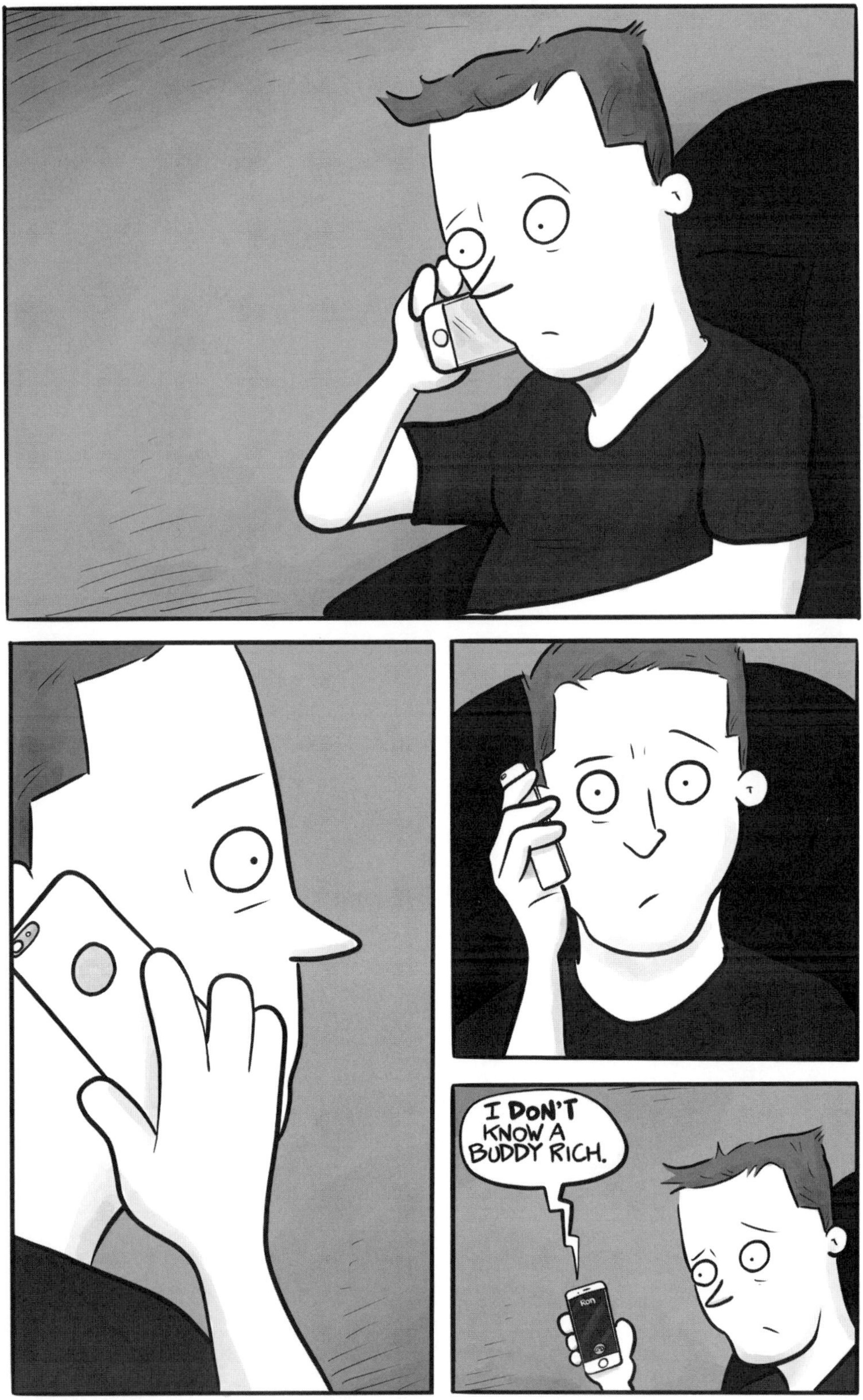
I DON'T KNOW A BUDDY RICH.
Ron

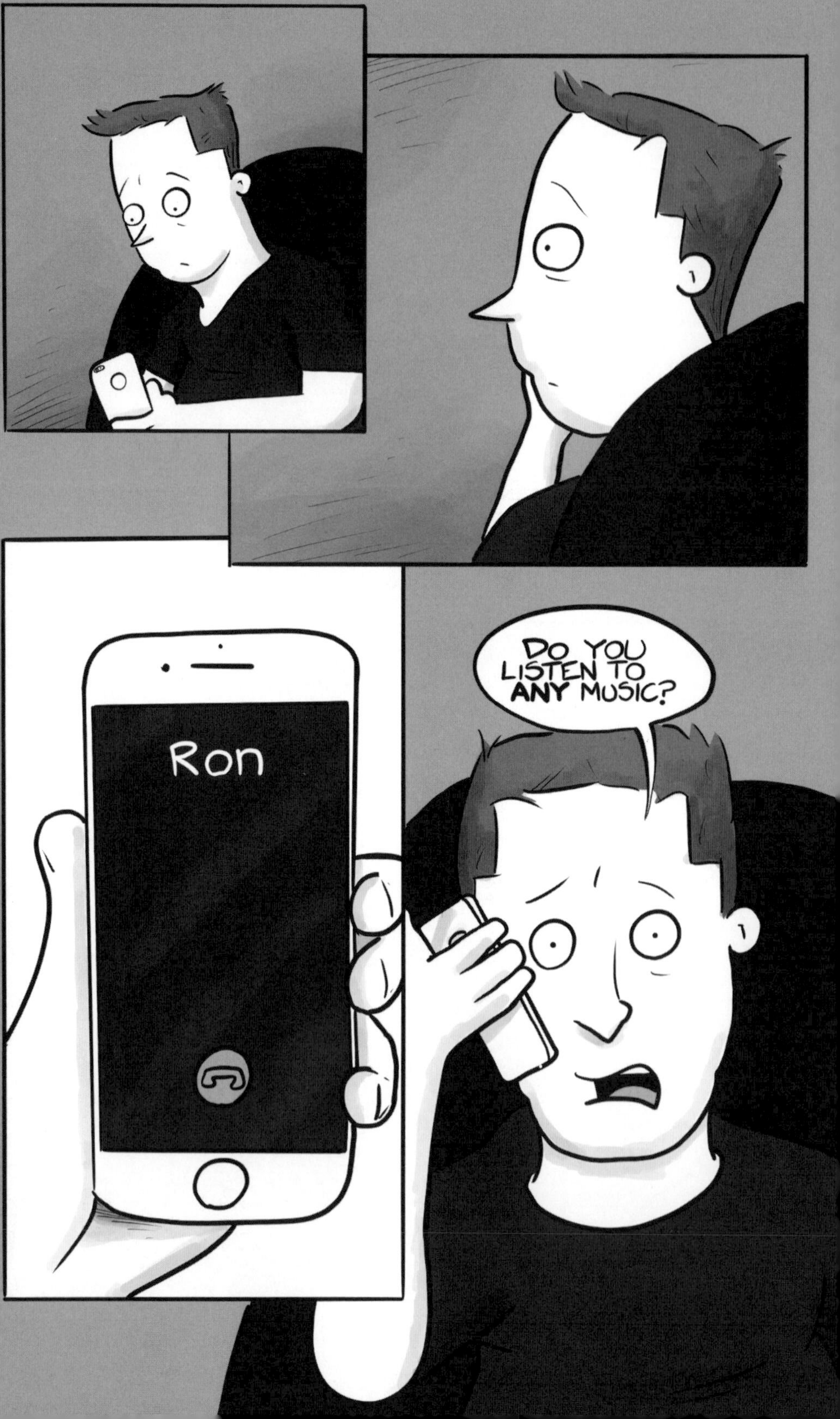
Ron
DO YOU LISTEN TO **ANY** MUSIC?

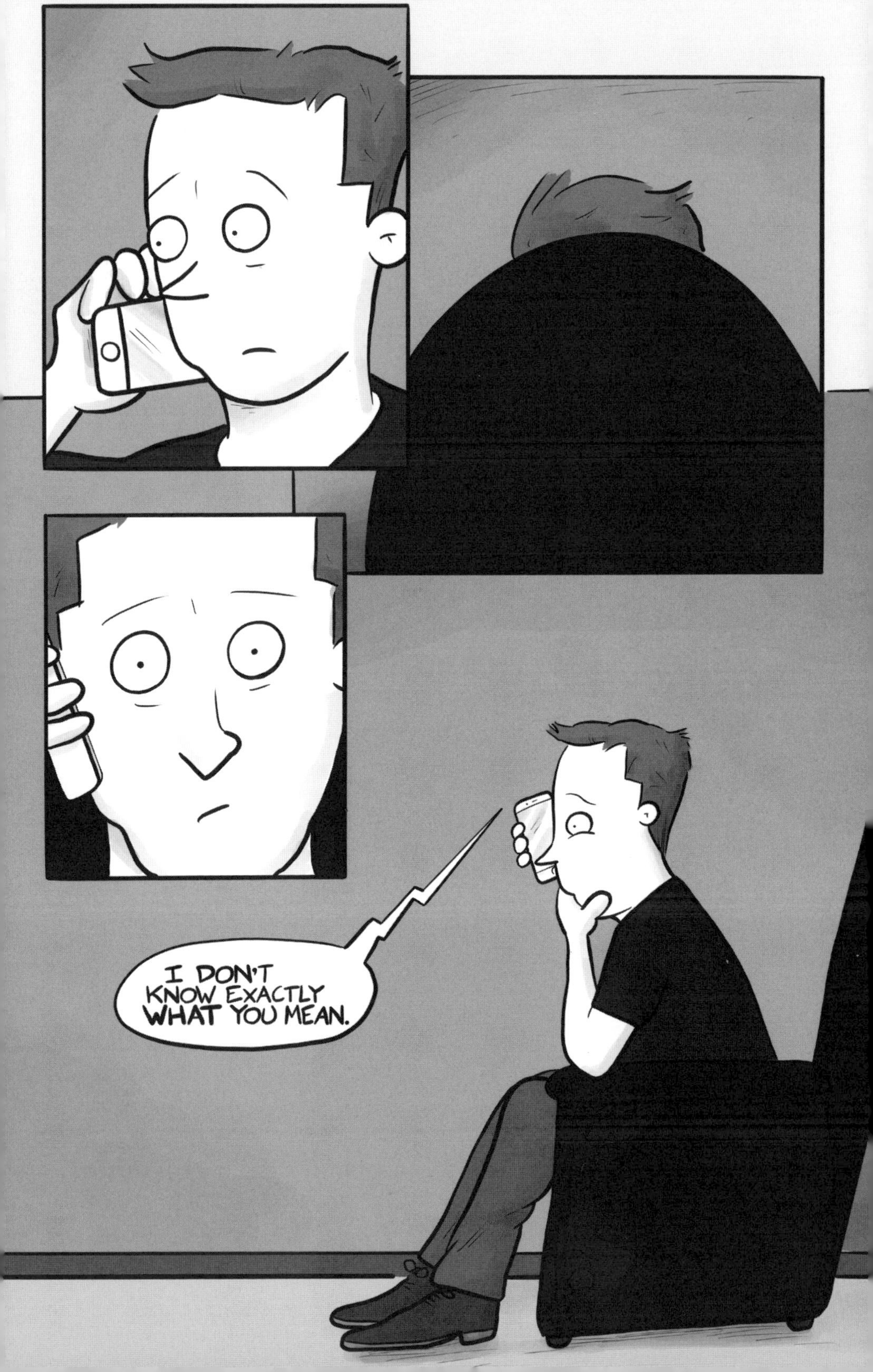
I DON'T KNOW EXACTLY WHAT YOU MEAN.

PART TWO
DRUMMING ALONG

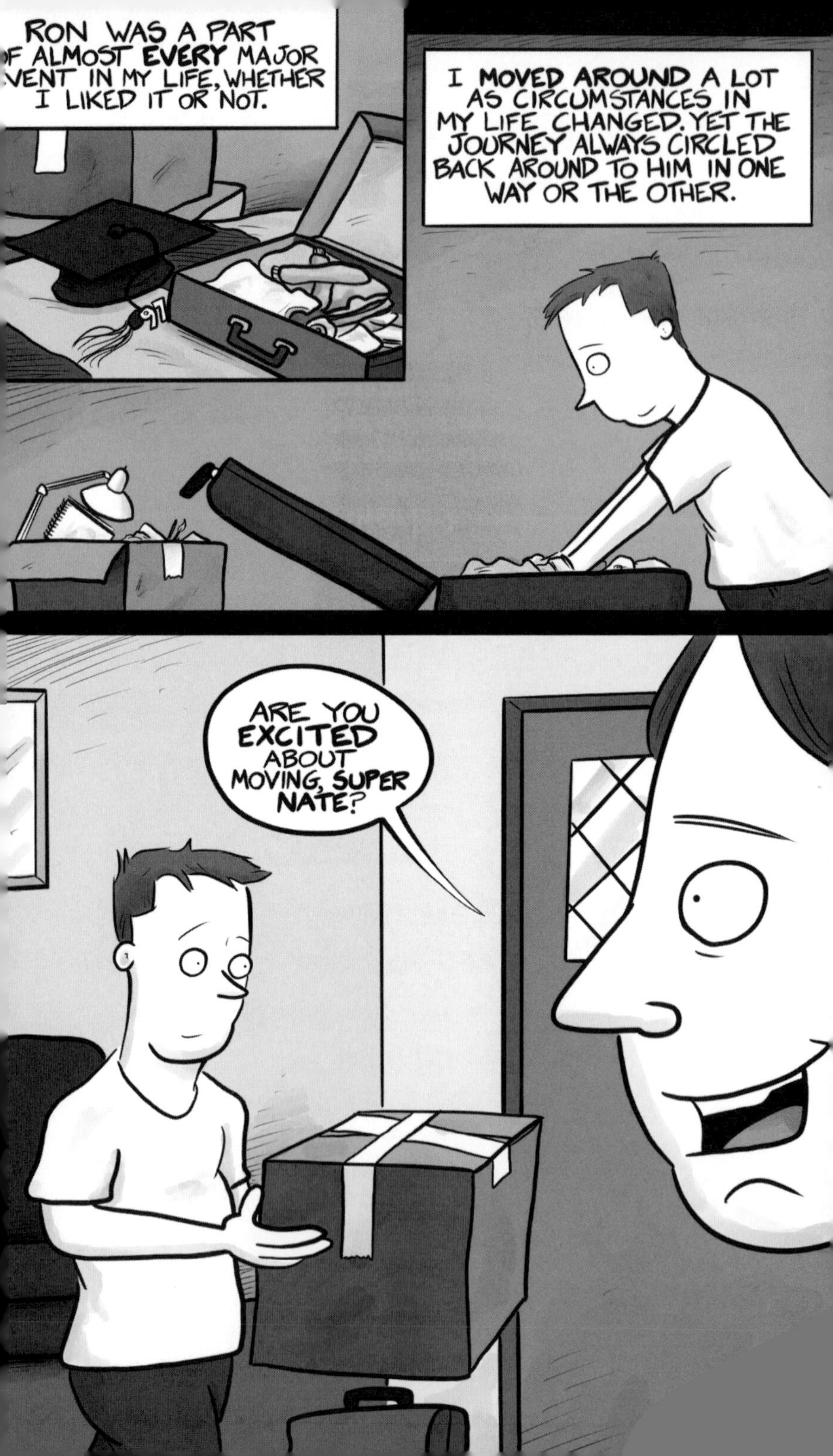

RON WAS A PART OF ALMOST EVERY MAJOR EVENT IN MY LIFE, WHETHER I LIKED IT OR NOT.
I MOVED AROUND A LOT AS CIRCUMSTANCES IN MY LIFE CHANGED. YET THE JOURNEY ALWAYS CIRCLED BACK AROUND TO HIM IN ONE WAY OR THE OTHER.
ARE YOU EXCITED ABOUT MOVING, SUPER NATE?

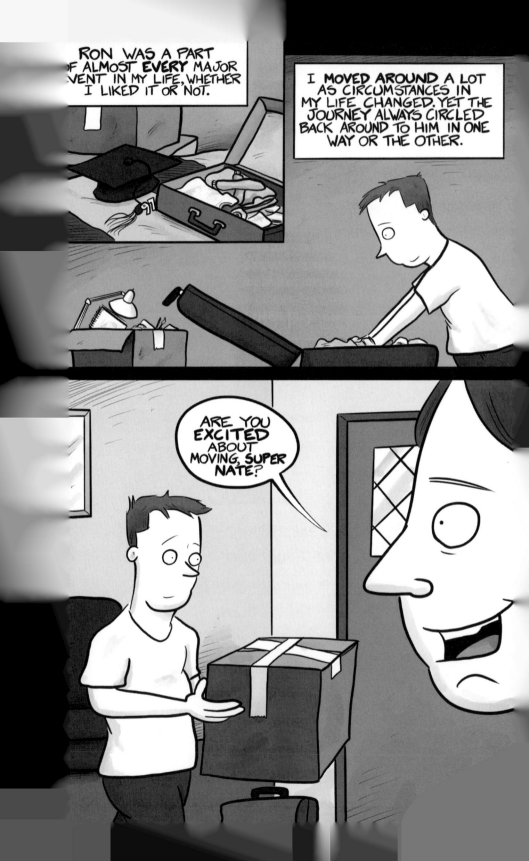

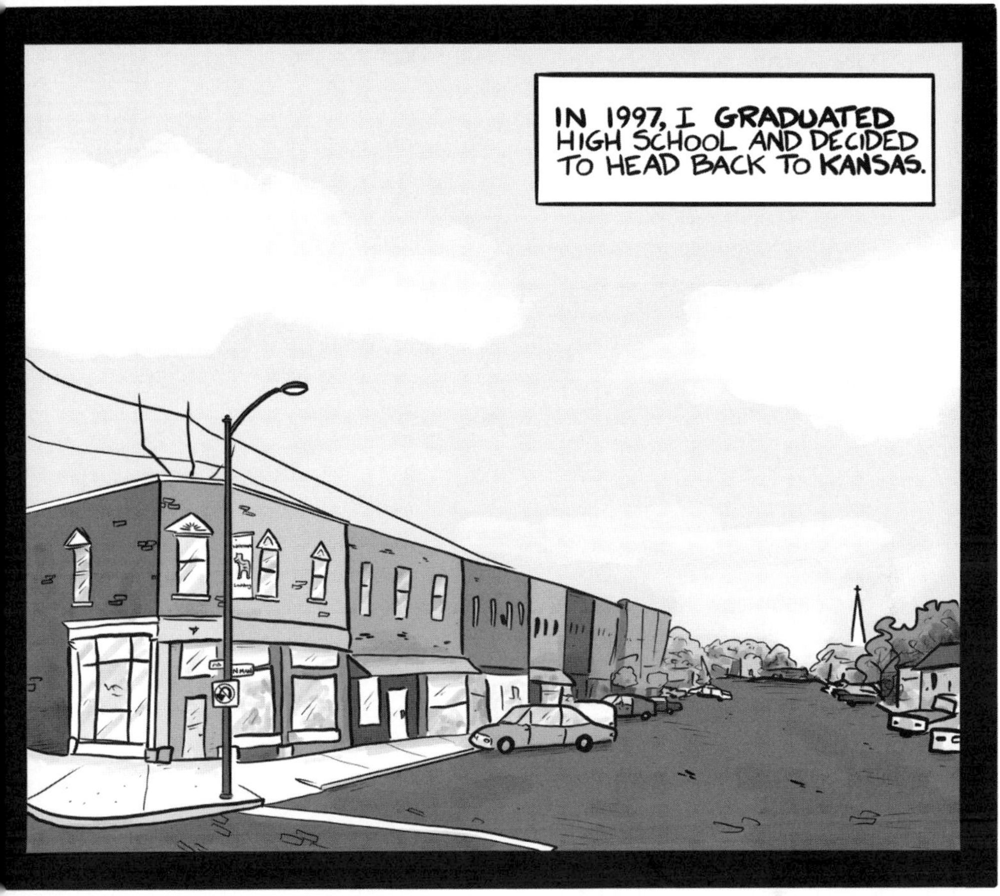
IN 1997, I GRADUATED HIGH SCHOOL AND DECIDED TO HEAD BACK TO KANSAS.

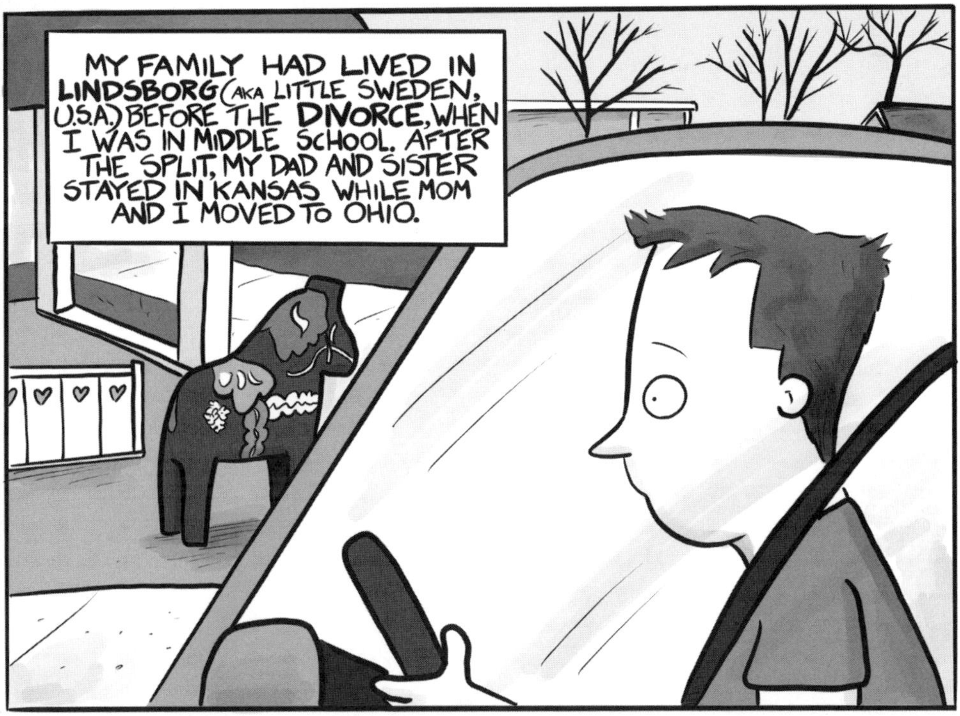
MY FAMILY HAD LIVED IN LINDSBORG (AKA LITTLE SWEDEN, U.S.A.) BEFORE THE DIVORCE, WHEN I WAS IN MIDDLE SCHOOL. AFTER THE SPLIT, MY DAD AND SISTER STAYED IN KANSAS WHILE MOM AND I MOVED TO OHIO.

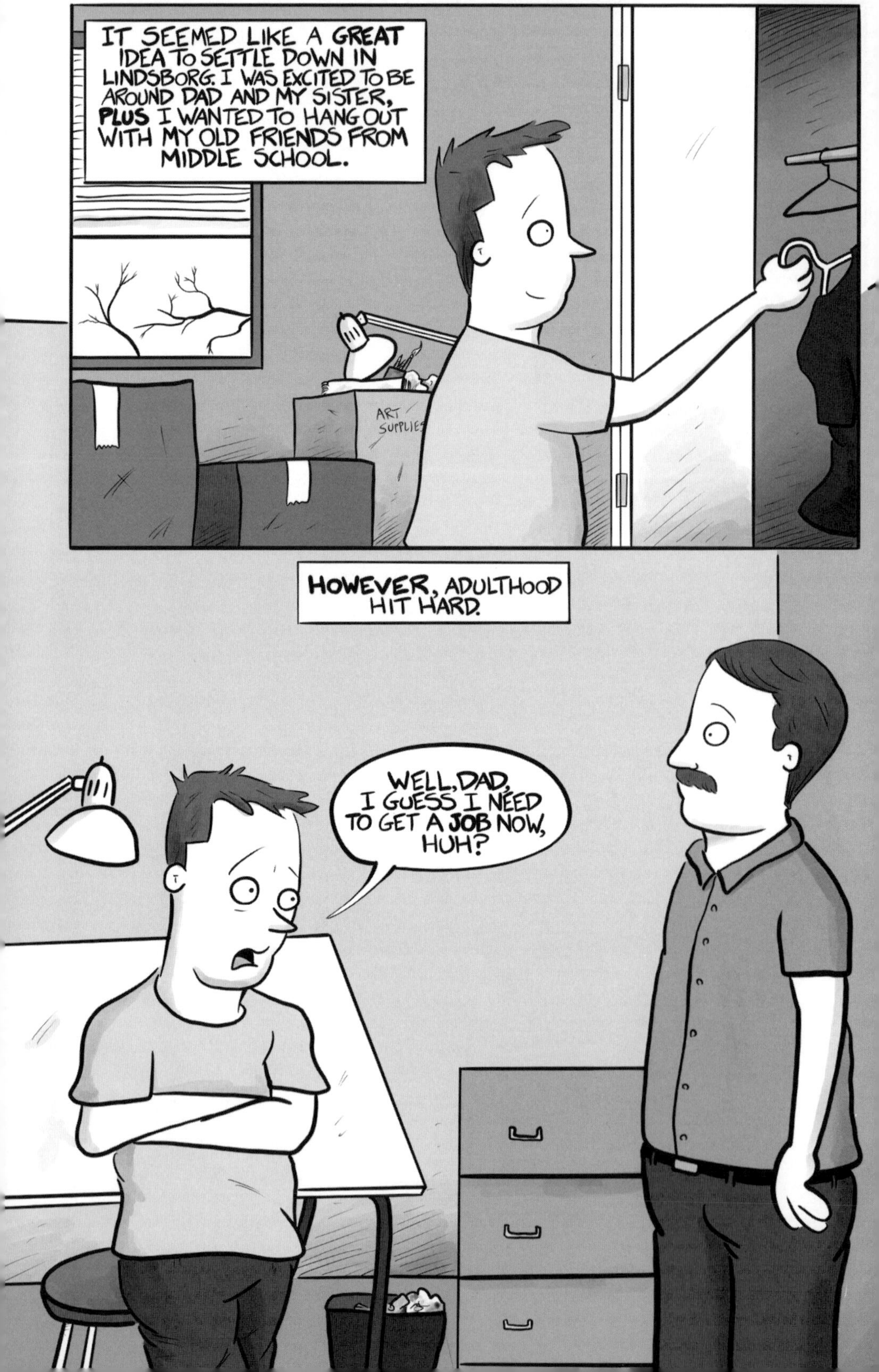
IT SEEMED LIKE A **GREAT** IDEA TO SETTLE DOWN IN LINDSBORG. I WAS EXCITED TO BE AROUND DAD AND MY SISTER, **PLUS** I WANTED TO HANG OUT WITH MY OLD FRIENDS FROM MIDDLE SCHOOL.
ART SUPPLIES
HOWEVER, ADULTHOOD HIT HARD.
WELL, DAD, I GUESS I NEED TO GET A **JOB** NOW, HUH?

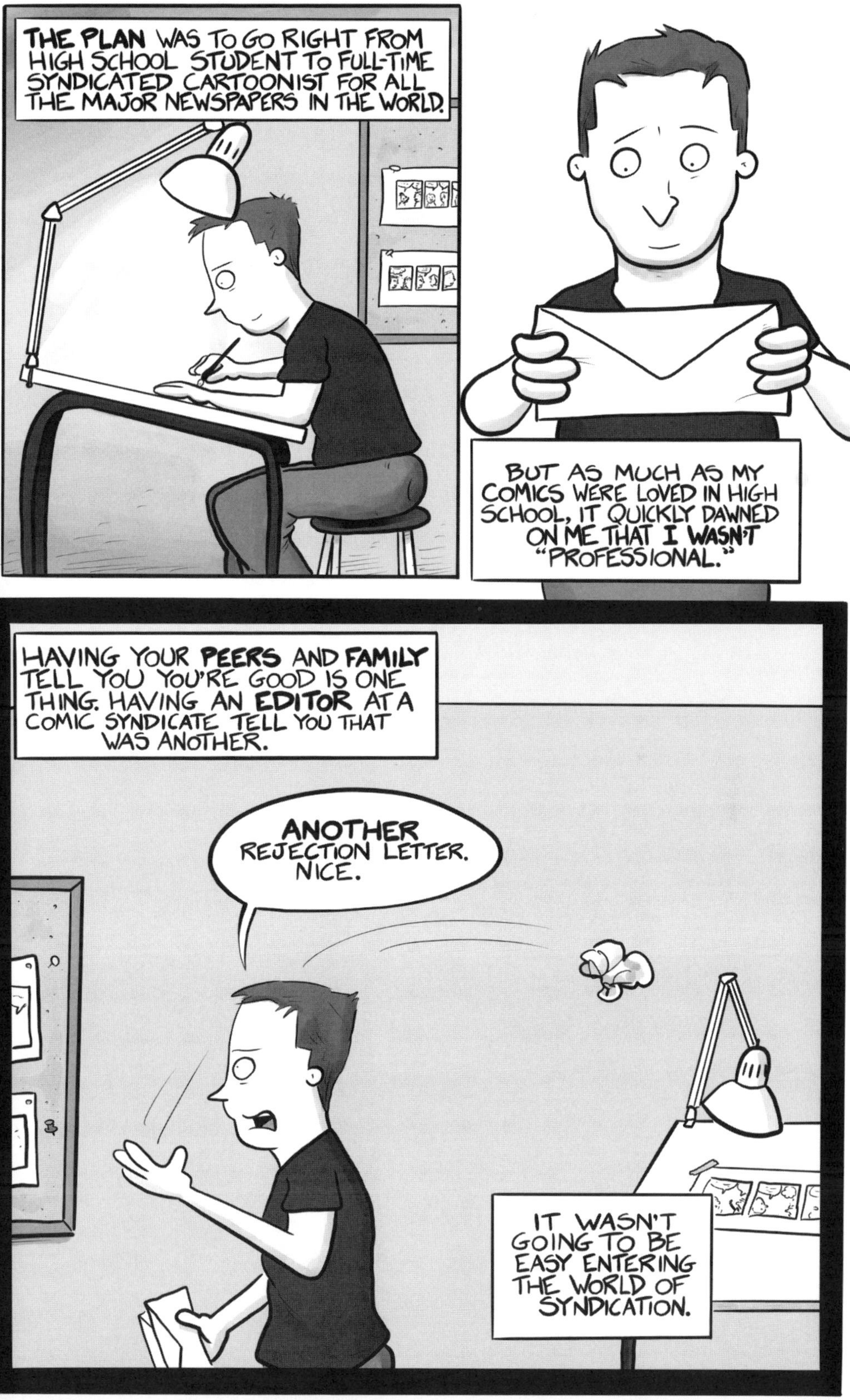

THE PLAN WAS TO GO RIGHT FROM HIGH SCHOOL STUDENT TO FULL-TIME SYNDICATED CARTOONIST FOR ALL THE MAJOR NEWSPAPERS IN THE WORLD.
BUT AS MUCH AS MY COMICS WERE LOVED IN HIGH SCHOOL, IT QUICKLY DAWNED ON ME THAT **I WASN'T** "PROFESSIONAL."
HAVING YOUR **PEERS** AND **FAMILY** TELL YOU YOU'RE GOOD IS ONE THING. HAVING AN **EDITOR** AT A COMIC SYNDICATE TELL YOU THAT WAS ANOTHER.
ANOTHER REJECTION LETTER. NICE.
IT WASN'T GOING TO BE EASY ENTERING THE WORLD OF SYNDICATION.

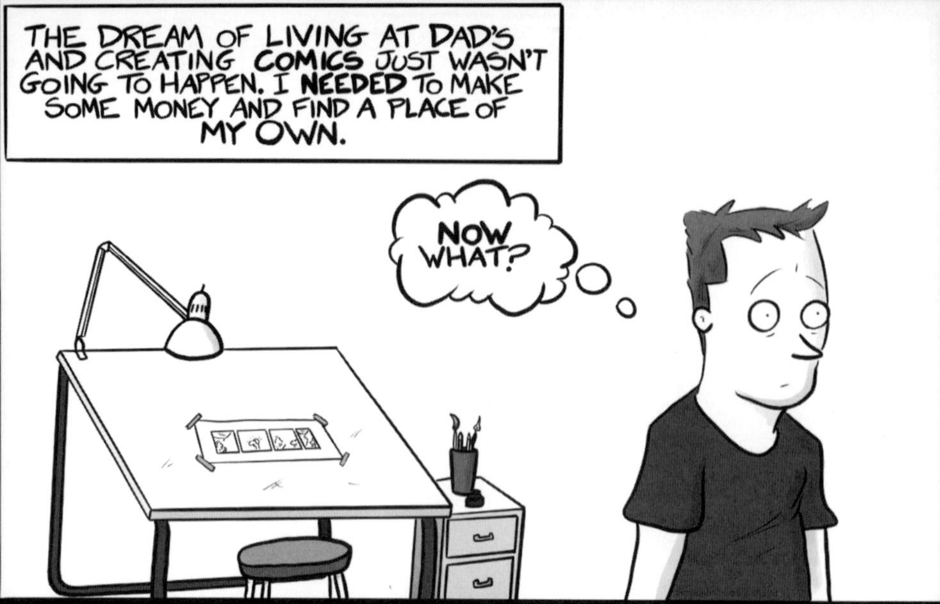
THE DREAM OF LIVING AT DAD'S AND CREATING COMICS JUST WASN'T GOING TO HAPPEN. I NEEDED TO MAKE SOME MONEY AND FIND A PLACE OF MY OWN.
NOW WHAT?

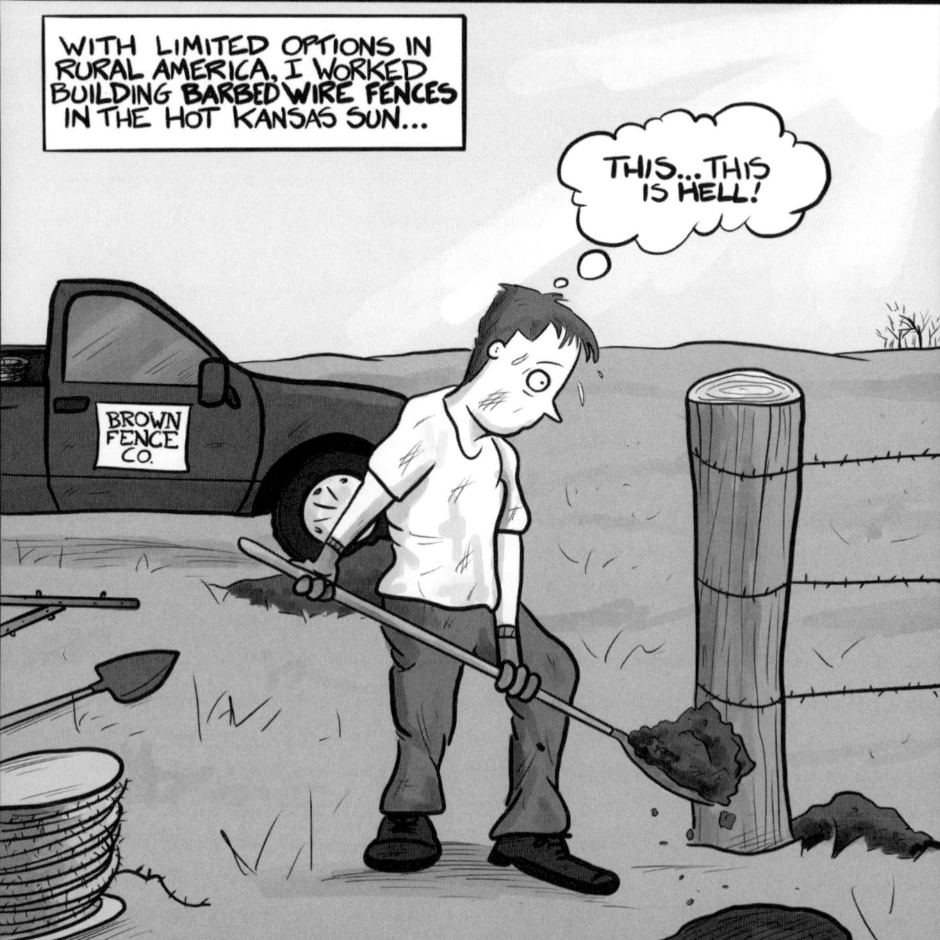
WITH LIMITED OPTIONS IN RURAL AMERICA, I WORKED BUILDING BARBED WIRE FENCES IN THE HOT KANSAS SUN...
THIS...THIS IS HELL!
BROWN FENCE CO.

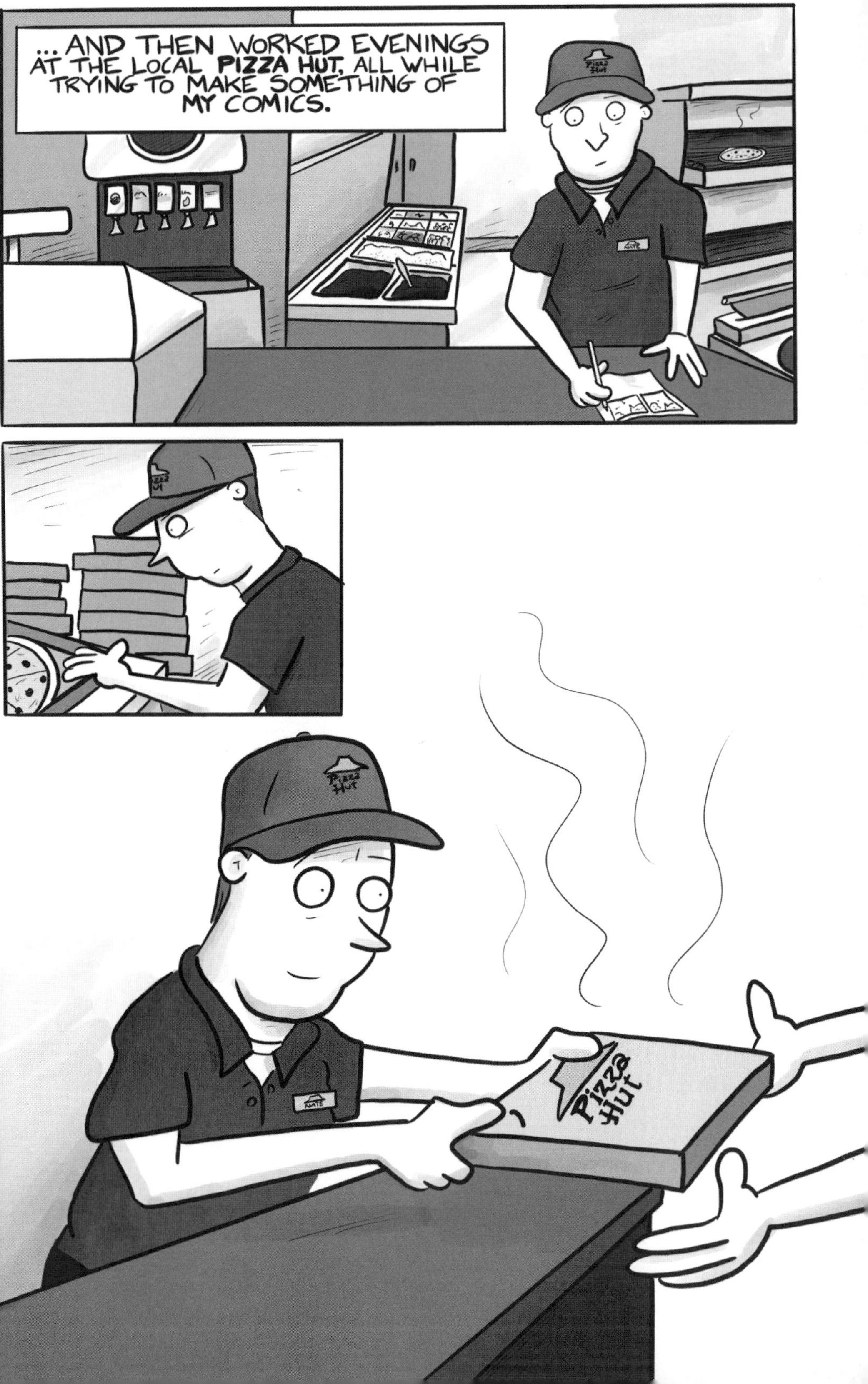
...AND THEN WORKED EVENINGS AT THE LOCAL PIZZA HUT, ALL WHILE TRYING TO MAKE SOMETHING OF MY COMICS.
Pizza Hut

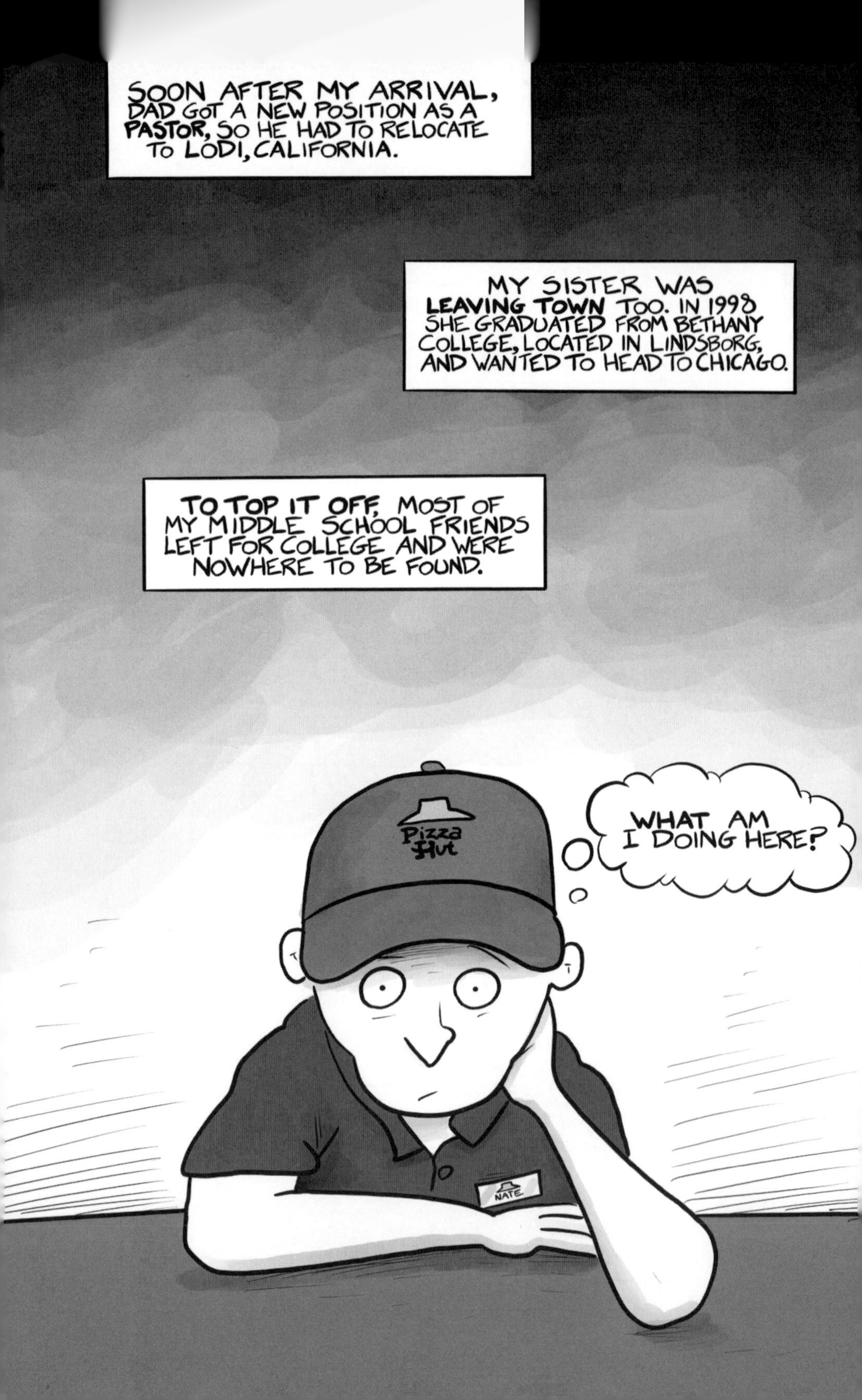
SOON AFTER MY ARRIVAL, DAD GOT A NEW POSITION AS A PASTOR, SO HE HAD TO RELOCATE TO LODI, CALIFORNIA.
MY SISTER WAS LEAVING TOWN TOO. IN 1998 SHE GRADUATED FROM BETHANY COLLEGE, LOCATED IN LINDSBORG, AND WANTED TO HEAD TO CHICAGO.
TO TOP IT OFF, MOST OF MY MIDDLE SCHOOL FRIENDS LEFT FOR COLLEGE AND WERE NOWHERE TO BE FOUND.
Pizza Hut
WHAT AM I DOING HERE?
NATE

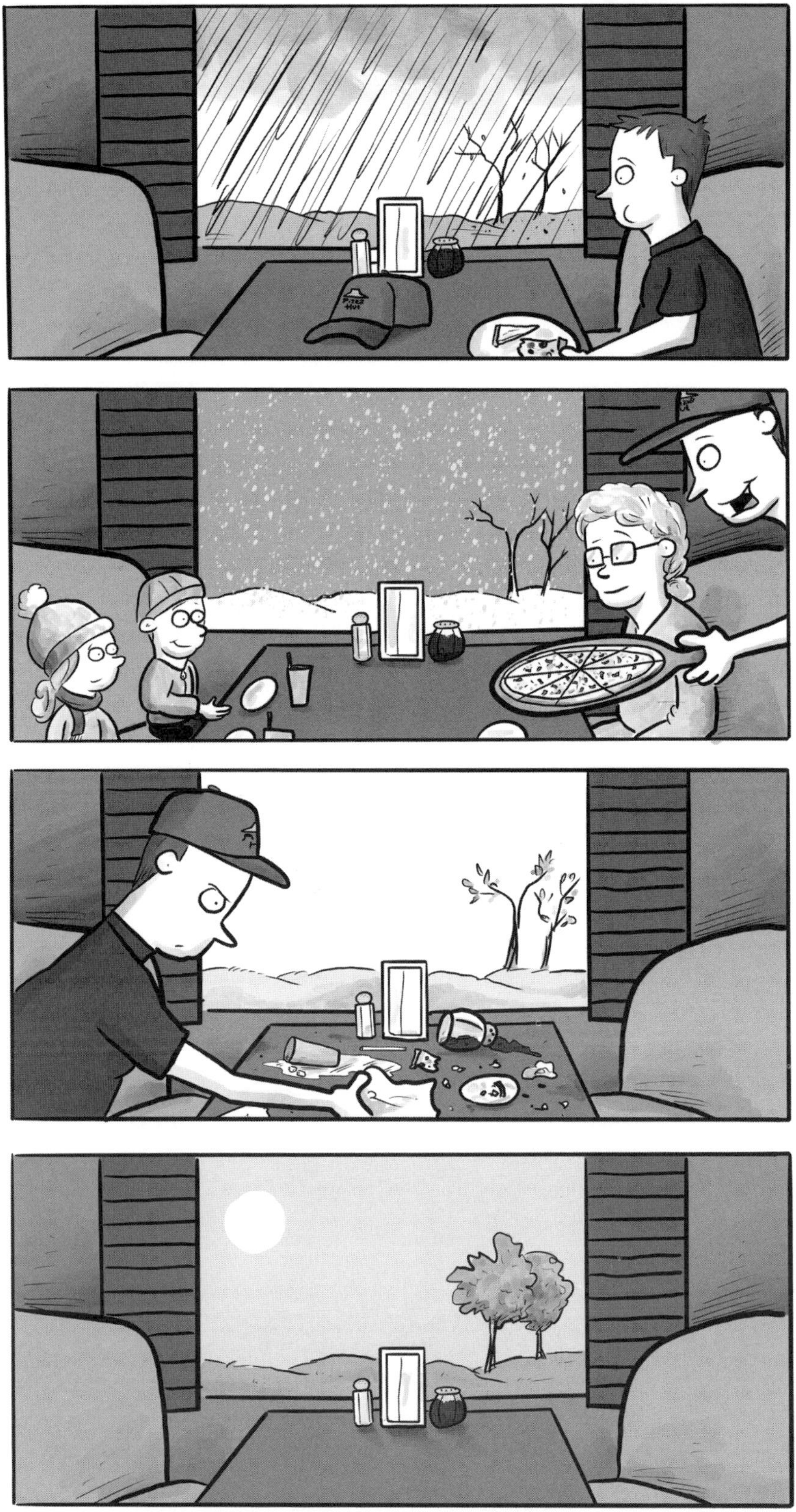
Pizza Hut

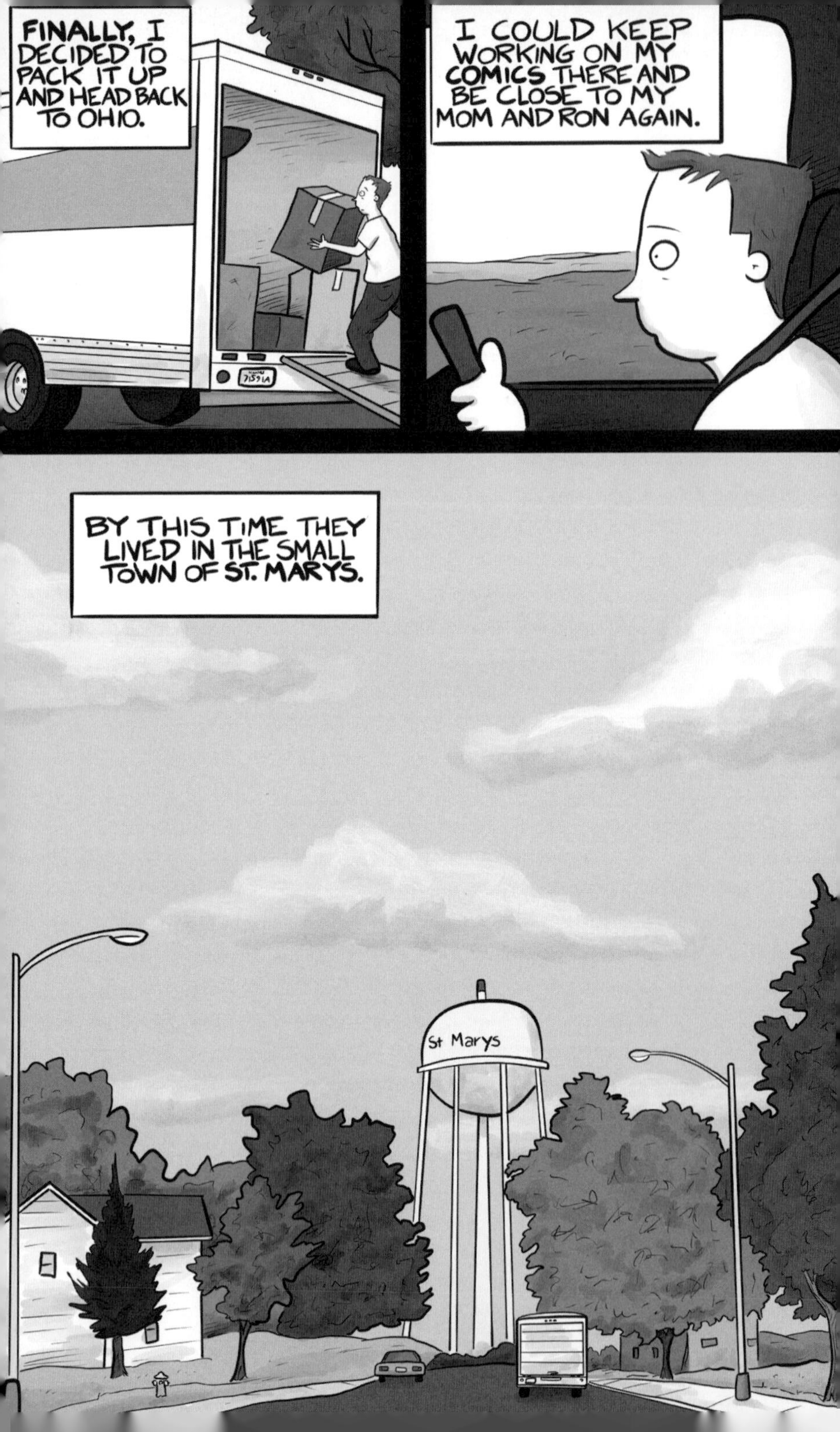
FINALLY, I DECIDED TO PACK IT UP AND HEAD BACK TO OHIO.
I COULD KEEP WORKING ON MY COMICS THERE AND BE CLOSE TO MY MOM AND RON AGAIN.
BY THIS TIME THEY LIVED IN THE SMALL TOWN OF ST. MARYS.
St Marys

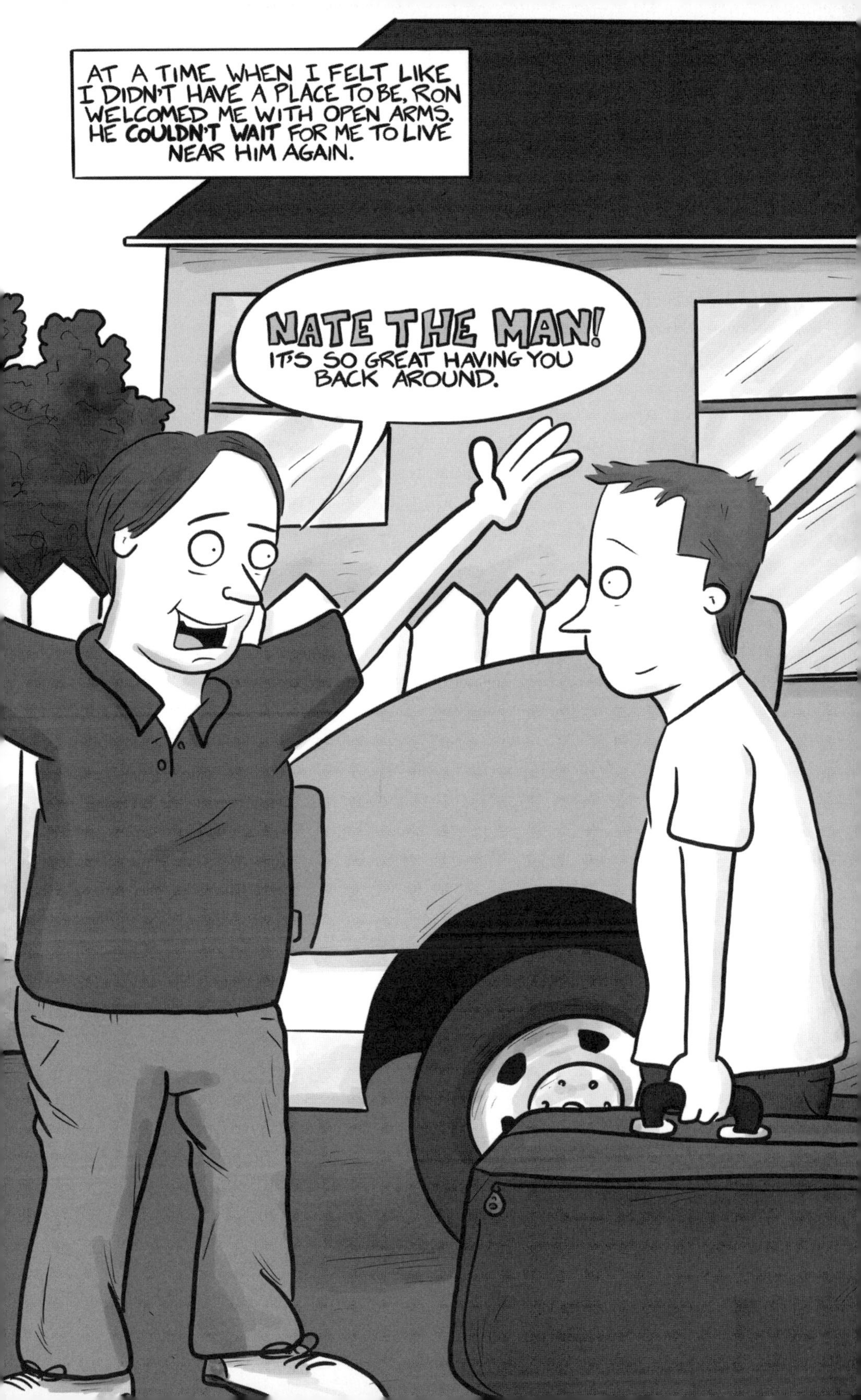
AT A TIME WHEN I FELT LIKE I DIDN'T HAVE A PLACE TO BE, RON WELCOMED ME WITH OPEN ARMS. HE **COULDN'T WAIT** FOR ME TO LIVE NEAR HIM AGAIN.
NATE THE MAN! IT'S SO GREAT HAVING YOU BACK AROUND.

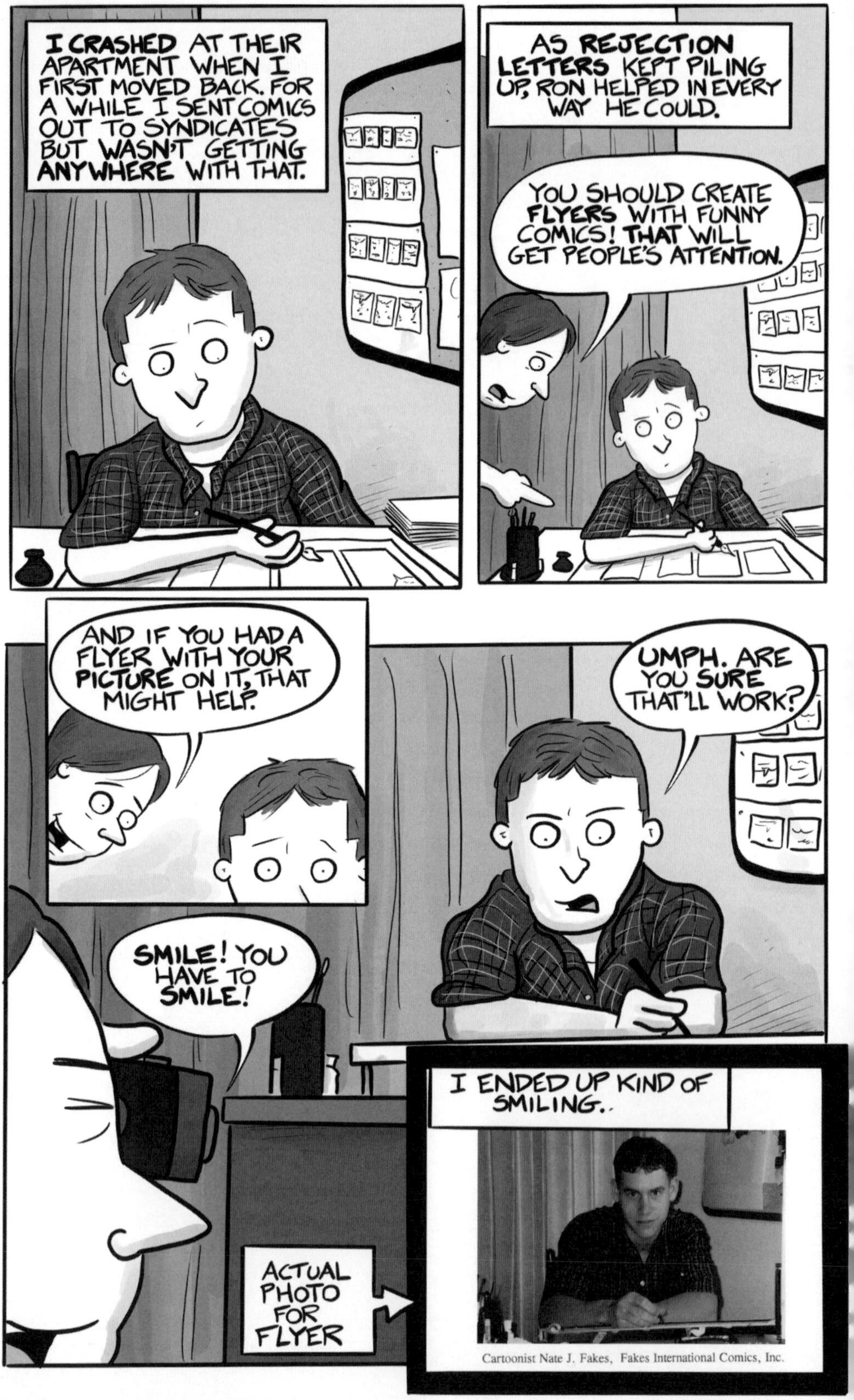
I CRASHED AT THEIR APARTMENT WHEN I FIRST MOVED BACK. FOR A WHILE I SENT COMICS OUT TO SYNDICATES BUT WASN'T GETTING ANYWHERE WITH THAT.
AS REJECTION LETTERS KEPT PILING UP, RON HELPED IN EVERY WAY HE COULD.
YOU SHOULD CREATE FLYERS WITH FUNNY COMICS! THAT WILL GET PEOPLE'S ATTENTION.
AND IF YOU HAD A FLYER WITH YOUR PICTURE ON IT, THAT MIGHT HELP.
UMPH. ARE YOU SURE THAT'LL WORK?
SMILE! YOU HAVE TO SMILE!
I ENDED UP KIND OF SMILING..
ACTUAL PHOTO FOR FLYER
Cartoonist Nate J. Fakes, Fakes International Comics, Inc.

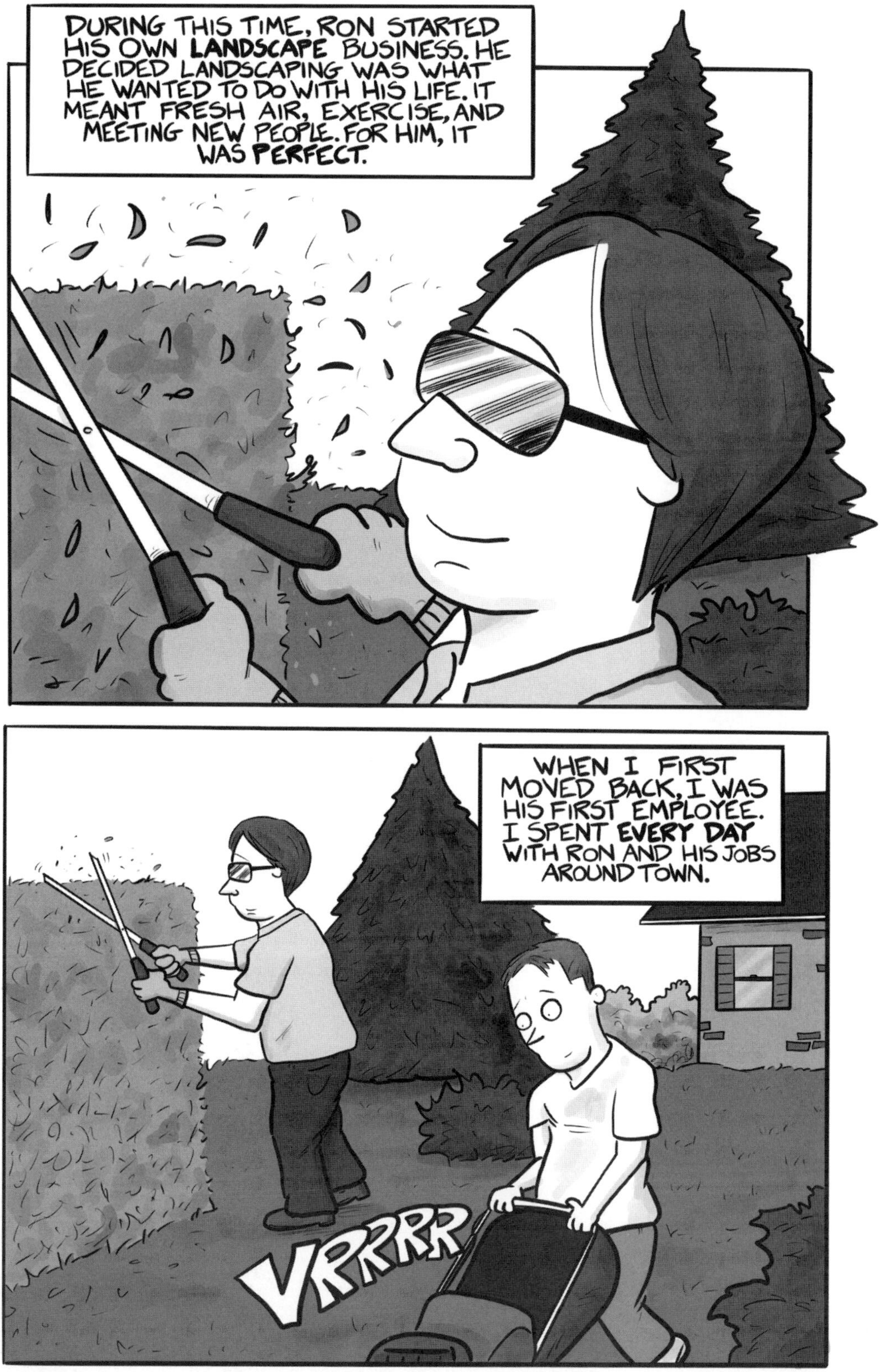
DURING THIS TIME, RON STARTED HIS OWN LANDSCAPE BUSINESS. HE DECIDED LANDSCAPING WAS WHAT HE WANTED TO DO WITH HIS LIFE. IT MEANT FRESH AIR, EXERCISE, AND MEETING NEW PEOPLE. FOR HIM, IT WAS PERFECT.
WHEN I FIRST MOVED BACK, I WAS HIS FIRST EMPLOYEE. I SPENT EVERY DAY WITH RON AND HIS JOBS AROUND TOWN.
VRRRRR

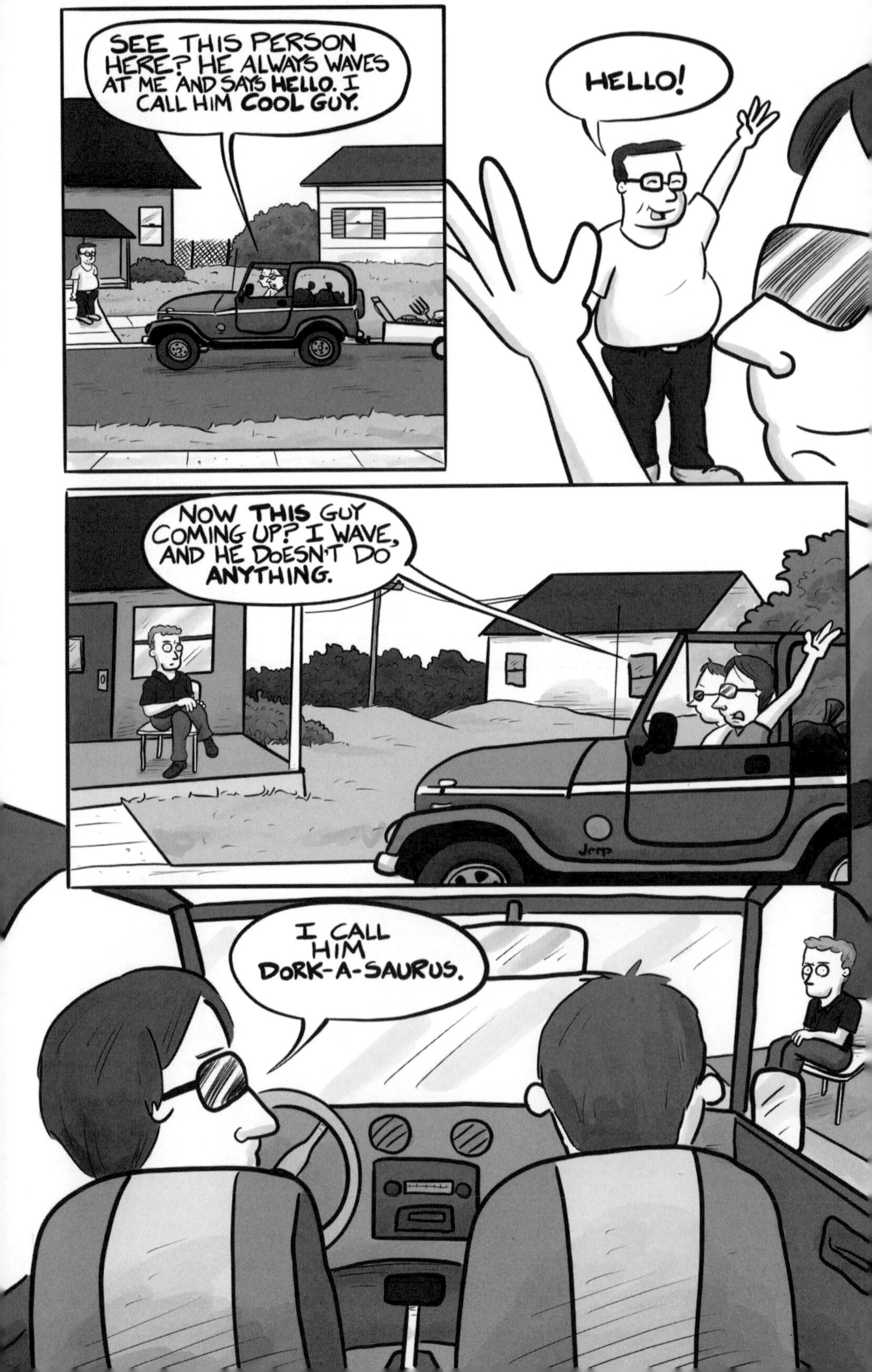
SEE THIS PERSON HERE? HE ALWAYS WAVES AT ME AND SAYS HELLO. I CALL HIM COOL GUY.
HELLO!
NOW THIS GUY COMING UP? I WAVE, AND HE DOESN'T DO ANYTHING.
Jeep
I CALL HIM DORK-A-SAURUS.

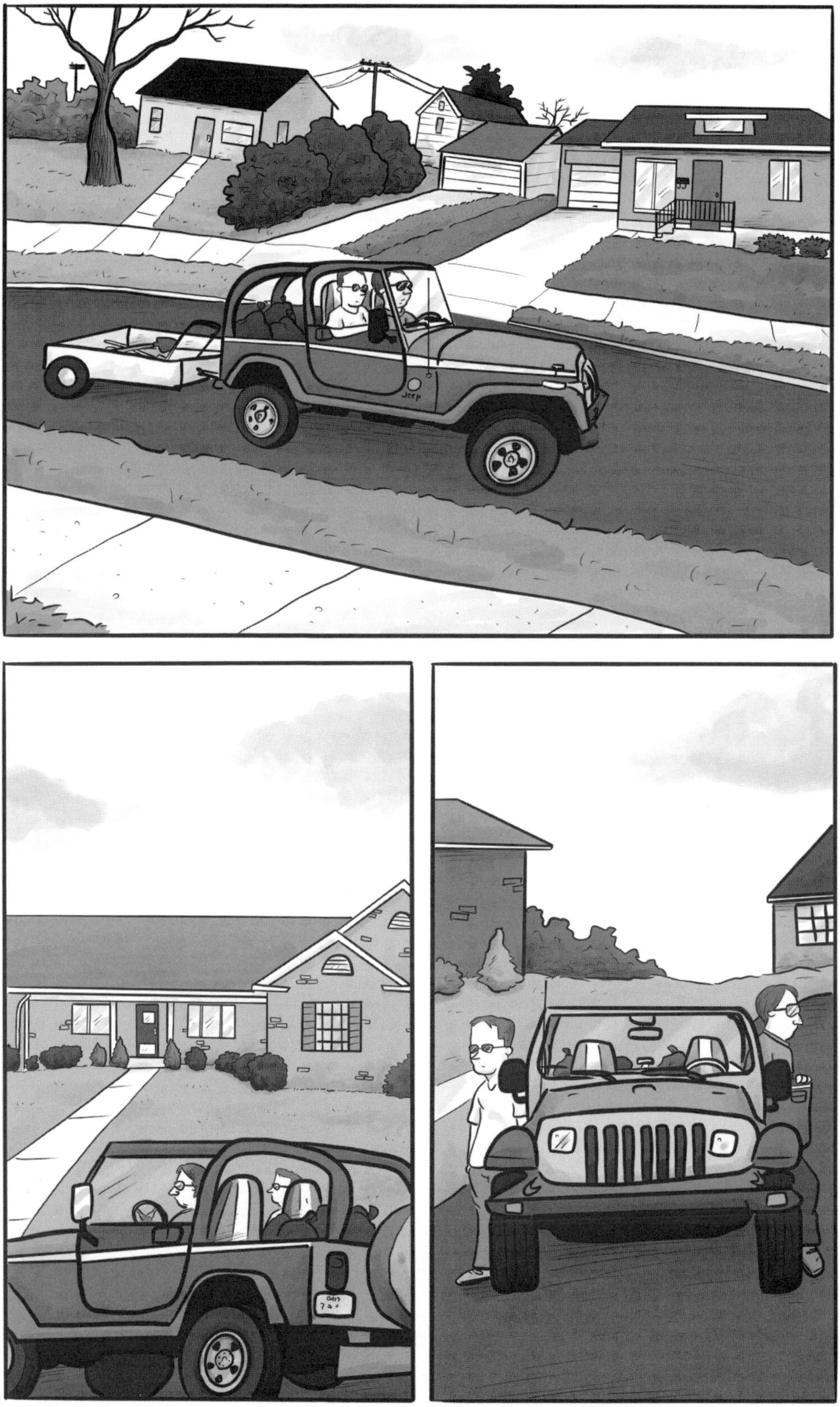

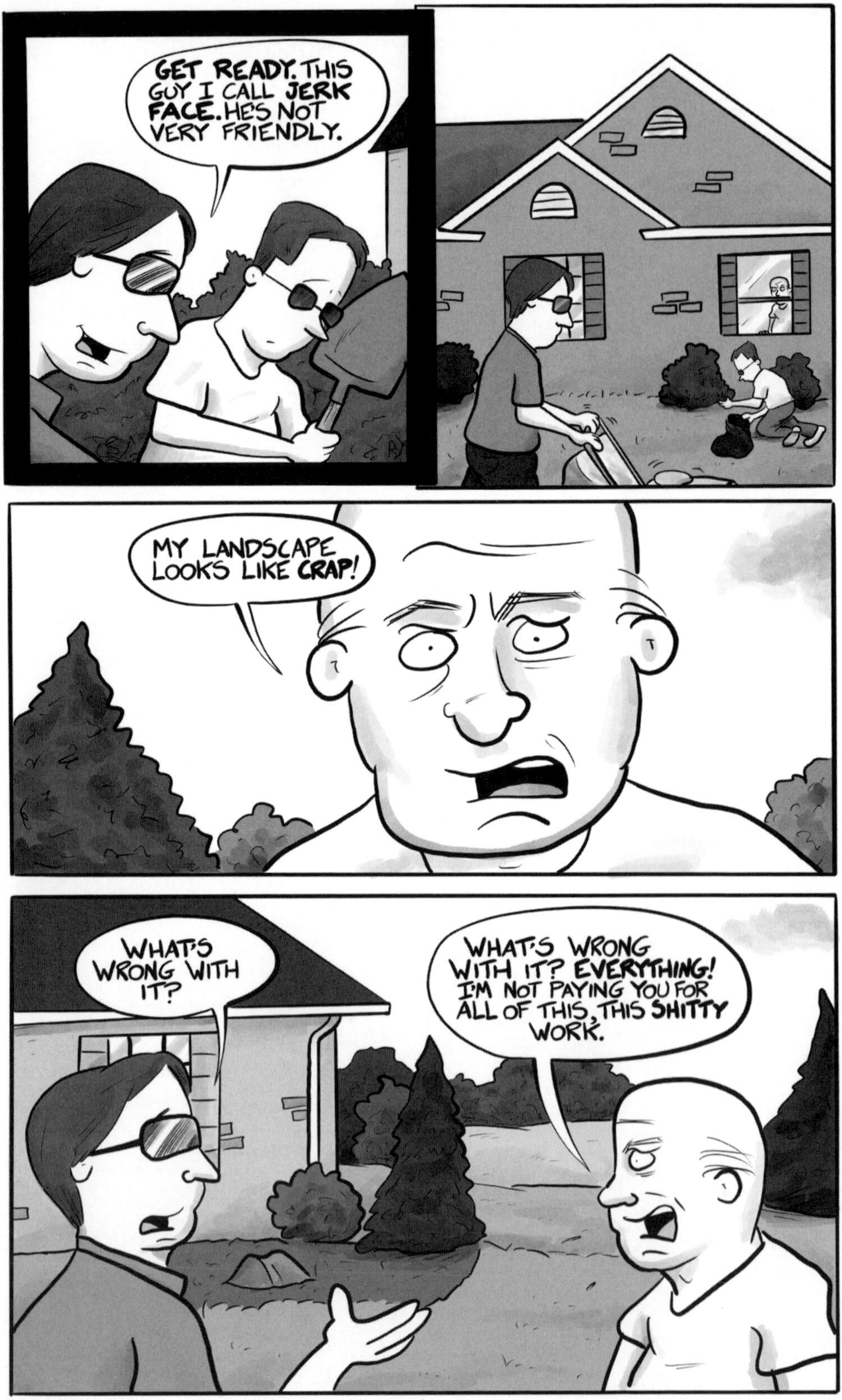
GET READY. THIS GUY I CALL JERK FACE. HE'S NOT VERY FRIENDLY.
MY LANDSCAPE LOOKS LIKE CRAP!
WHAT'S WRONG WITH IT?
WHAT'S WRONG WITH IT? EVERYTHING! I'M NOT PAYING YOU FOR ALL OF THIS, THIS SHITTY WORK.

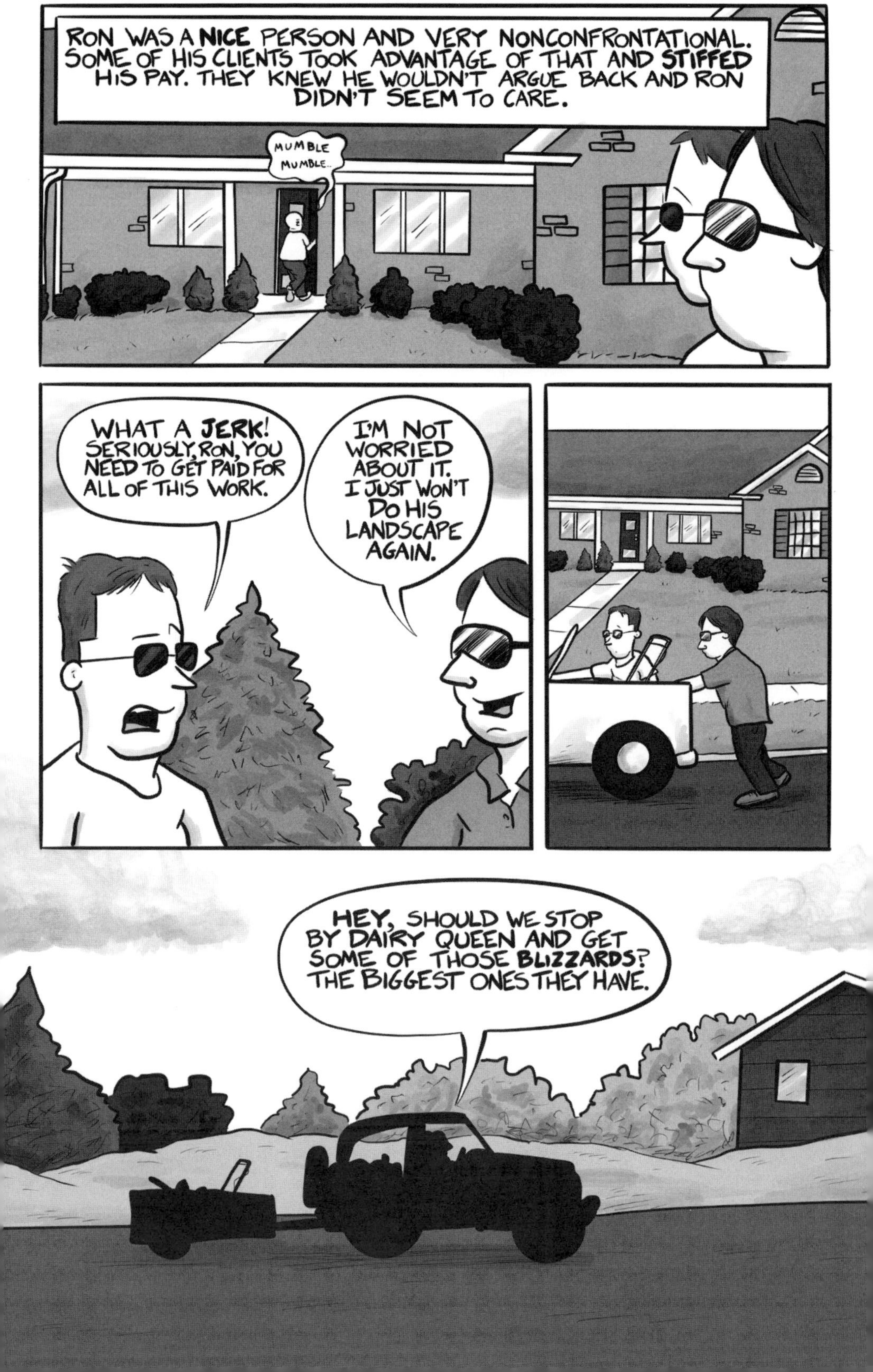
RON WAS A NICE PERSON AND VERY NONCONFRONTATIONAL. SOME OF HIS CLIENTS TOOK ADVANTAGE OF THAT AND STIFFED HIS PAY. THEY KNEW HE WOULDN'T ARGUE BACK AND RON DIDN'T SEEM TO CARE.
MUMBLE MUMBLE..
WHAT A JERK! SERIOUSLY, RON, YOU NEED TO GET PAID FOR ALL OF THIS WORK.
I'M NOT WORRIED ABOUT IT. I JUST WON'T DO HIS LANDSCAPE AGAIN.
HEY, SHOULD WE STOP BY DAIRY QUEEN AND GET SOME OF THOSE BLIZZARDS? THE BIGGEST ONES THEY HAVE.

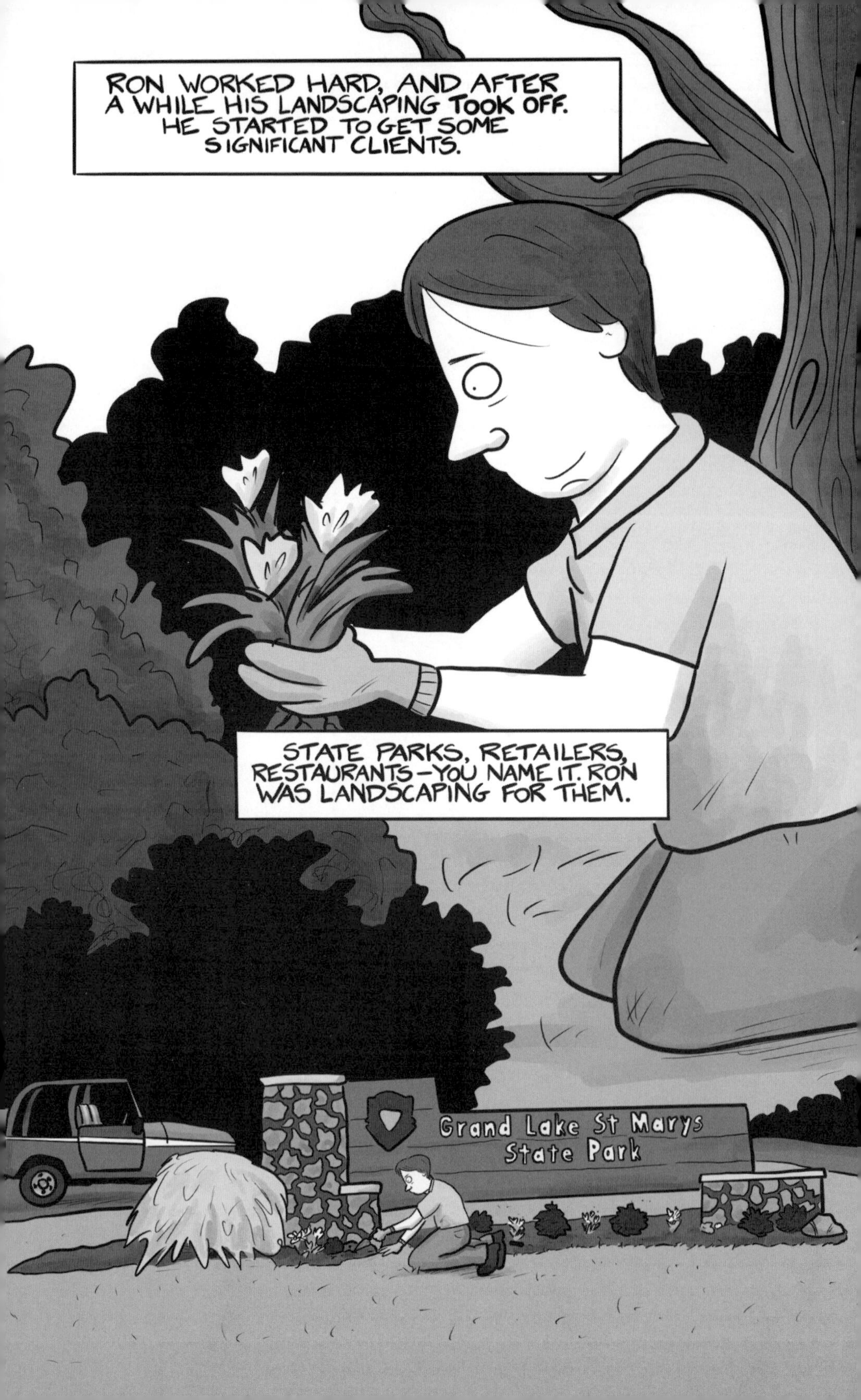
RON WORKED HARD, AND AFTER A WHILE HIS LANDSCAPING TOOK OFF. HE STARTED TO GET SOME SIGNIFICANT CLIENTS.
STATE PARKS, RETAILERS, RESTAURANTS–YOU NAME IT. RON WAS LANDSCAPING FOR THEM.
Grand Lake St Marys State Park

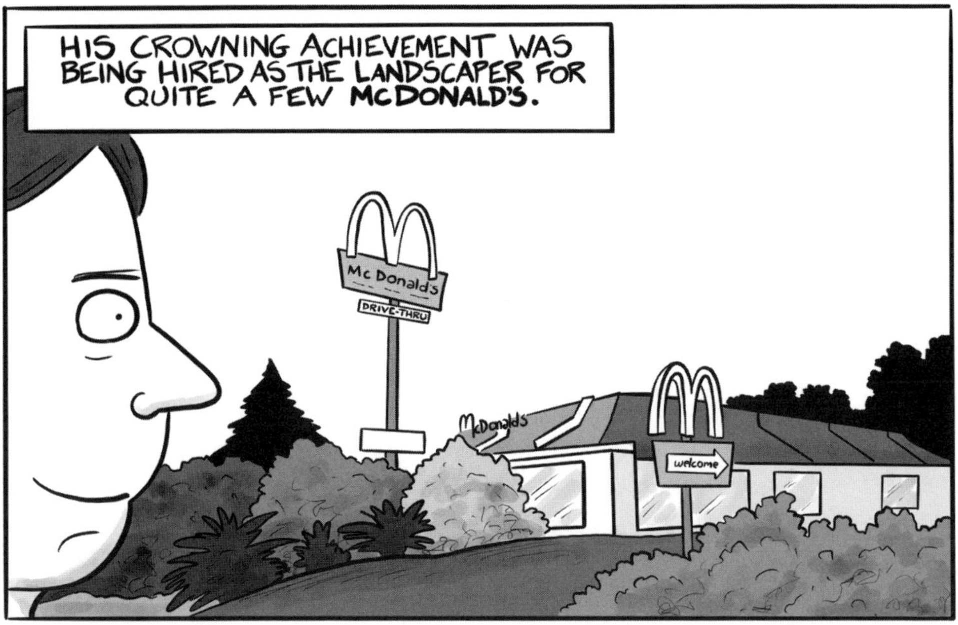
HIS CROWNING ACHIEVEMENT WAS BEING HIRED AS THE LANDSCAPER FOR QUITE A FEW McDONALD'S.
McDonald's
DRIVE-THRU
McDonald's
welcome

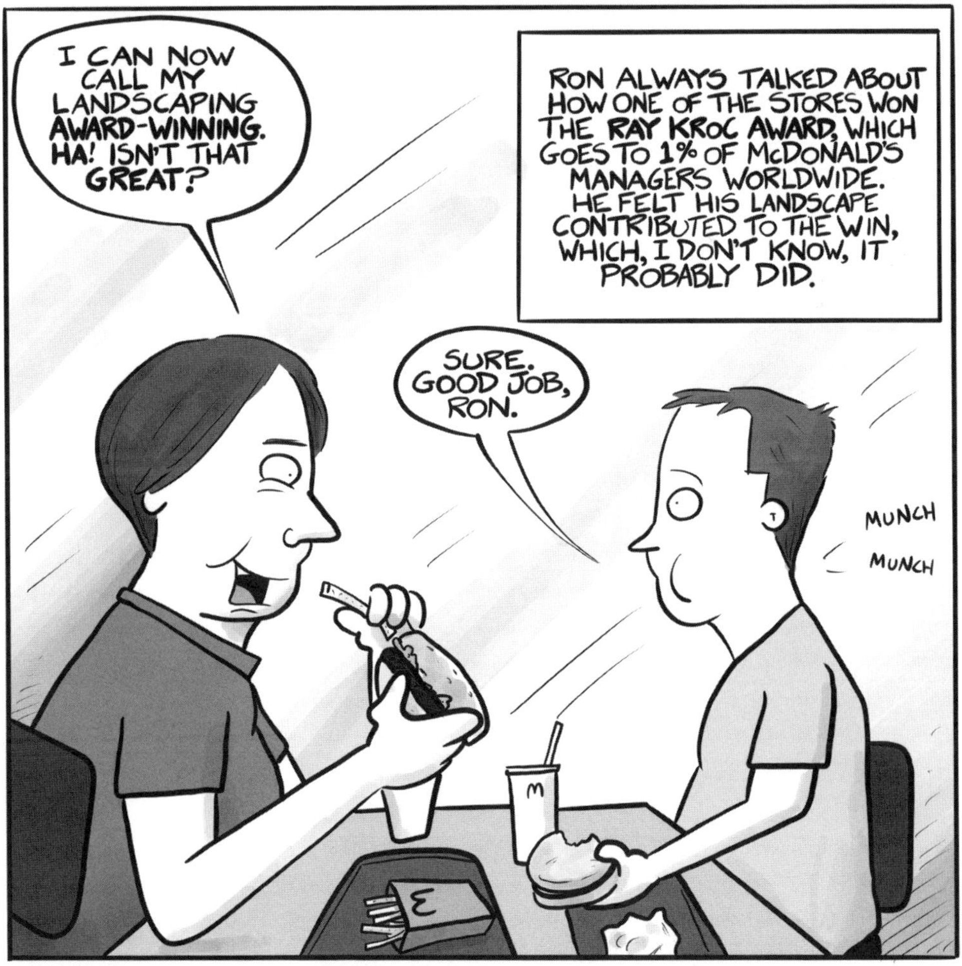
I CAN NOW CALL MY LANDSCAPING AWARD-WINNING. HA! ISN'T THAT GREAT?
RON ALWAYS TALKED ABOUT HOW ONE OF THE STORES WON THE RAY KROC AWARD, WHICH GOES TO 1% OF McDONALD'S MANAGERS WORLDWIDE. HE FELT HIS LANDSCAPE CONTRIBUTED TO THE WIN, WHICH, I DON'T KNOW, IT PROBABLY DID.
SURE. GOOD JOB, RON.
MUNCH
MUNCH

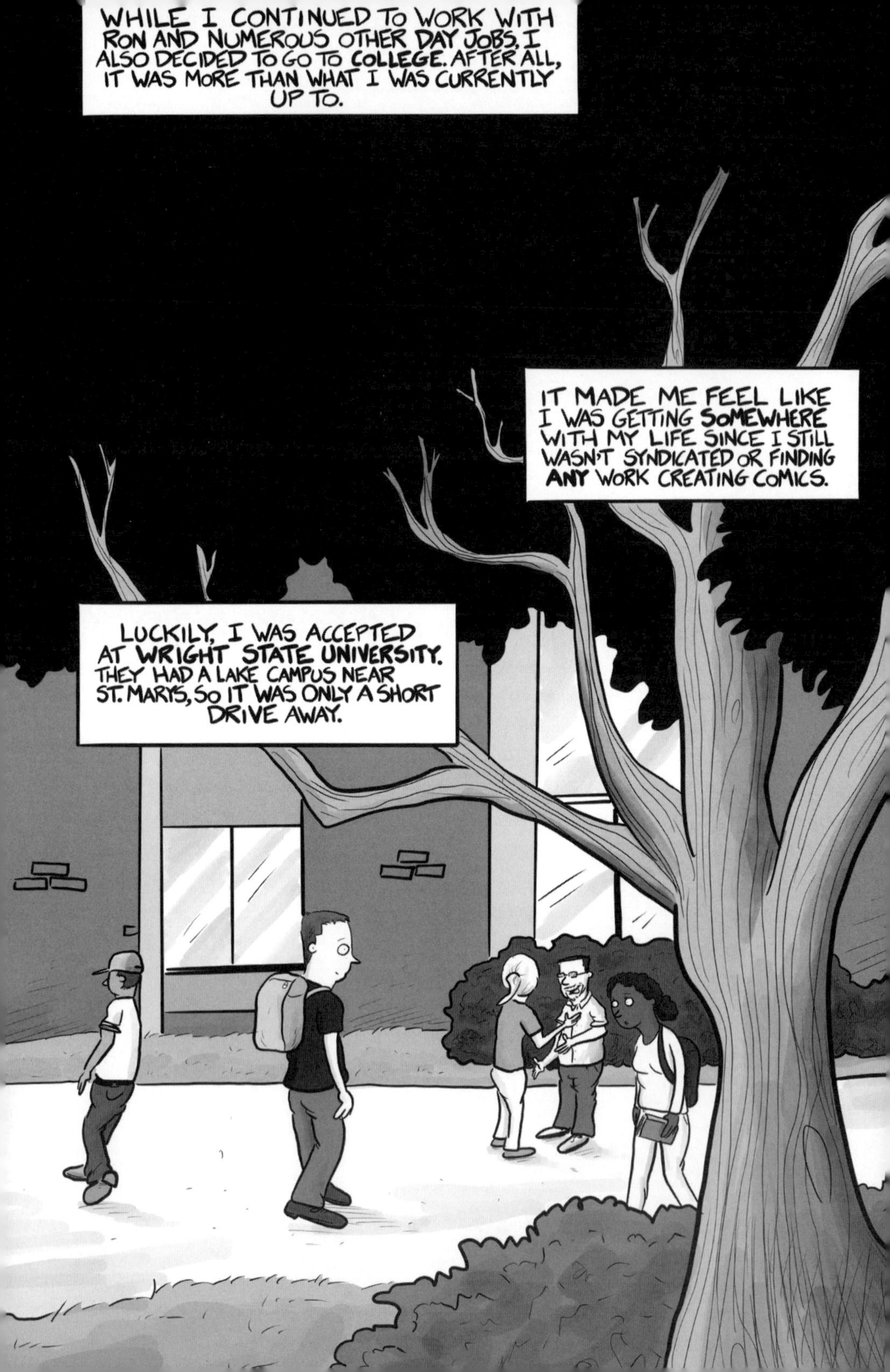
WHILE I CONTINUED TO WORK WITH RON AND NUMEROUS OTHER DAY JOBS, I ALSO DECIDED TO GO TO COLLEGE. AFTER ALL, IT WAS MORE THAN WHAT I WAS CURRENTLY UP TO.
IT MADE ME FEEL LIKE I WAS GETTING SOMEWHERE WITH MY LIFE SINCE I STILL WASN'T SYNDICATED OR FINDING ANY WORK CREATING COMICS.
LUCKILY, I WAS ACCEPTED AT WRIGHT STATE UNIVERSITY. THEY HAD A LAKE CAMPUS NEAR ST. MARYS, SO IT WAS ONLY A SHORT DRIVE AWAY.

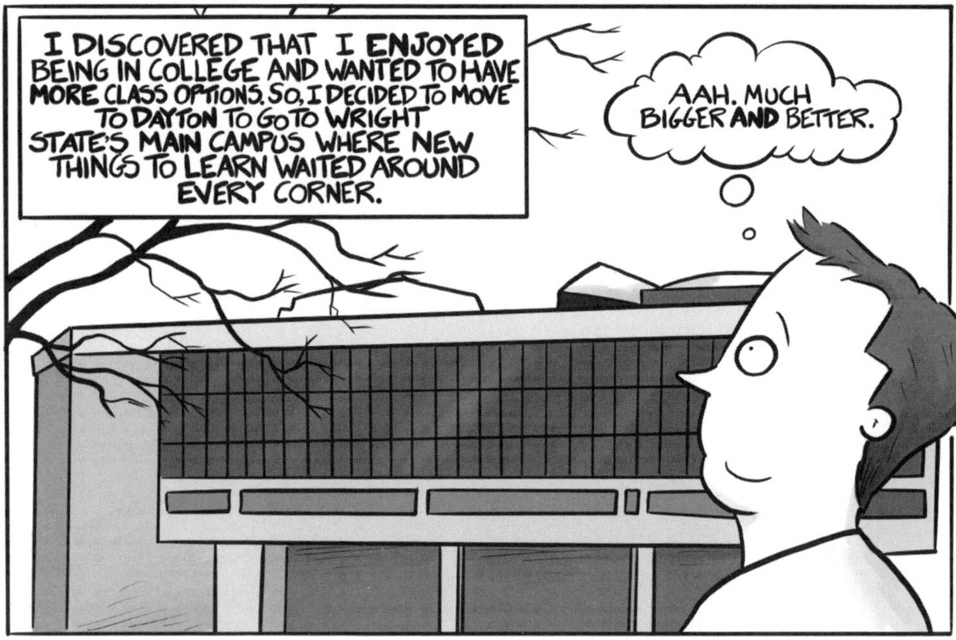
I DISCOVERED THAT I ENJOYED BEING IN COLLEGE AND WANTED TO HAVE MORE CLASS OPTIONS. SO, I DECIDED TO MOVE TO DAYTON TO GO TO WRIGHT STATE'S MAIN CAMPUS WHERE NEW THINGS TO LEARN WAITED AROUND EVERY CORNER.
AAH. MUCH BIGGER AND BETTER.

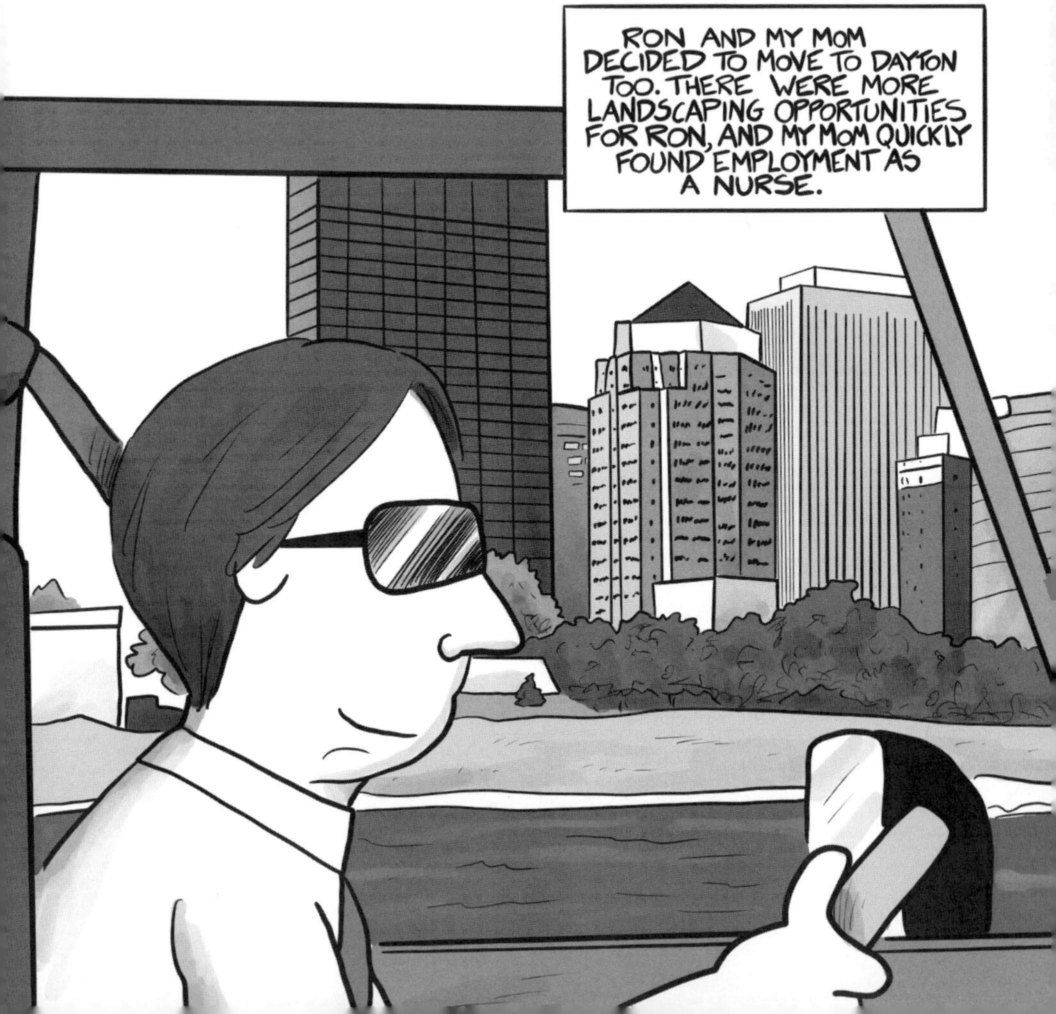
RON AND MY MOM DECIDED TO MOVE TO DAYTON TOO. THERE WERE MORE LANDSCAPING OPPORTUNITIES FOR RON, AND MY MOM QUICKLY FOUND EMPLOYMENT AS A NURSE.

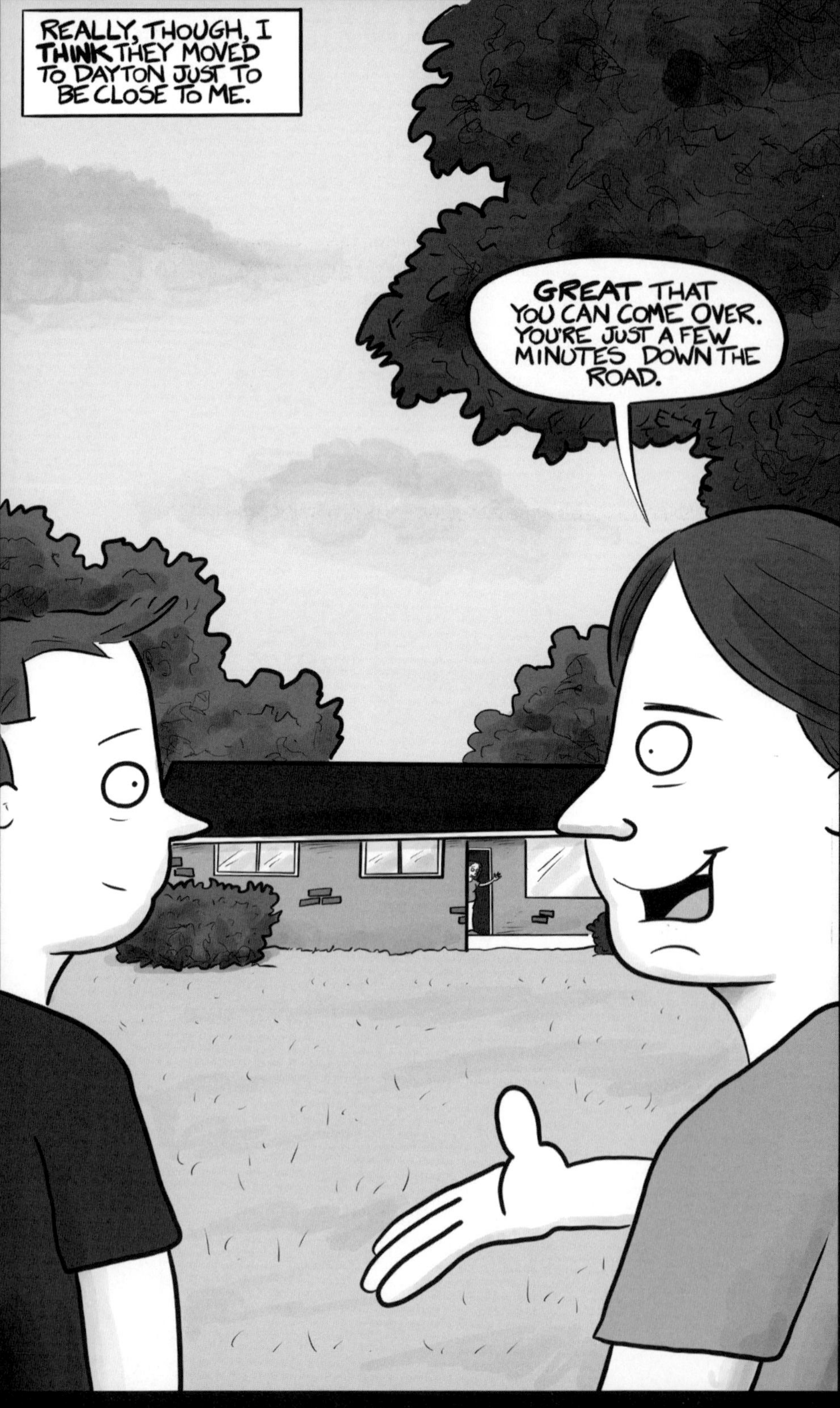
REALLY, THOUGH, I THINK THEY MOVED TO DAYTON JUST TO BE CLOSE TO ME.
GREAT THAT YOU CAN COME OVER. YOU'RE JUST A FEW MINUTES DOWN THE ROAD.

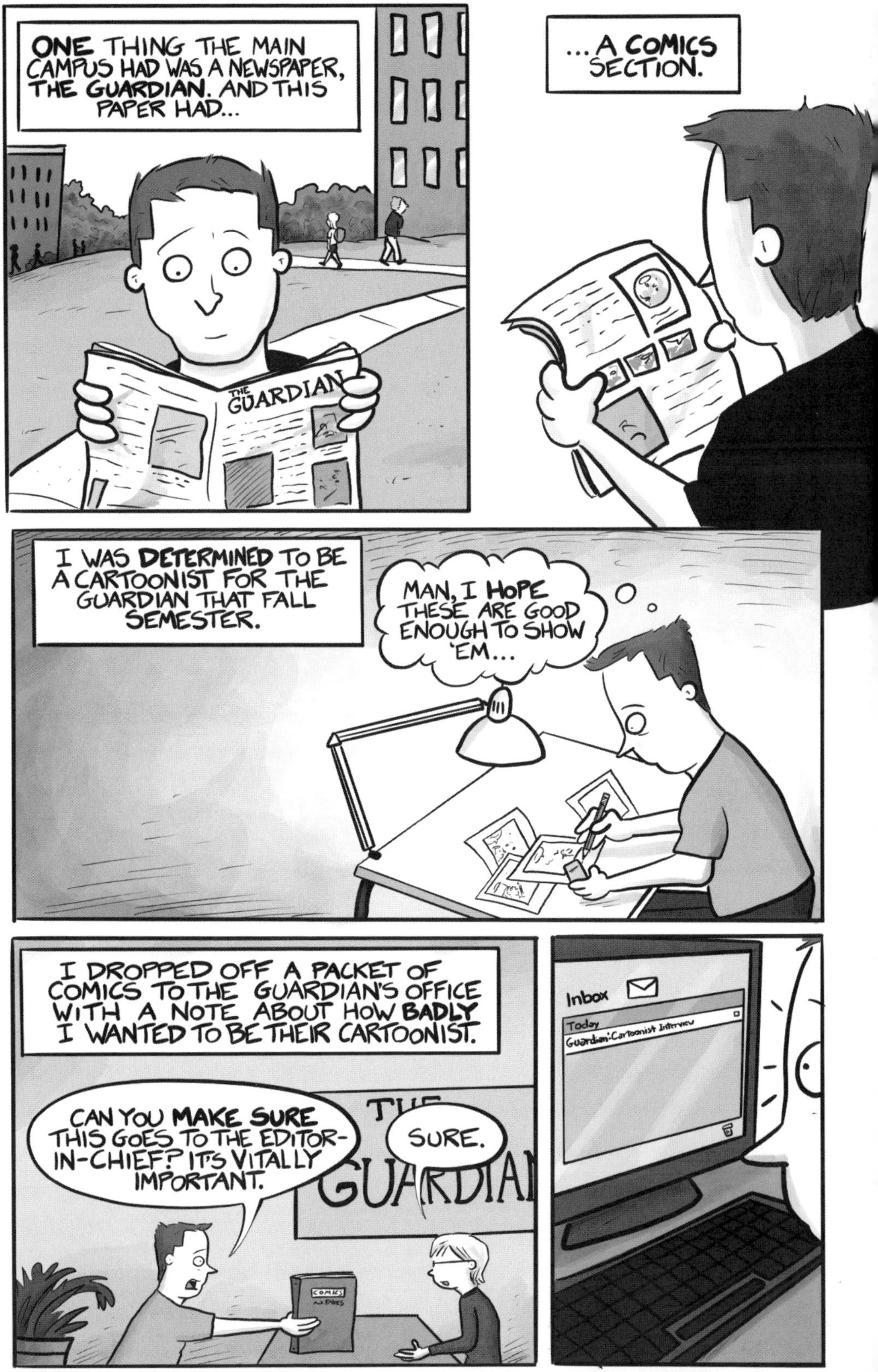
ONE THING THE MAIN CAMPUS HAD WAS A NEWSPAPER, THE GUARDIAN. AND THIS PAPER HAD...
THE GUARDIAN
...A COMICS SECTION.
I WAS DETERMINED TO BE A CARTOONIST FOR THE GUARDIAN THAT FALL SEMESTER.
MAN, I HOPE THESE ARE GOOD ENOUGH TO SHOW 'EM...
I DROPPED OFF A PACKET OF COMICS TO THE GUARDIAN'S OFFICE WITH A NOTE ABOUT HOW BADLY I WANTED TO BE THEIR CARTOONIST.
THE GUARDIAN
CAN YOU MAKE SURE THIS GOES TO THE EDITOR-IN-CHIEF? IT'S VITALLY IMPORTANT.
SURE.
Inbox
Today
Guardian: Cartoonist Interview

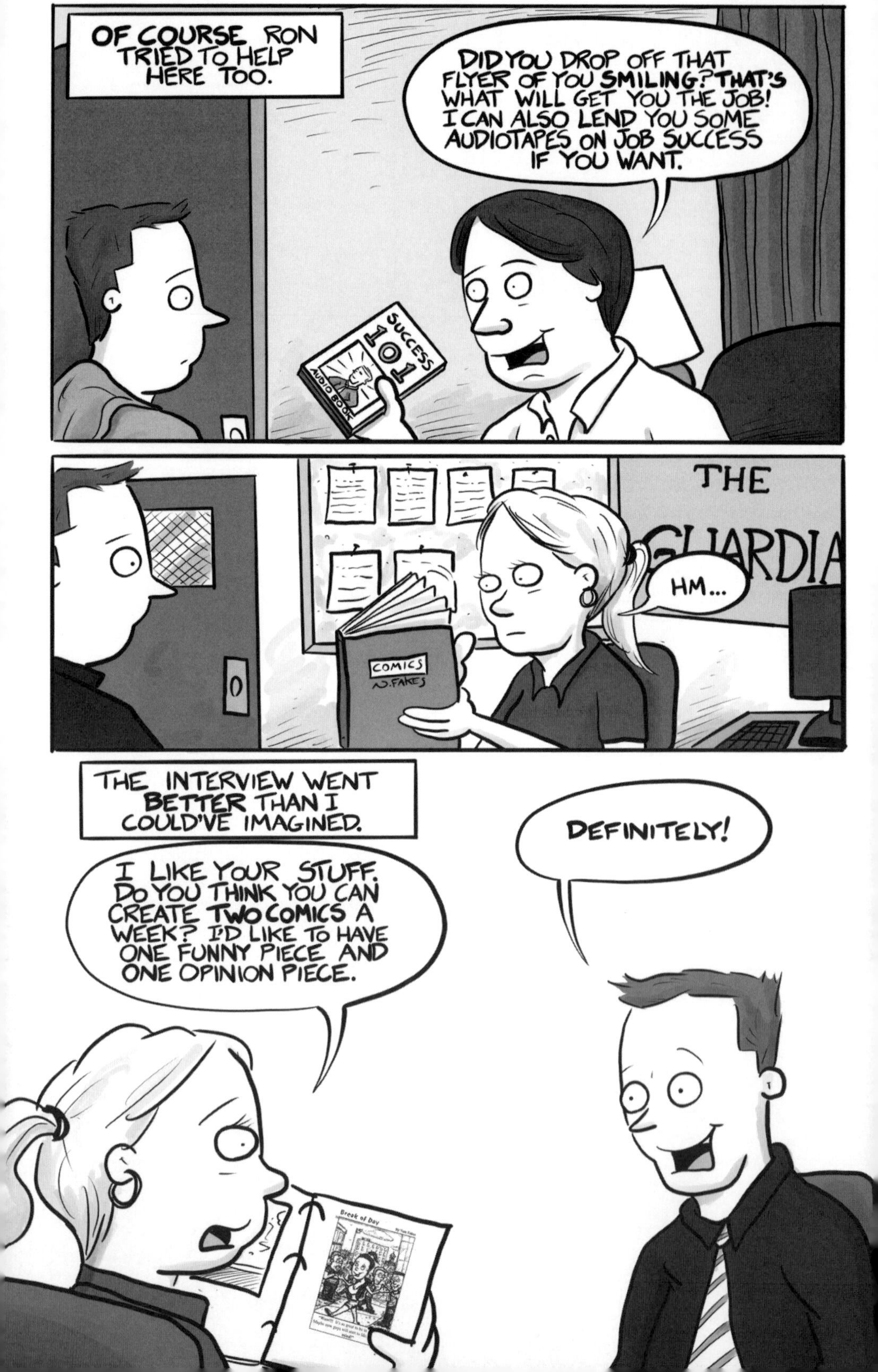
OF COURSE RON TRIED TO HELP HERE TOO.
DID YOU DROP OFF THAT FLYER OF YOU SMILING? THAT'S WHAT WILL GET YOU THE JOB! I CAN ALSO LEND YOU SOME AUDIOTAPES ON JOB SUCCESS IF YOU WANT.
SUCCESS 101
AUDIO BOOK
THE
GUARDIA
HM...
COMICS
N. FAKES
THE INTERVIEW WENT BETTER THAN I COULD'VE IMAGINED.
I LIKE YOUR STUFF. DO YOU THINK YOU CAN CREATE TWO COMICS A WEEK? I'D LIKE TO HAVE ONE FUNNY PIECE AND ONE OPINION PIECE.
DEFINITELY!
Break of Day

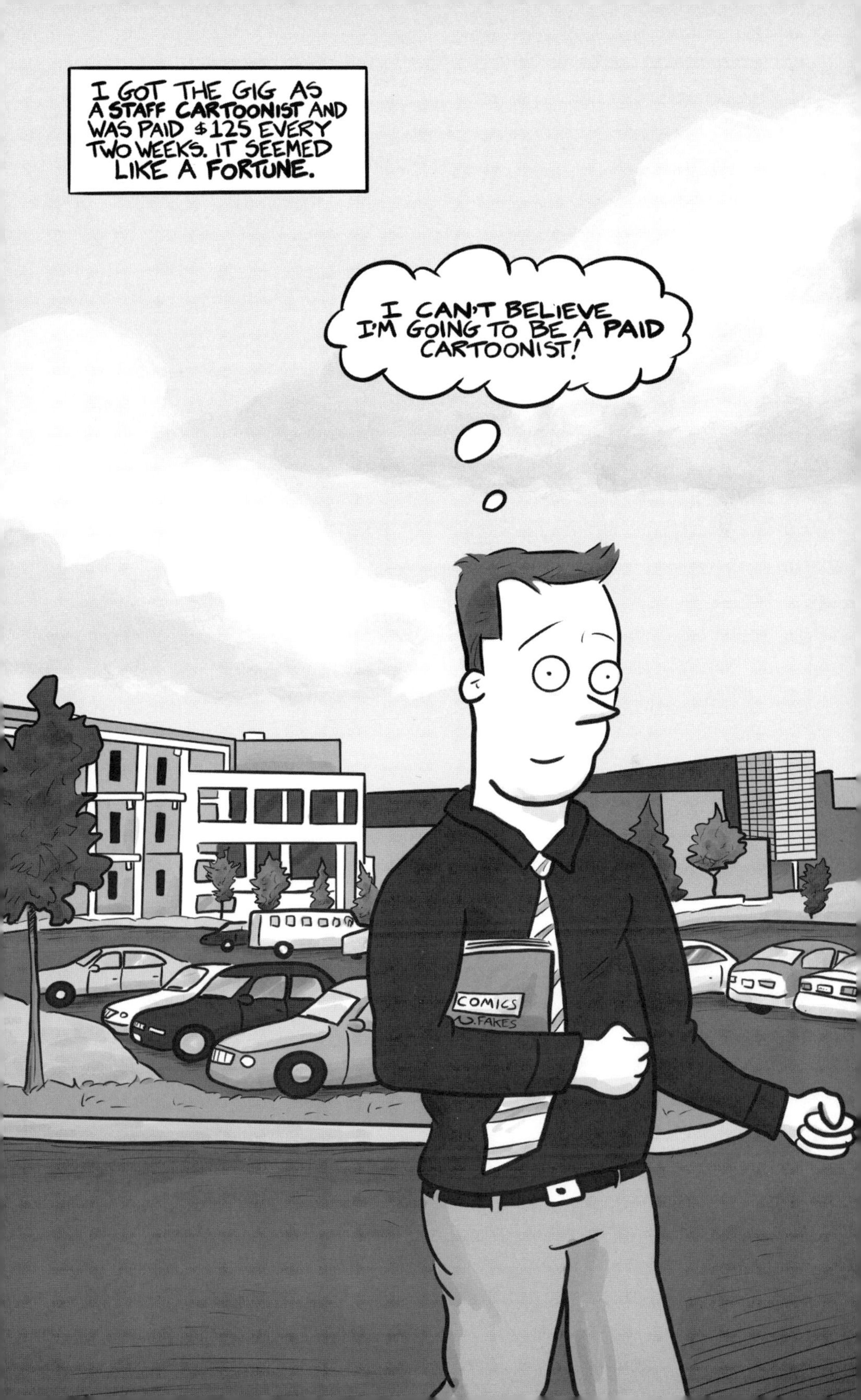
I GOT THE GIG AS A STAFF CARTOONIST AND WAS PAID $125 EVERY TWO WEEKS. IT SEEMED LIKE A FORTUNE.
I CAN'T BELIEVE I'M GOING TO BE A PAID CARTOONIST!
COMICS
M.J. FAKES

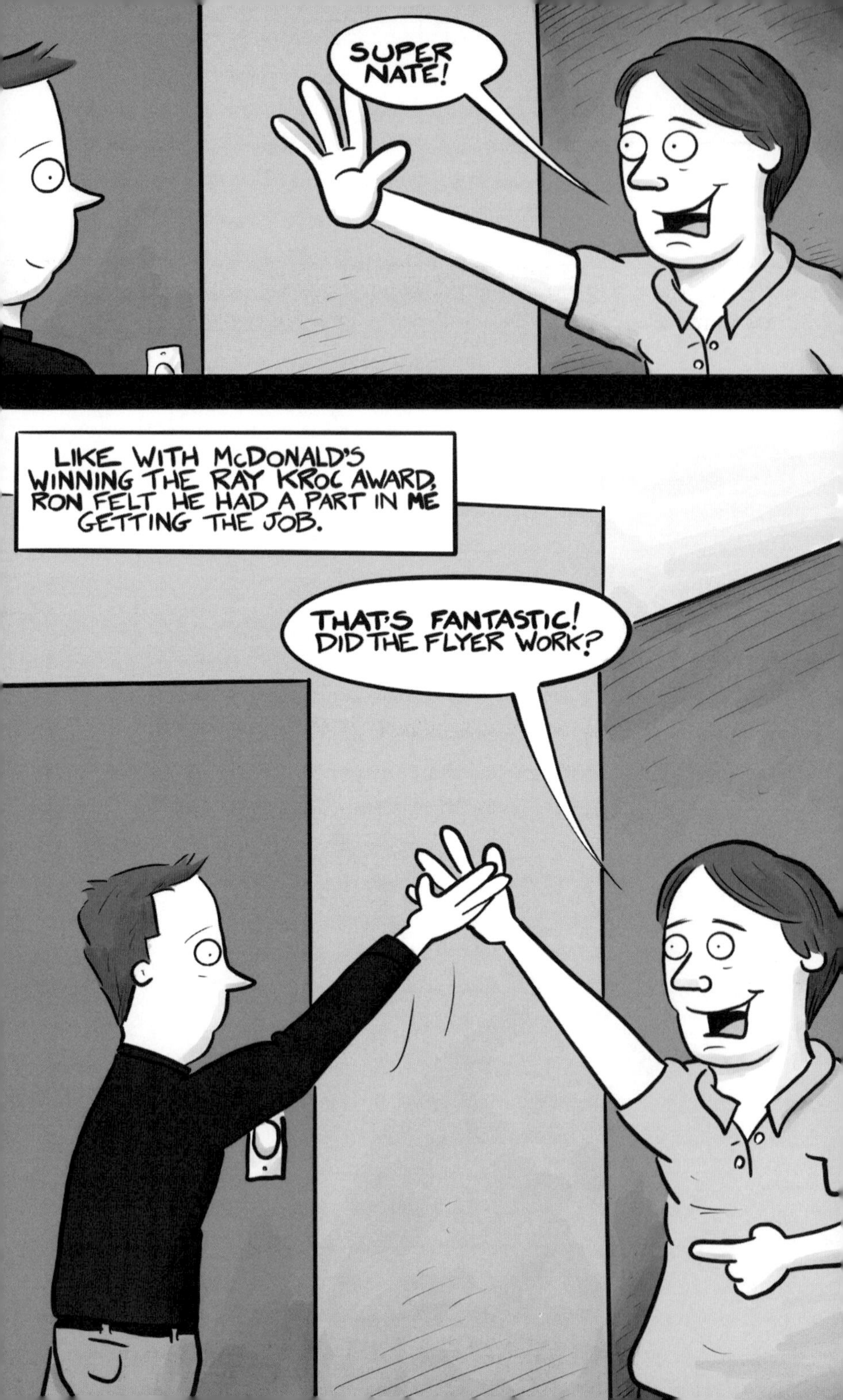
SUPER NATE!
LIKE WITH McDONALD'S WINNING THE RAY KROC AWARD, RON FELT HE HAD A PART IN ME GETTING THE JOB.
THAT'S FANTASTIC! DID THE FLYER WORK?

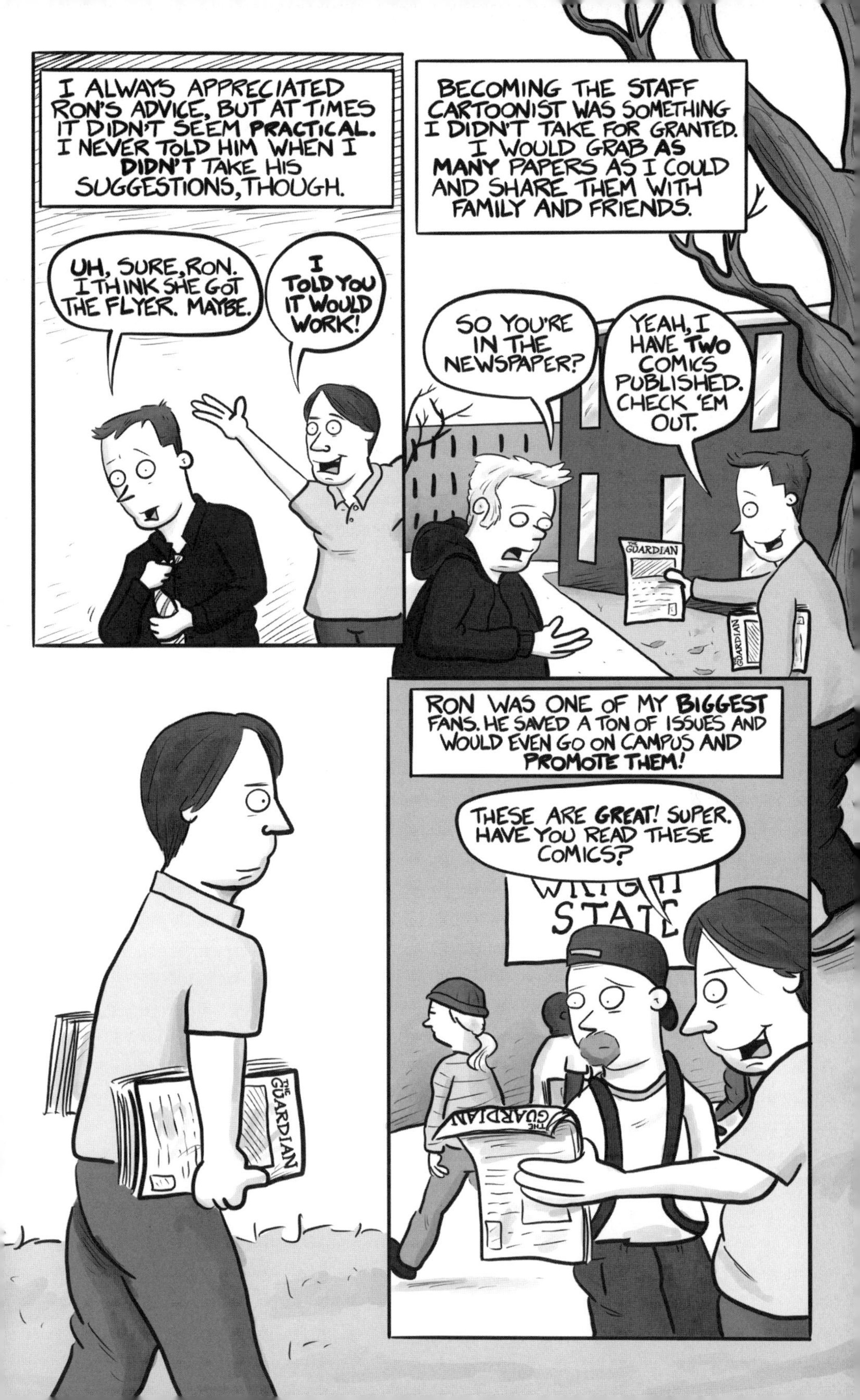
I ALWAYS APPRECIATED RON'S ADVICE, BUT AT TIMES IT DIDN'T SEEM PRACTICAL. I NEVER TOLD HIM WHEN I DIDN'T TAKE HIS SUGGESTIONS, THOUGH.
UH, SURE, RON. I THINK SHE GOT THE FLYER. MAYBE.
I TOLD YOU IT WOULD WORK!
BECOMING THE STAFF CARTOONIST WAS SOMETHING I DIDN'T TAKE FOR GRANTED. I WOULD GRAB AS MANY PAPERS AS I COULD AND SHARE THEM WITH FAMILY AND FRIENDS.
SO YOU'RE IN THE NEWSPAPER?
YEAH, I HAVE TWO COMICS PUBLISHED. CHECK 'EM OUT.
THE GUARDIAN
THE GUARDIAN
THE GUARDIAN
RON WAS ONE OF MY BIGGEST FANS. HE SAVED A TON OF ISSUES AND WOULD EVEN GO ON CAMPUS AND PROMOTE THEM!
THESE ARE GREAT! SUPER. HAVE YOU READ THESE COMICS?
STATE
THE GUARDIAN

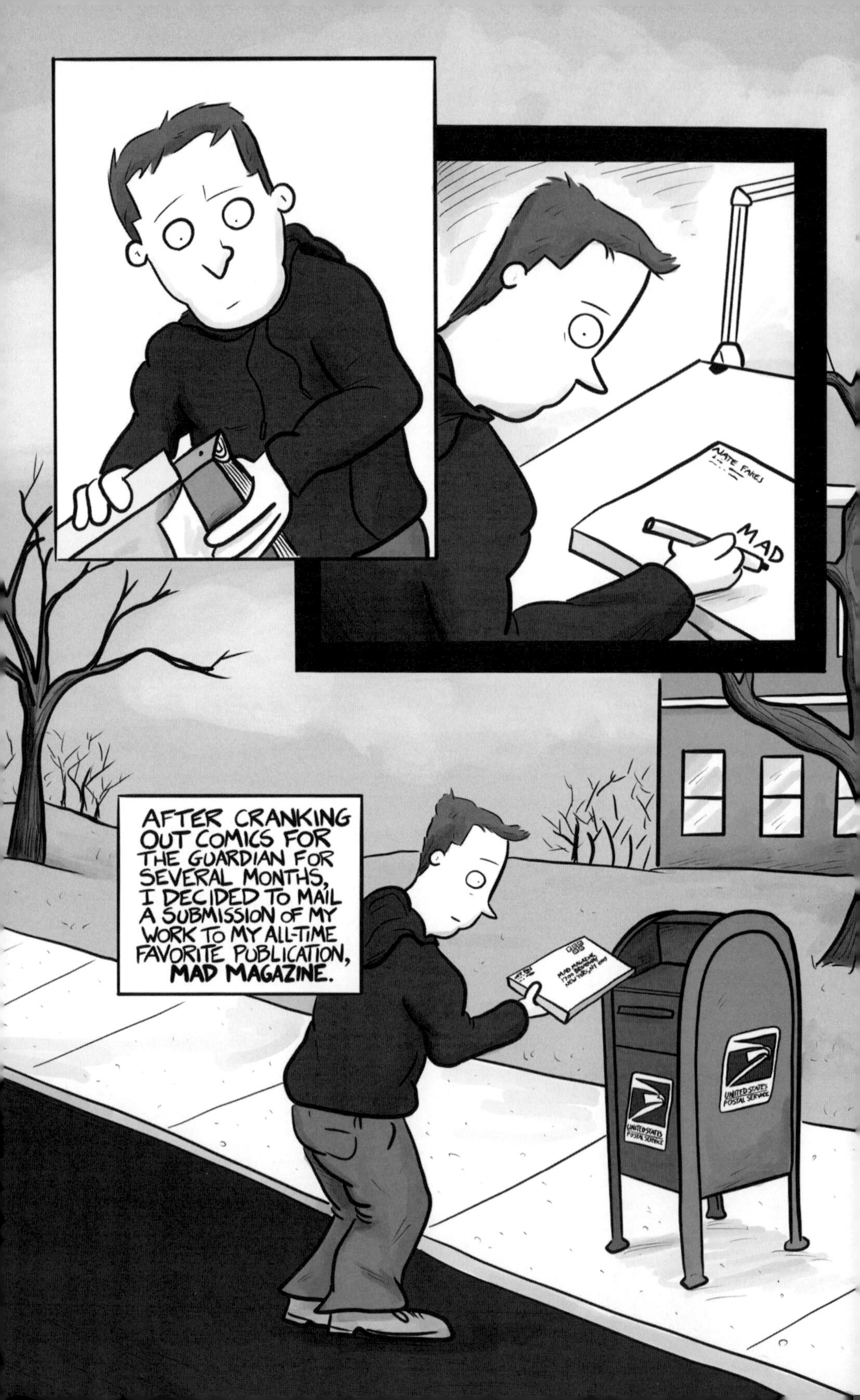
NATE FAKES
MAD
AFTER CRANKING OUT COMICS FOR THE GUARDIAN FOR SEVERAL MONTHS, I DECIDED TO MAIL A SUBMISSION OF MY WORK TO MY ALL-TIME FAVORITE PUBLICATION, MAD MAGAZINE.
UNITED STATES POSTAL SERVICE
UNITED STATES POSTAL SERVICE

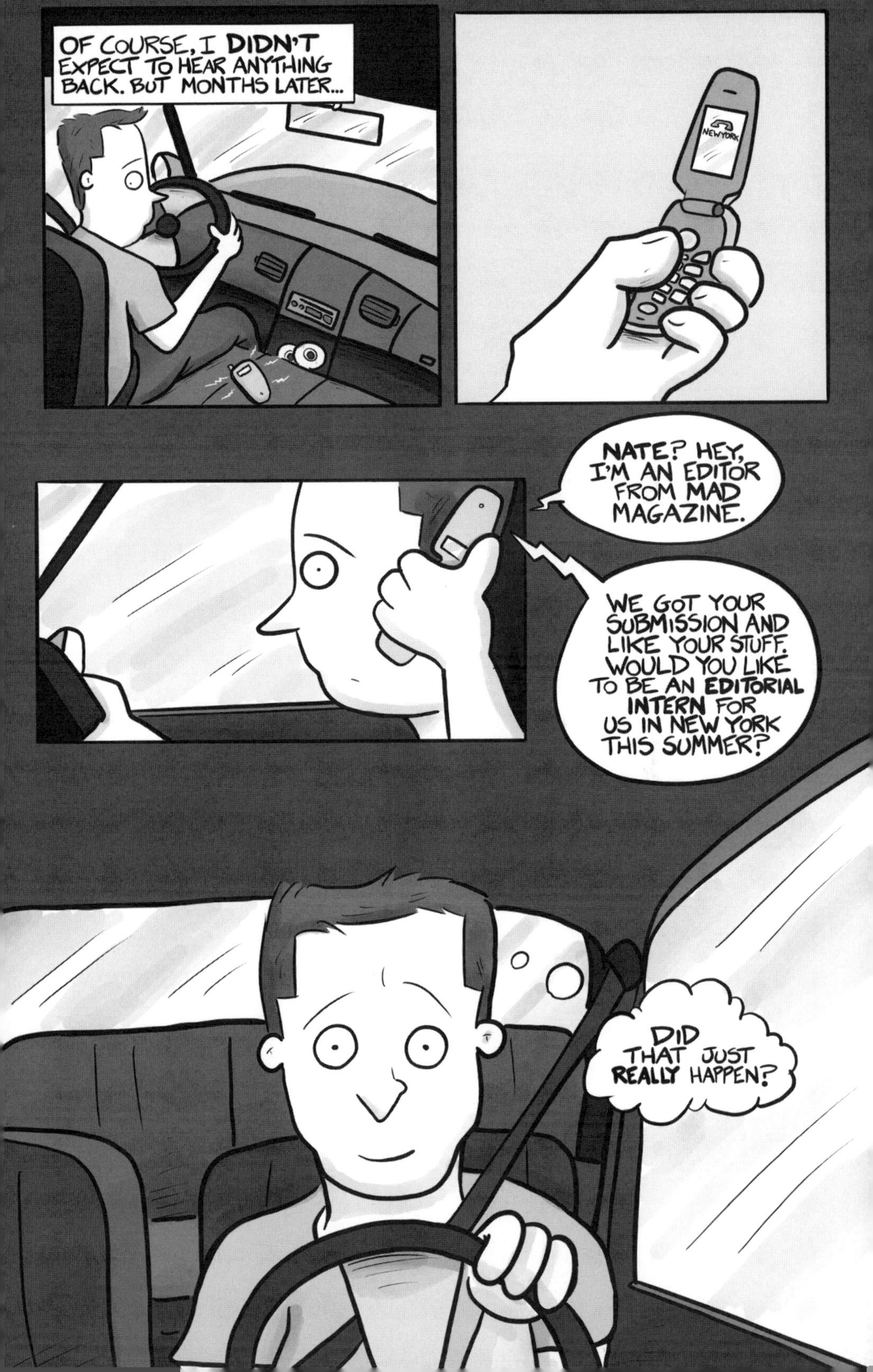
OF COURSE, I DIDN'T EXPECT TO HEAR ANYTHING BACK. BUT MONTHS LATER...
NEW YORK
NATE? HEY, I'M AN EDITOR FROM MAD MAGAZINE.
WE GOT YOUR SUBMISSION AND LIKE YOUR STUFF. WOULD YOU LIKE TO BE AN EDITORIAL INTERN FOR US IN NEW YORK THIS SUMMER?
DID THAT JUST REALLY HAPPEN?

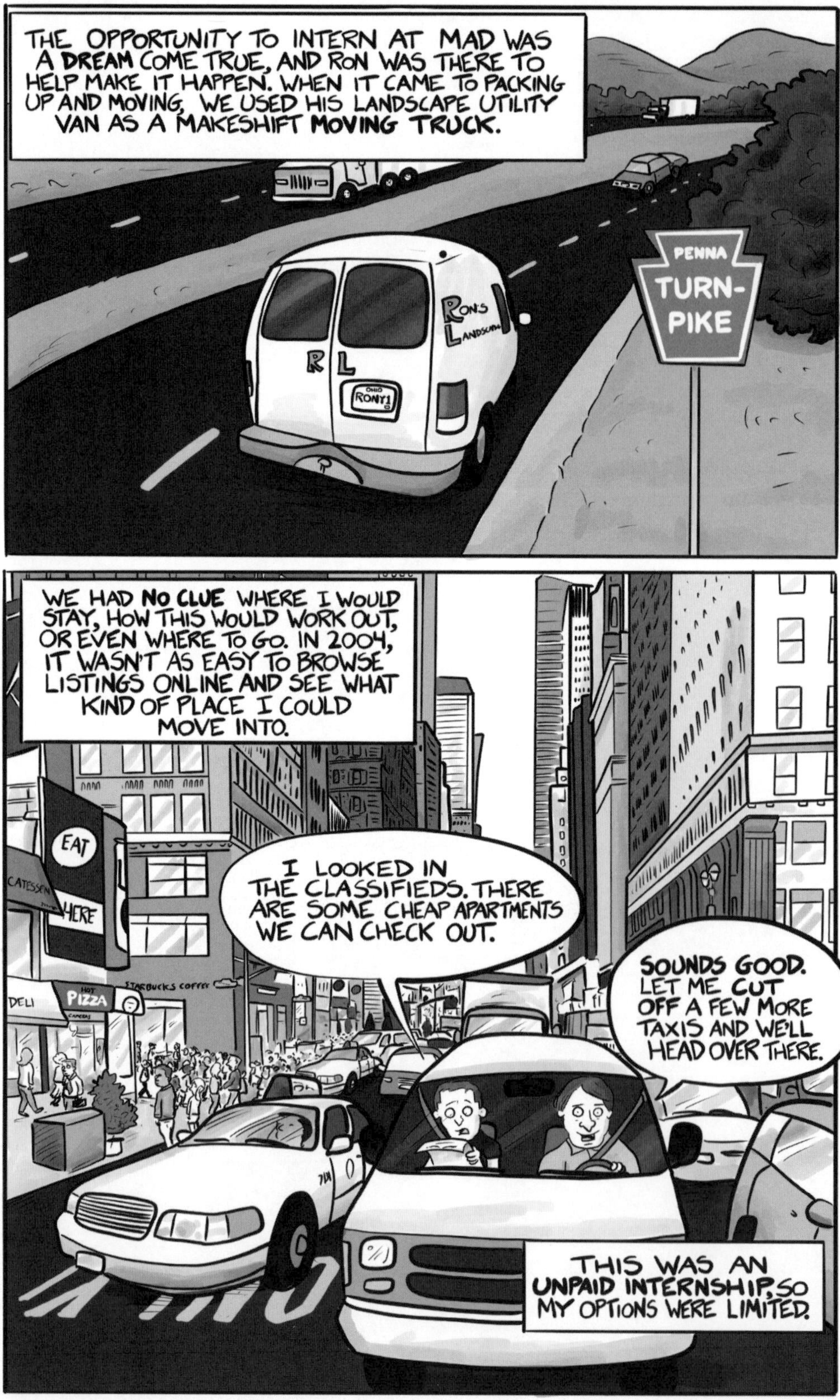
THE OPPORTUNITY TO INTERN AT MAD WAS A **DREAM** COME TRUE, AND RON WAS THERE TO HELP MAKE IT HAPPEN. WHEN IT CAME TO PACKING UP AND MOVING, WE USED HIS LANDSCAPE UTILITY VAN AS A MAKESHIFT **MOVING TRUCK**.
PENNA TURN-PIKE
RL
RONY1
WE HAD **NO CLUE** WHERE I WOULD STAY, HOW THIS WOULD WORK OUT, OR EVEN WHERE TO GO. IN 2004, IT WASN'T AS EASY TO BROWSE LISTINGS ONLINE AND SEE WHAT KIND OF PLACE I COULD MOVE INTO.
EAT
HERE
DELI
HOT PIZZA
STARBUCKS COFFEE
I LOOKED IN THE CLASSIFIEDS. THERE ARE SOME CHEAP APARTMENTS WE CAN CHECK OUT.
SOUNDS GOOD. LET ME **CUT** OFF A FEW MORE TAXIS AND WE'LL HEAD OVER THERE.
THIS WAS AN **UNPAID INTERNSHIP,** SO MY OPTIONS WERE LIMITED.

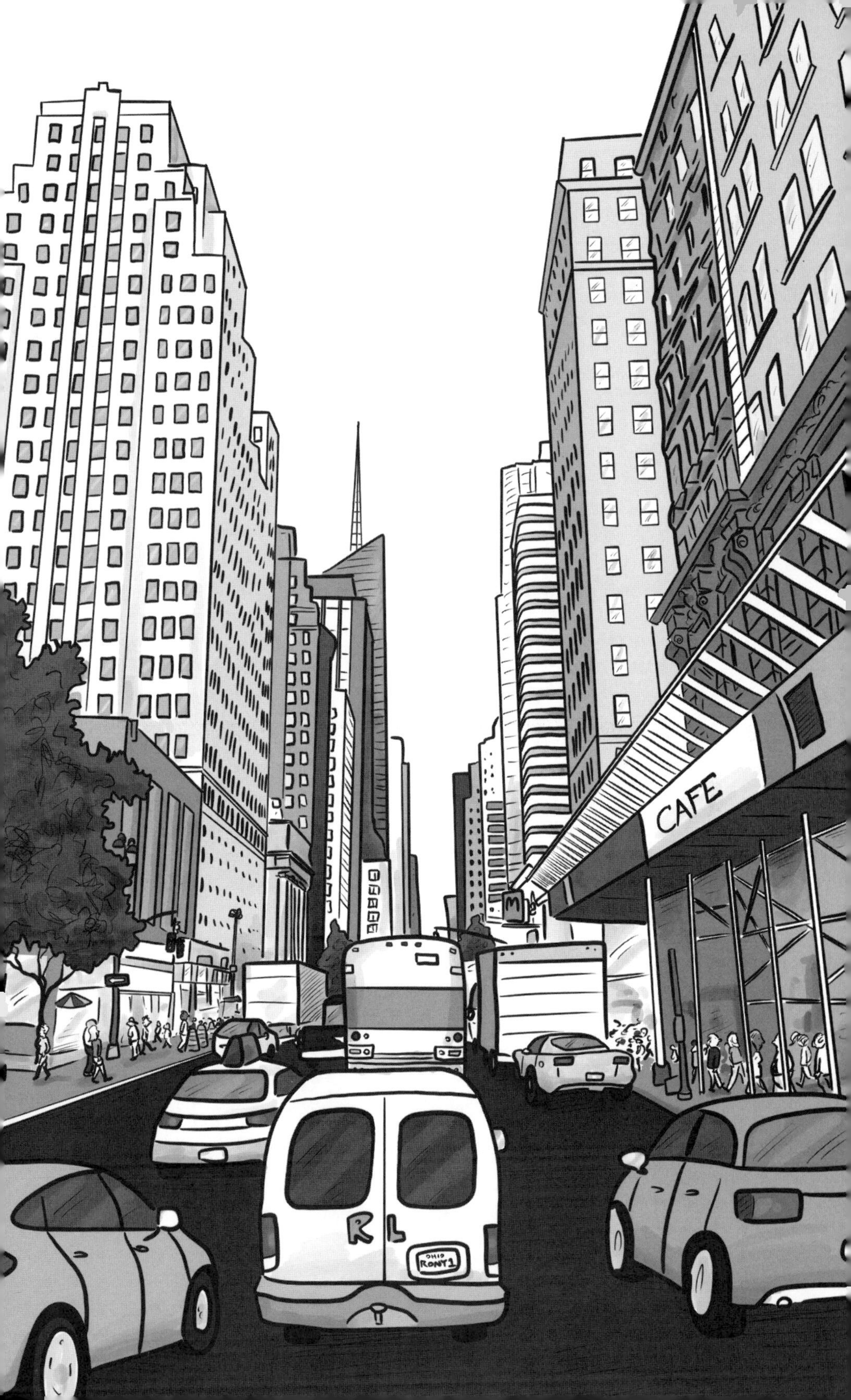
CAFE
M
R L
OHIO
RONY1

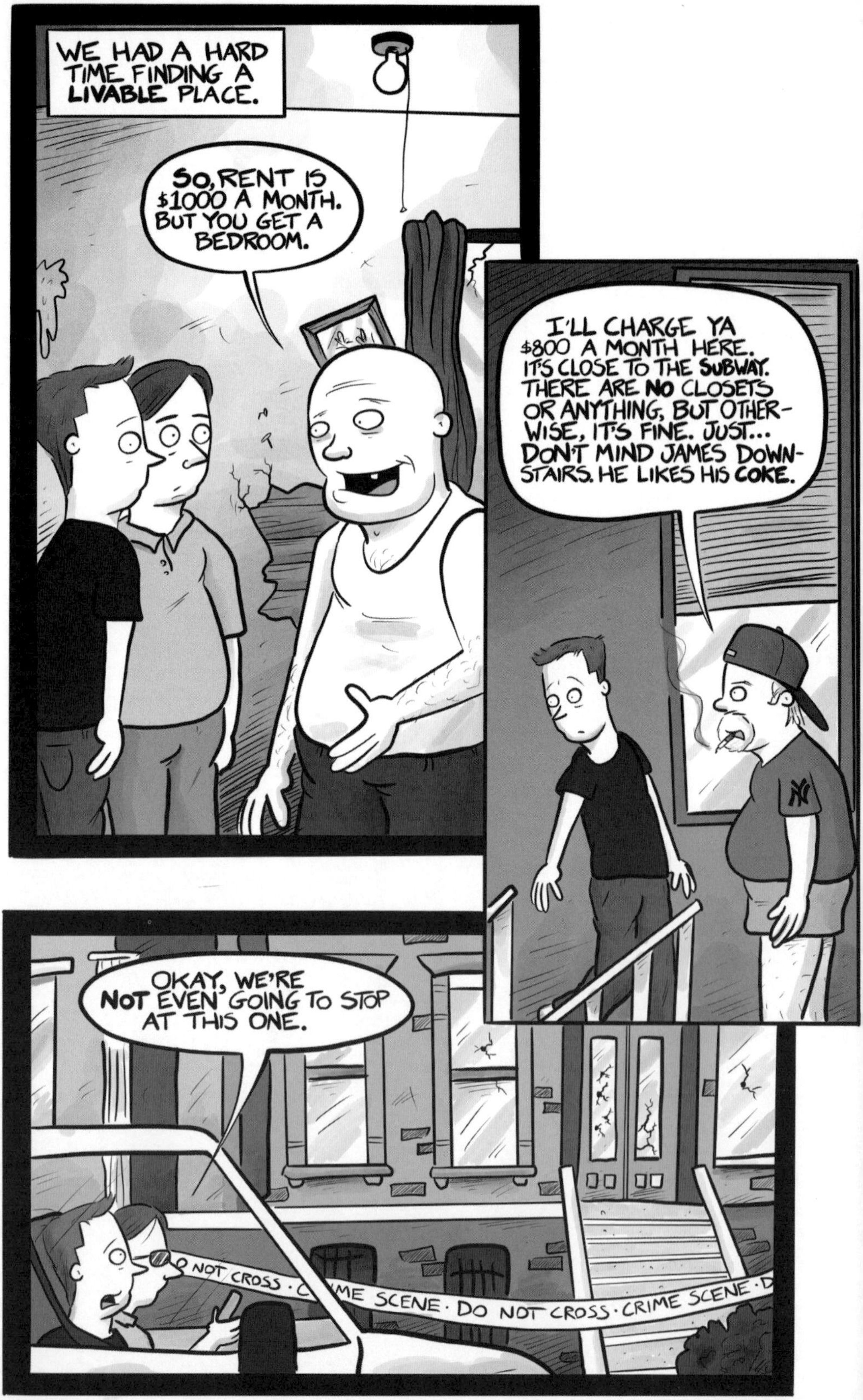
WE HAD A HARD TIME FINDING A LIVABLE PLACE.
SO, RENT IS $1000 A MONTH. BUT YOU GET A BEDROOM.
I'LL CHARGE YA $800 A MONTH HERE. IT'S CLOSE TO THE SUBWAY. THERE ARE NO CLOSETS OR ANYTHING, BUT OTHER-WISE, IT'S FINE. JUST... DON'T MIND JAMES DOWN-STAIRS. HE LIKES HIS COKE.
OKAY, WE'RE NOT EVEN GOING TO STOP AT THIS ONE.
CRIME SCENE · DO NOT CROSS · CRIME SCENE

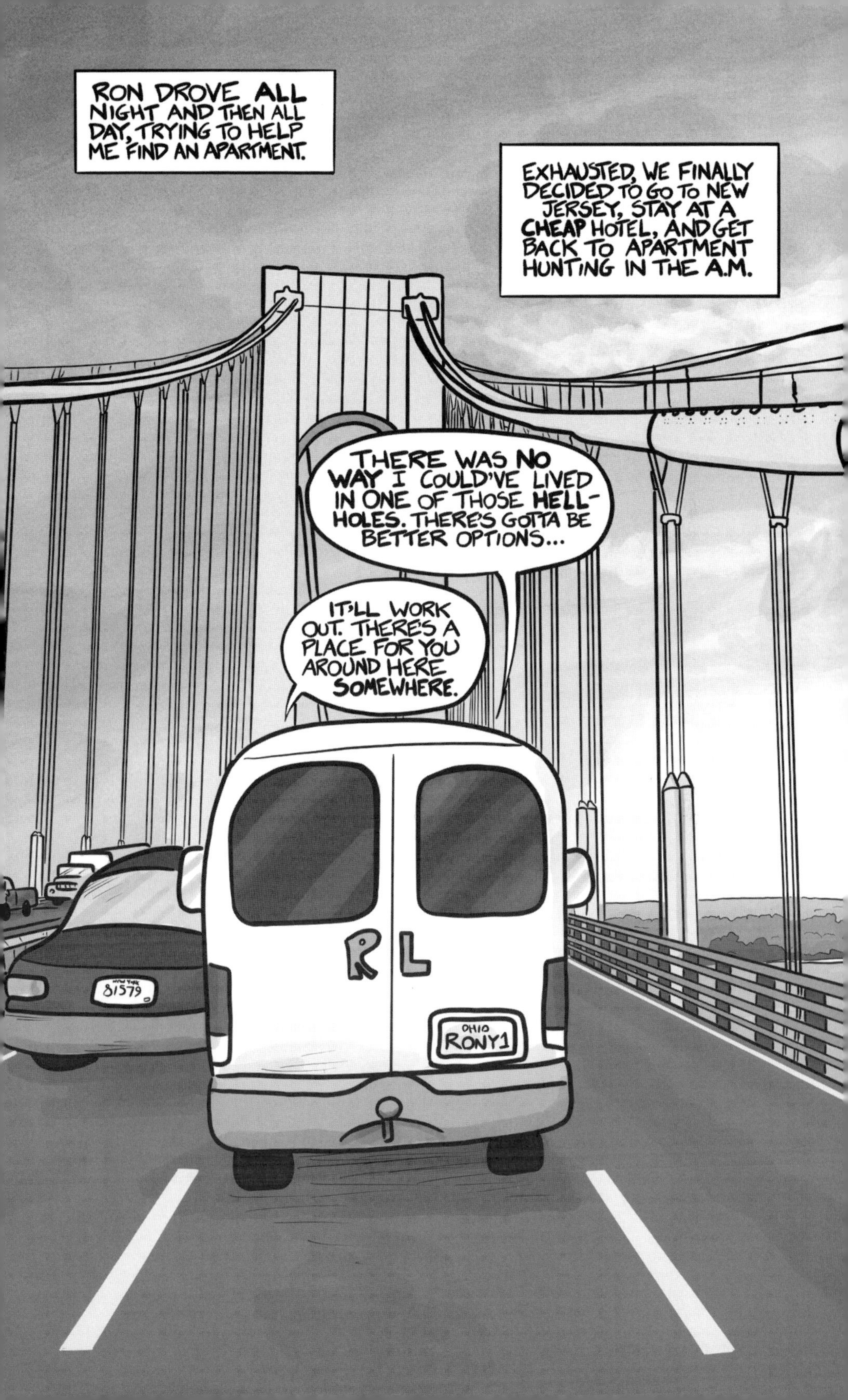
RON DROVE ALL NIGHT AND THEN ALL DAY, TRYING TO HELP ME FIND AN APARTMENT.
EXHAUSTED, WE FINALLY DECIDED TO GO TO NEW JERSEY, STAY AT A CHEAP HOTEL, AND GET BACK TO APARTMENT HUNTING IN THE A.M.
THERE WAS NO WAY I COULD'VE LIVED IN ONE OF THOSE HELL-HOLES. THERE'S GOTTA BE BETTER OPTIONS...
IT'LL WORK OUT. THERE'S A PLACE FOR YOU AROUND HERE SOMEWHERE.
RL
OHIO
RONY1
NEW YORK
81579

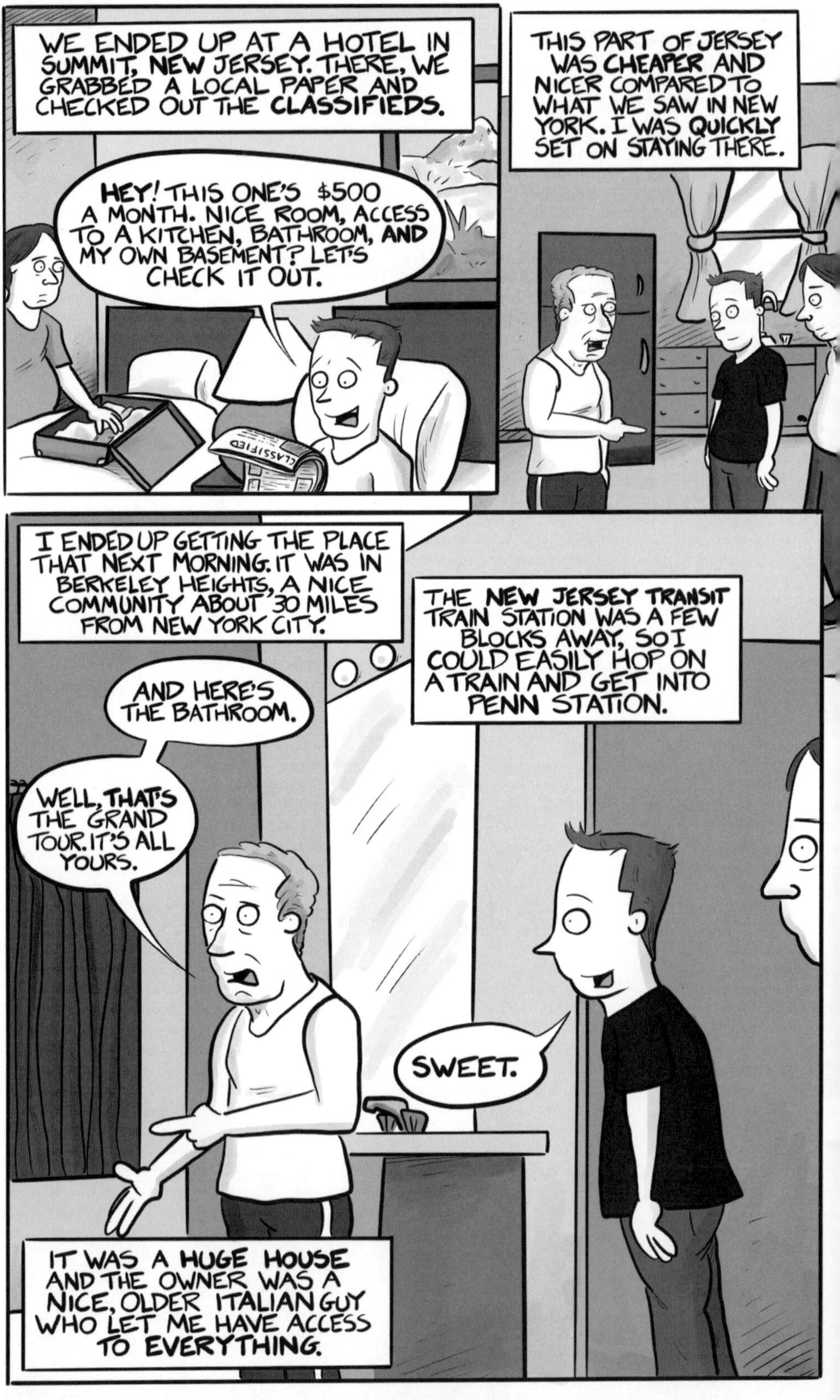
WE ENDED UP AT A HOTEL IN SUMMIT, NEW JERSEY. THERE, WE GRABBED A LOCAL PAPER AND CHECKED OUT THE CLASSIFIEDS.
HEY! THIS ONE'S $500 A MONTH. NICE ROOM, ACCESS TO A KITCHEN, BATHROOM, AND MY OWN BASEMENT? LET'S CHECK IT OUT.
CLASSIFIED
THIS PART OF JERSEY WAS CHEAPER AND NICER COMPARED TO WHAT WE SAW IN NEW YORK. I WAS QUICKLY SET ON STAYING THERE.
I ENDED UP GETTING THE PLACE THAT NEXT MORNING. IT WAS IN BERKELEY HEIGHTS, A NICE COMMUNITY ABOUT 30 MILES FROM NEW YORK CITY.
THE NEW JERSEY TRANSIT TRAIN STATION WAS A FEW BLOCKS AWAY, SO I COULD EASILY HOP ON A TRAIN AND GET INTO PENN STATION.
AND HERE'S THE BATHROOM.
WELL, THAT'S THE GRAND TOUR. IT'S ALL YOURS.
SWEET.
IT WAS A HUGE HOUSE AND THE OWNER WAS A NICE, OLDER ITALIAN GUY WHO LET ME HAVE ACCESS TO EVERYTHING.

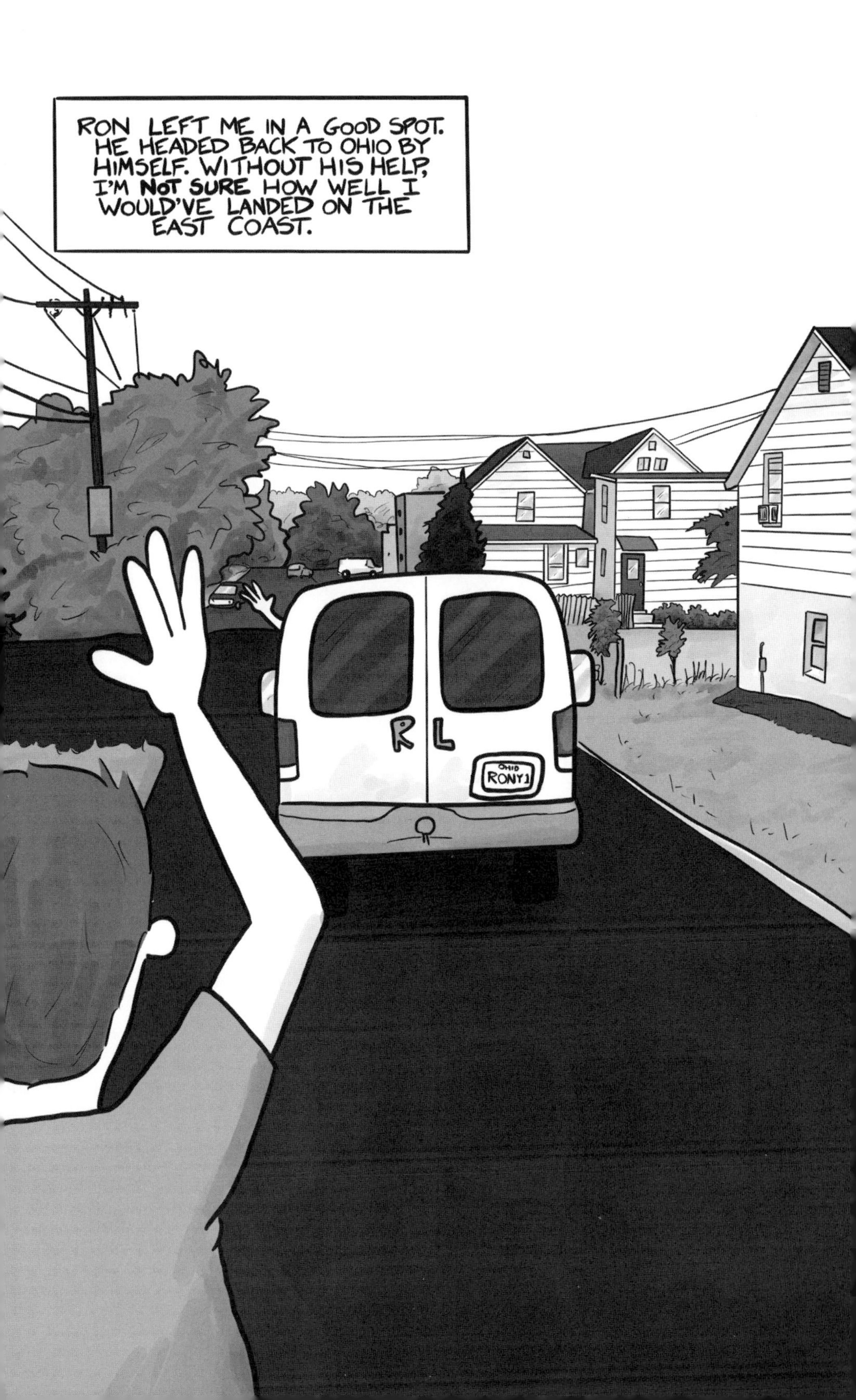
RON LEFT ME IN A GOOD SPOT. HE HEADED BACK TO OHIO BY HIMSELF. WITHOUT HIS HELP, I'M **NOT SURE** HOW WELL I WOULD'VE LANDED ON THE EAST COAST.
RL
OHIO
RONY1

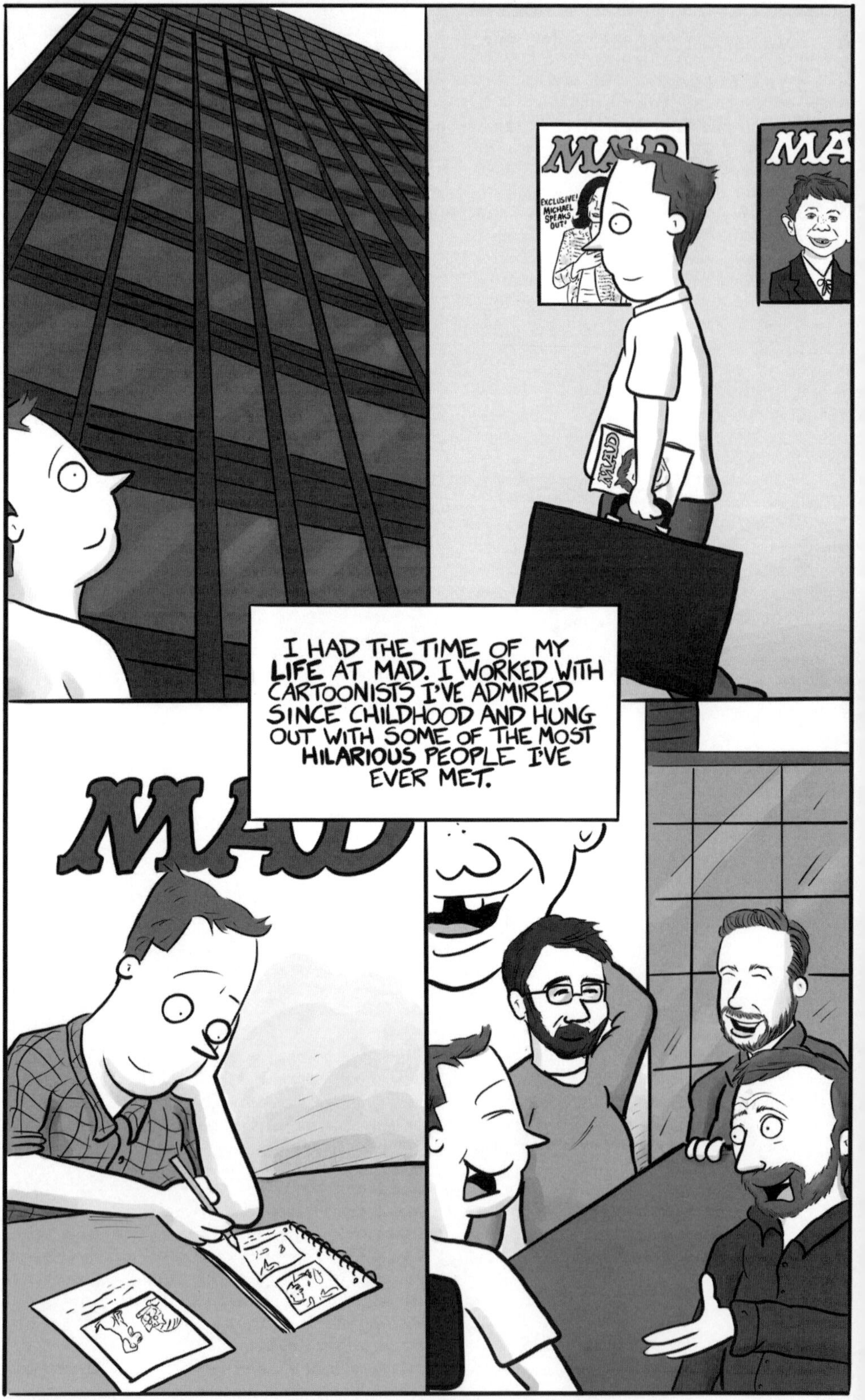
MAD
EXCLUSIVE! MICHAEL SPEAKS OUT!
MAD
MAD
I HAD THE TIME OF MY LIFE AT MAD. I WORKED WITH CARTOONISTS I'VE ADMIRED SINCE CHILDHOOD AND HUNG OUT WITH SOME OF THE MOST HILARIOUS PEOPLE I'VE EVER MET.
MAD

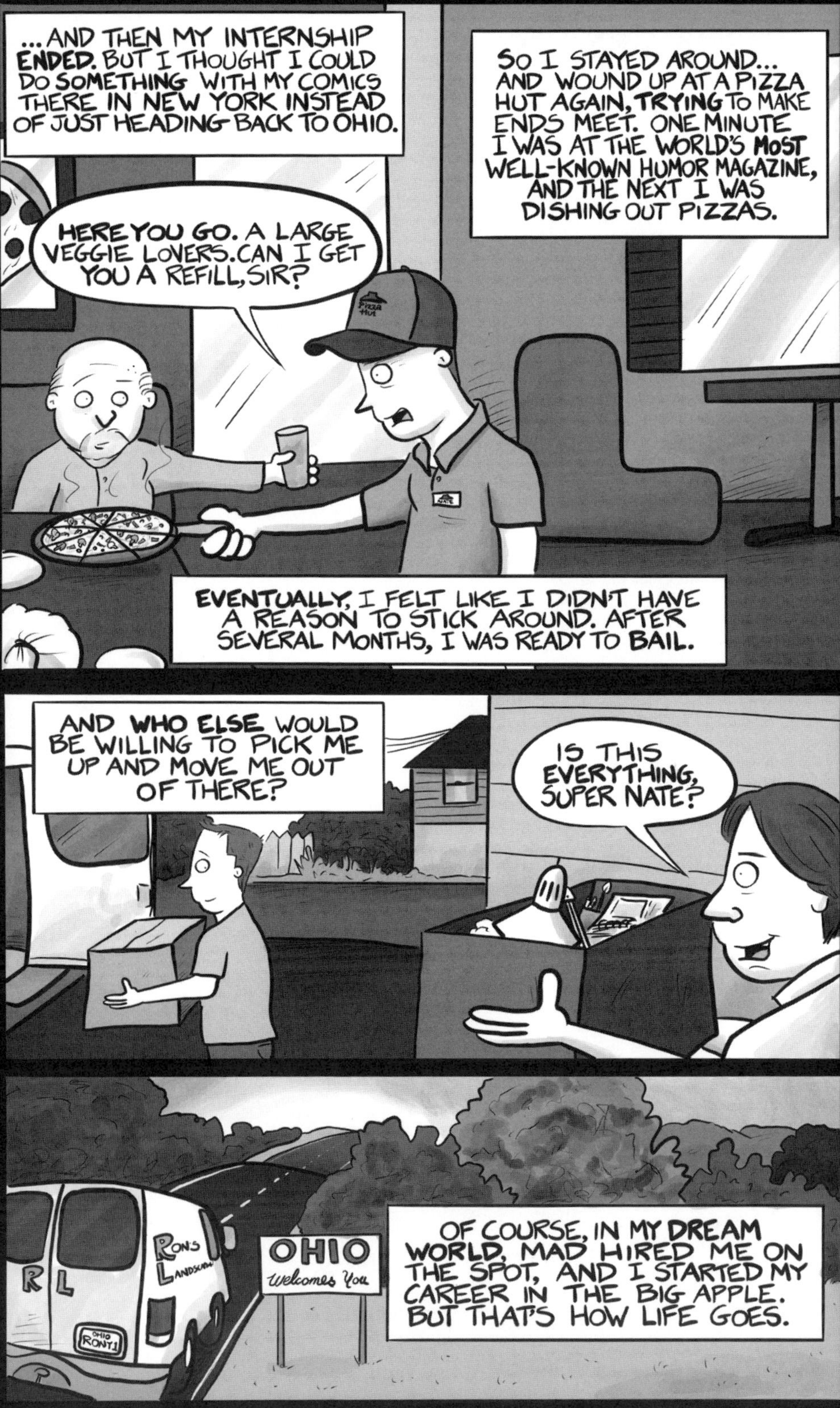
...AND THEN MY INTERNSHIP ENDED. BUT I THOUGHT I COULD DO SOMETHING WITH MY COMICS THERE IN NEW YORK INSTEAD OF JUST HEADING BACK TO OHIO.
SO I STAYED AROUND... AND WOUND UP AT A PIZZA HUT AGAIN, TRYING TO MAKE ENDS MEET. ONE MINUTE I WAS AT THE WORLD'S MOST WELL-KNOWN HUMOR MAGAZINE, AND THE NEXT I WAS DISHING OUT PIZZAS.
HERE YOU GO. A LARGE VEGGIE LOVERS. CAN I GET YOU A REFILL, SIR?
EVENTUALLY, I FELT LIKE I DIDN'T HAVE A REASON TO STICK AROUND. AFTER SEVERAL MONTHS, I WAS READY TO BAIL.
AND WHO ELSE WOULD BE WILLING TO PICK ME UP AND MOVE ME OUT OF THERE?
IS THIS EVERYTHING, SUPER NATE?
RL
OHIO
Welcomes You
OF COURSE, IN MY DREAM WORLD, MAD HIRED ME ON THE SPOT, AND I STARTED MY CAREER IN THE BIG APPLE. BUT THAT'S HOW LIFE GOES.

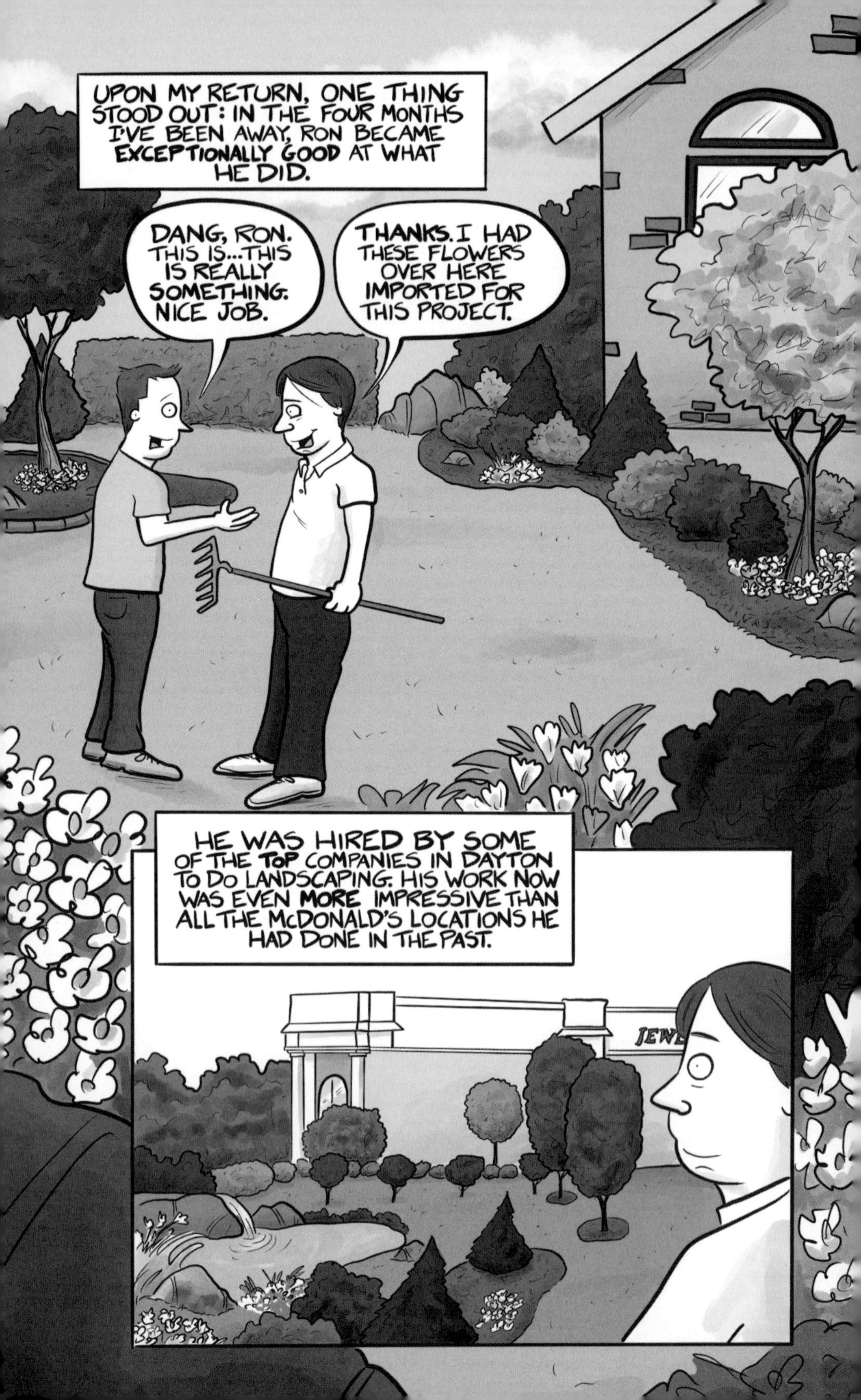
UPON MY RETURN, ONE THING STOOD OUT: IN THE FOUR MONTHS I'VE BEEN AWAY, RON BECAME **EXCEPTIONALLY GOOD** AT WHAT HE DID.
DANG, RON. THIS IS...THIS IS REALLY SOMETHING. NICE JOB.
THANKS. I HAD THESE FLOWERS OVER HERE IMPORTED FOR THIS PROJECT.
HE WAS HIRED BY SOME OF THE **TOP** COMPANIES IN DAYTON TO DO LANDSCAPING. HIS WORK NOW WAS EVEN **MORE** IMPRESSIVE THAN ALL THE McDONALD'S LOCATIONS HE HAD DONE IN THE PAST.

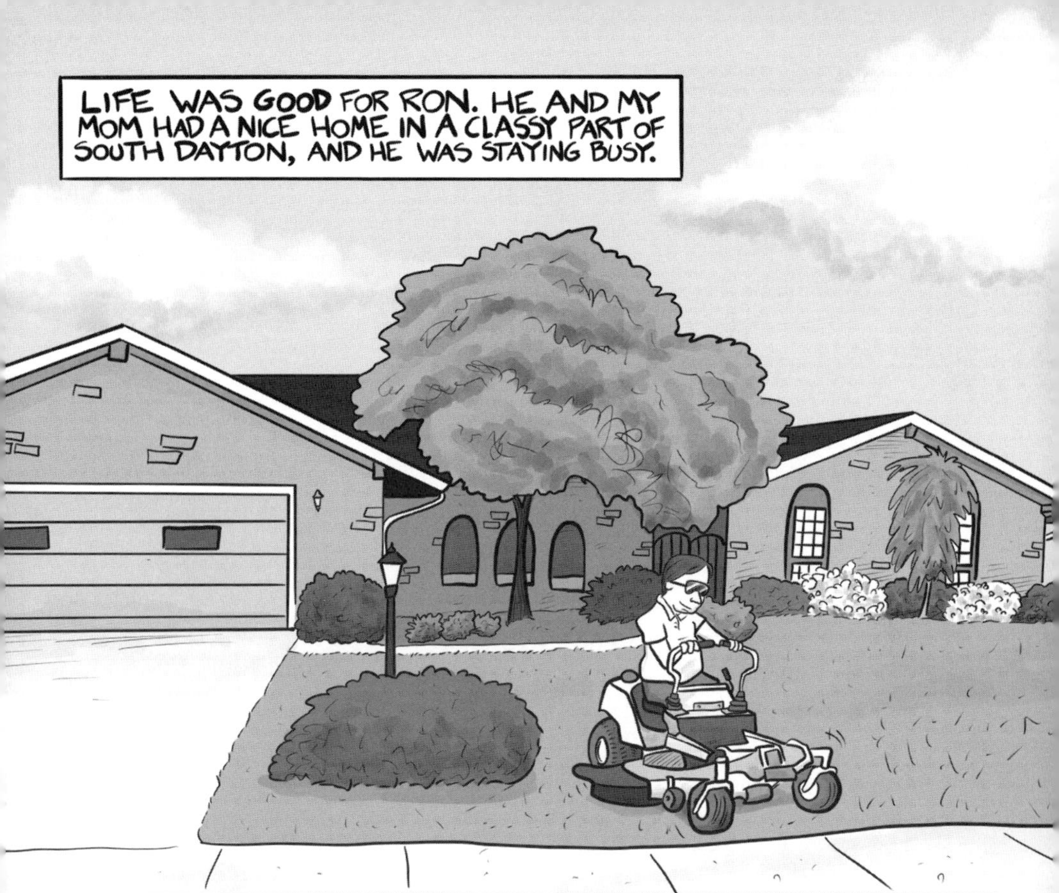
LIFE WAS GOOD FOR RON. HE AND MY MOM HAD A NICE HOME IN A CLASSY PART OF SOUTH DAYTON, AND HE WAS STAYING BUSY.

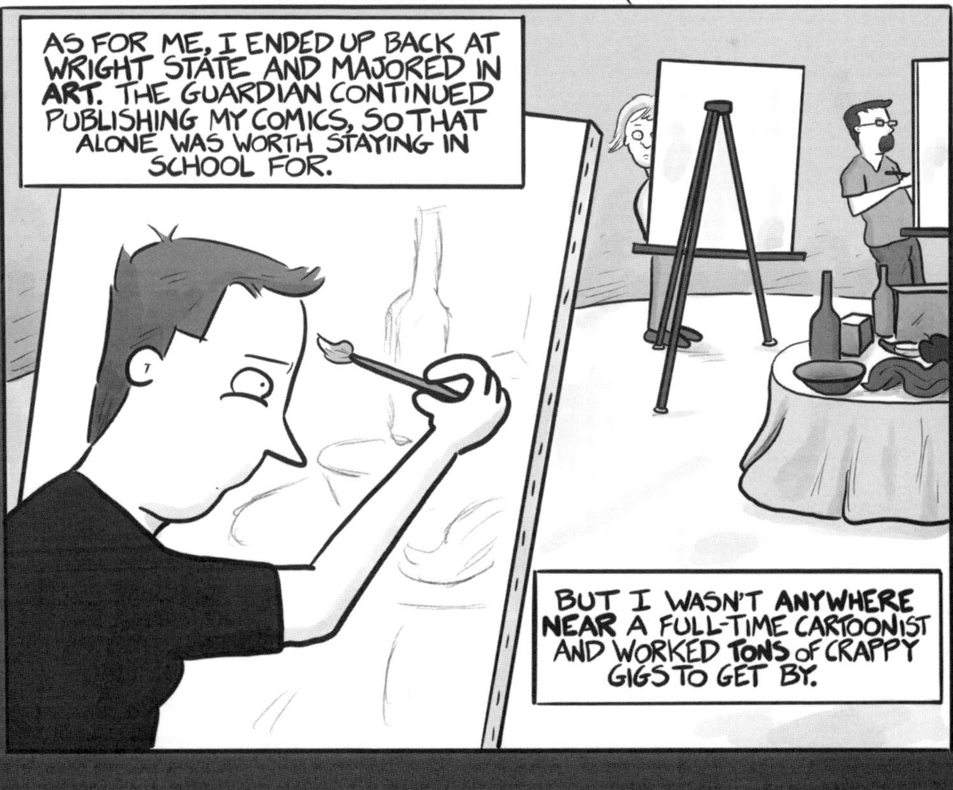
AS FOR ME, I ENDED UP BACK AT WRIGHT STATE AND MAJORED IN ART. THE GUARDIAN CONTINUED PUBLISHING MY COMICS, SO THAT ALONE WAS WORTH STAYING IN SCHOOL FOR.
BUT I WASN'T ANYWHERE NEAR A FULL-TIME CARTOONIST AND WORKED TONS OF CRAPPY GIGS TO GET BY.

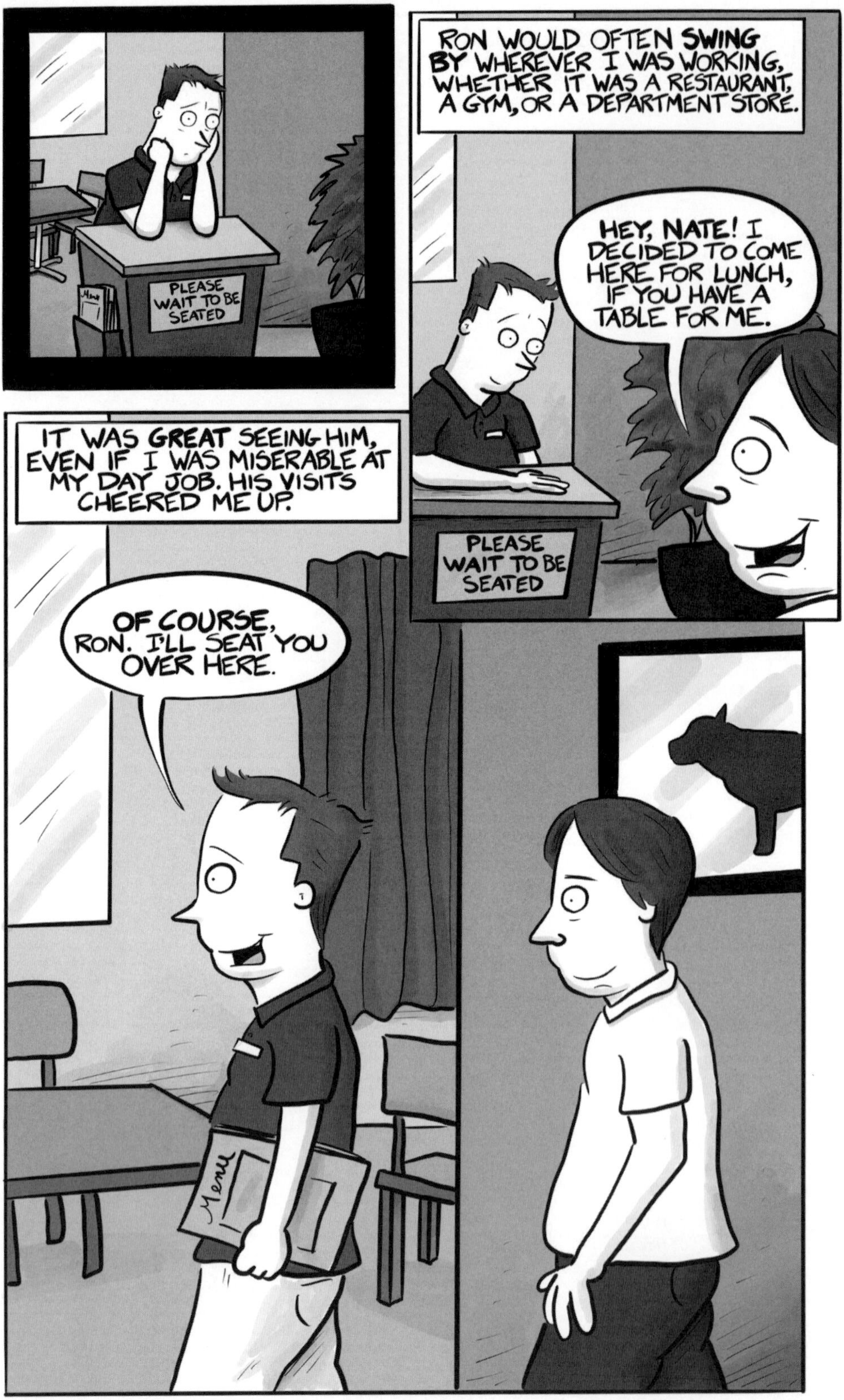
PLEASE WAIT TO BE SEATED
RON WOULD OFTEN SWING BY WHEREVER I WAS WORKING, WHETHER IT WAS A RESTAURANT, A GYM, OR A DEPARTMENT STORE.
HEY, NATE! I DECIDED TO COME HERE FOR LUNCH, IF YOU HAVE A TABLE FOR ME.
PLEASE WAIT TO BE SEATED
IT WAS GREAT SEEING HIM, EVEN IF I WAS MISERABLE AT MY DAY JOB. HIS VISITS CHEERED ME UP.
OF COURSE, RON. I'LL SEAT YOU OVER HERE.
Menu

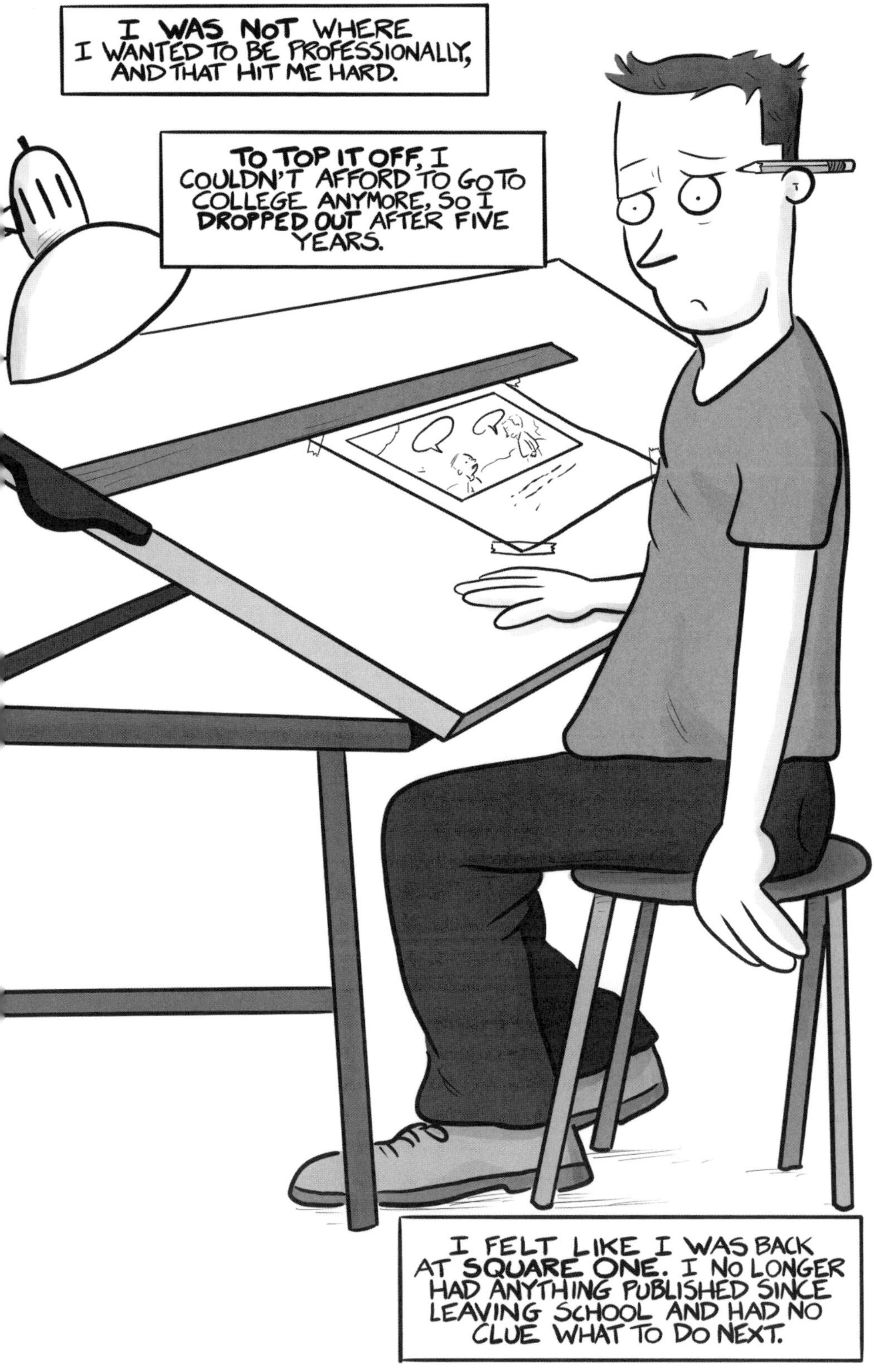
I WAS NOT WHERE I WANTED TO BE PROFESSIONALLY, AND THAT HIT ME HARD.
TO TOP IT OFF, I COULDN'T AFFORD TO GO TO COLLEGE ANYMORE, SO I DROPPED OUT AFTER FIVE YEARS.
I FELT LIKE I WAS BACK AT SQUARE ONE. I NO LONGER HAD ANYTHING PUBLISHED SINCE LEAVING SCHOOL AND HAD NO CLUE WHAT TO DO NEXT.

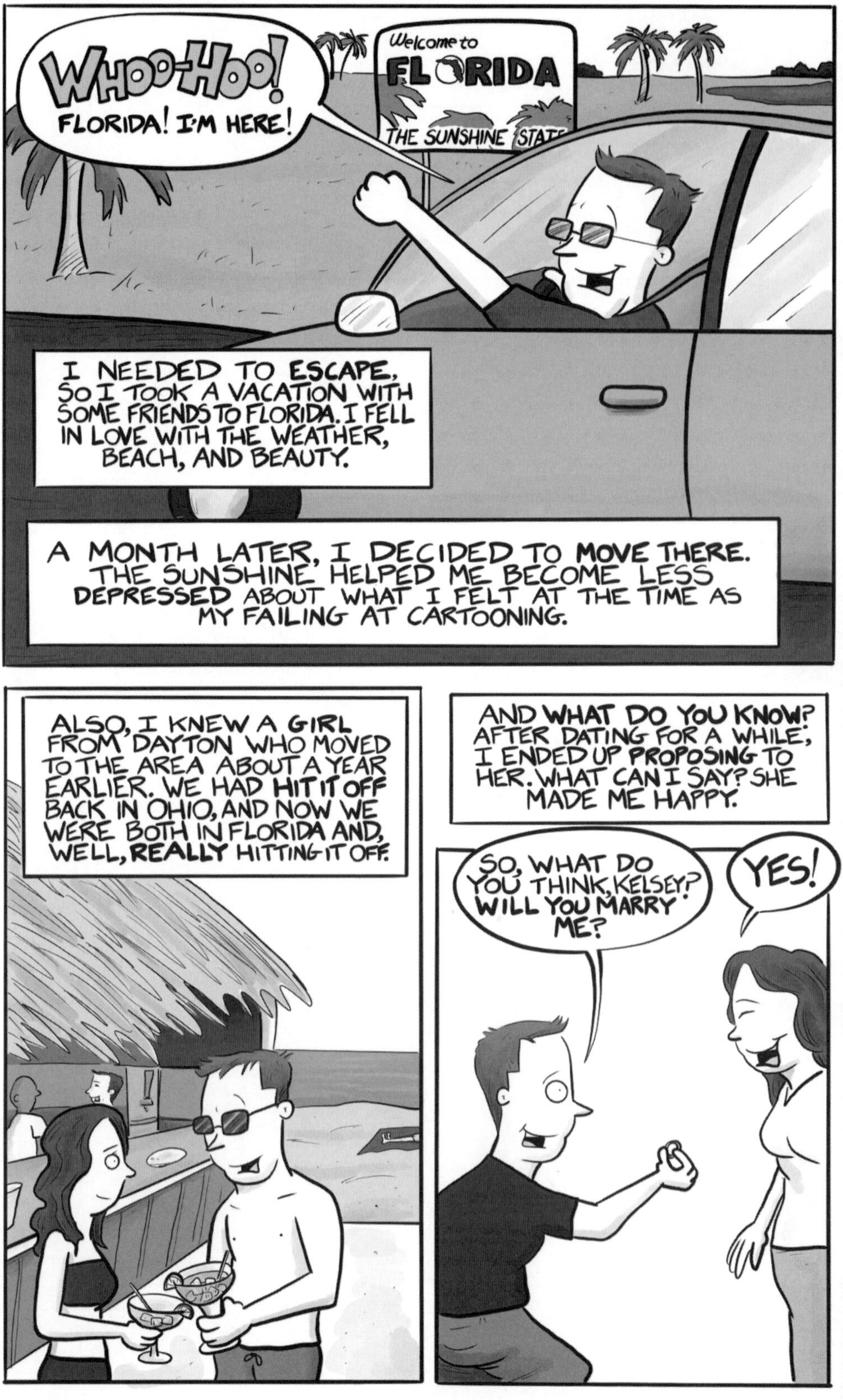
WHOO-HOO! FLORIDA! I'M HERE!
Welcome to FLORIDA THE SUNSHINE STATE
I NEEDED TO ESCAPE, SO I TOOK A VACATION WITH SOME FRIENDS TO FLORIDA. I FELL IN LOVE WITH THE WEATHER, BEACH, AND BEAUTY.
A MONTH LATER, I DECIDED TO MOVE THERE. THE SUNSHINE HELPED ME BECOME LESS DEPRESSED ABOUT WHAT I FELT AT THE TIME AS MY FAILING AT CARTOONING.
ALSO, I KNEW A GIRL FROM DAYTON WHO MOVED TO THE AREA ABOUT A YEAR EARLIER. WE HAD HIT IT OFF BACK IN OHIO, AND NOW WE WERE BOTH IN FLORIDA AND, WELL, REALLY HITTING IT OFF.
AND WHAT DO YOU KNOW? AFTER DATING FOR A WHILE, I ENDED UP PROPOSING TO HER. WHAT CAN I SAY? SHE MADE ME HAPPY.
SO, WHAT DO YOU THINK, KELSEY? WILL YOU MARRY ME?
YES!

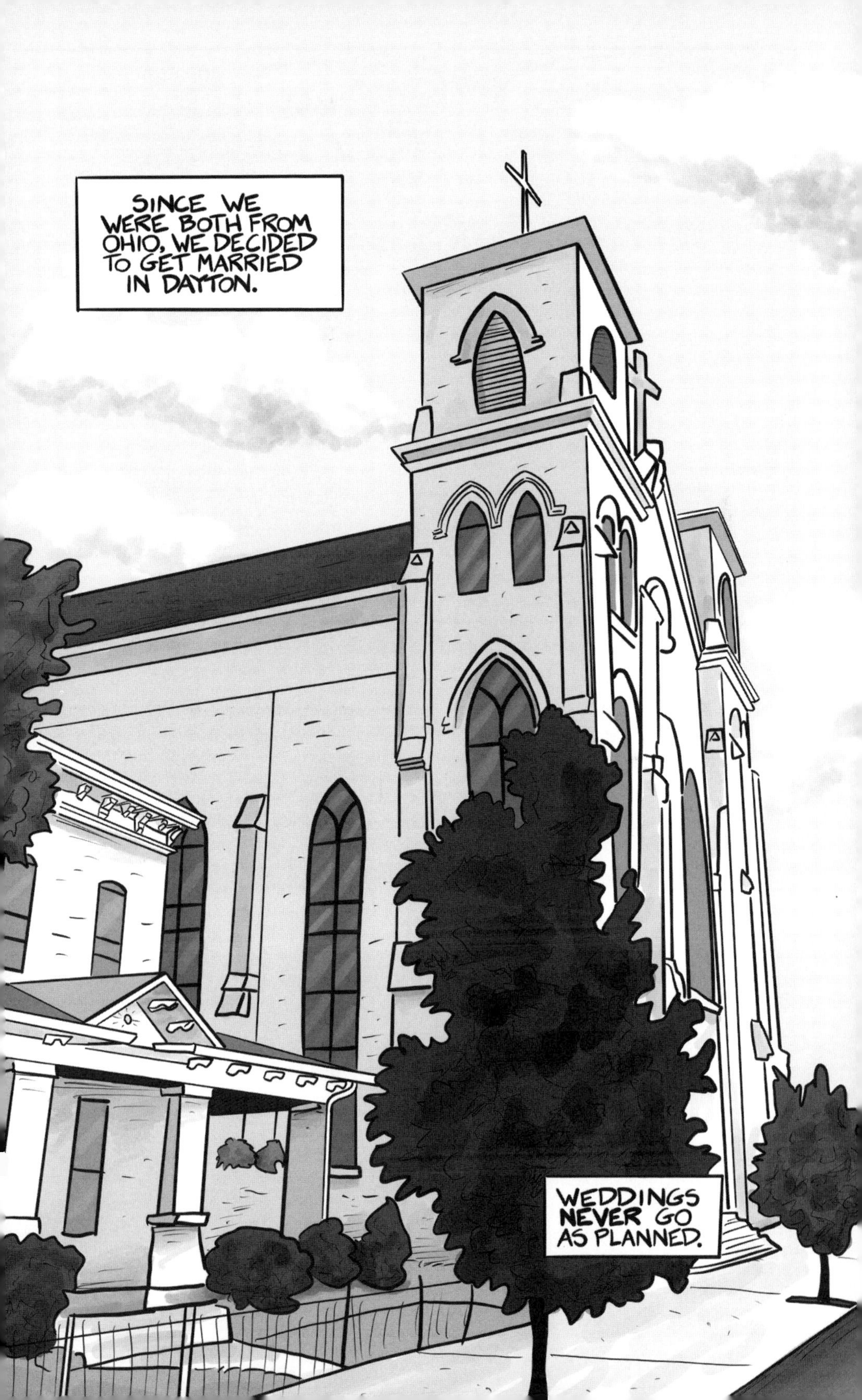
SINCE WE WERE BOTH FROM OHIO, WE DECIDED TO GET MARRIED IN DAYTON.
WEDDINGS **NEVER** GO AS PLANNED.

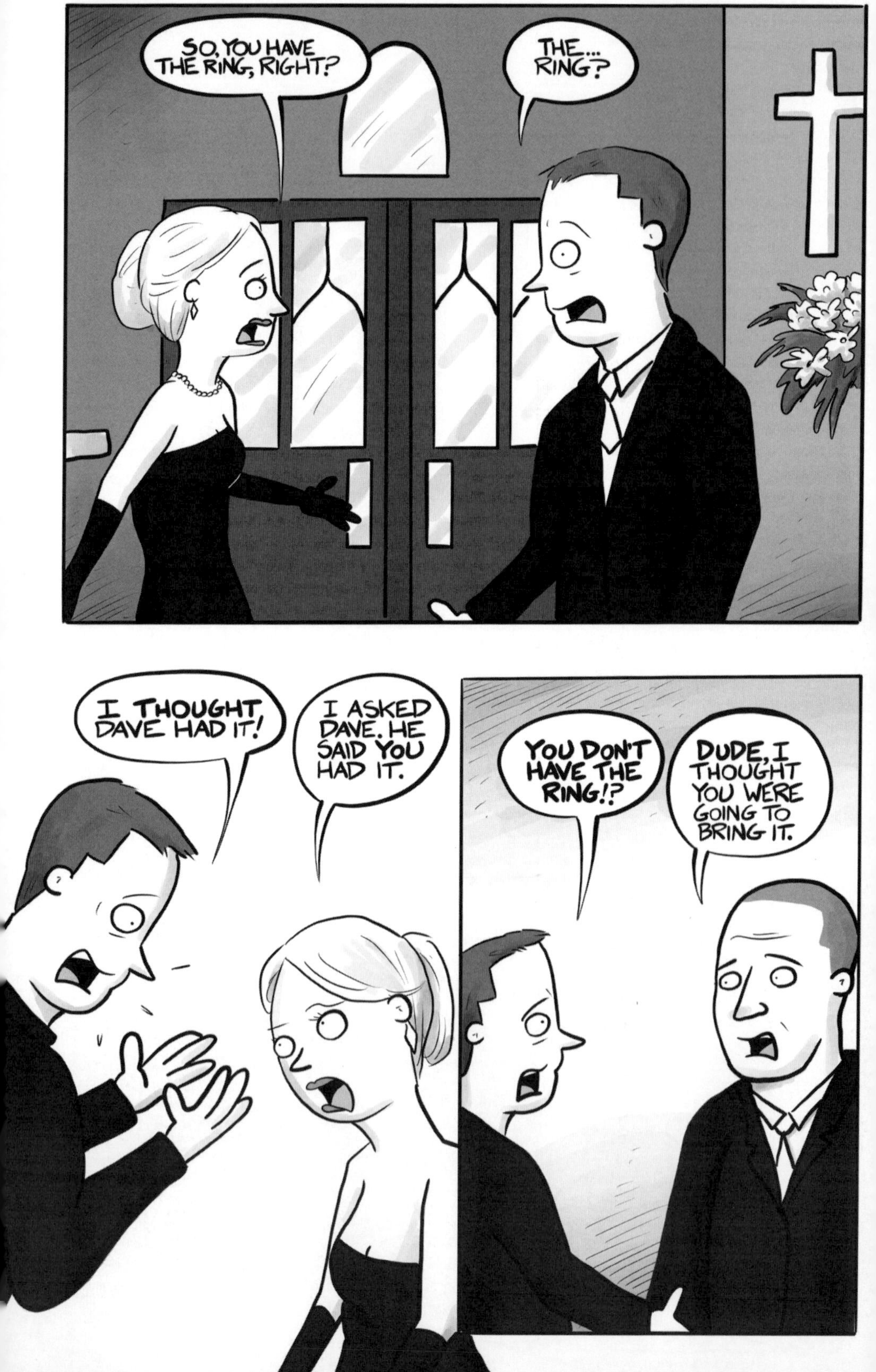
SO, YOU HAVE THE RING, RIGHT?
THE... RING?
I THOUGHT DAVE HAD IT!
I ASKED DAVE. HE SAID YOU HAD IT.
YOU DON'T HAVE THE RING!?
DUDE, I THOUGHT YOU WERE GOING TO BRING IT.

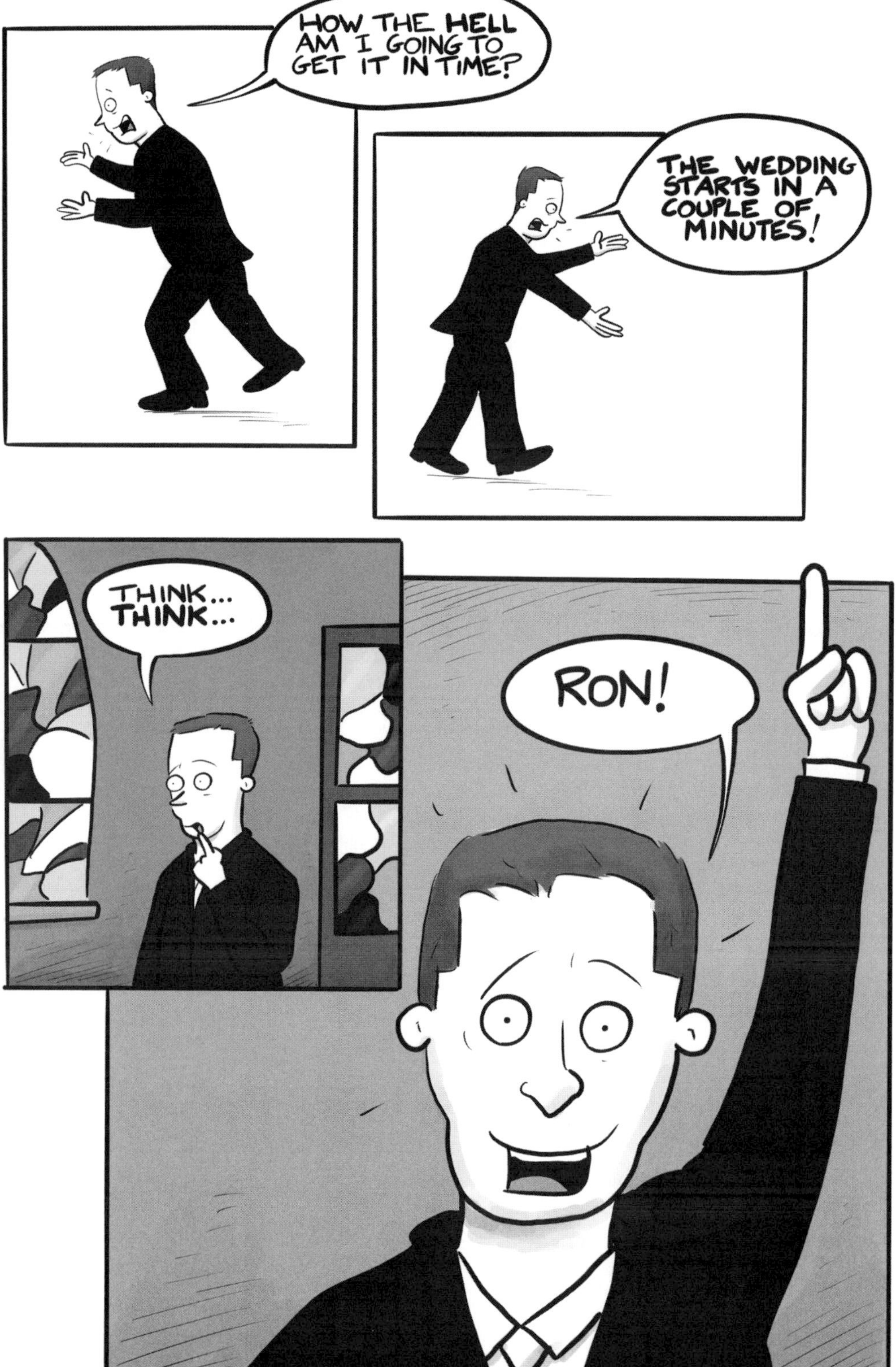
HOW THE HELL AM I GOING TO GET IT IN TIME?
THE WEDDING STARTS IN A COUPLE OF MINUTES!
THINK... THINK...
RON!

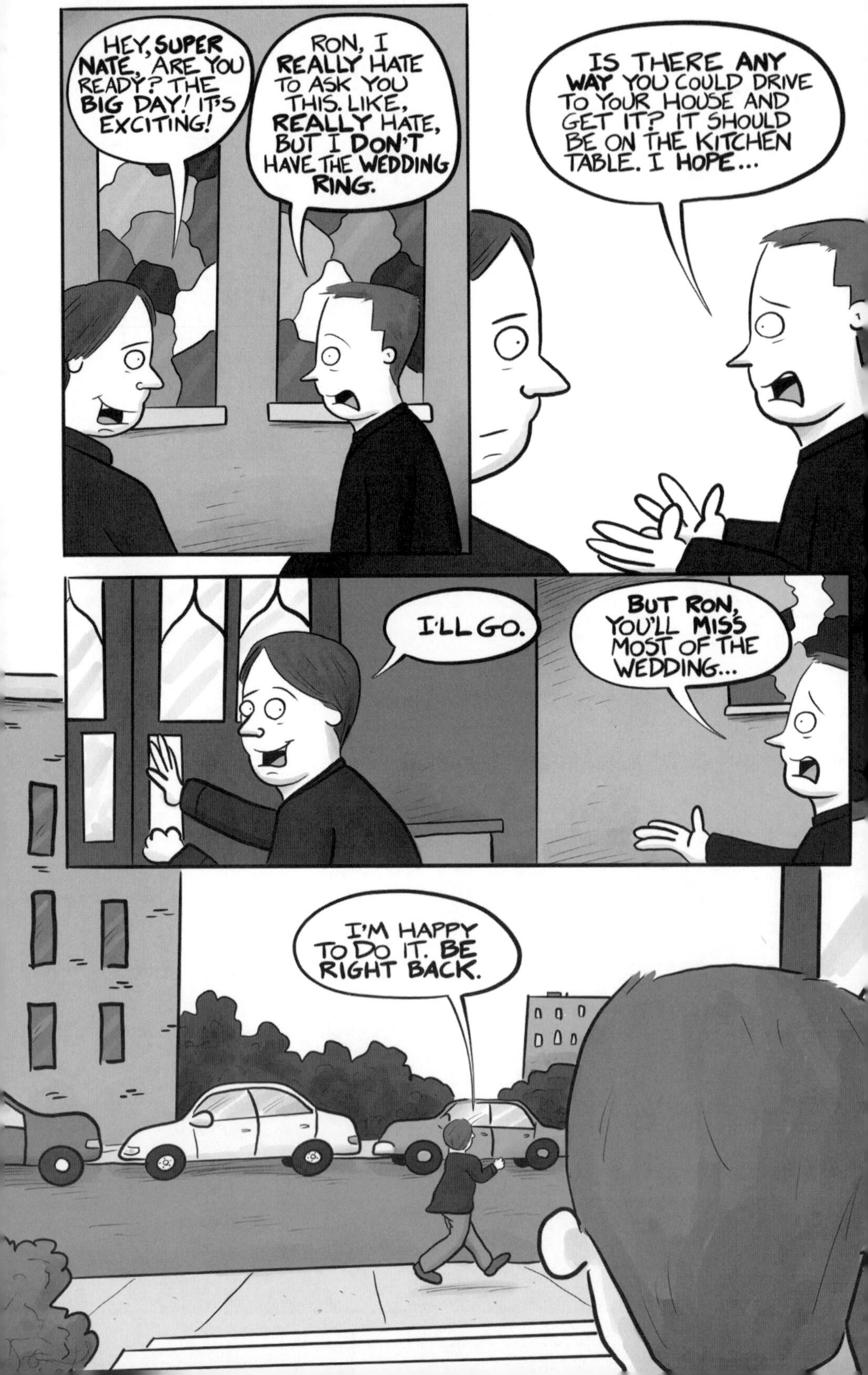
HEY, SUPER NATE, ARE YOU READY? THE BIG DAY! IT'S EXCITING!
RON, I REALLY HATE TO ASK YOU THIS. LIKE, REALLY HATE, BUT I DON'T HAVE THE WEDDING RING.
IS THERE ANY WAY YOU COULD DRIVE TO YOUR HOUSE AND GET IT? IT SHOULD BE ON THE KITCHEN TABLE. I HOPE...
I'LL GO.
BUT RON, YOU'LL MISS MOST OF THE WEDDING...
I'M HAPPY TO DO IT. BE RIGHT BACK.

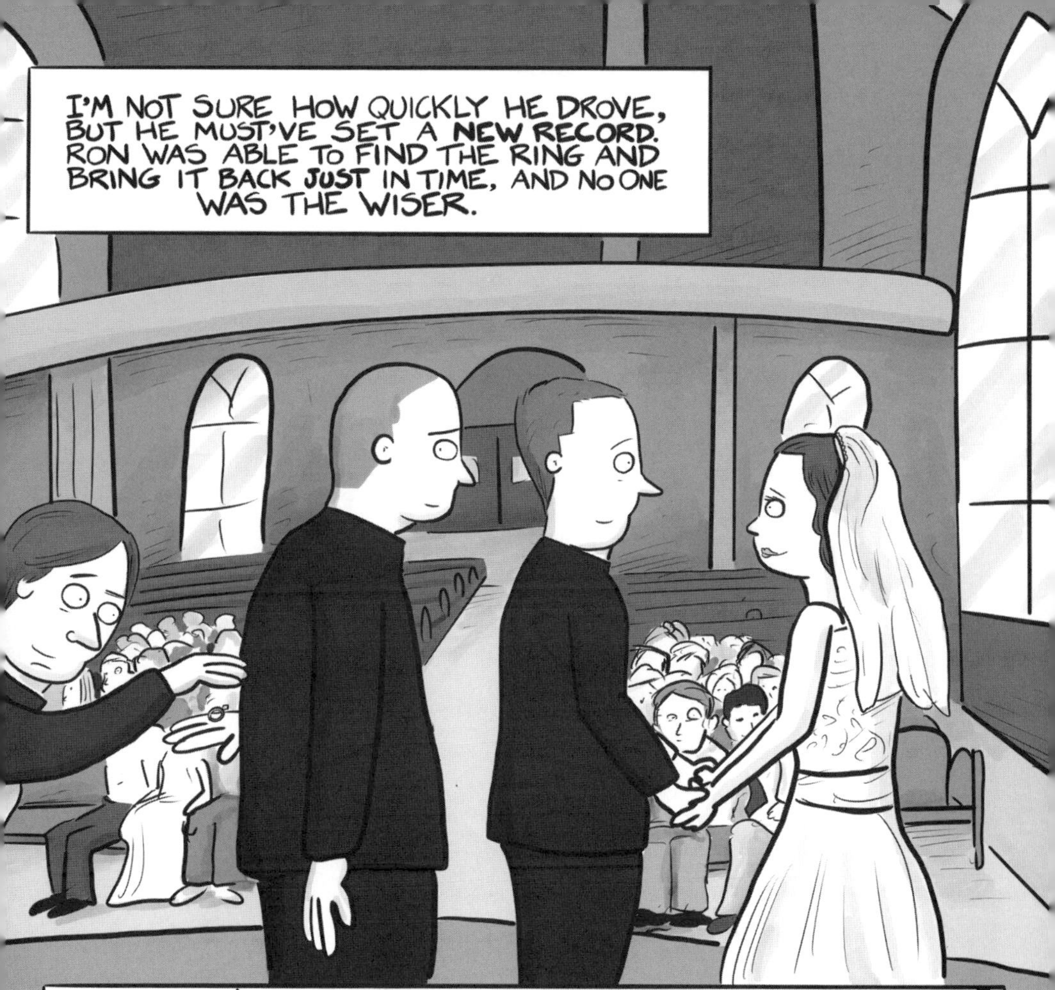
I'M NOT SURE HOW QUICKLY HE DROVE, BUT HE MUST'VE SET A NEW RECORD. RON WAS ABLE TO FIND THE RING AND BRING IT BACK JUST IN TIME, AND NO ONE WAS THE WISER.

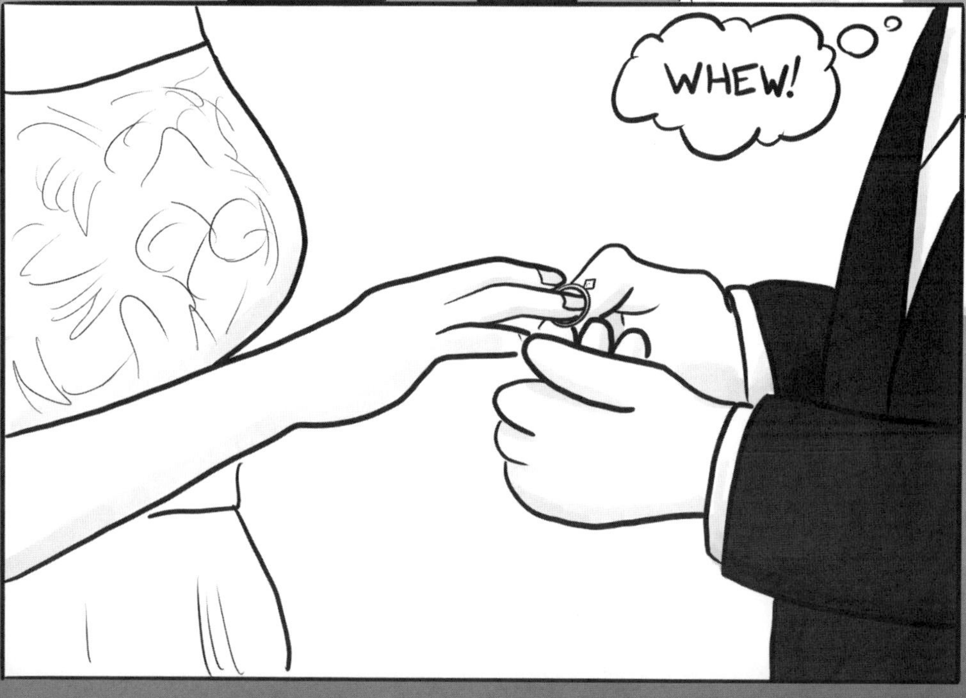
WHEW!

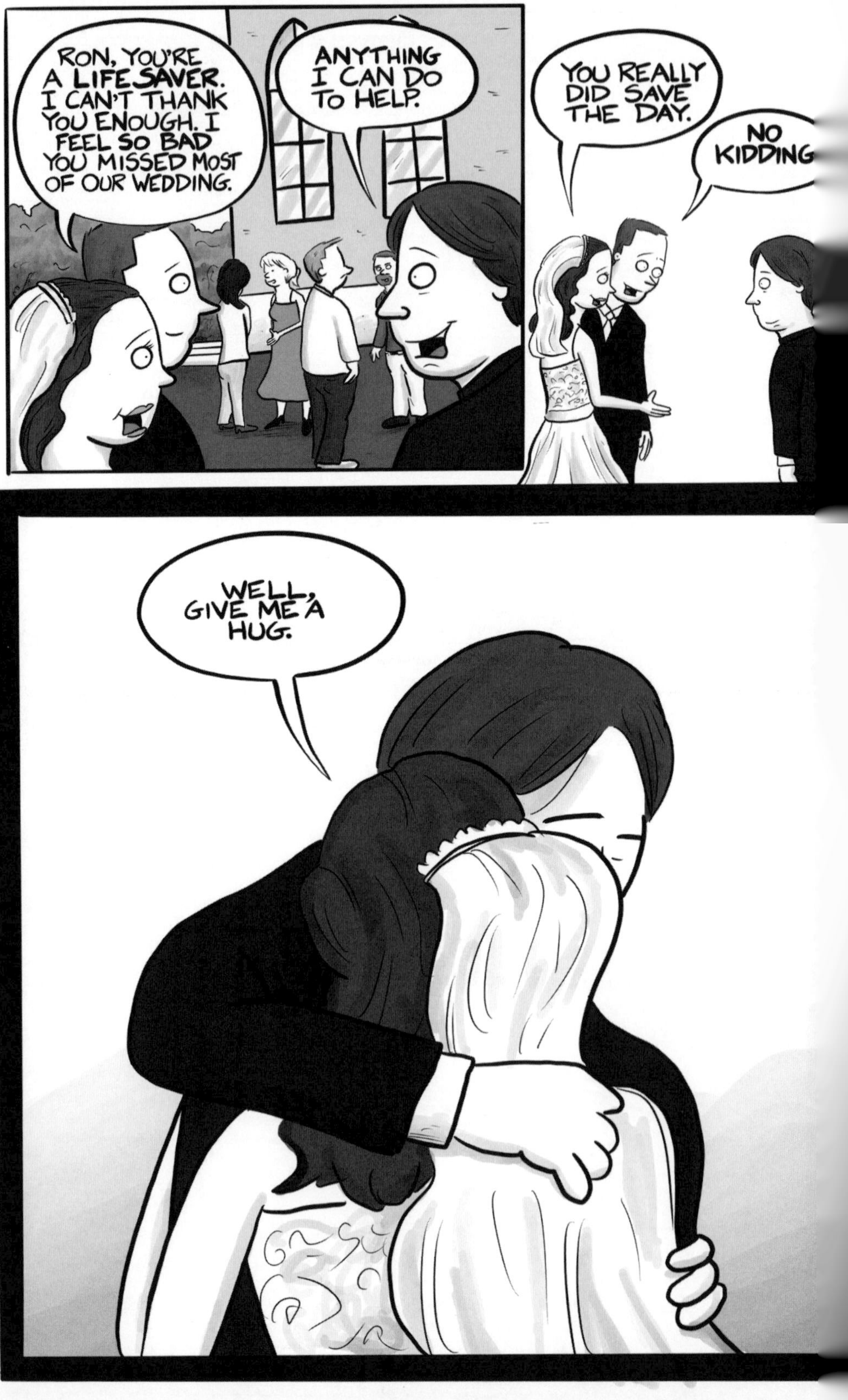
RON, YOU'RE A **LIFESAVER**. I CAN'T THANK YOU ENOUGH. I FEEL SO BAD YOU MISSED MOST OF OUR WEDDING.
ANYTHING I CAN DO TO HELP.
YOU REALLY DID SAVE THE DAY.
NO KIDDING
WELL, GIVE ME A HUG.

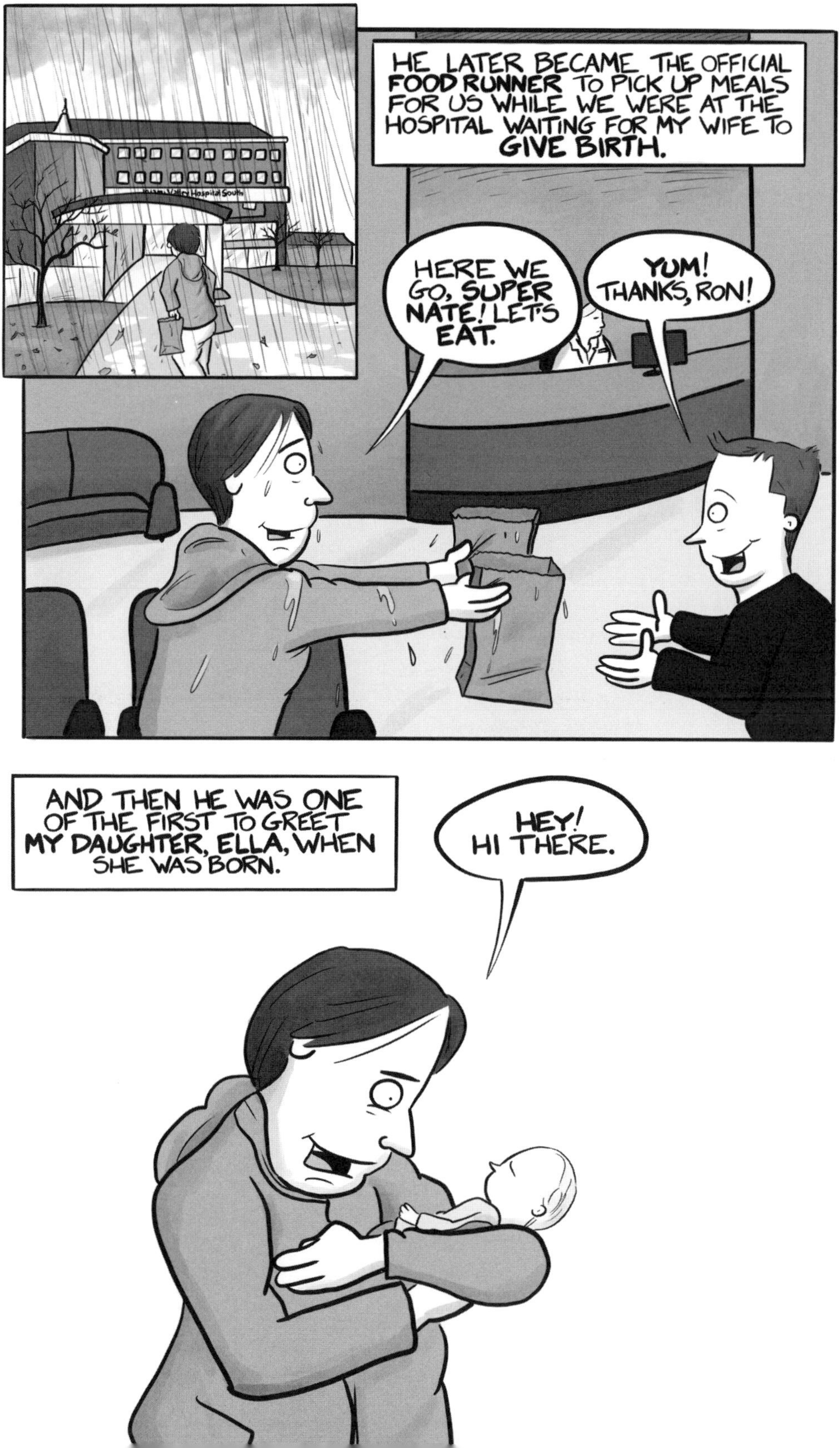
HE LATER BECAME THE OFFICIAL FOOD RUNNER TO PICK UP MEALS FOR US WHILE WE WERE AT THE HOSPITAL WAITING FOR MY WIFE TO GIVE BIRTH.
HERE WE GO, SUPER NATE! LET'S EAT.
YUM! THANKS, RON!
AND THEN HE WAS ONE OF THE FIRST TO GREET MY DAUGHTER, ELLA, WHEN SHE WAS BORN.
HEY! HI THERE.

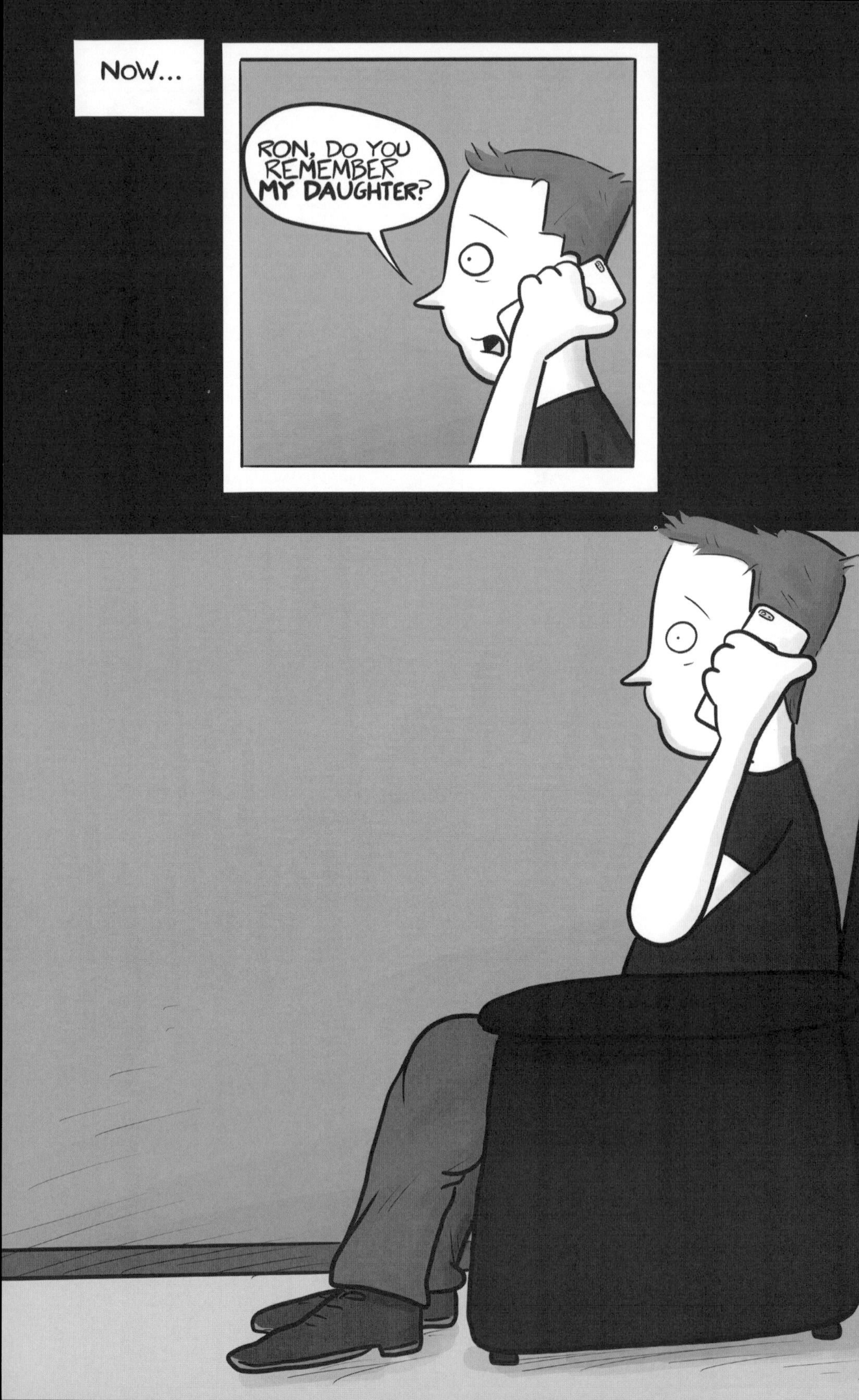
NOW...
RON, DO YOU REMEMBER **MY DAUGHTER?**

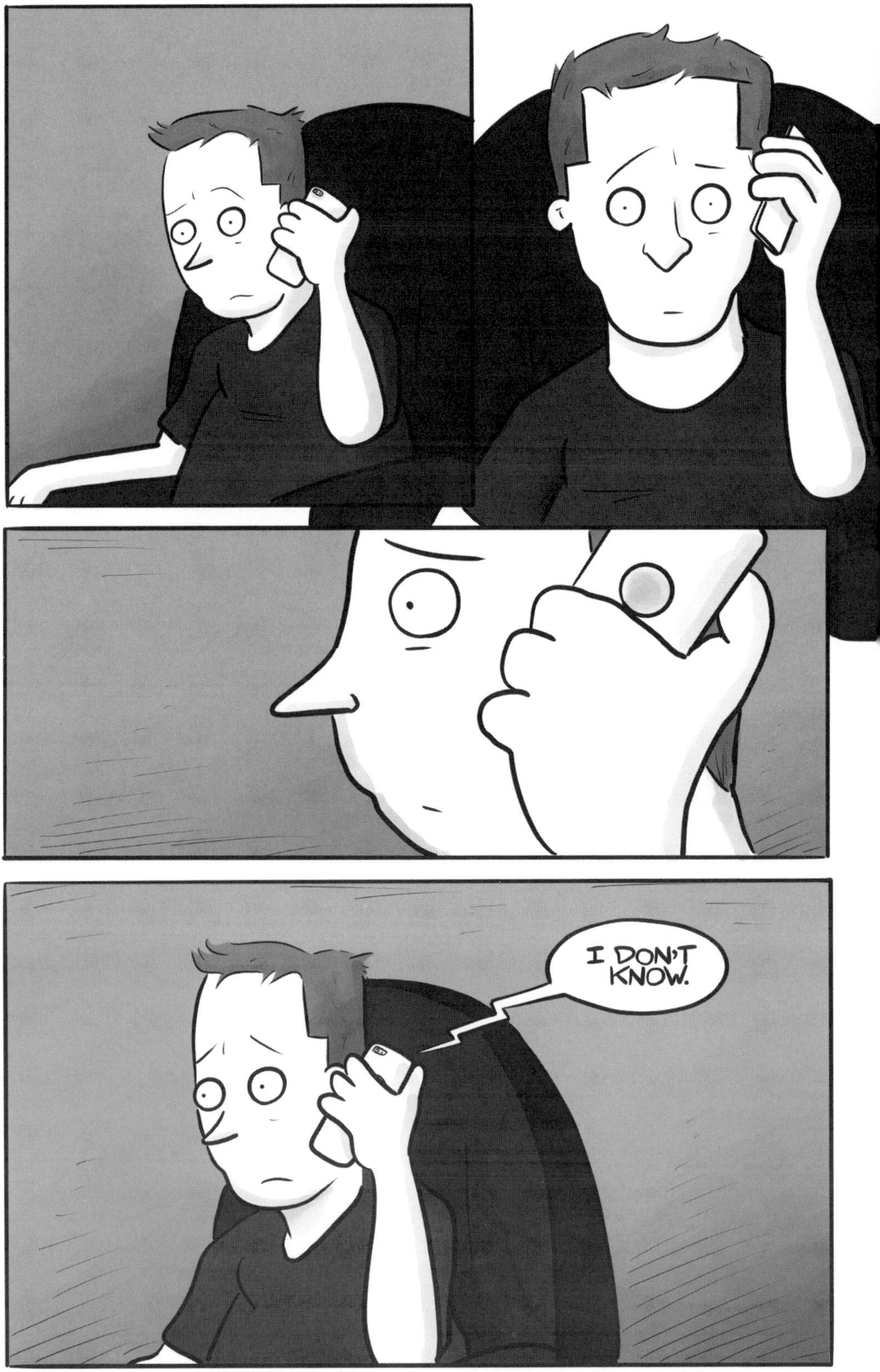
I DON'T KNOW.

PART THREE

THE SLIP

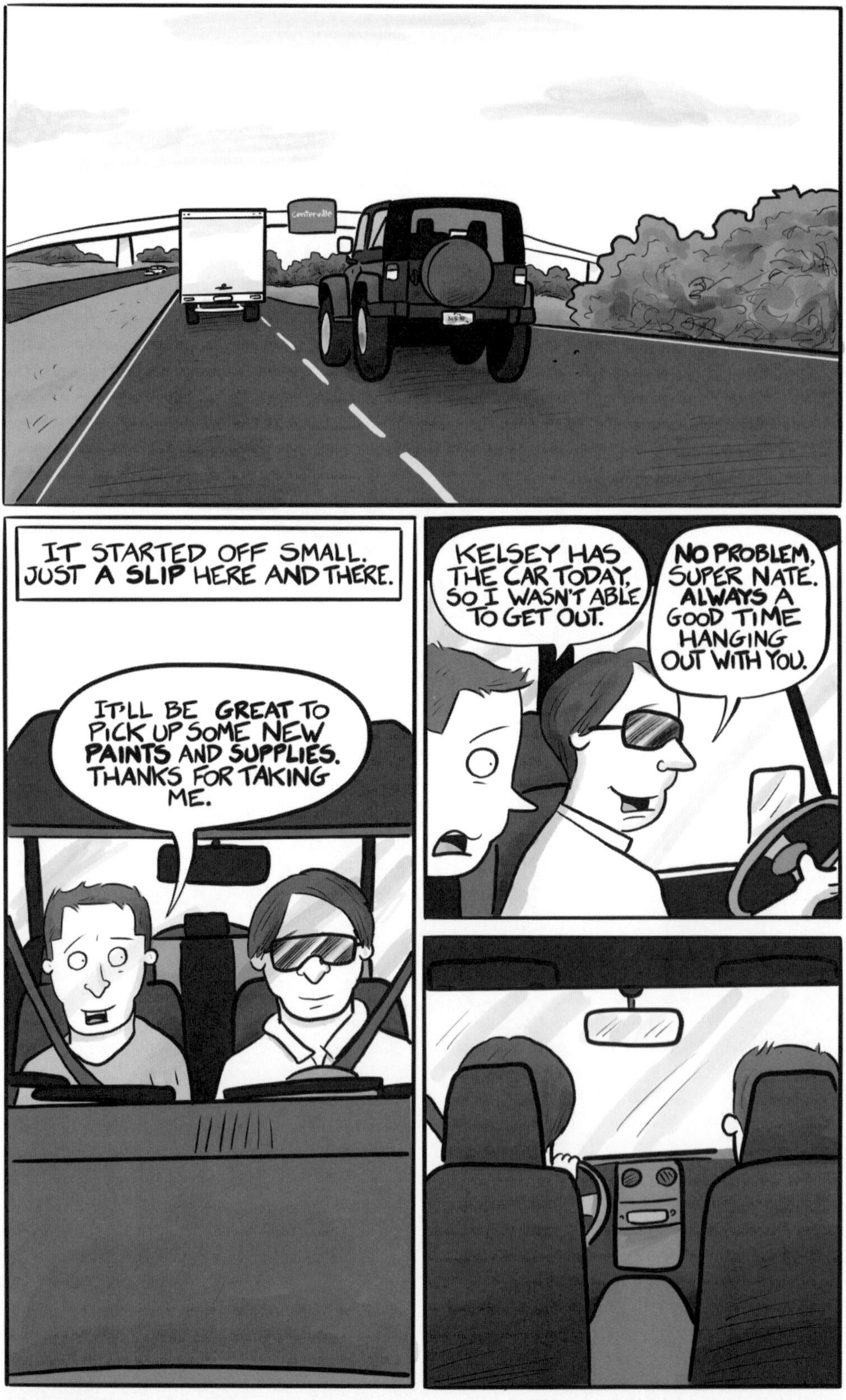
Centerville
IT STARTED OFF SMALL. JUST A SLIP HERE AND THERE.
IT'LL BE GREAT TO PICK UP SOME NEW PAINTS AND SUPPLIES. THANKS FOR TAKING ME.
KELSEY HAS THE CAR TODAY, SO I WASN'T ABLE TO GET OUT.
NO PROBLEM, SUPER NATE. ALWAYS A GOOD TIME HANGING OUT WITH YOU.

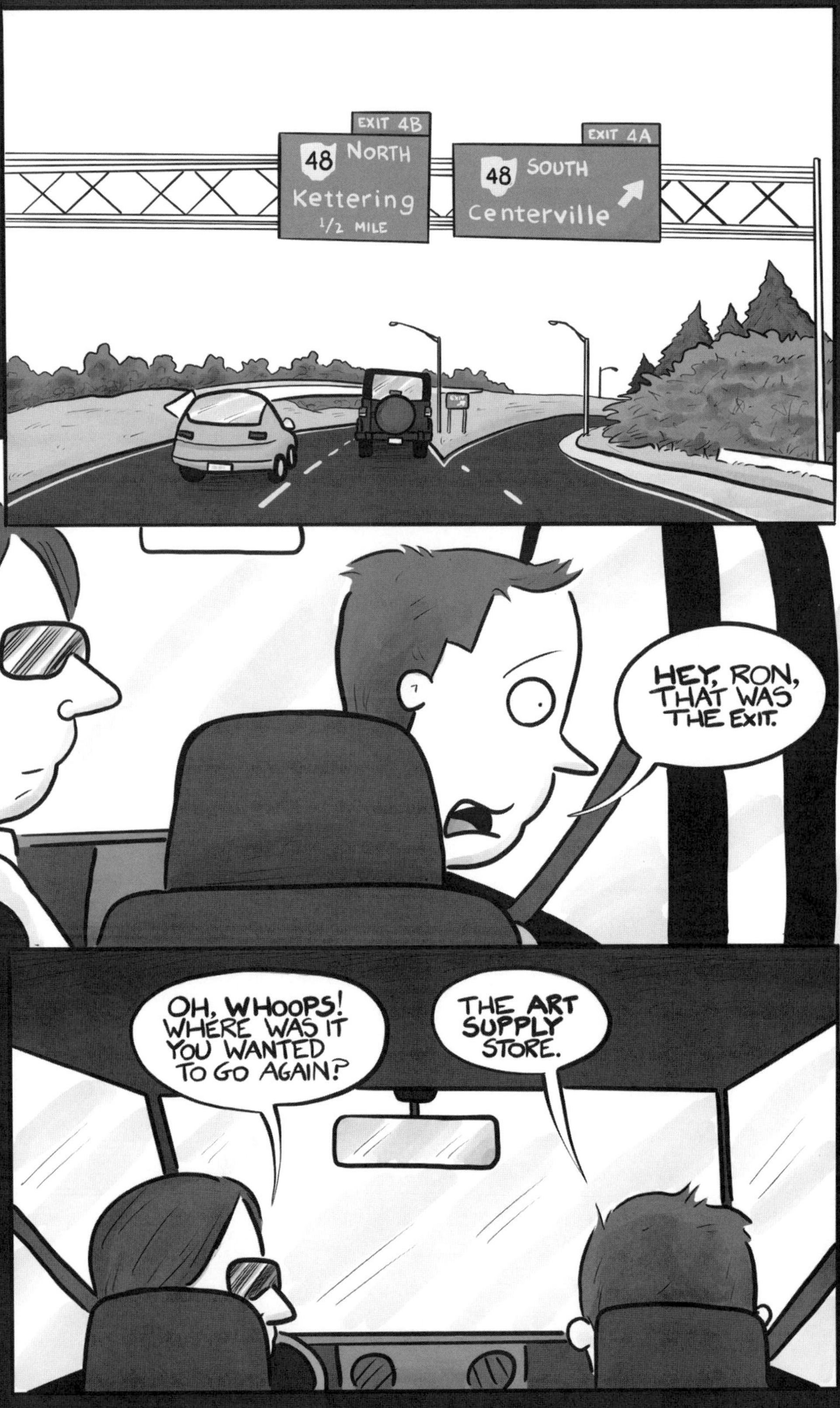
EXIT 4B
48 NORTH
Kettering
1/2 MILE
EXIT 4A
48 SOUTH
Centerville
HEY, RON, THAT WAS THE EXIT.
OH, WHOOPS! WHERE WAS IT YOU WANTED TO GO AGAIN?
THE ART SUPPLY STORE.

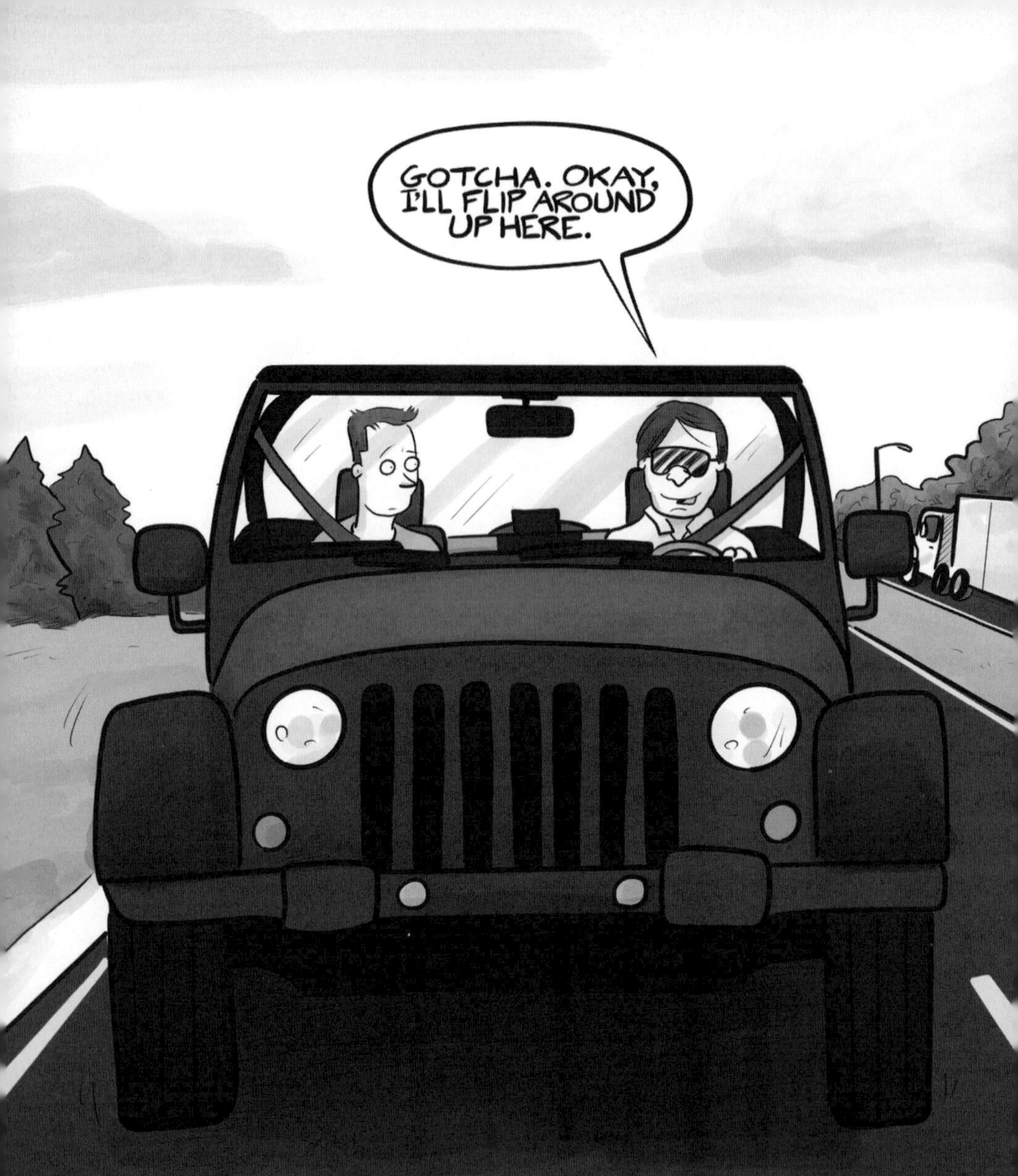
GOTCHA. OKAY, I'LL FLIP AROUND UP HERE.

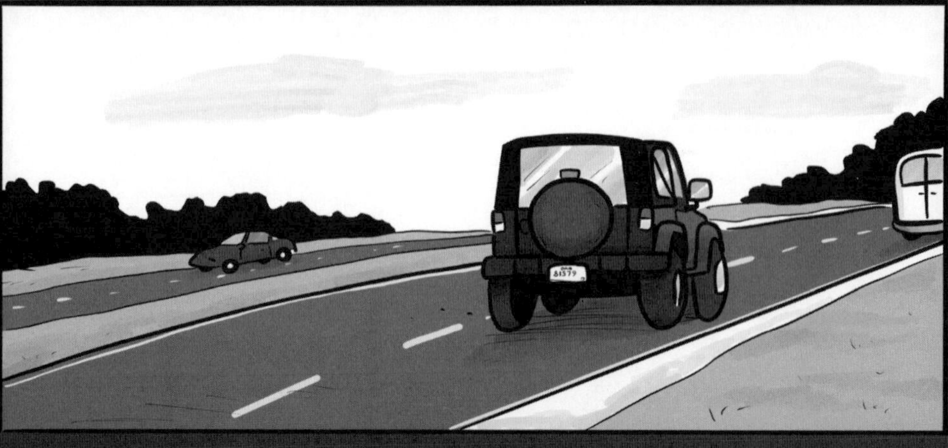

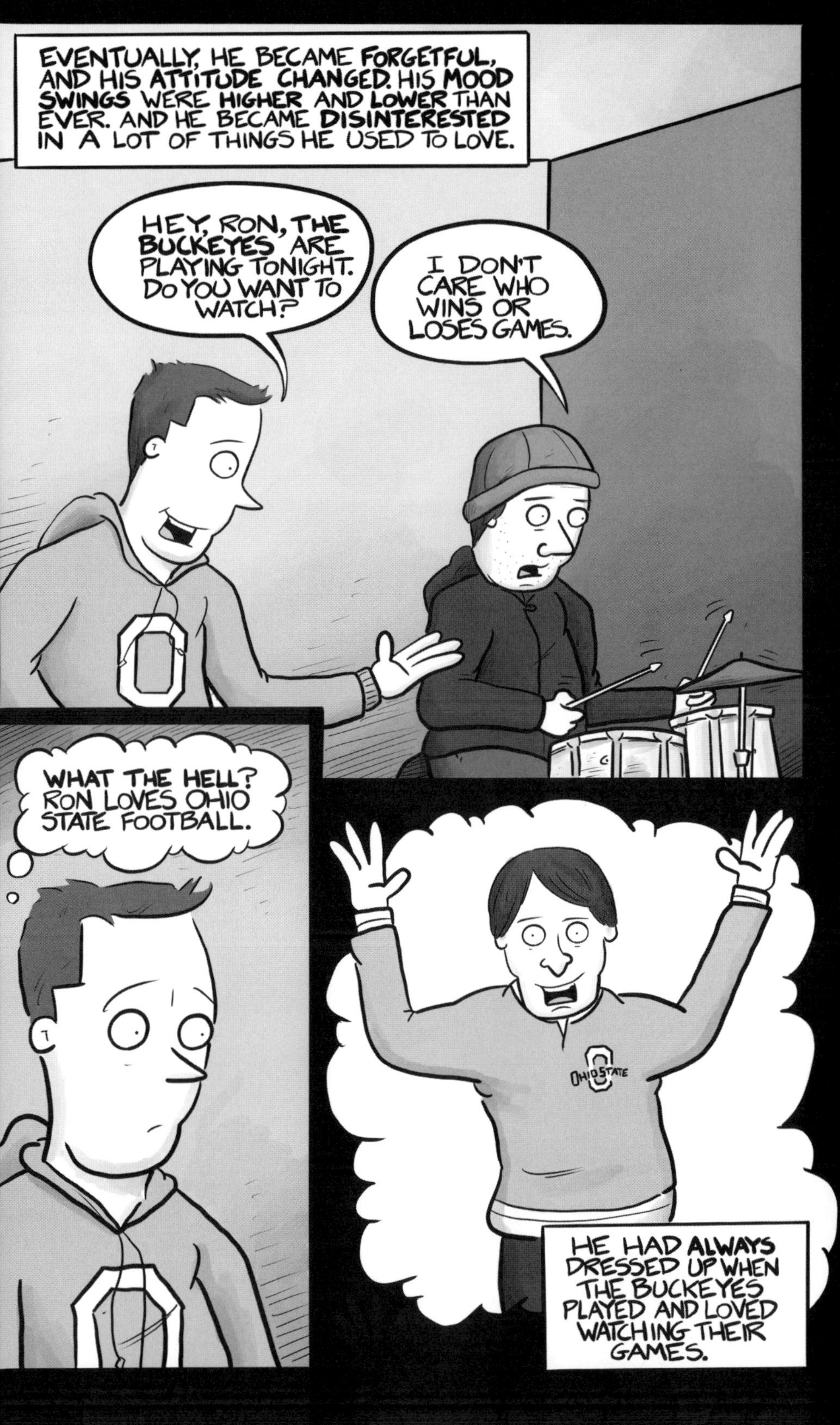
EVENTUALLY, HE BECAME FORGETFUL, AND HIS ATTITUDE CHANGED. HIS MOOD SWINGS WERE HIGHER AND LOWER THAN EVER. AND HE BECAME DISINTERESTED IN A LOT OF THINGS HE USED TO LOVE.
HEY, RON, THE BUCKEYES ARE PLAYING TONIGHT. DO YOU WANT TO WATCH?
I DON'T CARE WHO WINS OR LOSES GAMES.
WHAT THE HELL? RON LOVES OHIO STATE FOOTBALL.
OHIO STATE
HE HAD ALWAYS DRESSED UP WHEN THE BUCKEYES PLAYED AND LOVED WATCHING THEIR GAMES.

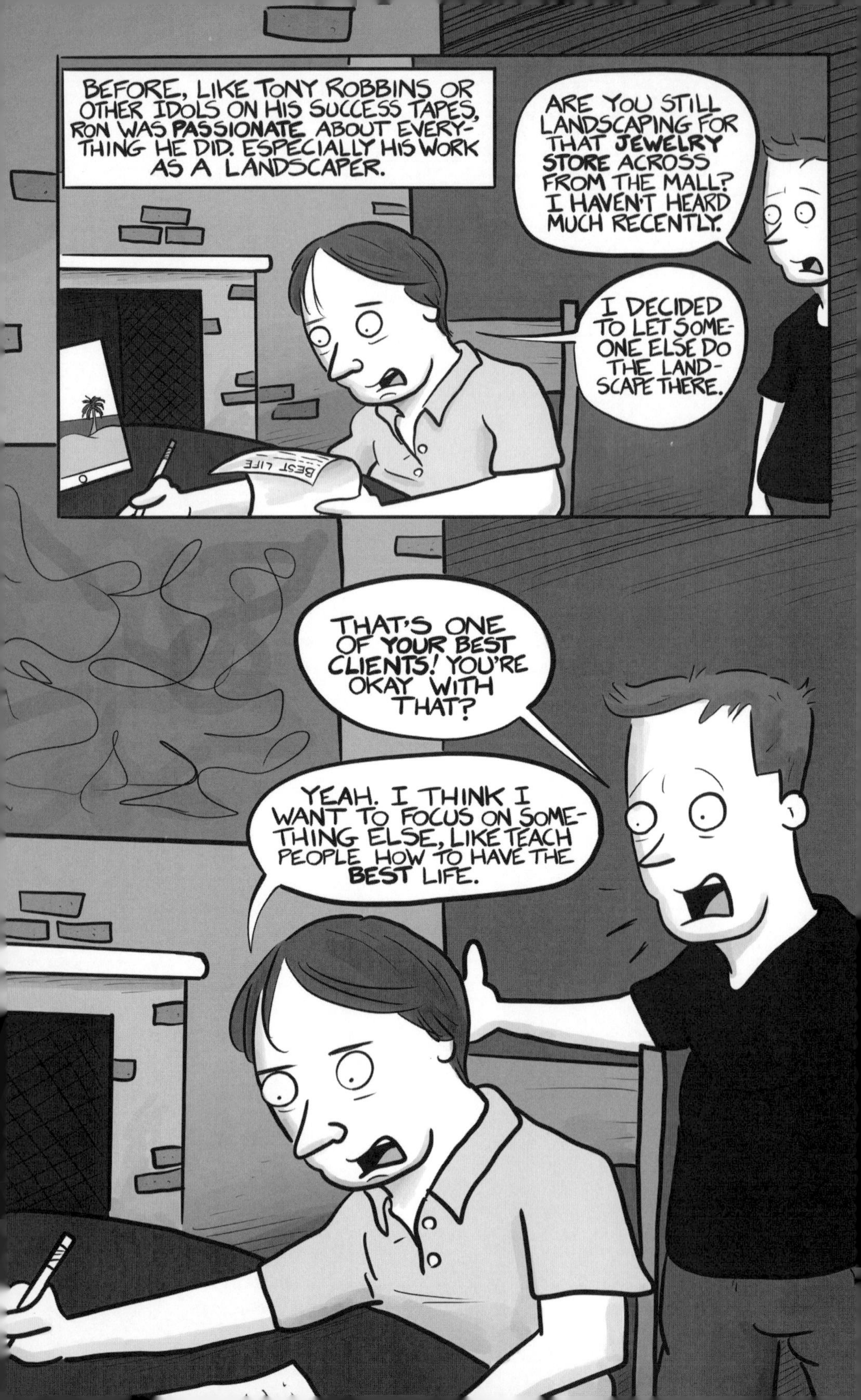
BEFORE, LIKE TONY ROBBINS OR OTHER IDOLS ON HIS SUCCESS TAPES, RON WAS PASSIONATE ABOUT EVERYTHING HE DID. ESPECIALLY HIS WORK AS A LANDSCAPER.
ARE YOU STILL LANDSCAPING FOR THAT JEWELRY STORE ACROSS FROM THE MALL? I HAVEN'T HEARD MUCH RECENTLY.
I DECIDED TO LET SOMEONE ELSE DO THE LANDSCAPE THERE.
BEST LIFE
THAT'S ONE OF YOUR BEST CLIENTS! YOU'RE OKAY WITH THAT?
YEAH. I THINK I WANT TO FOCUS ON SOMETHING ELSE, LIKE TEACH PEOPLE HOW TO HAVE THE BEST LIFE.

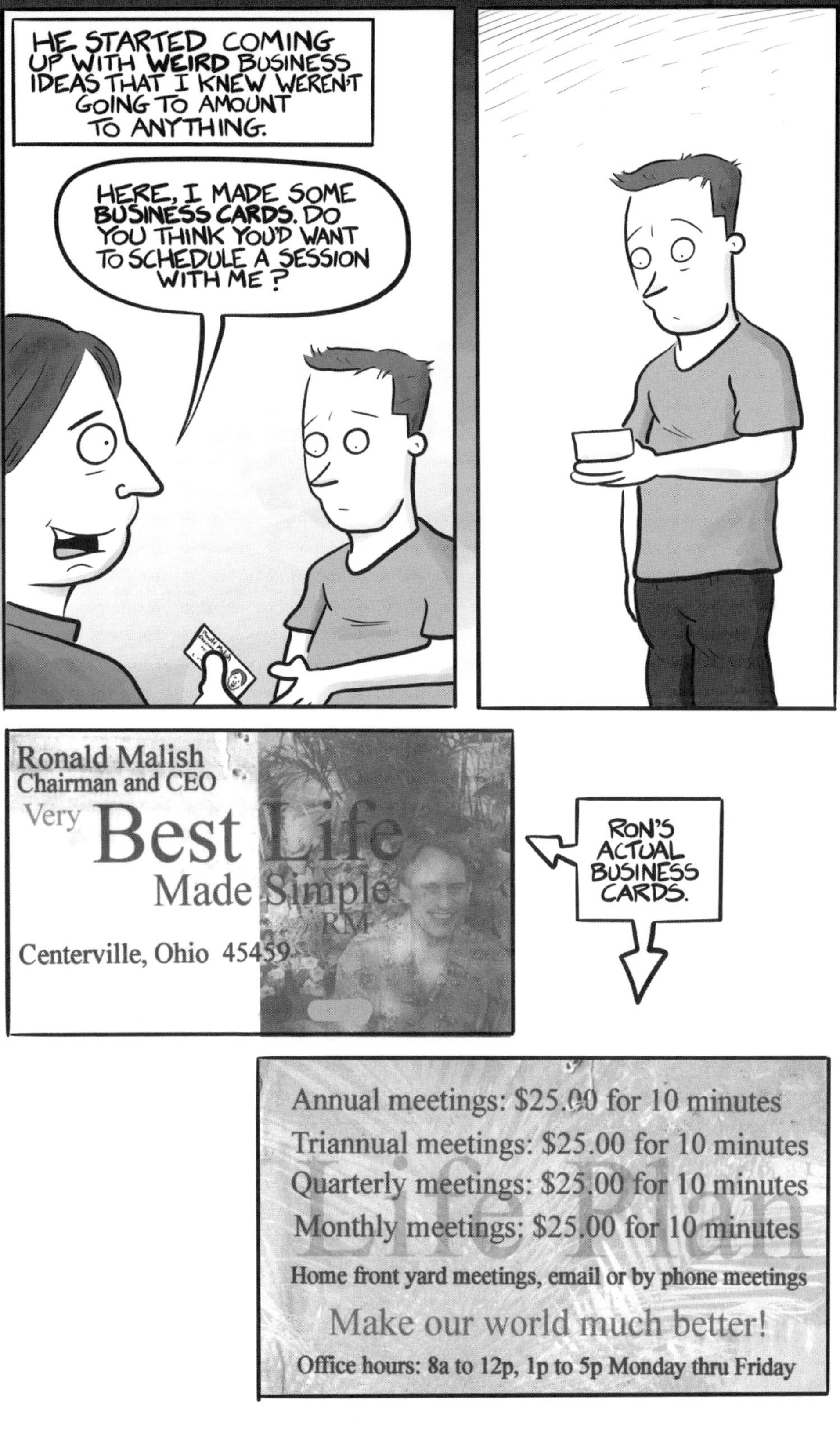
HE STARTED COMING UP WITH WEIRD BUSINESS IDEAS THAT I KNEW WEREN'T GOING TO AMOUNT TO ANYTHING.
HERE, I MADE SOME BUSINESS CARDS. DO YOU THINK YOU'D WANT TO SCHEDULE A SESSION WITH ME?
Ronald Malish
Chairman and CEO
Very Best Life
Made Simple
RM
Centerville, Ohio 45459
RON'S ACTUAL BUSINESS CARDS.
Life Plan
Annual meetings: $25.00 for 10 minutes
Triannual meetings: $25.00 for 10 minutes
Quarterly meetings: $25.00 for 10 minutes
Monthly meetings: $25.00 for 10 minutes
Home front yard meetings, email or by phone meetings
Make our world much better!
Office hours: 8a to 12p, 1p to 5p Monday thru Friday

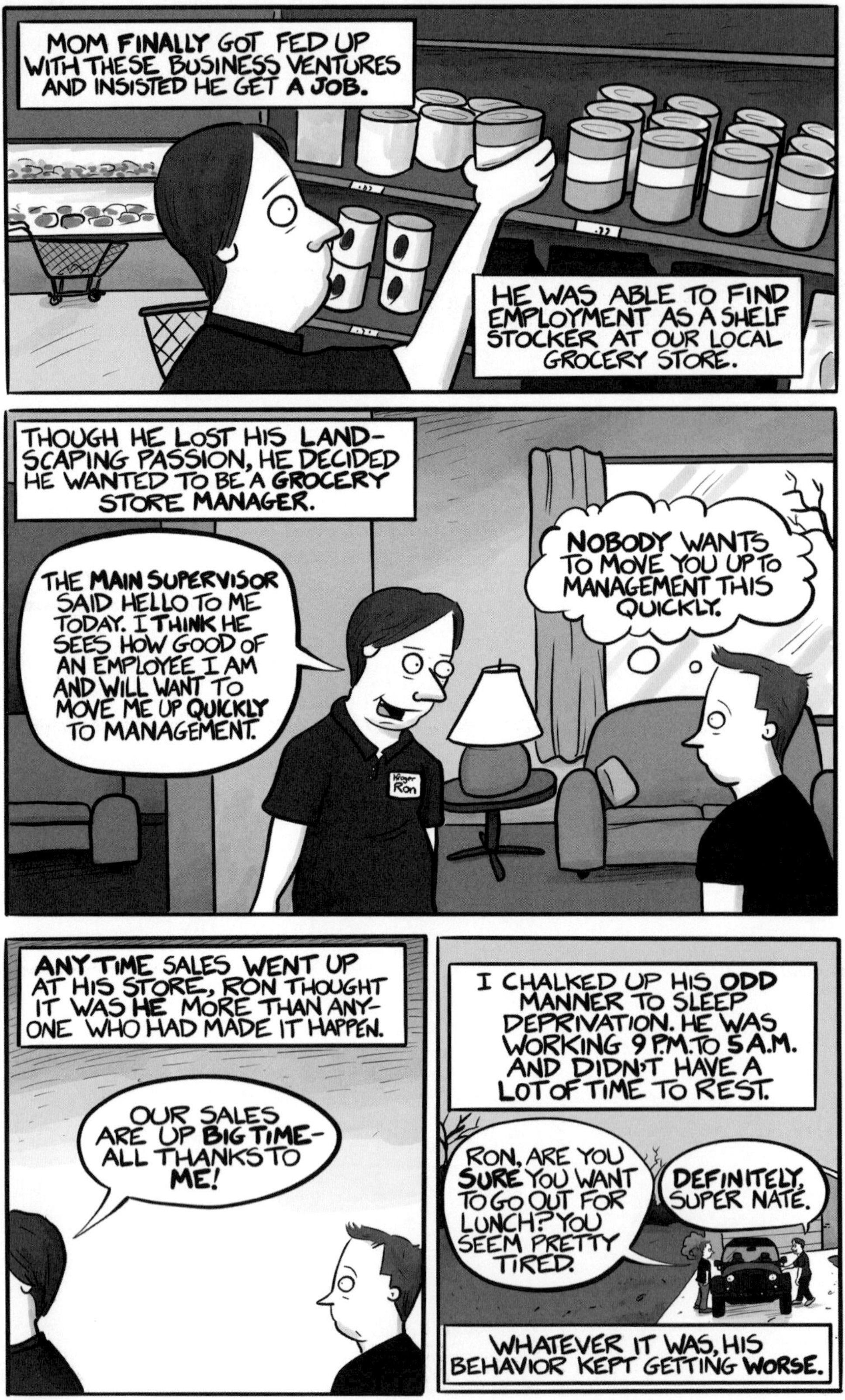
MOM FINALLY GOT FED UP WITH THESE BUSINESS VENTURES AND INSISTED HE GET A JOB.
HE WAS ABLE TO FIND EMPLOYMENT AS A SHELF STOCKER AT OUR LOCAL GROCERY STORE.
THOUGH HE LOST HIS LAND-SCAPING PASSION, HE DECIDED HE WANTED TO BE A GROCERY STORE MANAGER.
THE MAIN SUPERVISOR SAID HELLO TO ME TODAY. I THINK HE SEES HOW GOOD OF AN EMPLOYEE I AM AND WILL WANT TO MOVE ME UP QUICKLY TO MANAGEMENT.
Kroger Ron
NOBODY WANTS TO MOVE YOU UP TO MANAGEMENT THIS QUICKLY.
ANY TIME SALES WENT UP AT HIS STORE, RON THOUGHT IT WAS HE MORE THAN ANY-ONE WHO HAD MADE IT HAPPEN.
OUR SALES ARE UP BIG TIME- ALL THANKS TO ME!
I CHALKED UP HIS ODD MANNER TO SLEEP DEPRIVATION. HE WAS WORKING 9 P.M. TO 5 A.M. AND DIDN'T HAVE A LOT OF TIME TO REST.
RON, ARE YOU SURE YOU WANT TO GO OUT FOR LUNCH? YOU SEEM PRETTY TIRED.
DEFINITELY, SUPER NATE.
WHATEVER IT WAS, HIS BEHAVIOR KEPT GETTING WORSE.

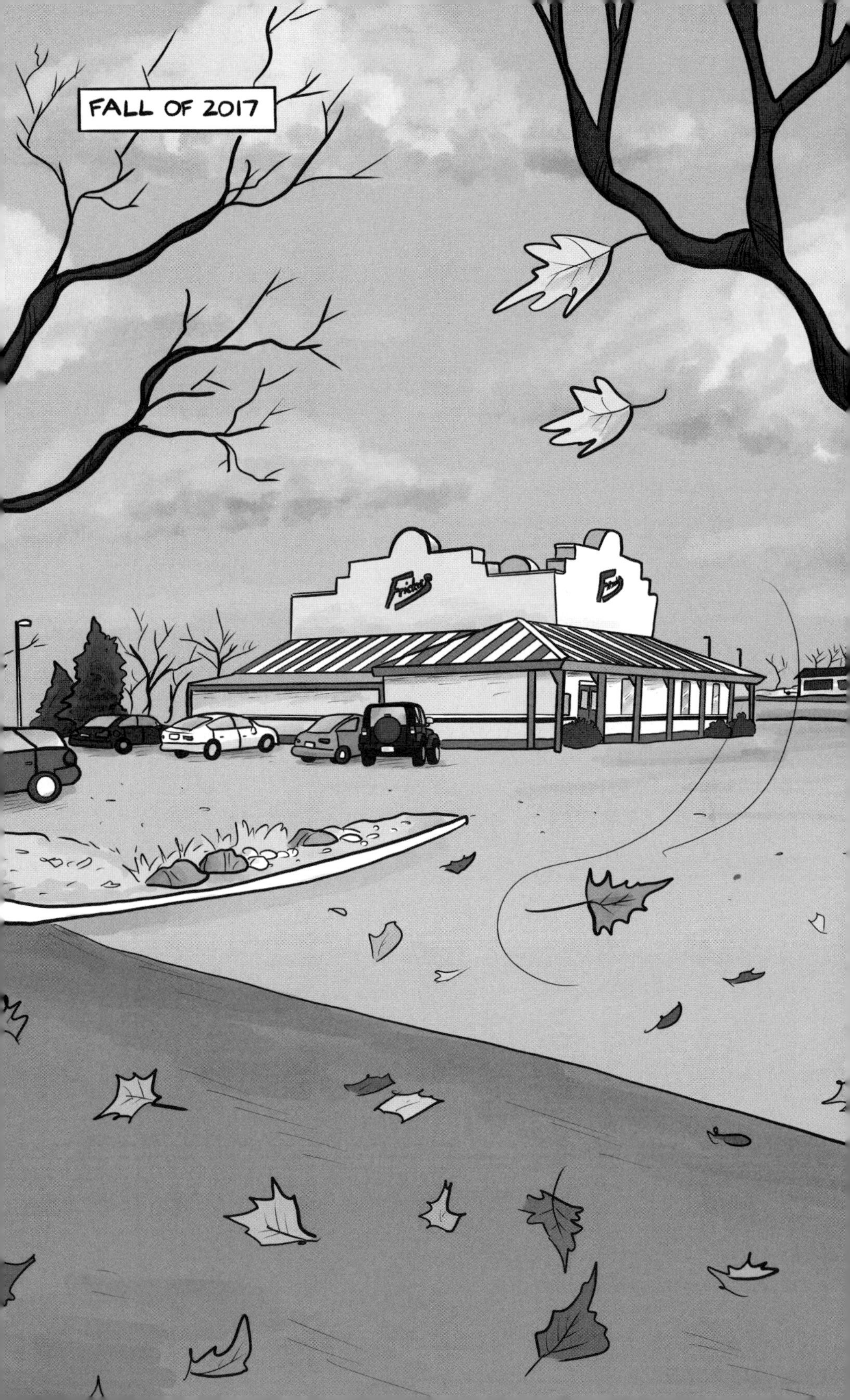
FALL OF 2017

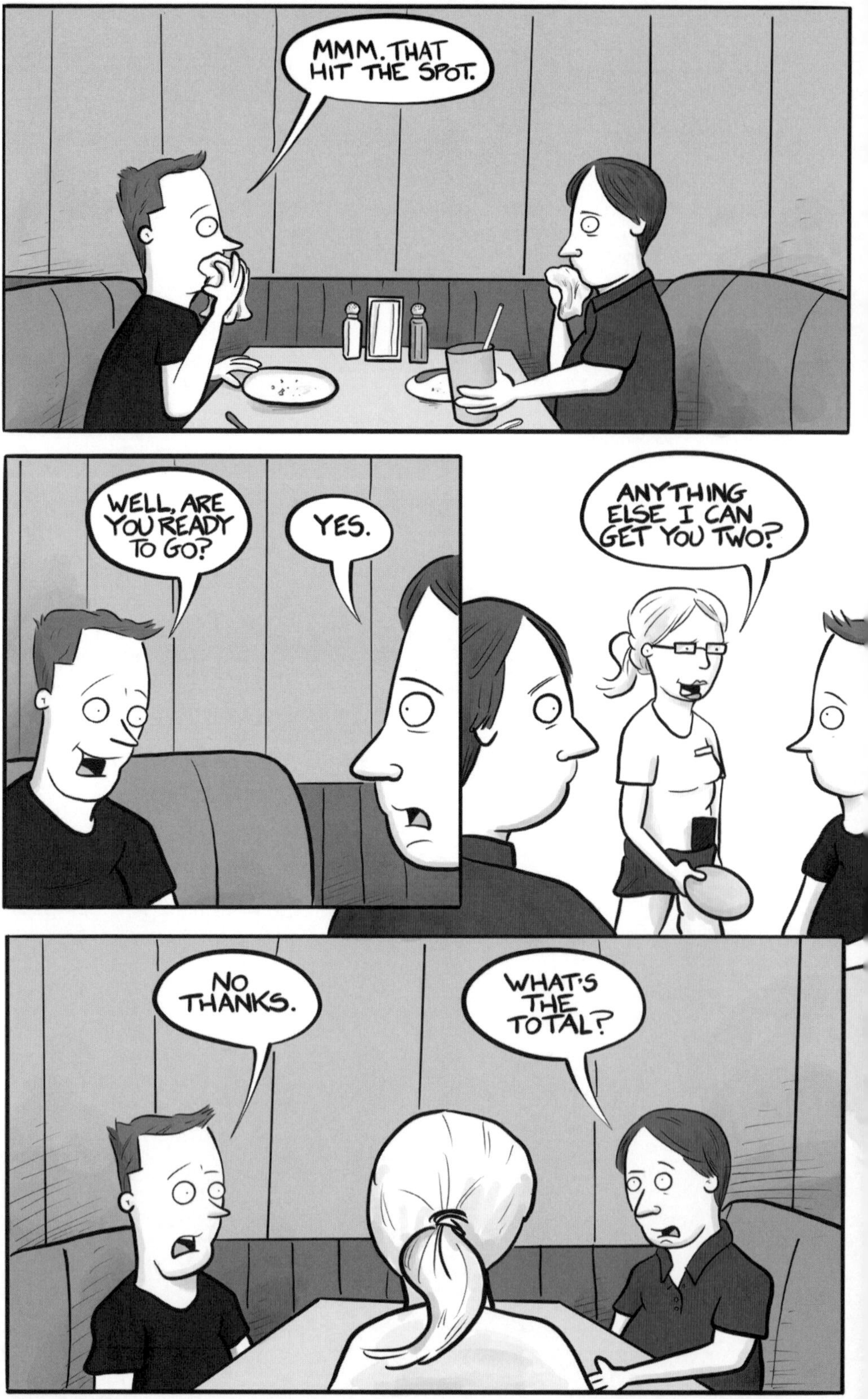
MMM. THAT HIT THE SPOT.
WELL, ARE YOU READY TO GO?
YES.
ANYTHING ELSE I CAN GET YOU TWO?
NO THANKS.
WHAT'S THE TOTAL?

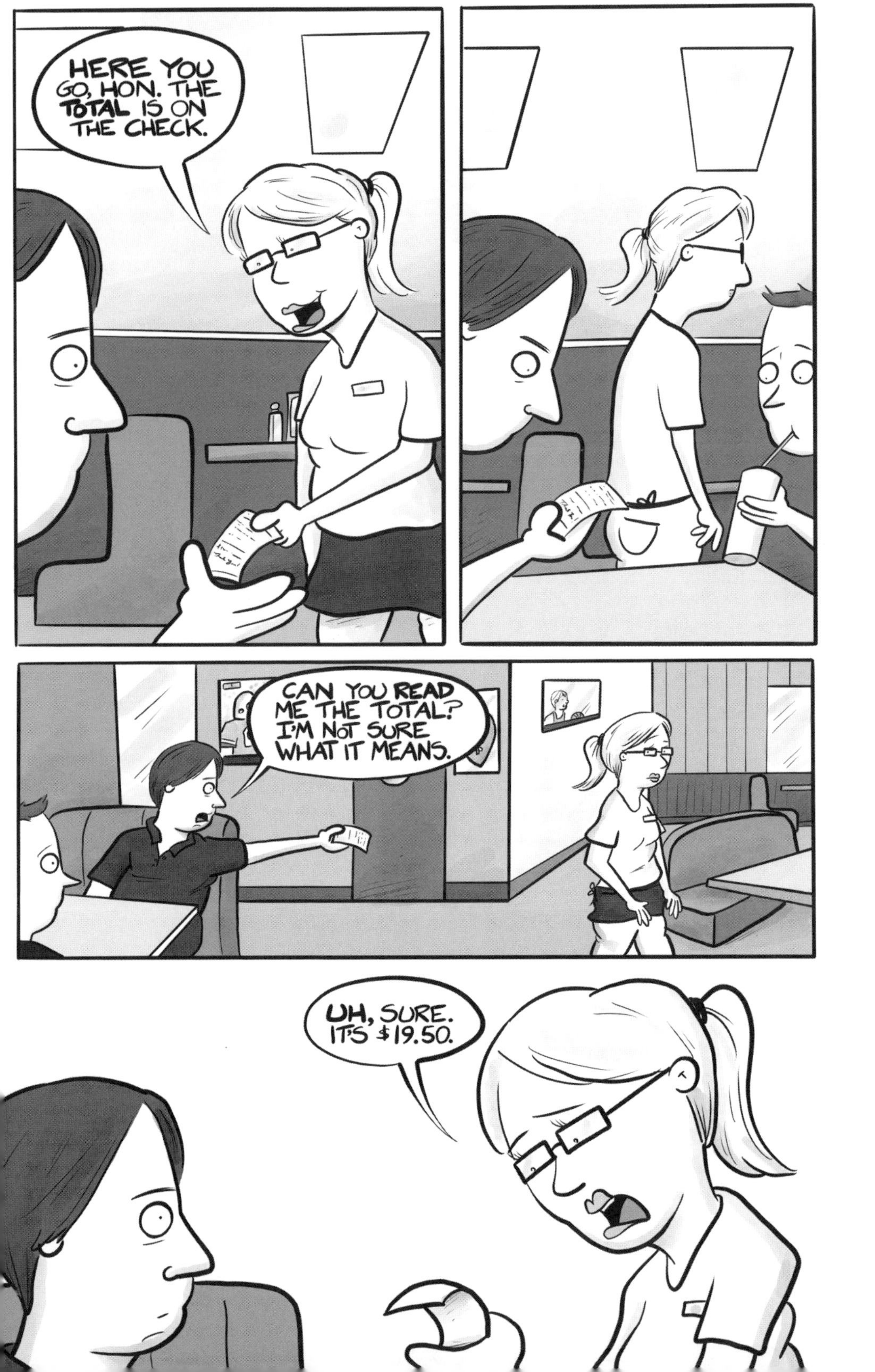
HERE YOU GO, HON. THE TOTAL IS ON THE CHECK.
CAN YOU READ ME THE TOTAL? I'M NOT SURE WHAT IT MEANS.
UH, SURE. IT'S $19.50.

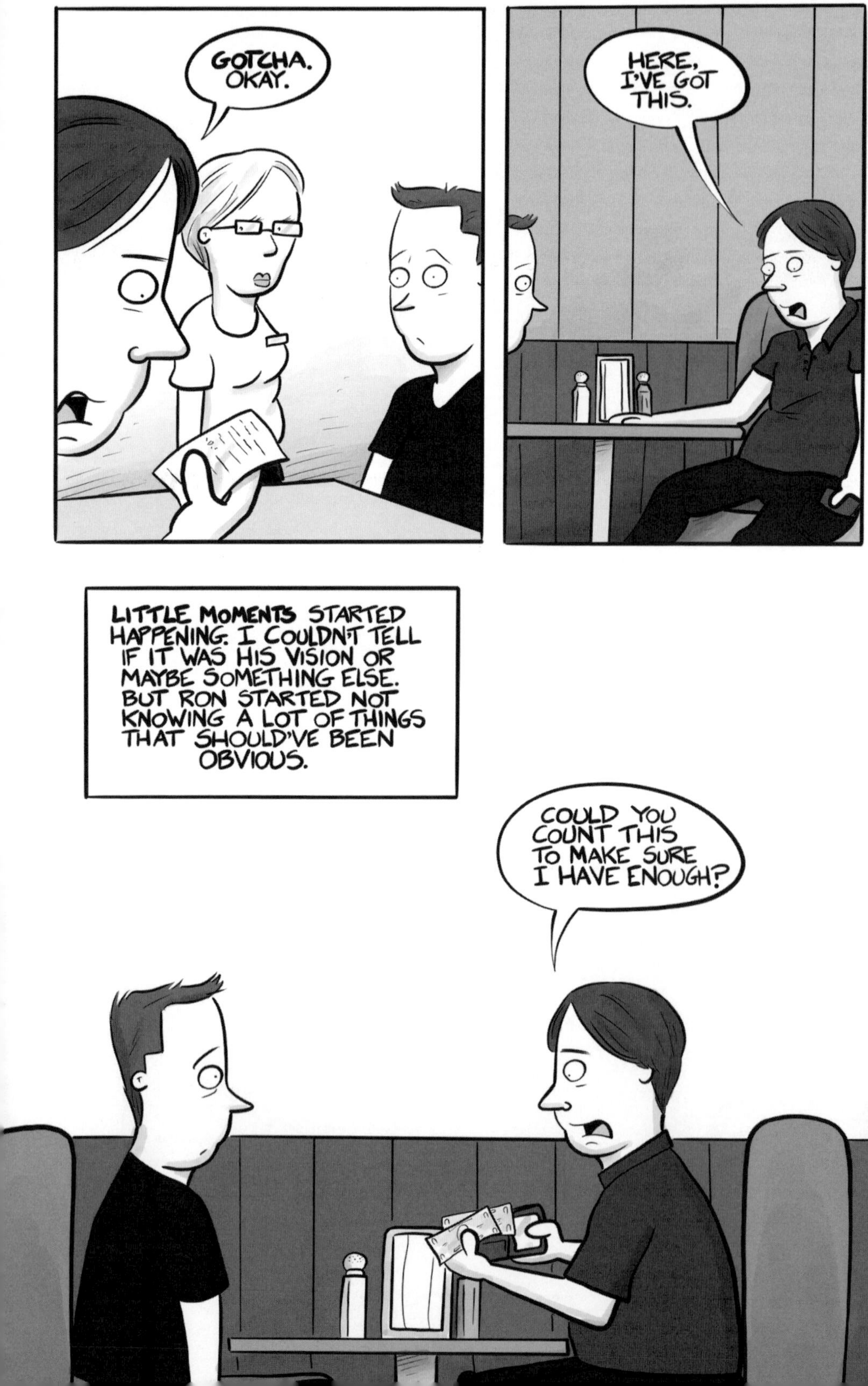
GOTCHA. OKAY.
HERE, I'VE GOT THIS.
LITTLE MOMENTS STARTED HAPPENING. I COULDN'T TELL IF IT WAS HIS VISION OR MAYBE SOMETHING ELSE. BUT RON STARTED NOT KNOWING A LOT OF THINGS THAT SHOULD'VE BEEN OBVIOUS.
COULD YOU COUNT THIS TO MAKE SURE I HAVE ENOUGH?

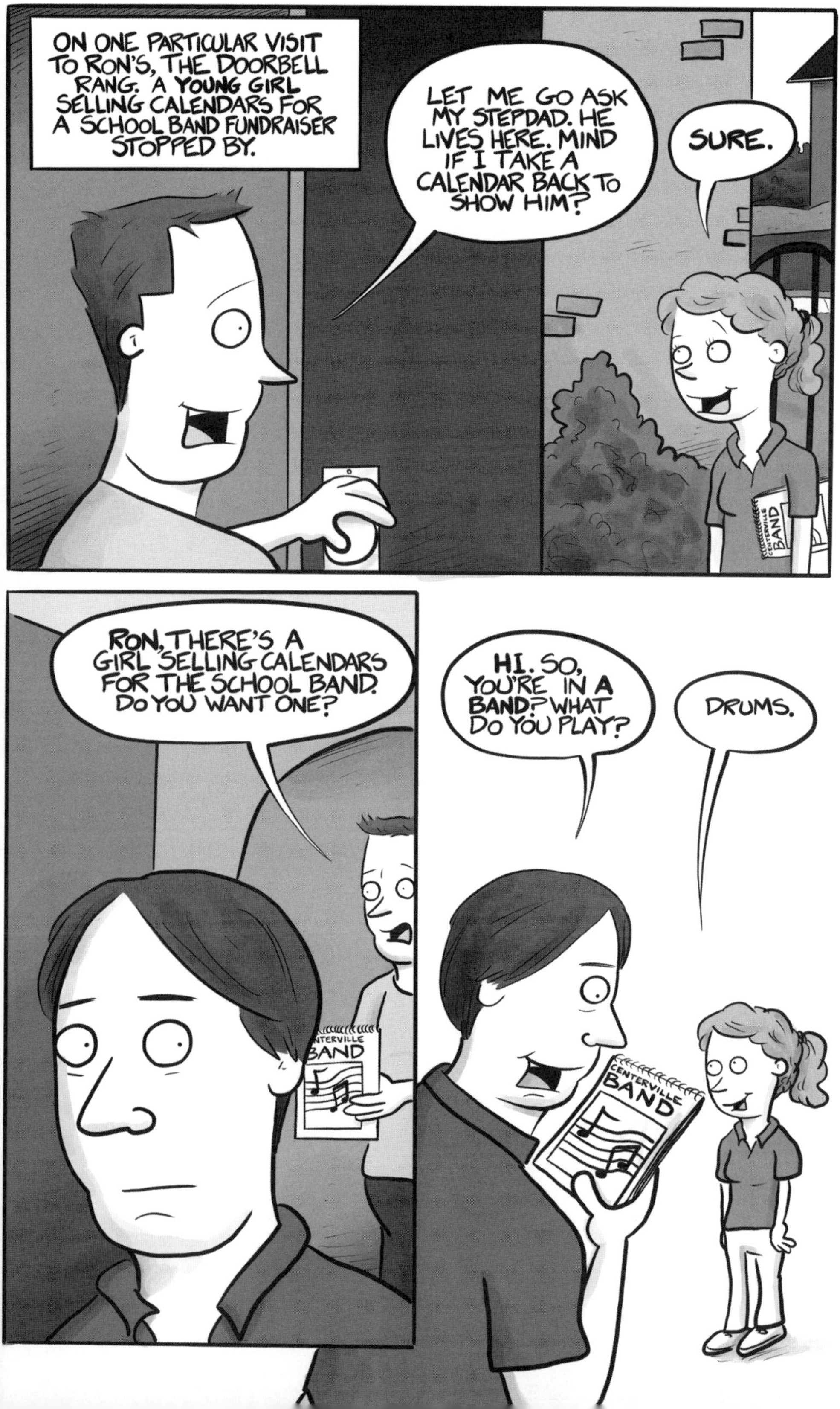
ON ONE PARTICULAR VISIT TO RON'S, THE DOORBELL RANG. A **YOUNG GIRL** SELLING CALENDARS FOR A SCHOOL BAND FUNDRAISER STOPPED BY.
LET ME GO ASK MY STEPDAD. HE LIVES HERE. MIND IF I TAKE A CALENDAR BACK TO SHOW HIM?
SURE.
CENTERVILLE BAND
RON, THERE'S A GIRL SELLING CALENDARS FOR THE SCHOOL BAND. DO YOU WANT ONE?
HI. SO, YOU'RE IN A BAND? WHAT DO YOU PLAY?
DRUMS.
CENTERVILLE BAND
CENTERVILLE BAND

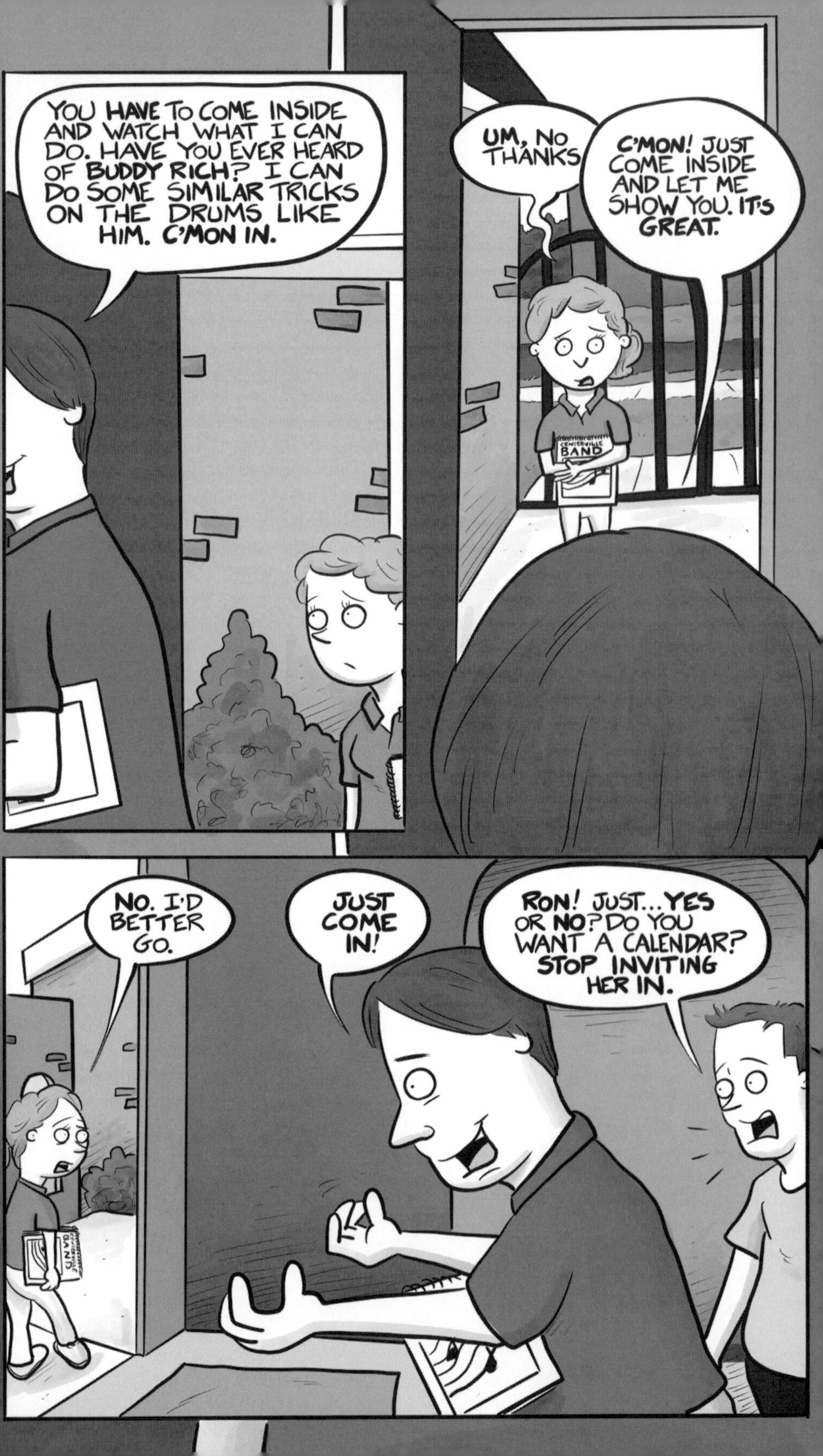
YOU HAVE TO COME INSIDE AND WATCH WHAT I CAN DO. HAVE YOU EVER HEARD OF BUDDY RICH? I CAN DO SOME SIMILAR TRICKS ON THE DRUMS LIKE HIM. C'MON IN.
UM, NO THANKS.
C'MON! JUST COME INSIDE AND LET ME SHOW YOU. IT'S GREAT.
CENTERVILLE BAND
NO. I'D BETTER GO.
JUST COME IN!
RON! JUST... YES OR NO? DO YOU WANT A CALENDAR? STOP INVITING HER IN.

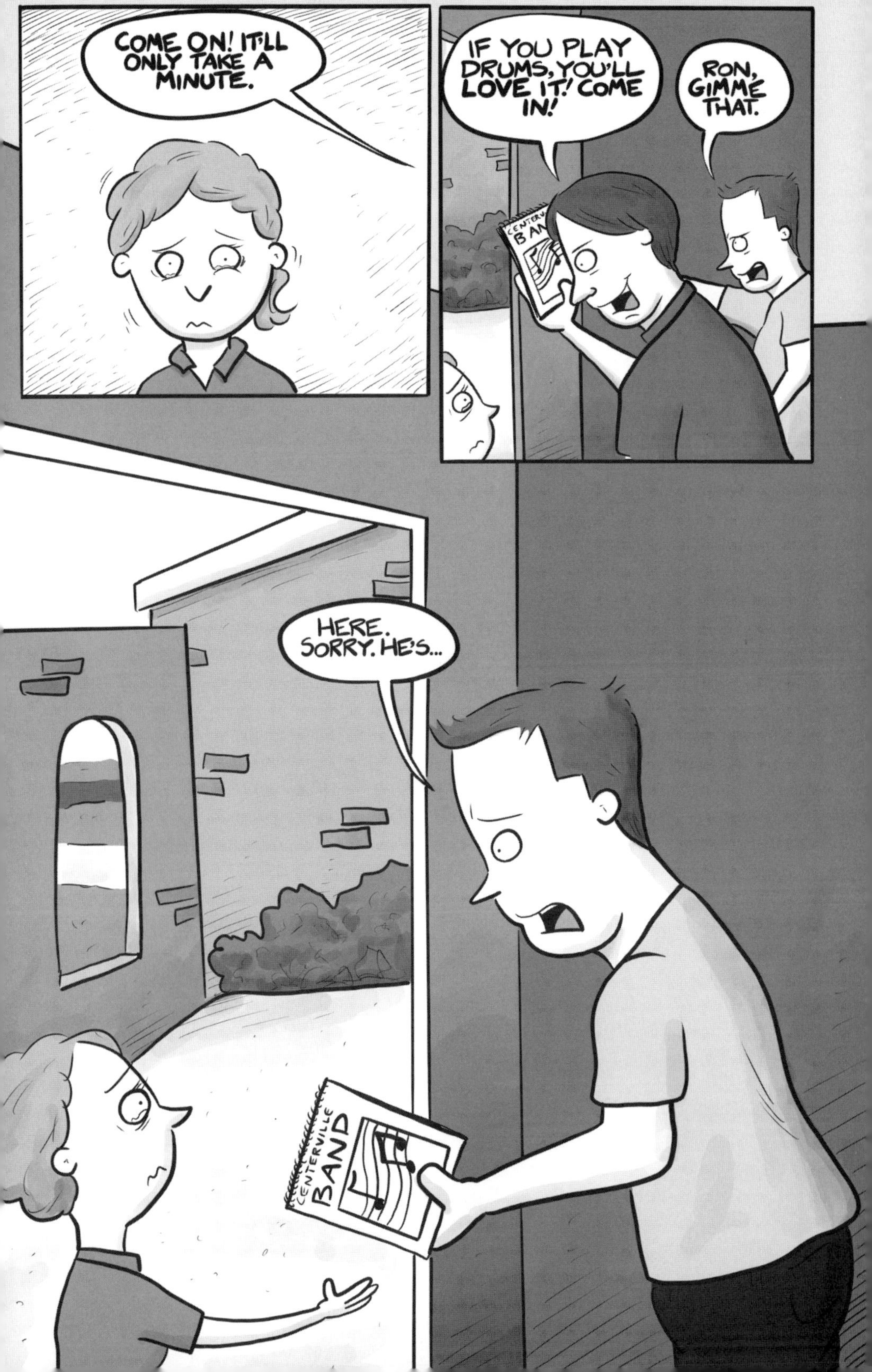
COME ON! IT'LL ONLY TAKE A MINUTE.
IF YOU PLAY DRUMS, YOU'LL LOVE IT! COME IN!
RON, GIMME THAT.
CENTERVILLE BAND
HERE. SORRY. HE'S...
CENTERVILLE BAND

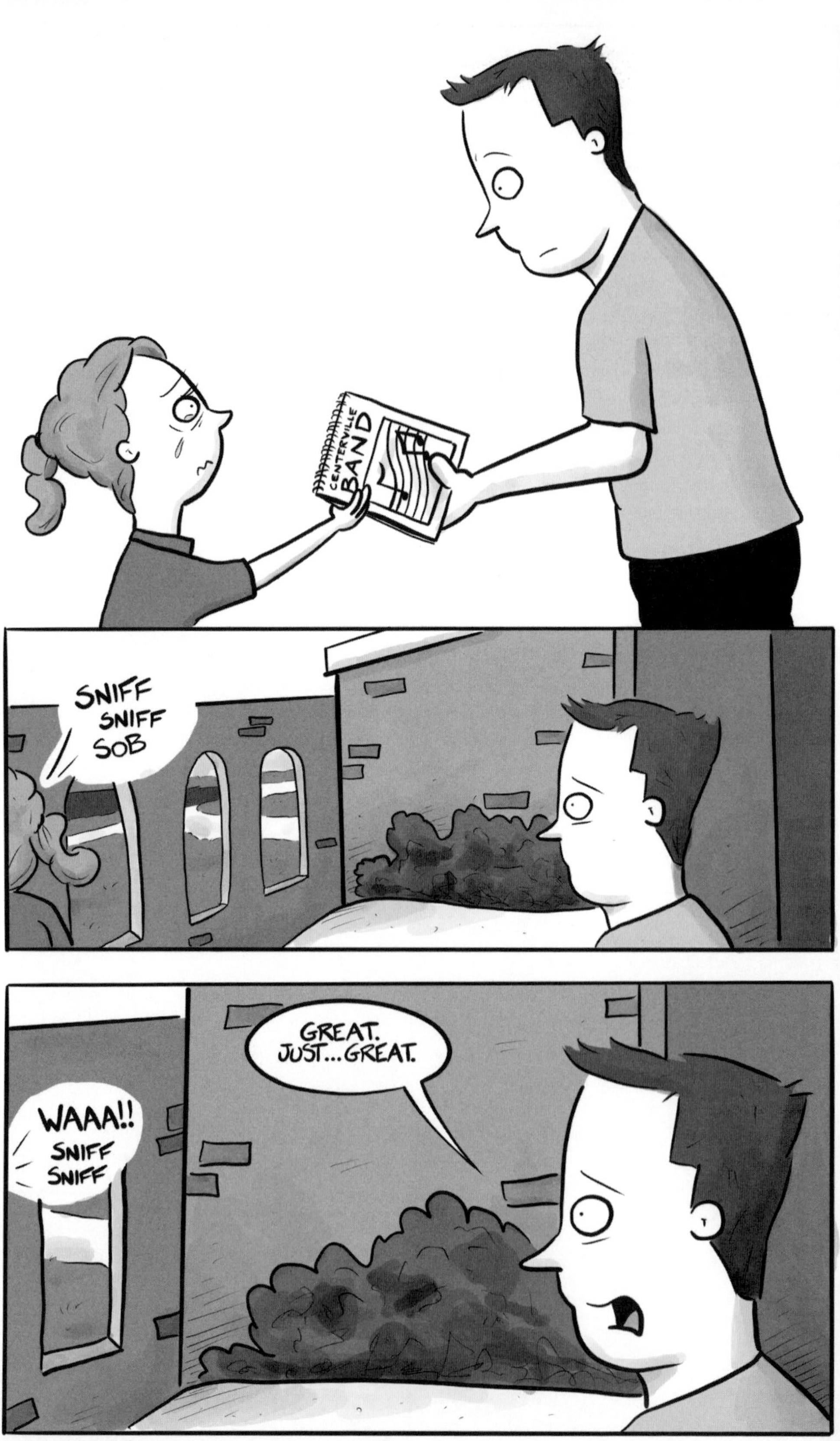
CENTERVILLE BAND
SNIFF SNIFF SOB
GREAT. JUST...GREAT.
WAAA!! SNIFF SNIFF

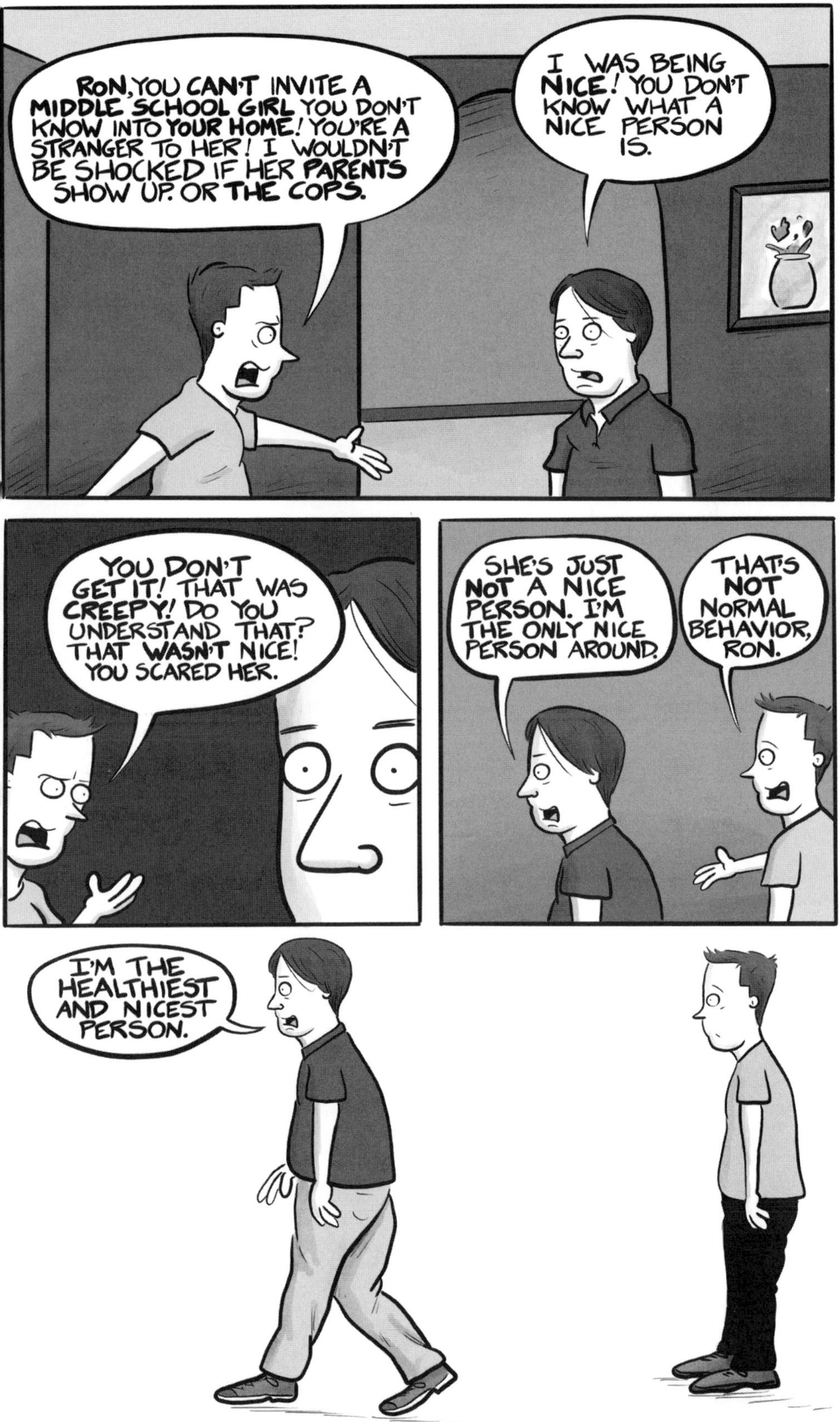
RON, YOU CAN'T INVITE A MIDDLE SCHOOL GIRL YOU DON'T KNOW INTO YOUR HOME! YOU'RE A STRANGER TO HER! I WOULDN'T BE SHOCKED IF HER PARENTS SHOW UP. OR THE COPS.
I WAS BEING NICE! YOU DON'T KNOW WHAT A NICE PERSON IS.
YOU DON'T GET IT! THAT WAS CREEPY! DO YOU UNDERSTAND THAT? THAT WASN'T NICE! YOU SCARED HER.
SHE'S JUST NOT A NICE PERSON. I'M THE ONLY NICE PERSON AROUND.
THAT'S NOT NORMAL BEHAVIOR, RON.
I'M THE HEALTHIEST AND NICEST PERSON.

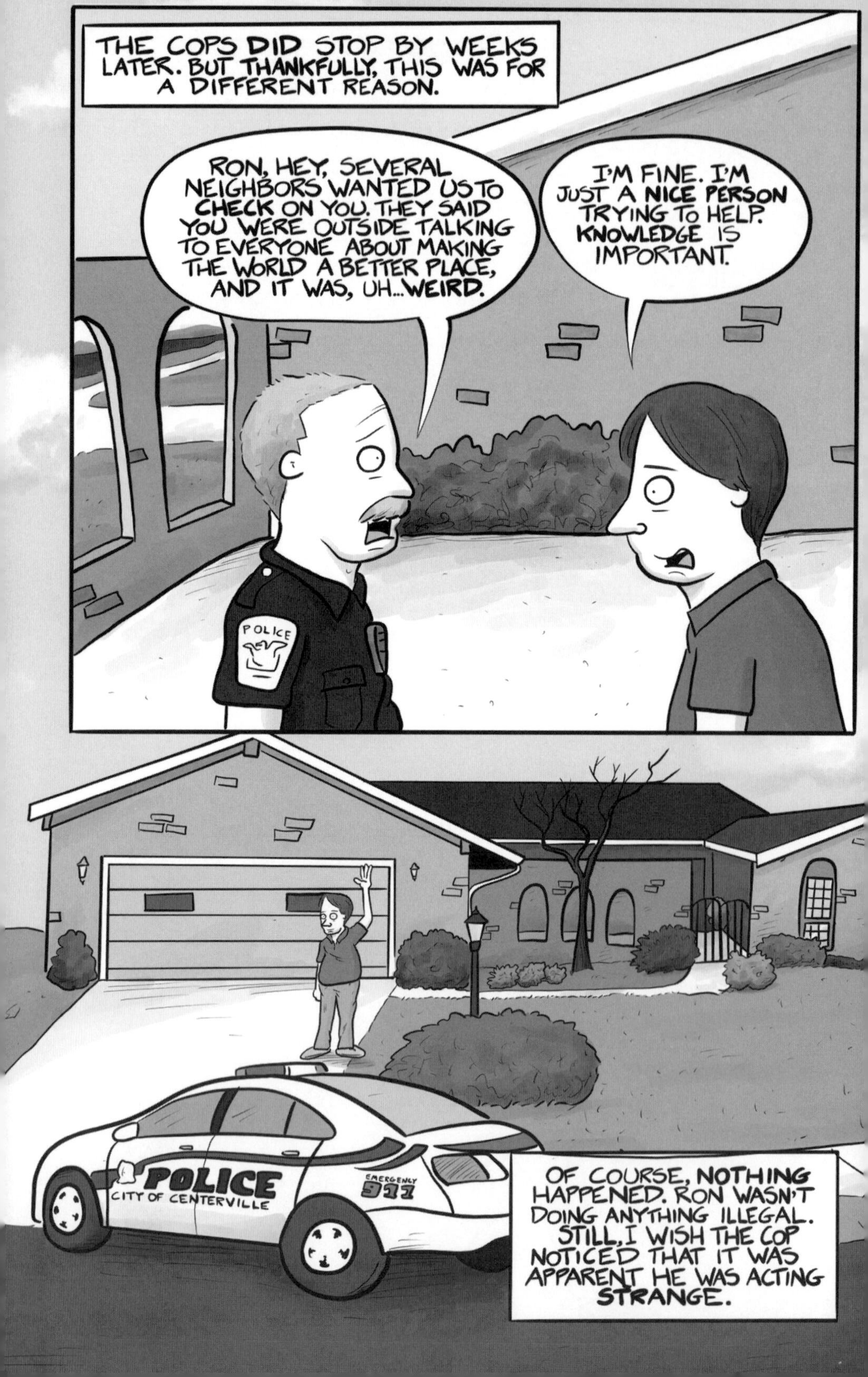
THE COPS DID STOP BY WEEKS LATER. BUT THANKFULLY, THIS WAS FOR A DIFFERENT REASON.
RON, HEY, SEVERAL NEIGHBORS WANTED US TO CHECK ON YOU. THEY SAID YOU WERE OUTSIDE TALKING TO EVERYONE ABOUT MAKING THE WORLD A BETTER PLACE, AND IT WAS, UH...WEIRD.
I'M FINE. I'M JUST A NICE PERSON TRYING TO HELP. KNOWLEDGE IS IMPORTANT.
POLICE
POLICE
CITY OF CENTERVILLE
EMERGENCY 911
OF COURSE, NOTHING HAPPENED. RON WASN'T DOING ANYTHING ILLEGAL. STILL, I WISH THE COP NOTICED THAT IT WAS APPARENT HE WAS ACTING STRANGE.

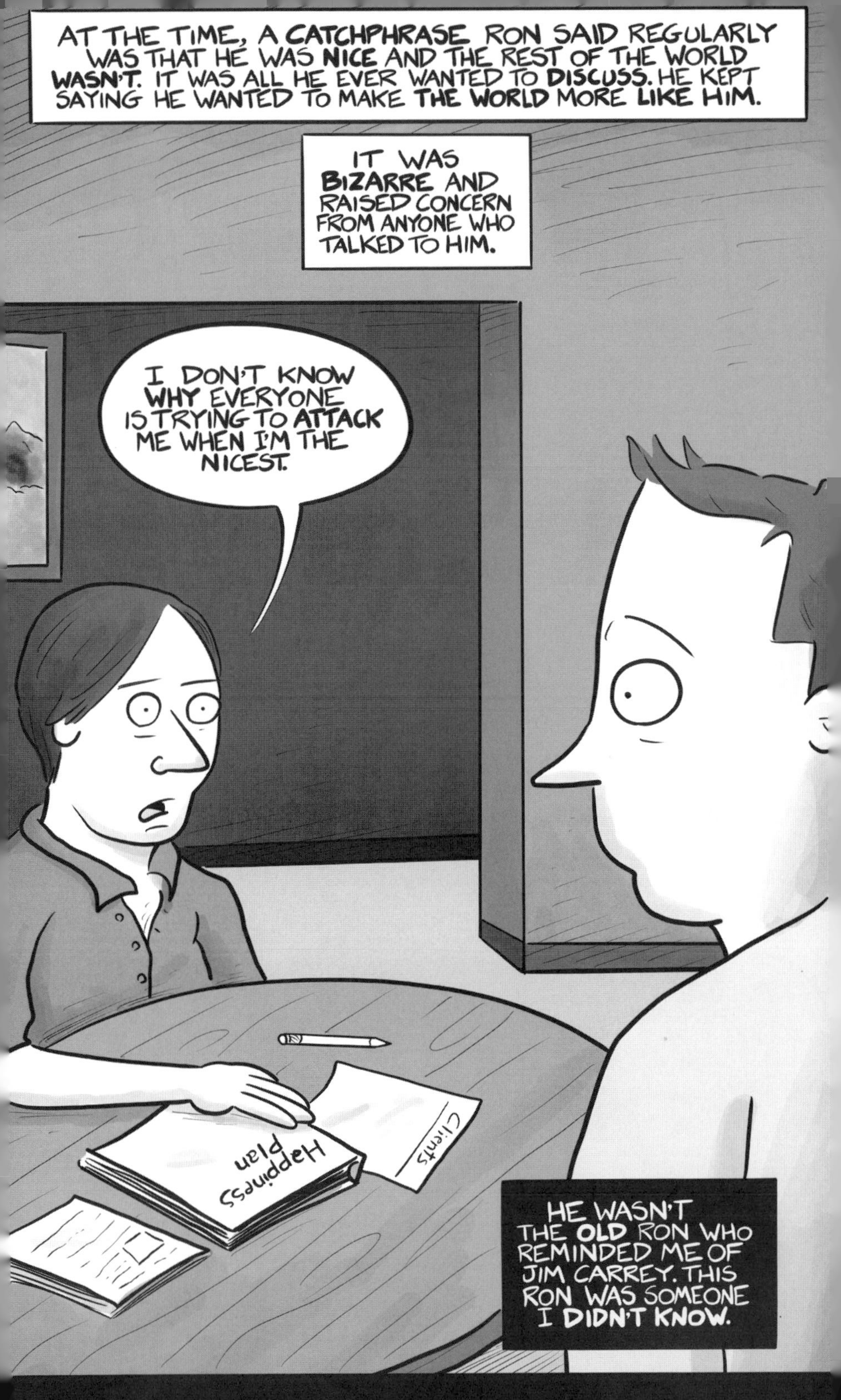
AT THE TIME, A CATCHPHRASE RON SAID REGULARLY WAS THAT HE WAS NICE AND THE REST OF THE WORLD WASN'T. IT WAS ALL HE EVER WANTED TO DISCUSS. HE KEPT SAYING HE WANTED TO MAKE THE WORLD MORE LIKE HIM.
IT WAS BIZARRE AND RAISED CONCERN FROM ANYONE WHO TALKED TO HIM.
I DON'T KNOW WHY EVERYONE IS TRYING TO ATTACK ME WHEN I'M THE NICEST.
Happiness Plan
Clients
HE WASN'T THE OLD RON WHO REMINDED ME OF JIM CARREY. THIS RON WAS SOMEONE I DIDN'T KNOW.

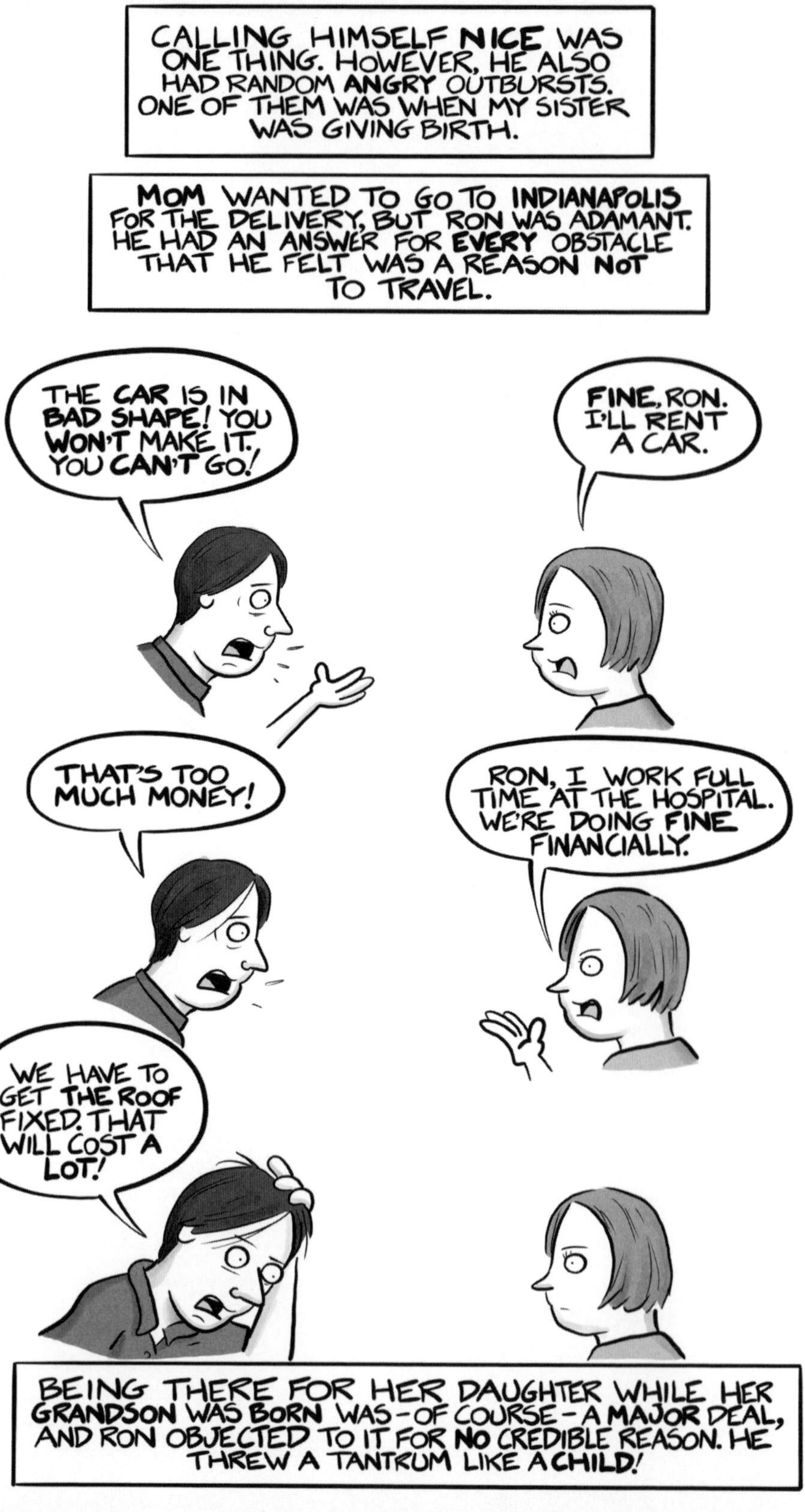
CALLING HIMSELF NICE WAS ONE THING. HOWEVER, HE ALSO HAD RANDOM ANGRY OUTBURSTS. ONE OF THEM WAS WHEN MY SISTER WAS GIVING BIRTH.
MOM WANTED TO GO TO INDIANAPOLIS FOR THE DELIVERY, BUT RON WAS ADAMANT. HE HAD AN ANSWER FOR EVERY OBSTACLE THAT HE FELT WAS A REASON NOT TO TRAVEL.
THE CAR IS IN BAD SHAPE! YOU WON'T MAKE IT. YOU CAN'T GO!
FINE, RON. I'LL RENT A CAR.
THAT'S TOO MUCH MONEY!
RON, I WORK FULL TIME AT THE HOSPITAL. WE'RE DOING FINE FINANCIALLY.
WE HAVE TO GET THE ROOF FIXED. THAT WILL COST A LOT!
BEING THERE FOR HER DAUGHTER WHILE HER GRANDSON WAS BORN WAS—OF COURSE—A MAJOR DEAL, AND RON OBJECTED TO IT FOR NO CREDIBLE REASON. HE THREW A TANTRUM LIKE A CHILD!

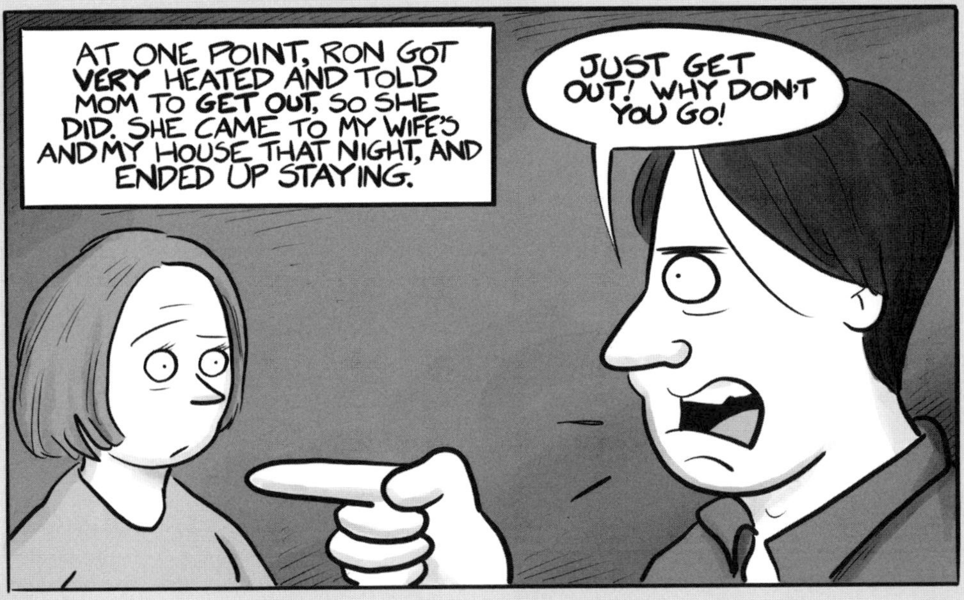
AT ONE POINT, RON GOT VERY HEATED AND TOLD MOM TO GET OUT, SO SHE DID. SHE CAME TO MY WIFE'S AND MY HOUSE THAT NIGHT, AND ENDED UP STAYING.
JUST GET OUT! WHY DON'T YOU GO!

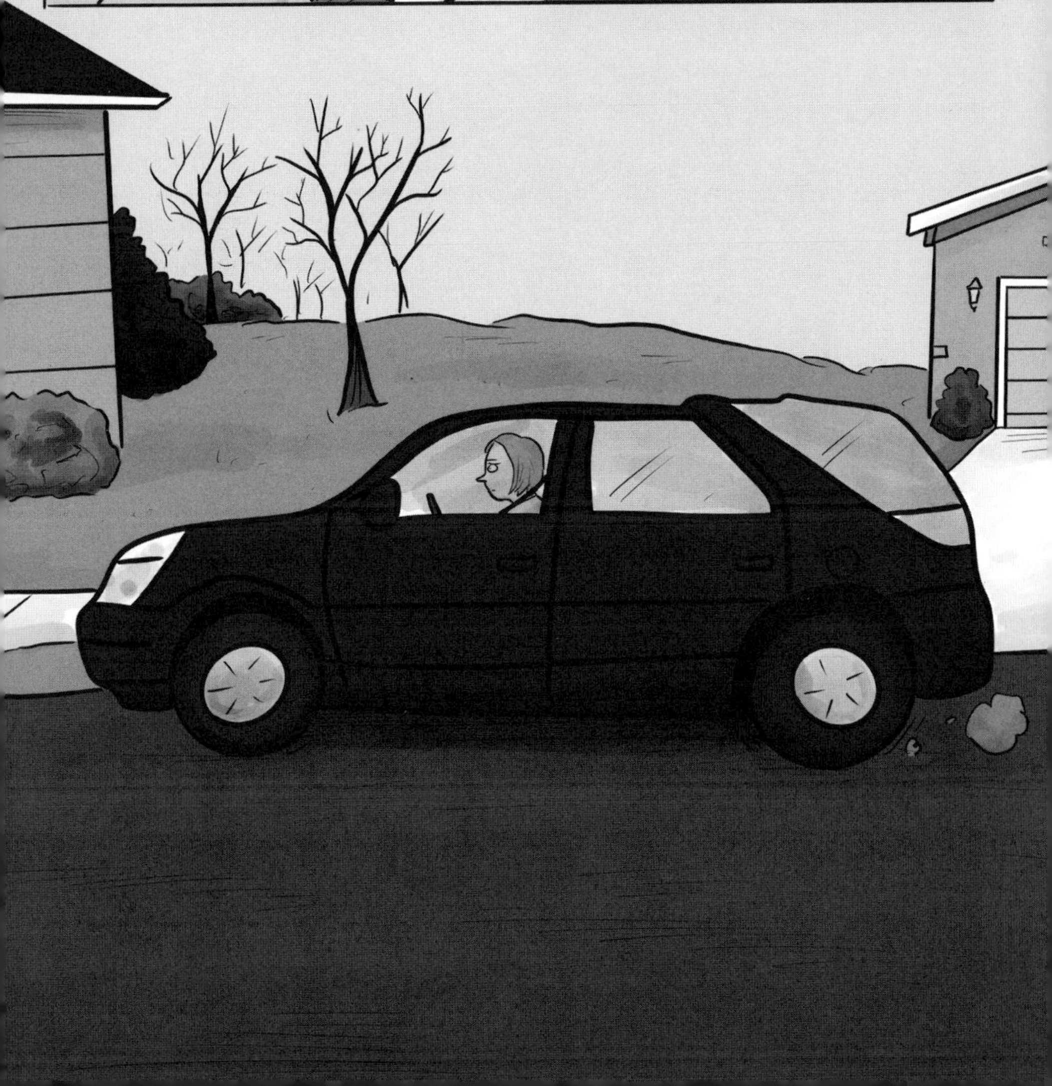

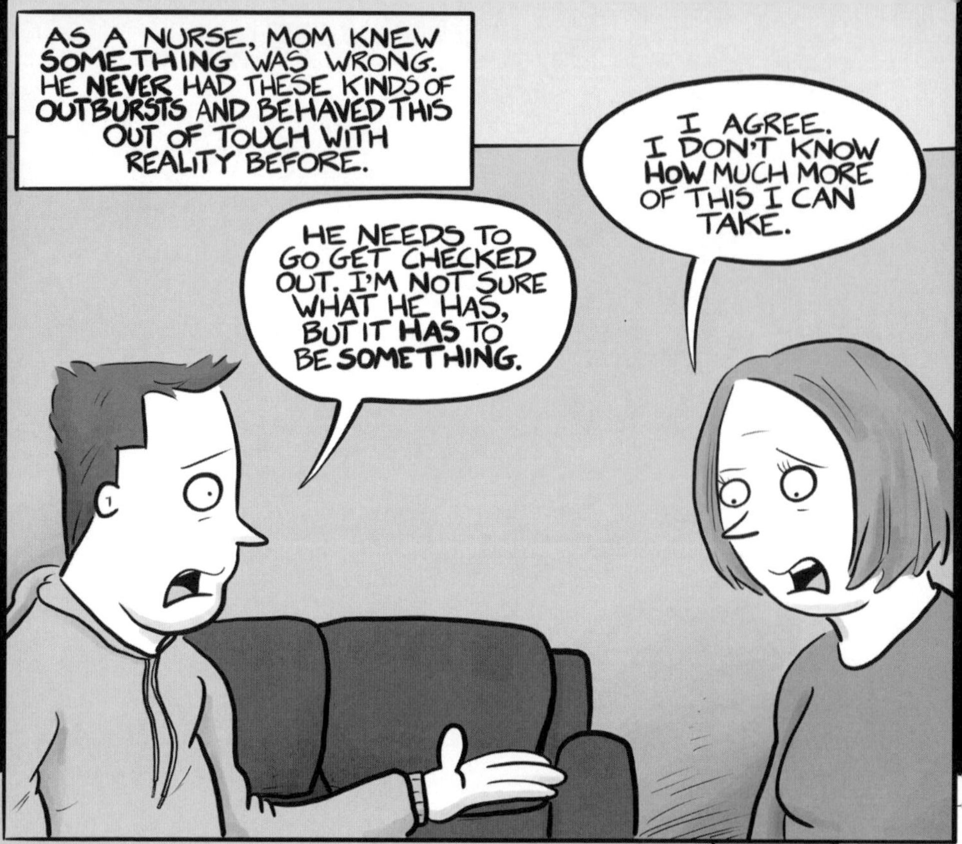
AS A NURSE, MOM KNEW SOMETHING WAS WRONG. HE NEVER HAD THESE KINDS OF OUTBURSTS AND BEHAVED THIS OUT OF TOUCH WITH REALITY BEFORE.
HE NEEDS TO GO GET CHECKED OUT. I'M NOT SURE WHAT HE HAS, BUT IT HAS TO BE SOMETHING.
I AGREE. I DON'T KNOW HOW MUCH MORE OF THIS I CAN TAKE.

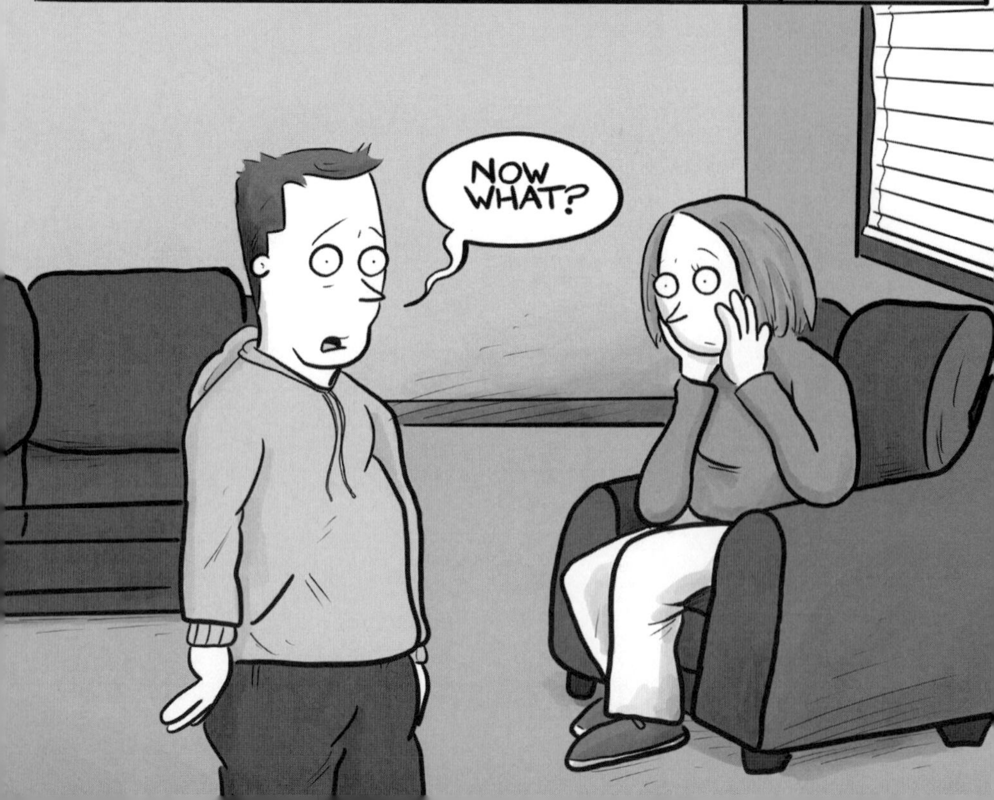
NOW WHAT?

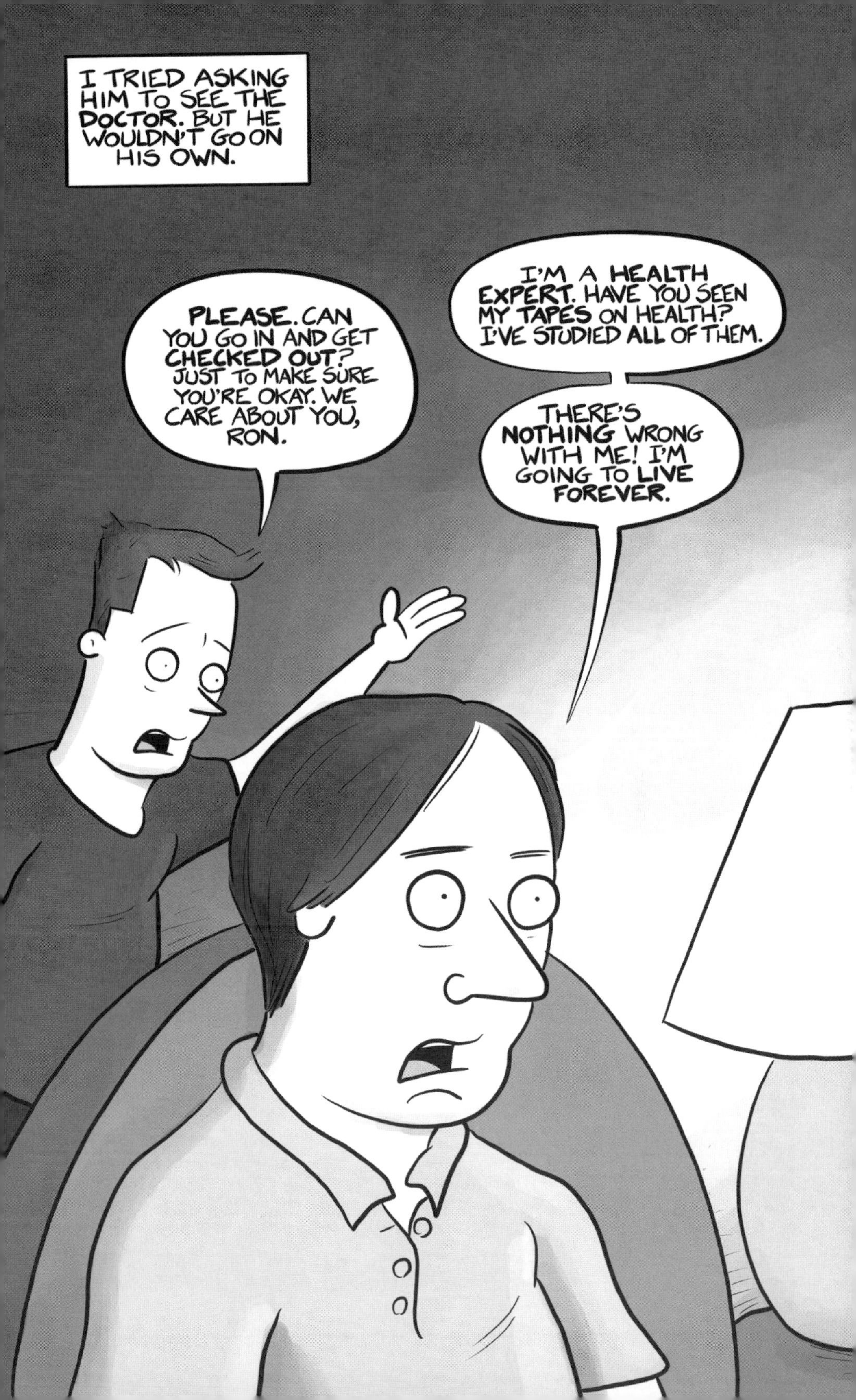
I TRIED ASKING HIM TO SEE THE DOCTOR. BUT HE WOULDN'T GO ON HIS OWN.
PLEASE. CAN YOU GO IN AND GET CHECKED OUT? JUST TO MAKE SURE YOU'RE OKAY. WE CARE ABOUT YOU, RON.
I'M A HEALTH EXPERT. HAVE YOU SEEN MY TAPES ON HEALTH? I'VE STUDIED ALL OF THEM.
THERE'S NOTHING WRONG WITH ME! I'M GOING TO LIVE FOREVER.

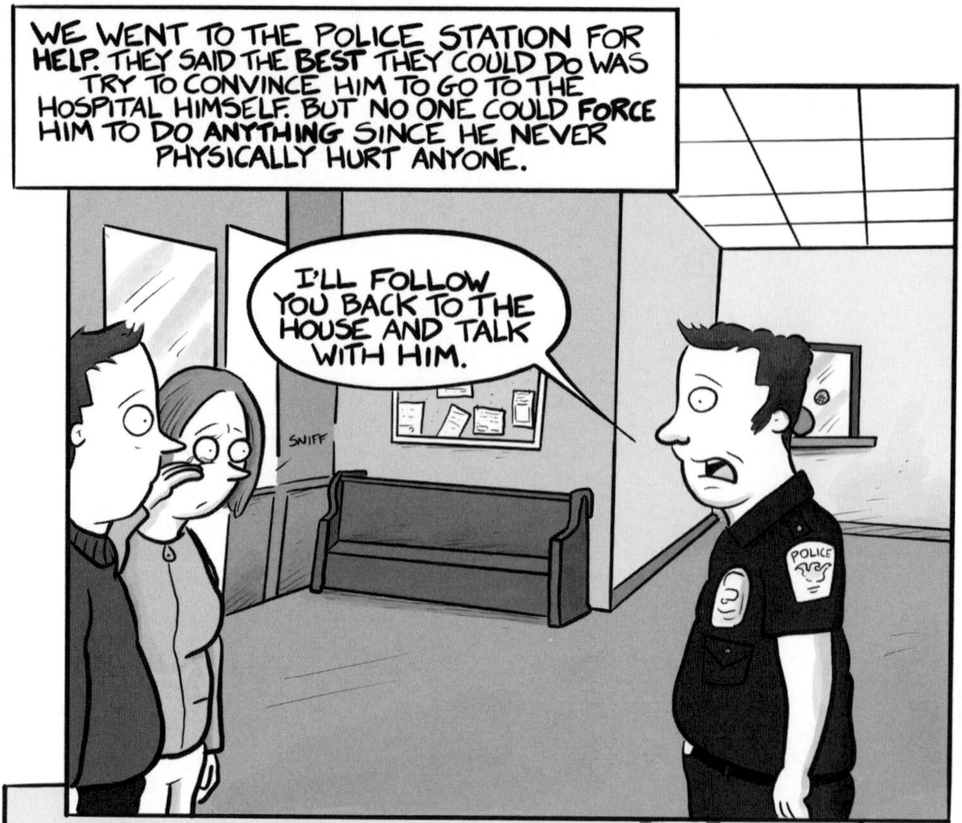
WE WENT TO THE POLICE STATION FOR HELP. THEY SAID THE BEST THEY COULD DO WAS TRY TO CONVINCE HIM TO GO TO THE HOSPITAL HIMSELF. BUT NO ONE COULD FORCE HIM TO DO ANYTHING SINCE HE NEVER PHYSICALLY HURT ANYONE.
I'LL FOLLOW YOU BACK TO THE HOUSE AND TALK WITH HIM.
SNIFF
POLICE

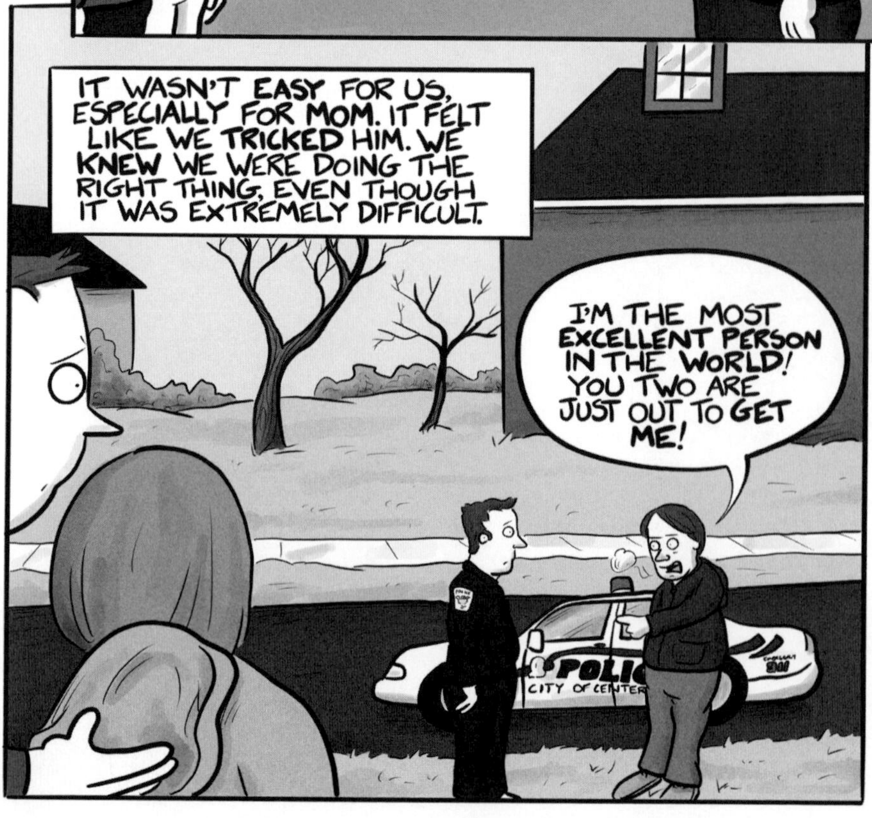
IT WASN'T EASY FOR US, ESPECIALLY FOR MOM. IT FELT LIKE WE TRICKED HIM. WE KNEW WE WERE DOING THE RIGHT THING, EVEN THOUGH IT WAS EXTREMELY DIFFICULT.
I'M THE MOST EXCELLENT PERSON IN THE WORLD! YOU TWO ARE JUST OUT TO GET ME!
POLIC
CITY OF CENTER

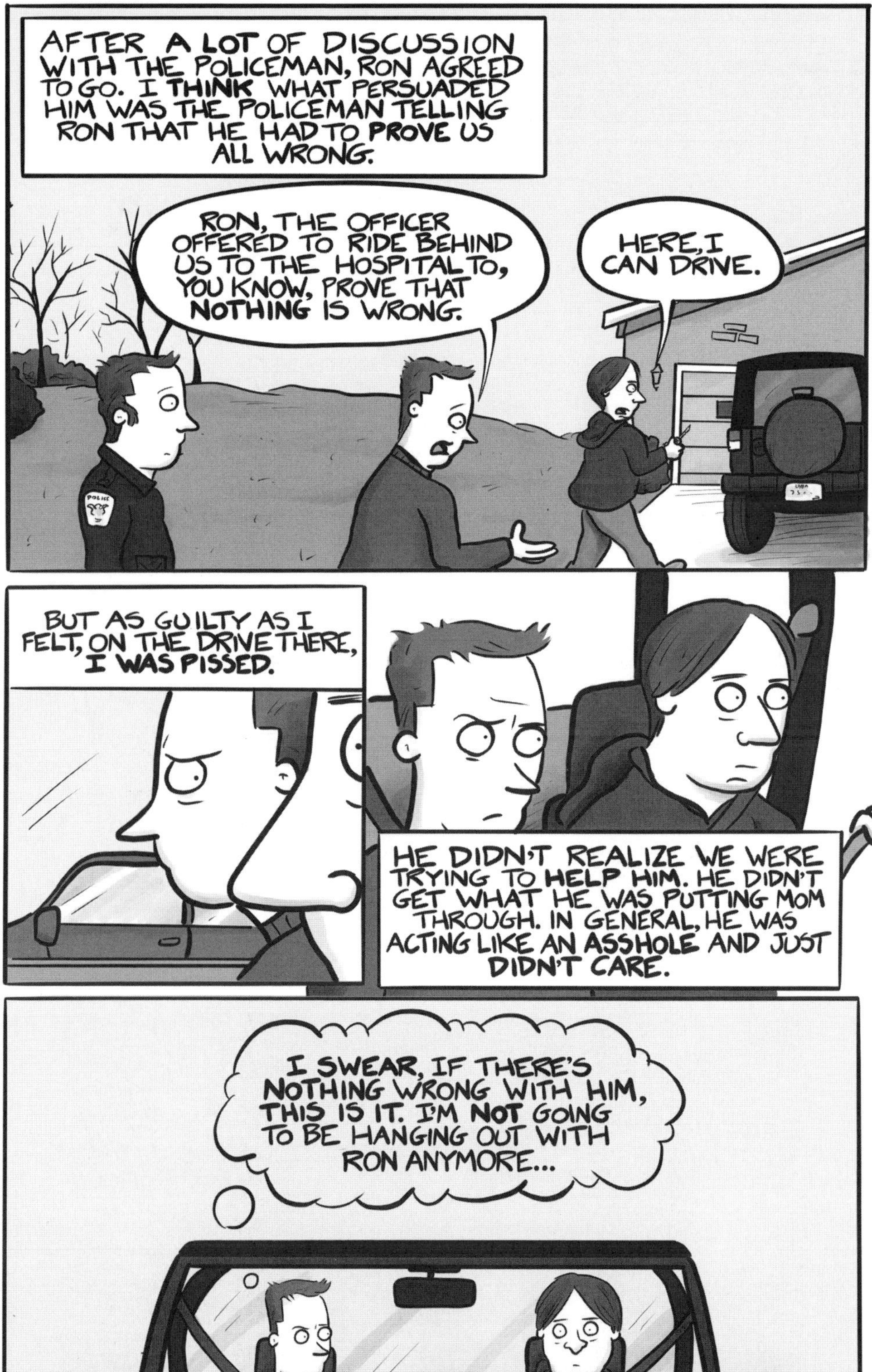
AFTER A LOT OF DISCUSSION WITH THE POLICEMAN, RON AGREED TO GO. I THINK WHAT PERSUADED HIM WAS THE POLICEMAN TELLING RON THAT HE HAD TO PROVE US ALL WRONG.
RON, THE OFFICER OFFERED TO RIDE BEHIND US TO THE HOSPITAL TO, YOU KNOW, PROVE THAT NOTHING IS WRONG.
HERE, I CAN DRIVE.
POLICE
BUT AS GUILTY AS I FELT, ON THE DRIVE THERE, I WAS PISSED.
HE DIDN'T REALIZE WE WERE TRYING TO HELP HIM. HE DIDN'T GET WHAT HE WAS PUTTING MOM THROUGH. IN GENERAL, HE WAS ACTING LIKE AN ASSHOLE AND JUST DIDN'T CARE.
I SWEAR, IF THERE'S NOTHING WRONG WITH HIM, THIS IS IT. I'M NOT GOING TO BE HANGING OUT WITH RON ANYMORE...

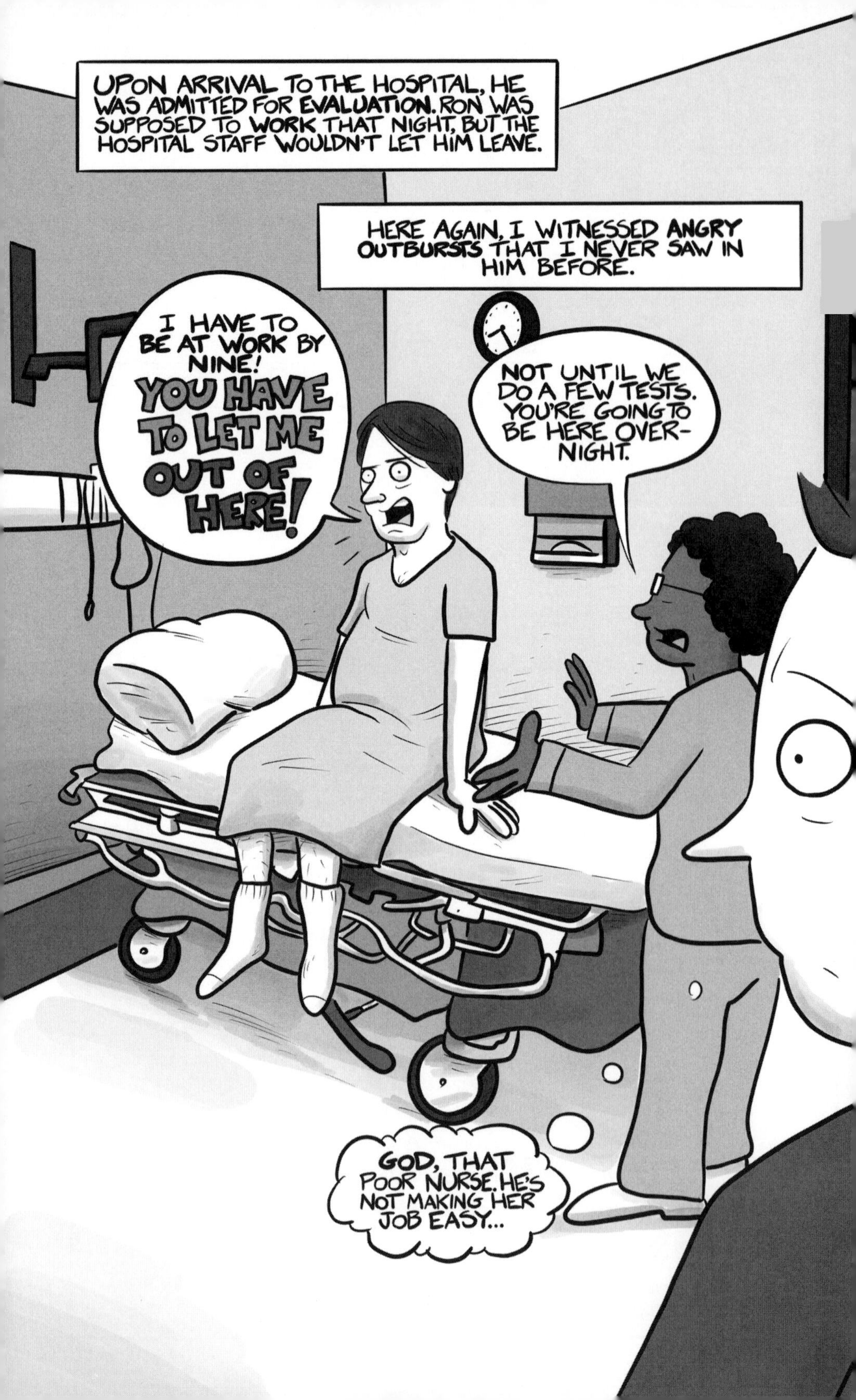

UPON ARRIVAL TO THE HOSPITAL, HE WAS ADMITTED FOR EVALUATION. RON WAS SUPPOSED TO WORK THAT NIGHT, BUT THE HOSPITAL STAFF WOULDN'T LET HIM LEAVE.
HERE AGAIN, I WITNESSED ANGRY OUTBURSTS THAT I NEVER SAW IN HIM BEFORE.
I HAVE TO BE AT WORK BY NINE! YOU HAVE TO LET ME OUT OF HERE!
NOT UNTIL WE DO A FEW TESTS. YOU'RE GOING TO BE HERE OVER-NIGHT.
GOD, THAT POOR NURSE. HE'S NOT MAKING HER JOB EASY...

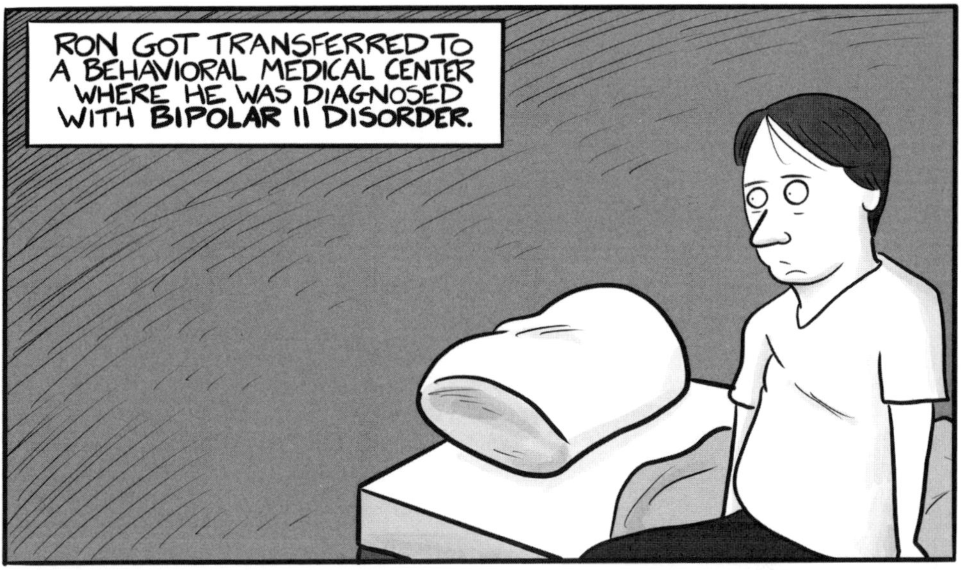
RON GOT TRANSFERRED TO A BEHAVIORAL MEDICAL CENTER WHERE HE WAS DIAGNOSED WITH BIPOLAR II DISORDER.

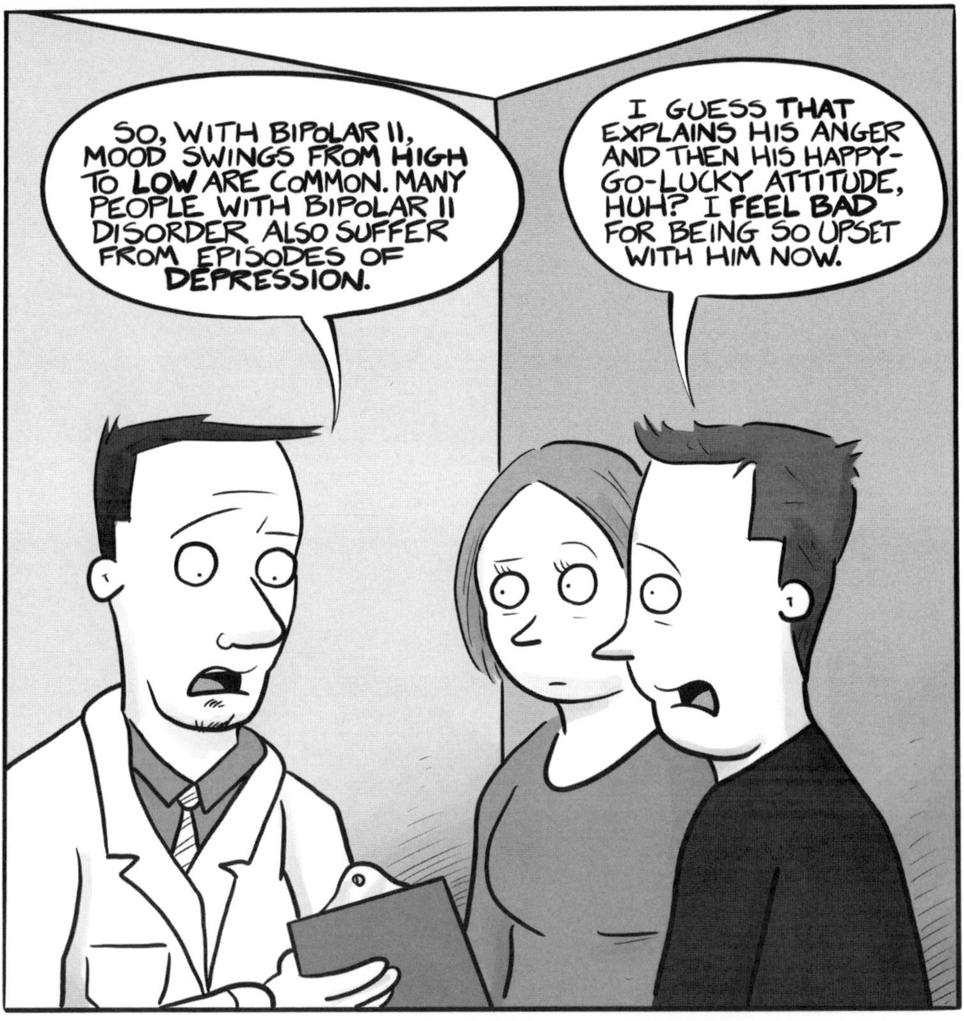
SO, WITH BIPOLAR II, MOOD SWINGS FROM HIGH TO LOW ARE COMMON. MANY PEOPLE WITH BIPOLAR II DISORDER ALSO SUFFER FROM EPISODES OF DEPRESSION.
I GUESS THAT EXPLAINS HIS ANGER AND THEN HIS HAPPY-GO-LUCKY ATTITUDE, HUH? I FEEL BAD FOR BEING SO UPSET WITH HIM NOW.

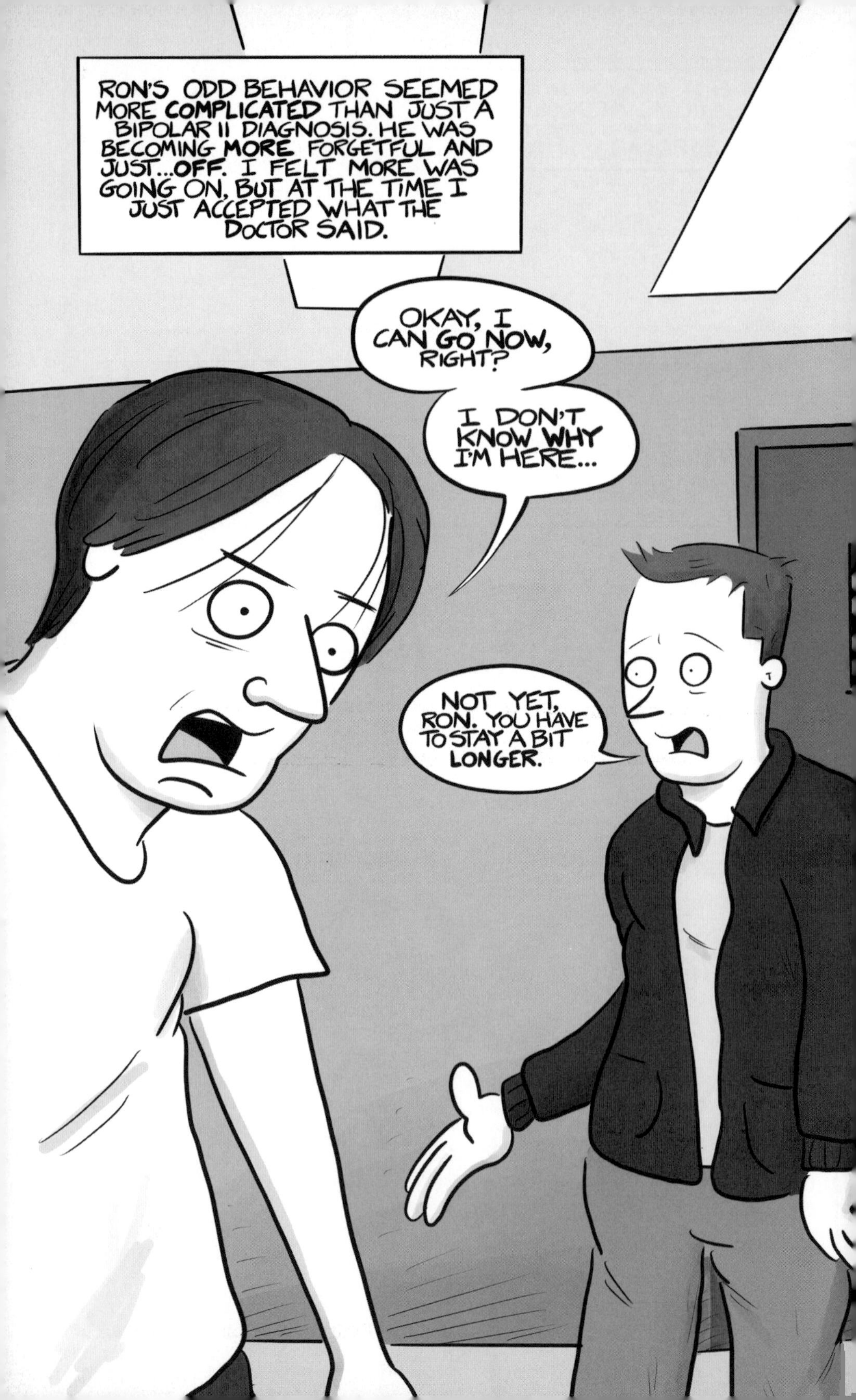
RON'S ODD BEHAVIOR SEEMED MORE **COMPLICATED** THAN JUST A BIPOLAR II DIAGNOSIS. HE WAS BECOMING **MORE** FORGETFUL AND JUST...**OFF**. I FELT MORE WAS GOING ON, BUT AT THE TIME I JUST ACCEPTED WHAT THE DOCTOR SAID.
OKAY, I CAN **GO NOW**, RIGHT?
I DON'T KNOW **WHY** I'M HERE...
NOT YET, RON. YOU HAVE TO STAY A BIT **LONGER**.

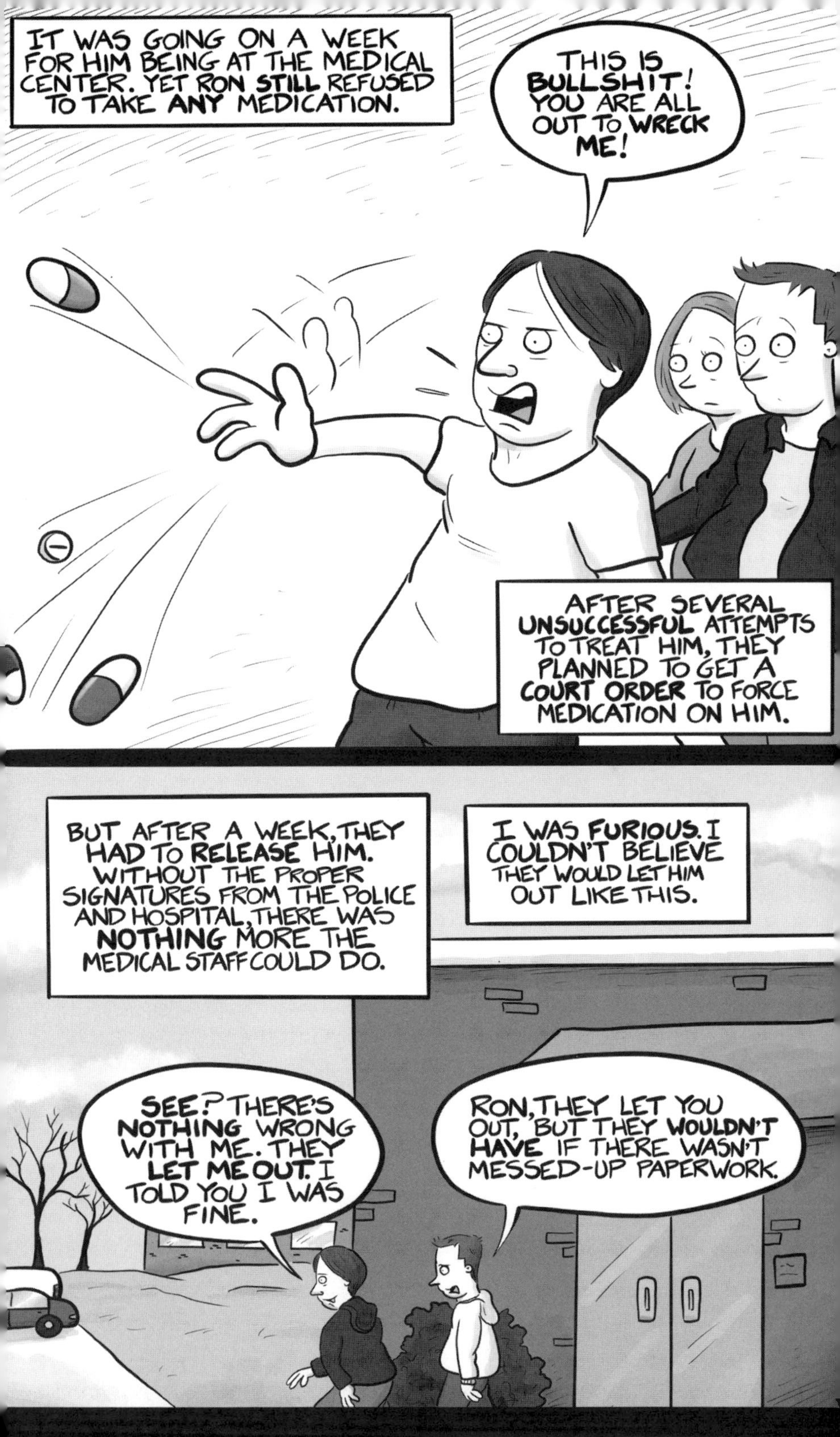
IT WAS GOING ON A WEEK FOR HIM BEING AT THE MEDICAL CENTER. YET RON STILL REFUSED TO TAKE ANY MEDICATION.
THIS IS BULLSHIT! YOU ARE ALL OUT TO WRECK ME!
AFTER SEVERAL UNSUCCESSFUL ATTEMPTS TO TREAT HIM, THEY PLANNED TO GET A COURT ORDER TO FORCE MEDICATION ON HIM.
BUT AFTER A WEEK, THEY HAD TO RELEASE HIM. WITHOUT THE PROPER SIGNATURES FROM THE POLICE AND HOSPITAL, THERE WAS NOTHING MORE THE MEDICAL STAFF COULD DO.
I WAS FURIOUS. I COULDN'T BELIEVE THEY WOULD LET HIM OUT LIKE THIS.
SEE? THERE'S NOTHING WRONG WITH ME. THEY LET ME OUT. I TOLD YOU I WAS FINE.
RON, THEY LET YOU OUT, BUT THEY WOULDN'T HAVE IF THERE WASN'T MESSED-UP PAPERWORK.

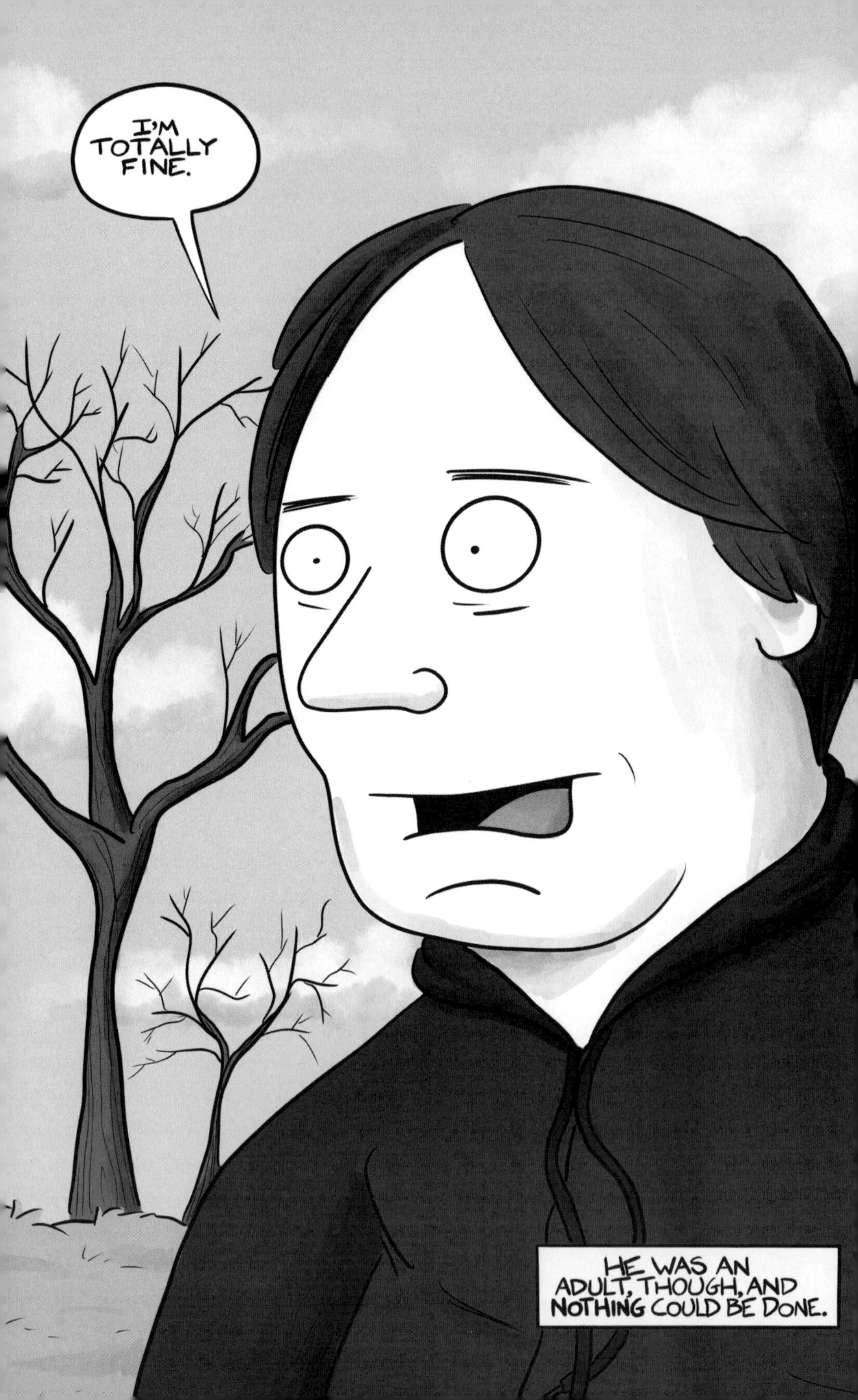
I'M TOTALLY FINE.
HE WAS AN ADULT, THOUGH, AND NOTHING COULD BE DONE.

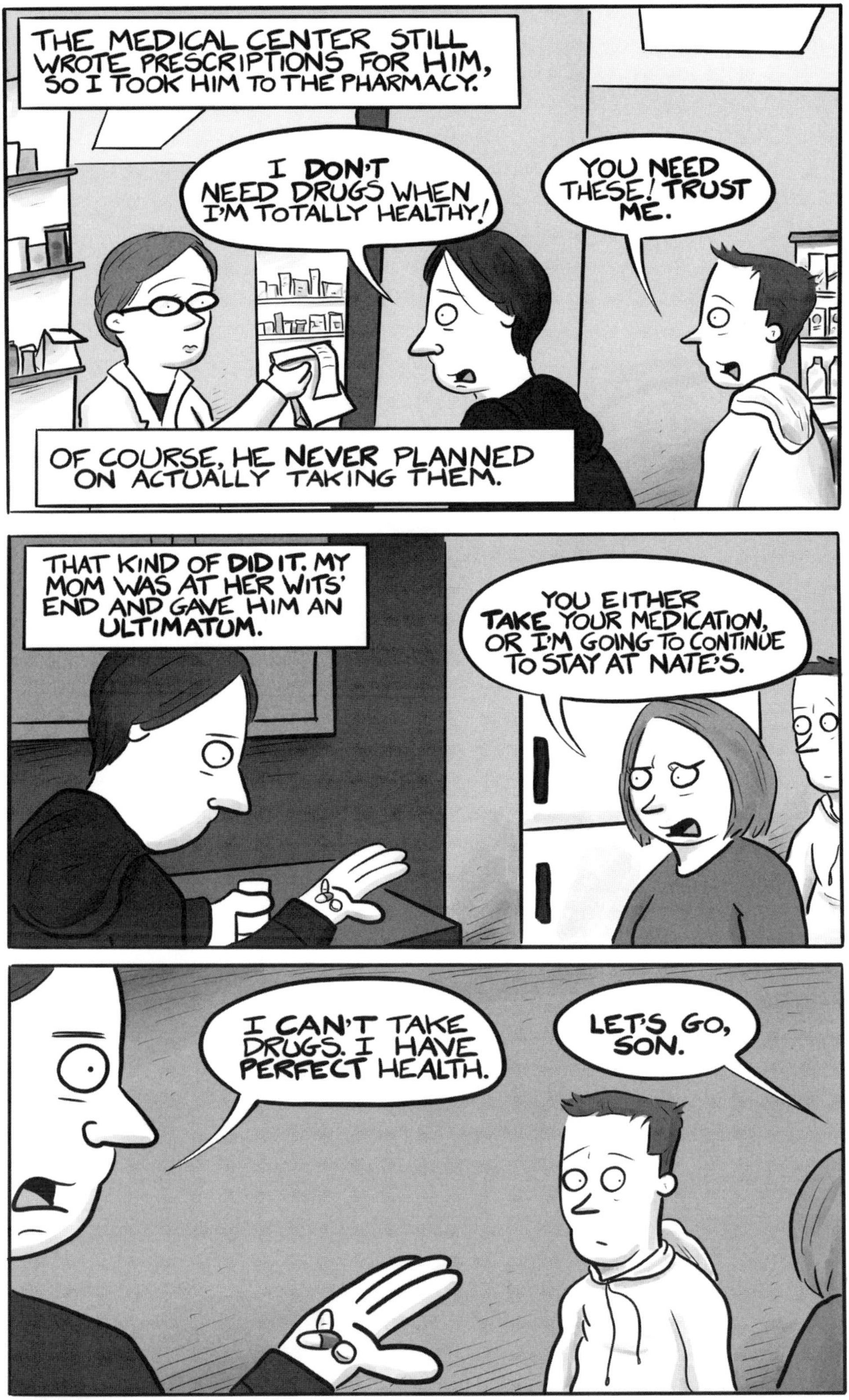
THE MEDICAL CENTER STILL WROTE PRESCRIPTIONS FOR HIM, SO I TOOK HIM TO THE PHARMACY.
I DON'T NEED DRUGS WHEN I'M TOTALLY HEALTHY!
YOU NEED THESE! TRUST ME.
OF COURSE, HE NEVER PLANNED ON ACTUALLY TAKING THEM.
THAT KIND OF DID IT. MY MOM WAS AT HER WITS' END AND GAVE HIM AN ULTIMATUM.
YOU EITHER TAKE YOUR MEDICATION, OR I'M GOING TO CONTINUE TO STAY AT NATE'S.
I CAN'T TAKE DRUGS. I HAVE PERFECT HEALTH.
LET'S GO, SON.

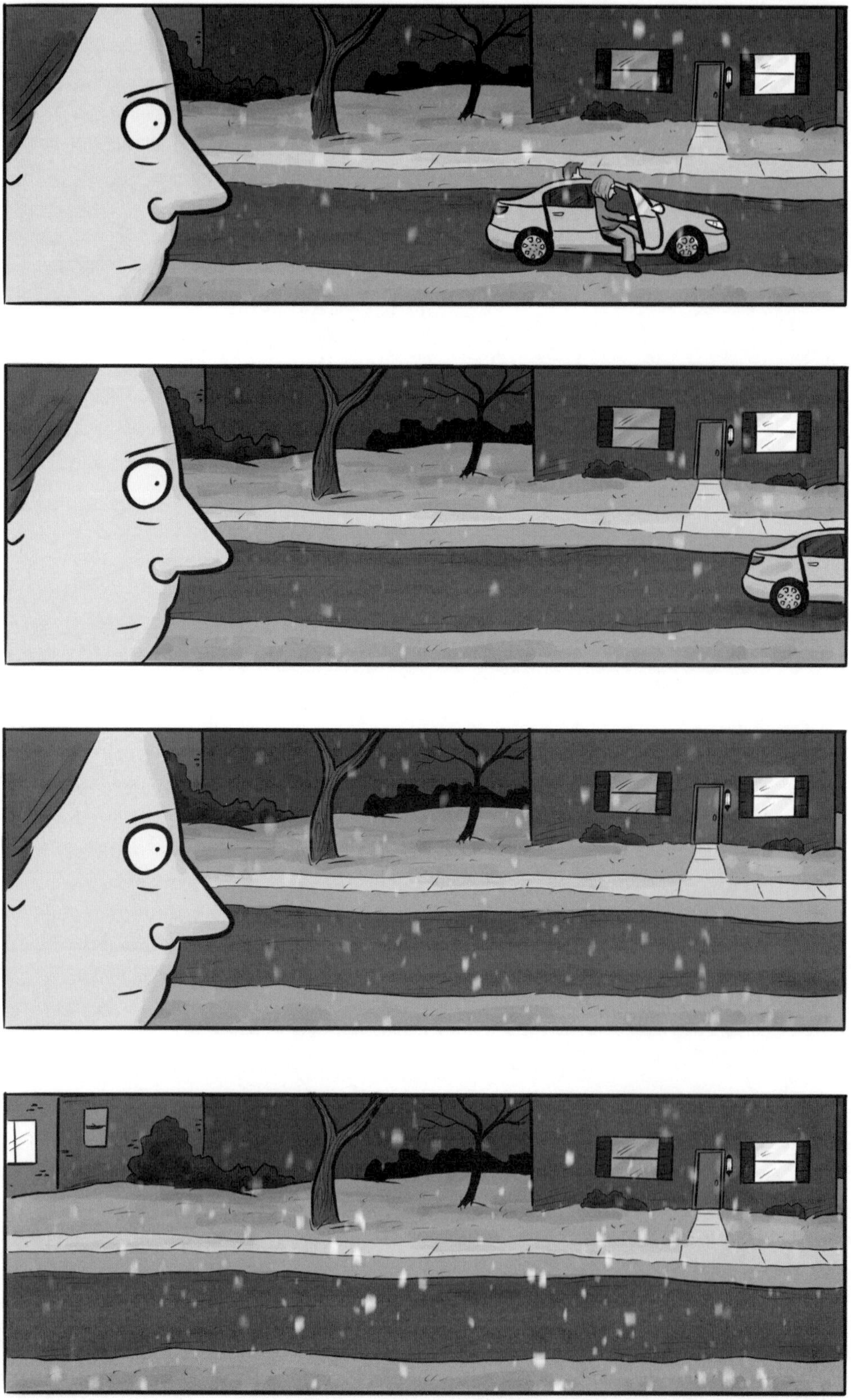

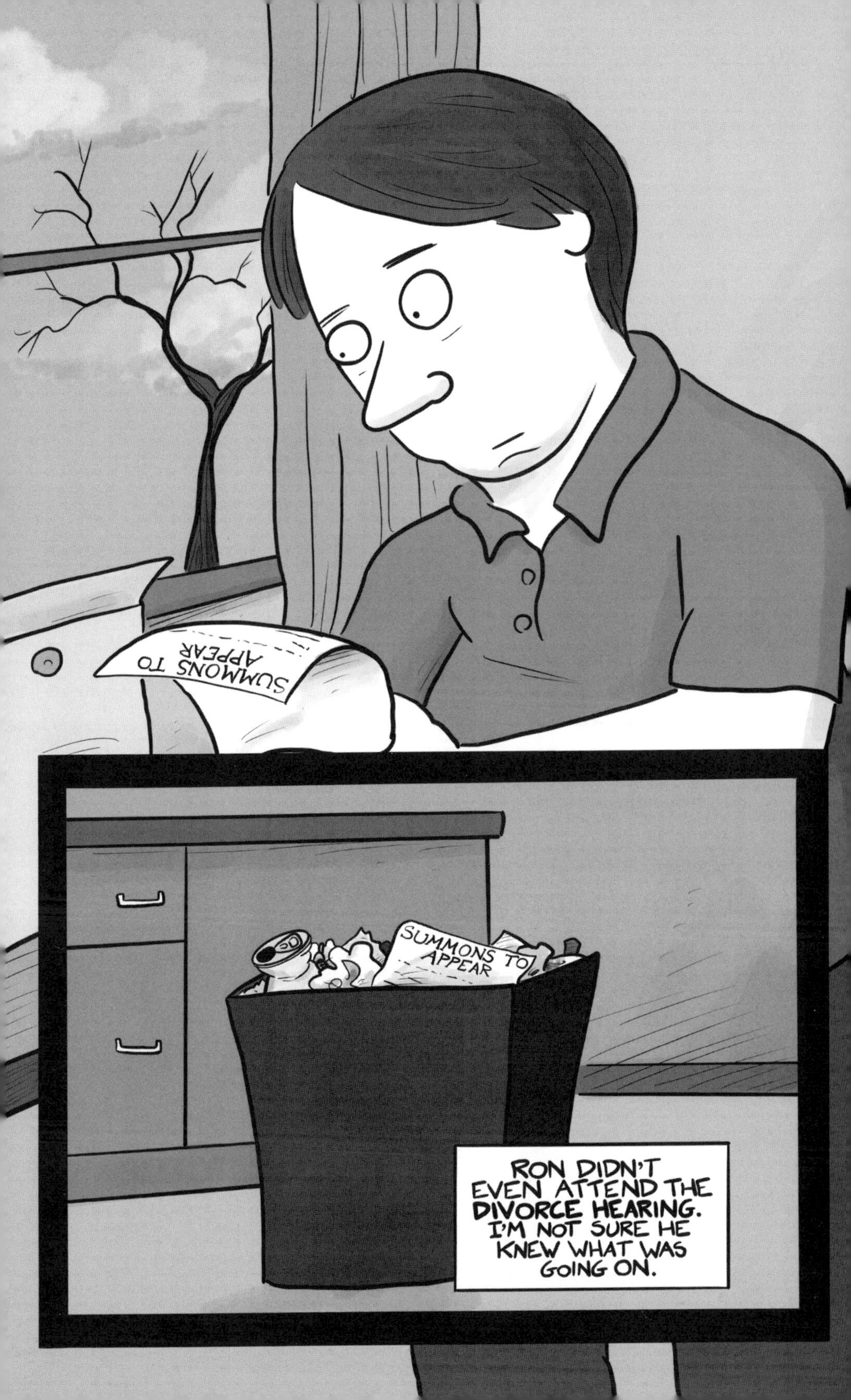
SUMMONS TO APPEAR
SUMMONS TO APPEAR
RON DIDN'T EVEN ATTEND THE DIVORCE HEARING. I'M NOT SURE HE KNEW WHAT WAS GOING ON.

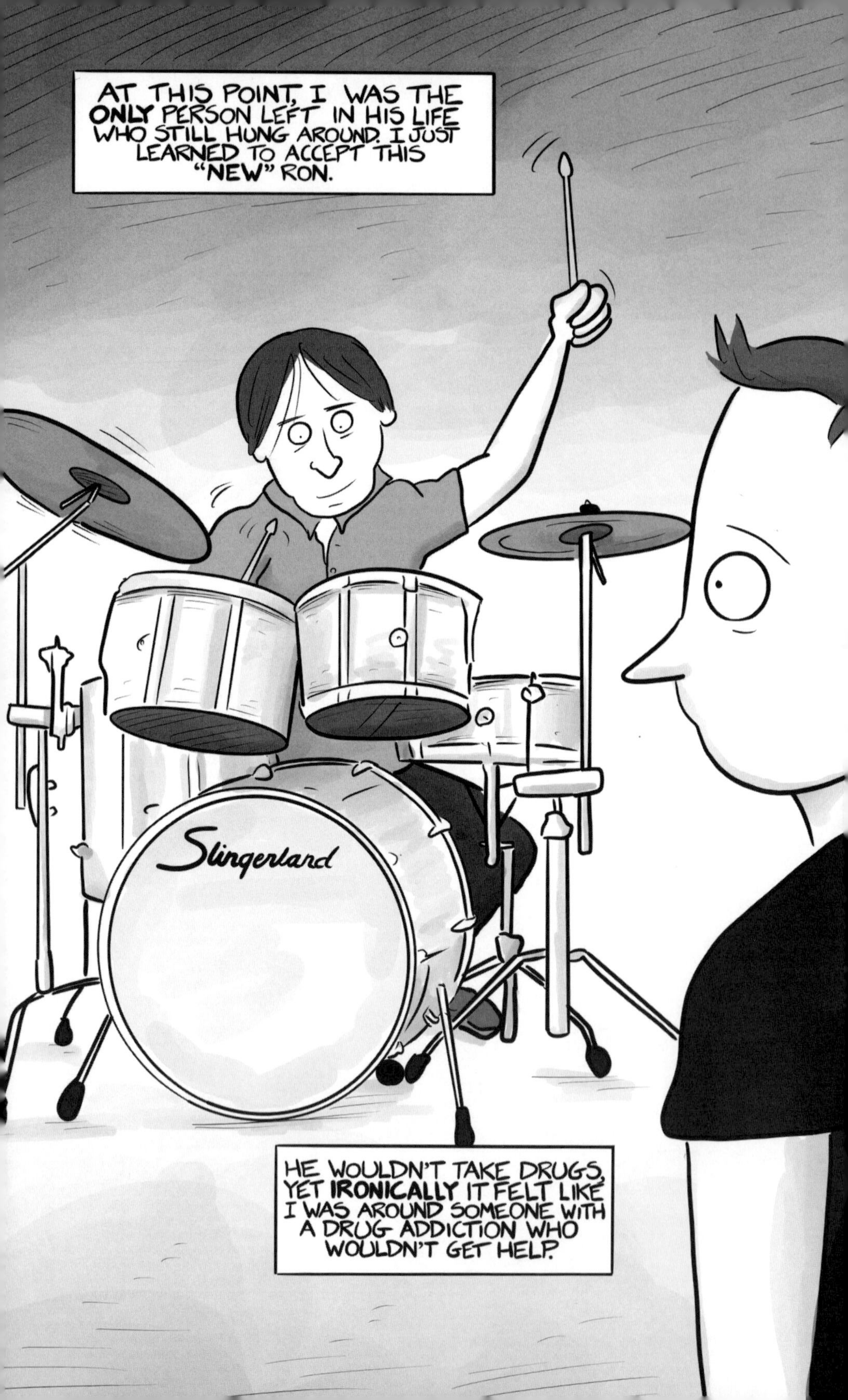
AT THIS POINT, I WAS THE ONLY PERSON LEFT IN HIS LIFE WHO STILL HUNG AROUND. I JUST LEARNED TO ACCEPT THIS "NEW" RON.
Slingerland
HE WOULDN'T TAKE DRUGS, YET IRONICALLY IT FELT LIKE I WAS AROUND SOMEONE WITH A DRUG ADDICTION WHO WOULDN'T GET HELP.

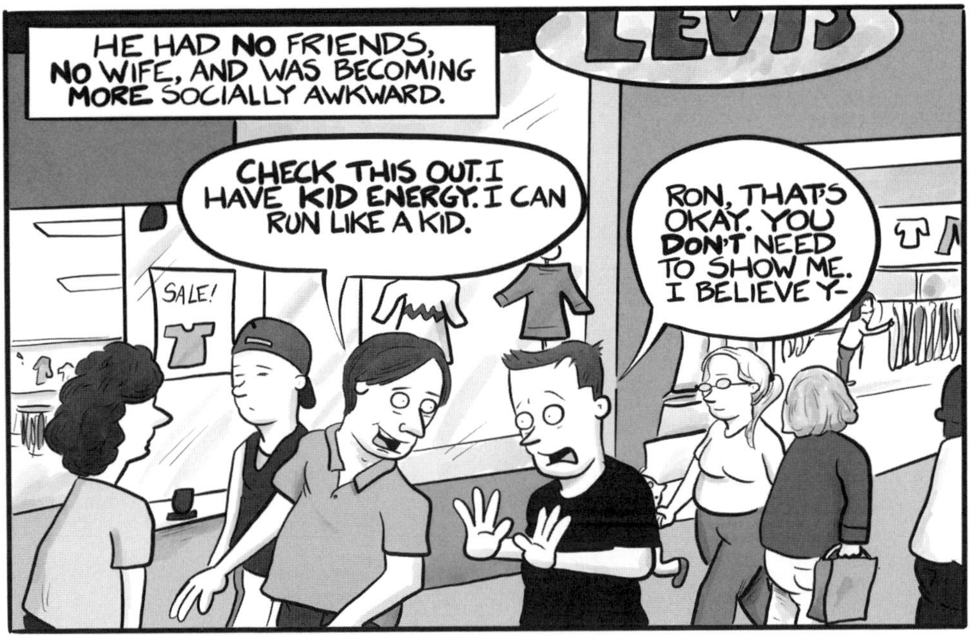
HE HAD NO FRIENDS, NO WIFE, AND WAS BECOMING MORE SOCIALLY AWKWARD.
CHECK THIS OUT. I HAVE KID ENERGY. I CAN RUN LIKE A KID.
RON, THAT'S OKAY. YOU DON'T NEED TO SHOW ME. I BELIEVE Y-
SALE!

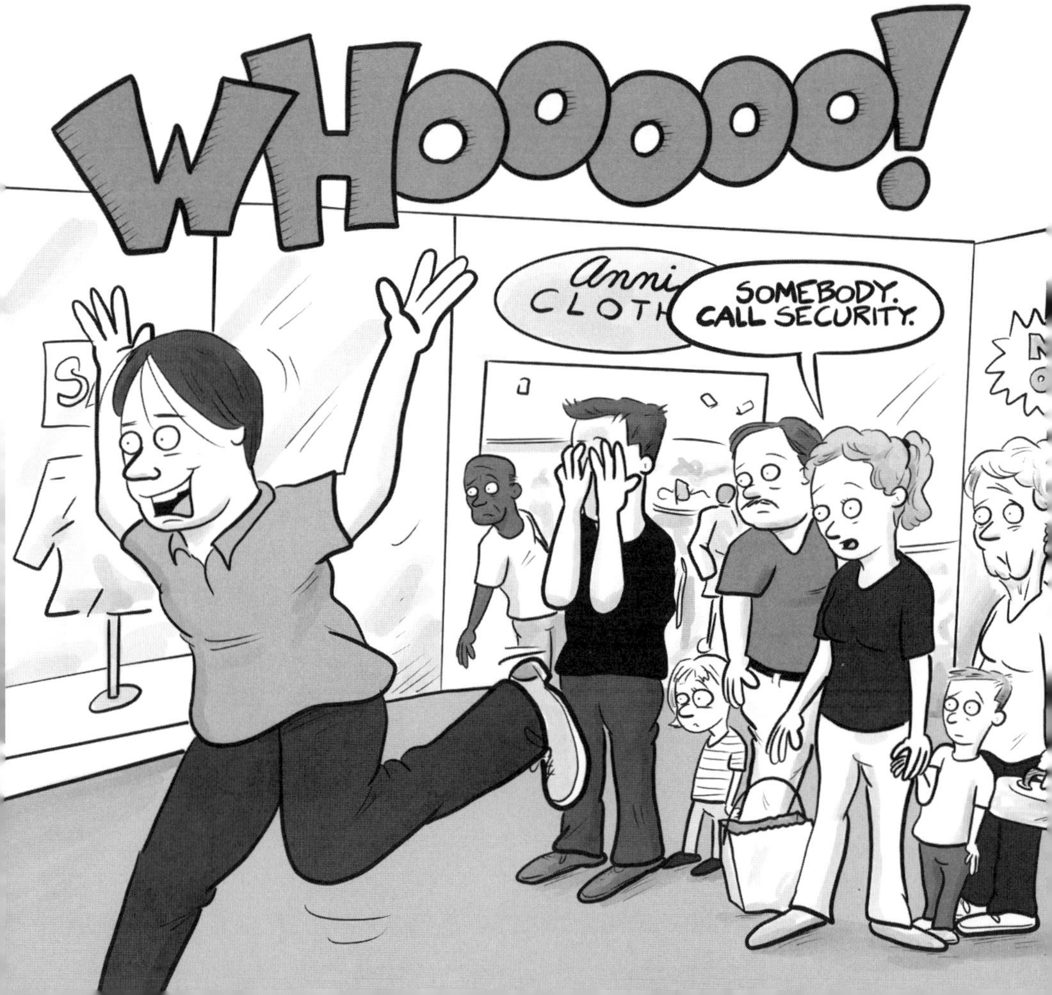
WHOOOOO!
SOMEBODY. CALL SECURITY.

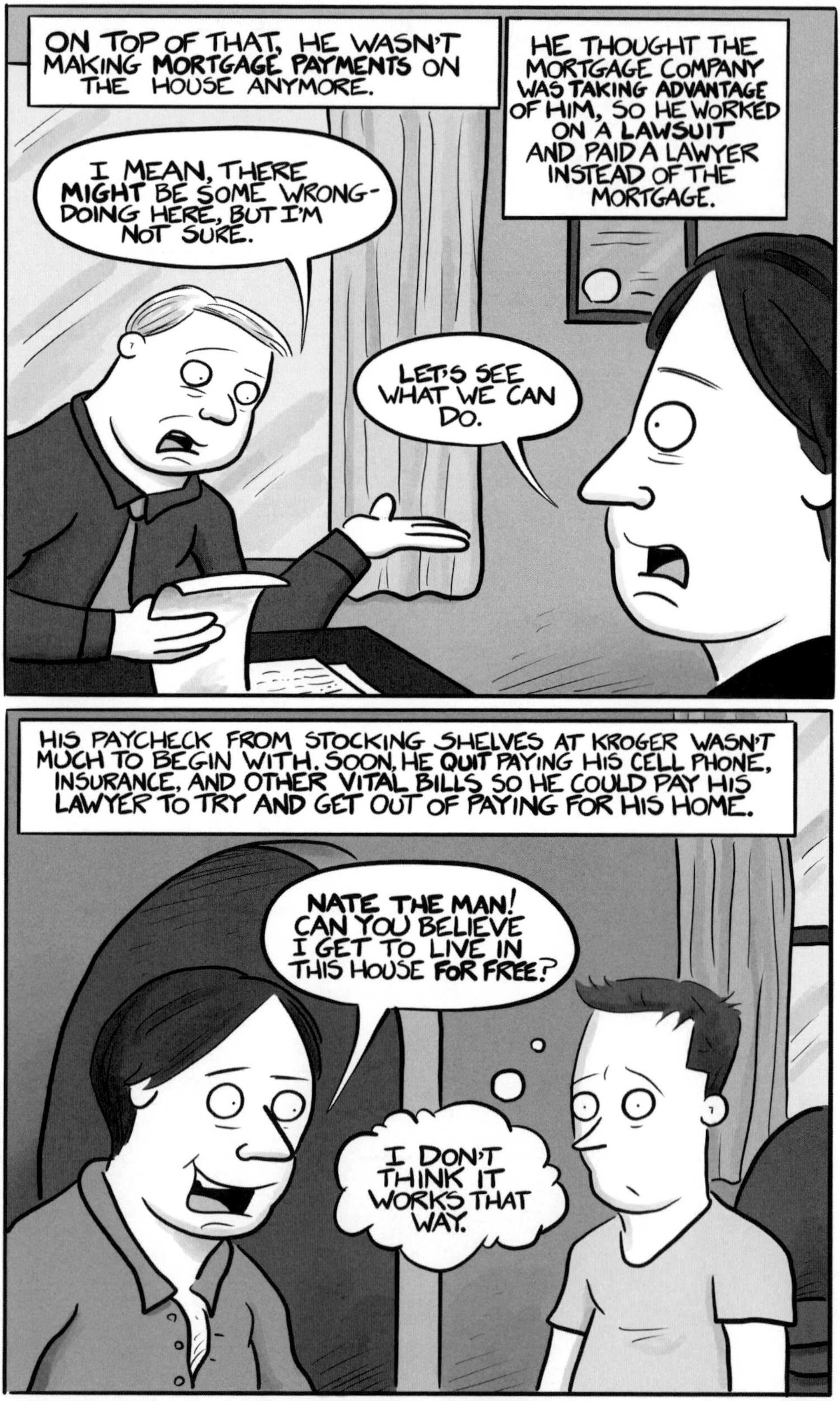
ON TOP OF THAT, HE WASN'T MAKING **MORTGAGE PAYMENTS** ON THE HOUSE ANYMORE.
HE THOUGHT THE MORTGAGE COMPANY WAS **TAKING ADVANTAGE** OF HIM, SO HE WORKED ON A **LAWSUIT** AND PAID A LAWYER INSTEAD OF THE MORTGAGE.
I MEAN, THERE **MIGHT** BE SOME WRONG-DOING HERE, BUT I'M NOT SURE.
LET'S SEE WHAT WE CAN DO.
HIS PAYCHECK FROM STOCKING SHELVES AT KROGER WASN'T MUCH TO BEGIN WITH. SOON, HE **QUIT** PAYING HIS CELL PHONE, INSURANCE, AND OTHER VITAL BILLS SO HE COULD PAY HIS LAWYER TO TRY AND GET OUT OF PAYING FOR HIS HOME.
NATE THE MAN! CAN YOU BELIEVE I GET TO LIVE IN THIS HOUSE **FOR FREE?**
I DON'T THINK IT WORKS THAT WAY.

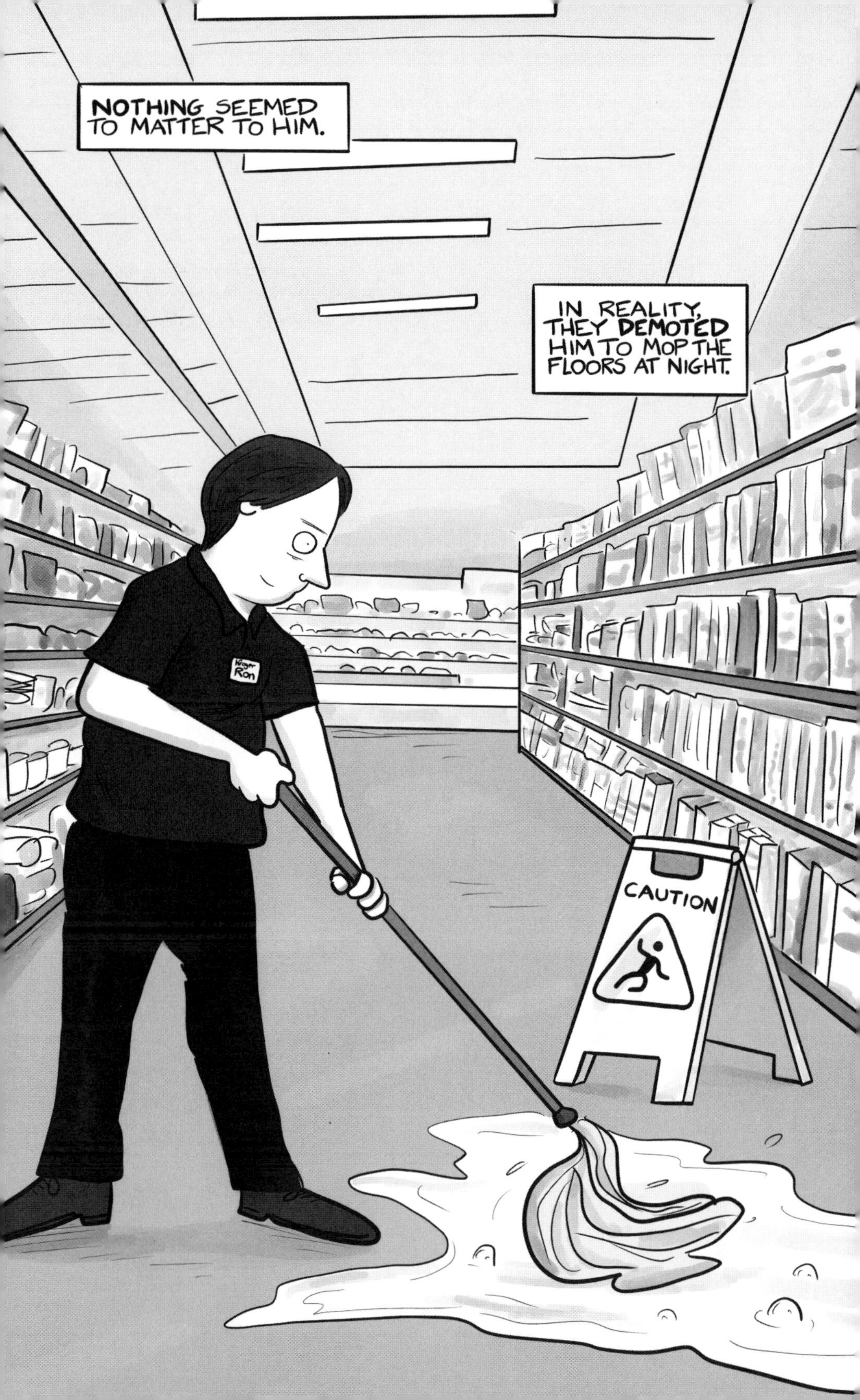
NOTHING SEEMED TO MATTER TO HIM.
IN REALITY, THEY DEMOTED HIM TO MOP THE FLOORS AT NIGHT.
Kroger Ron
CAUTION

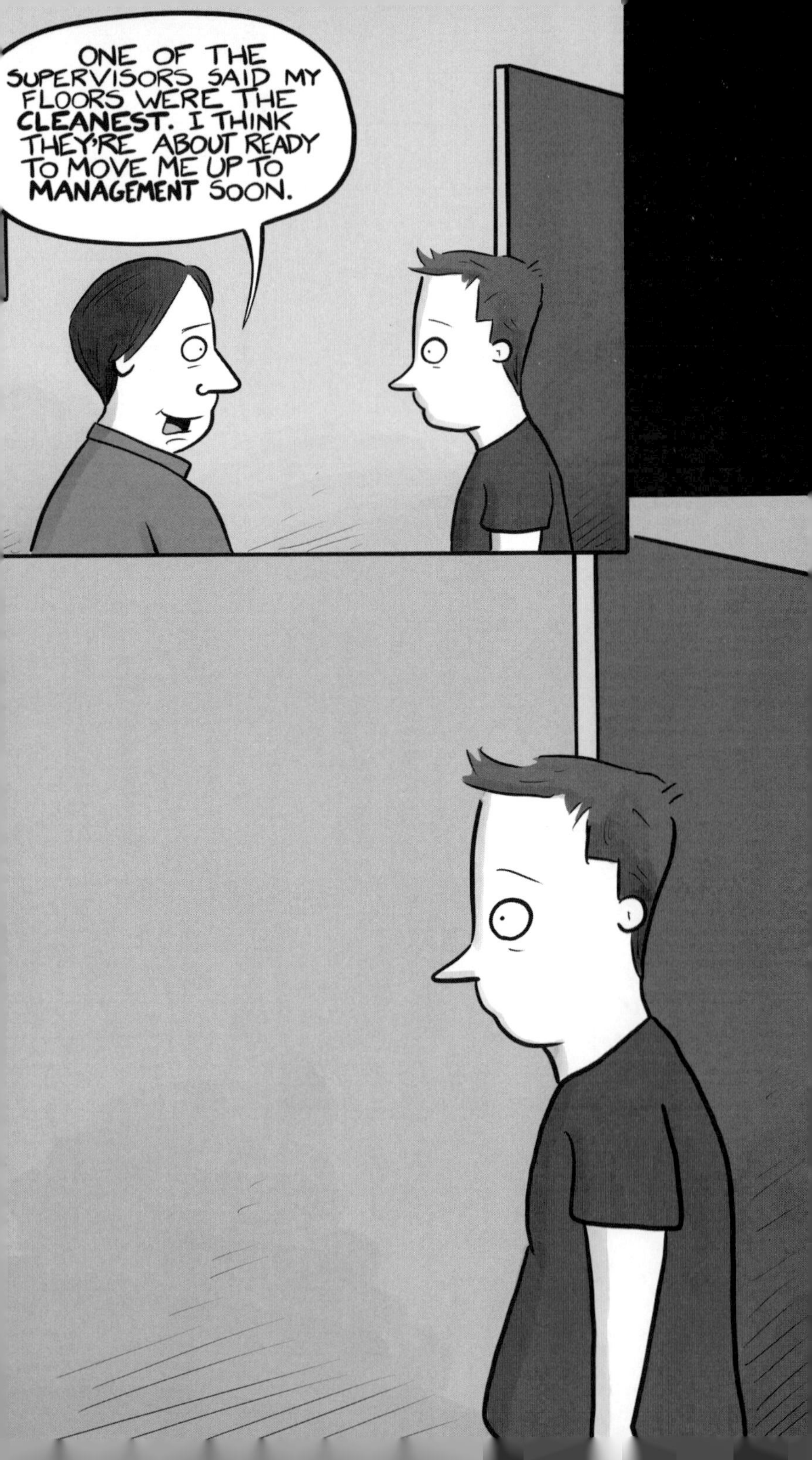
ONE OF THE SUPERVISORS SAID MY FLOORS WERE THE **CLEANEST**. I THINK THEY'RE ABOUT READY TO MOVE ME UP TO **MANAGEMENT** SOON.

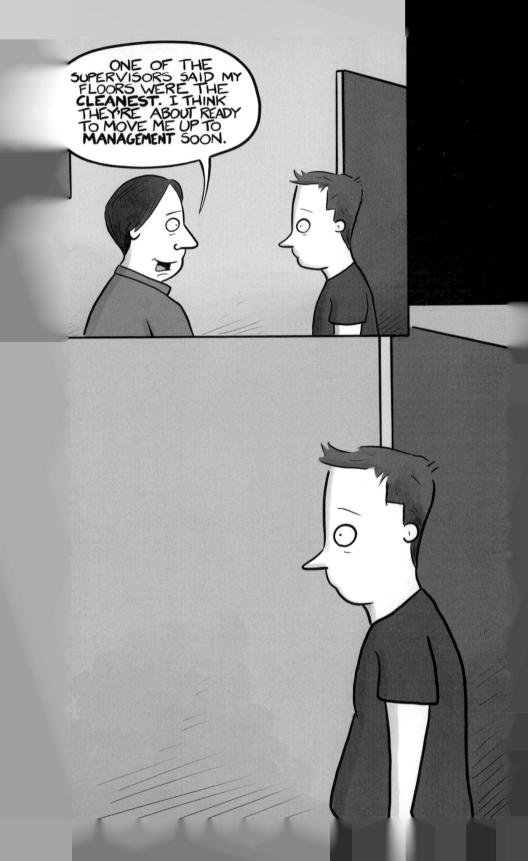

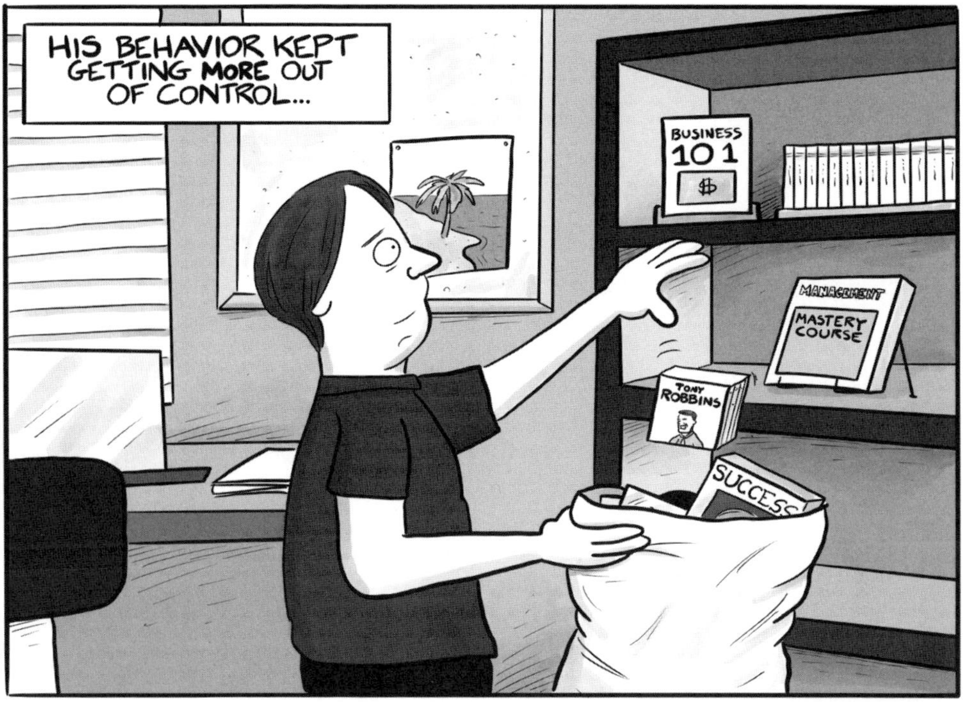
HIS BEHAVIOR KEPT GETTING **MORE** OUT OF CONTROL...
BUSINESS 101 $
MANAGEMENT MASTERY COURSE
TONY ROBBINS
SUCCESS

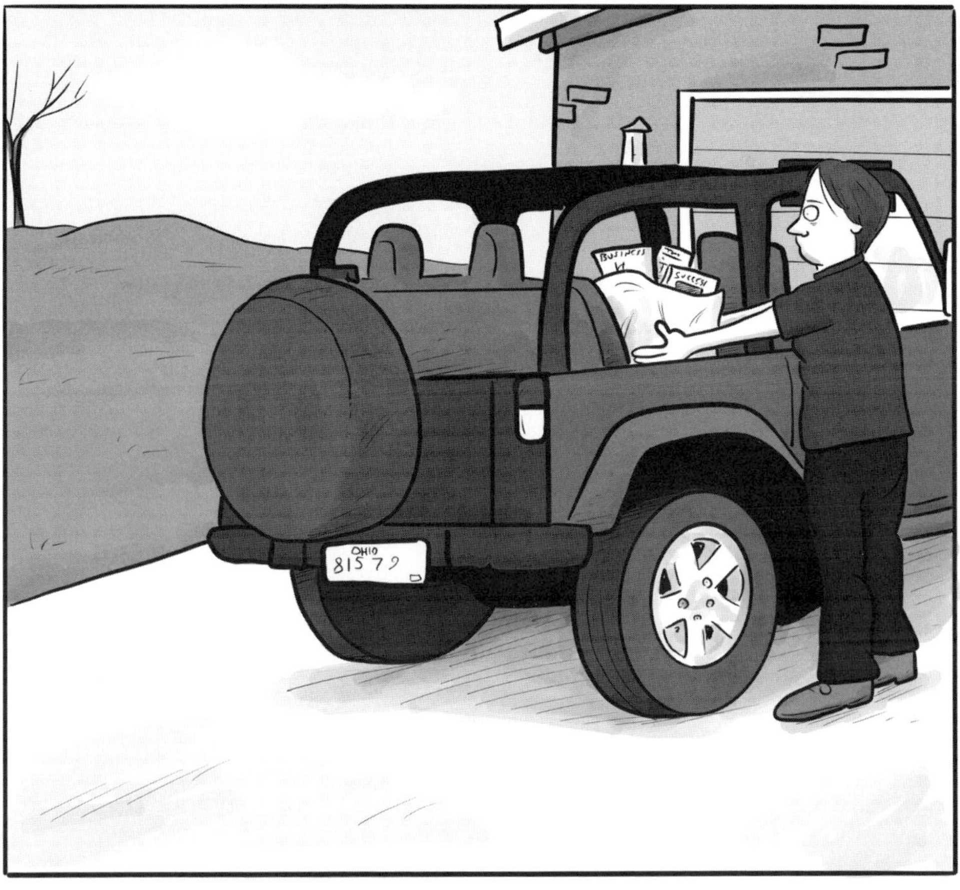

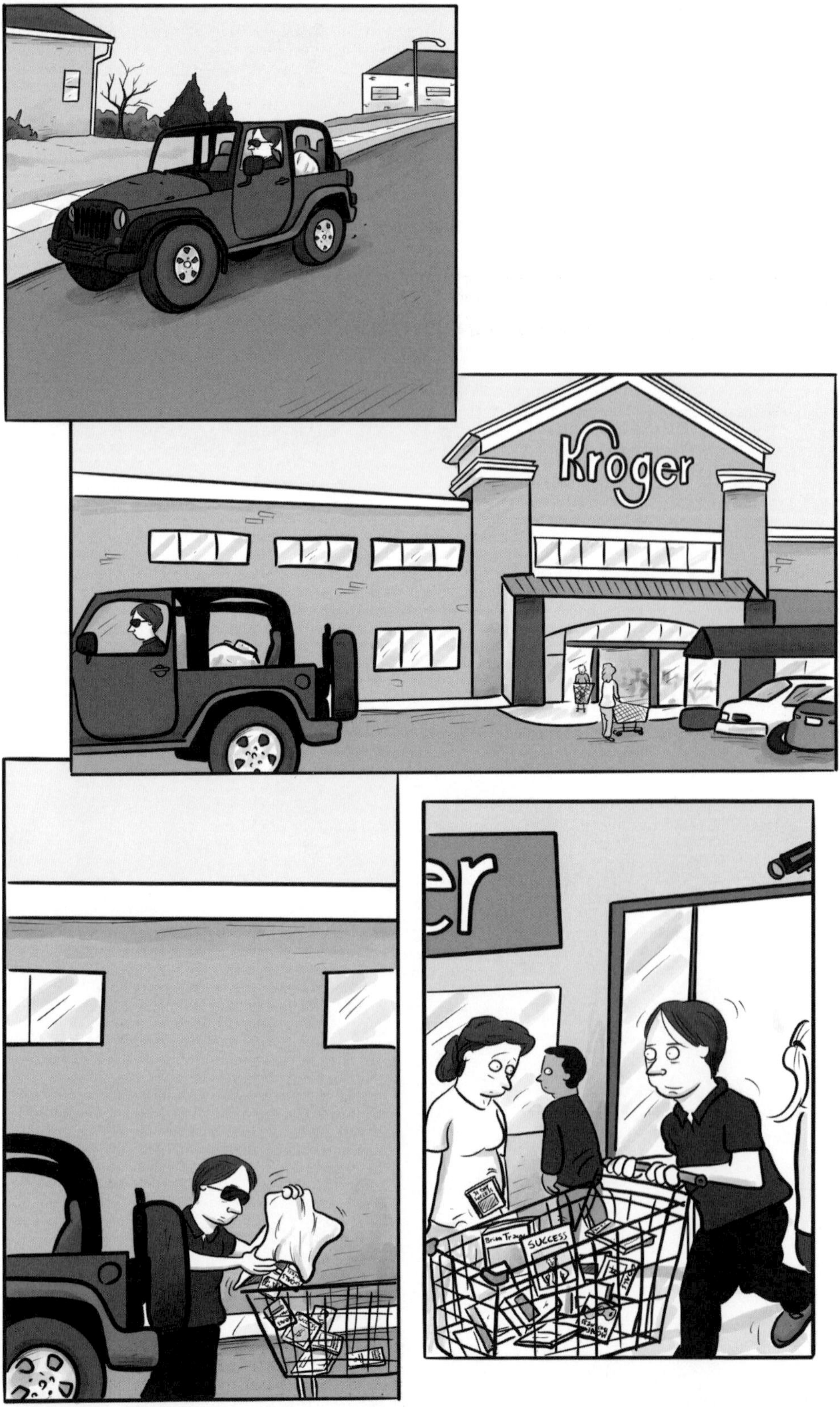

Kroger
er
SUCCESS

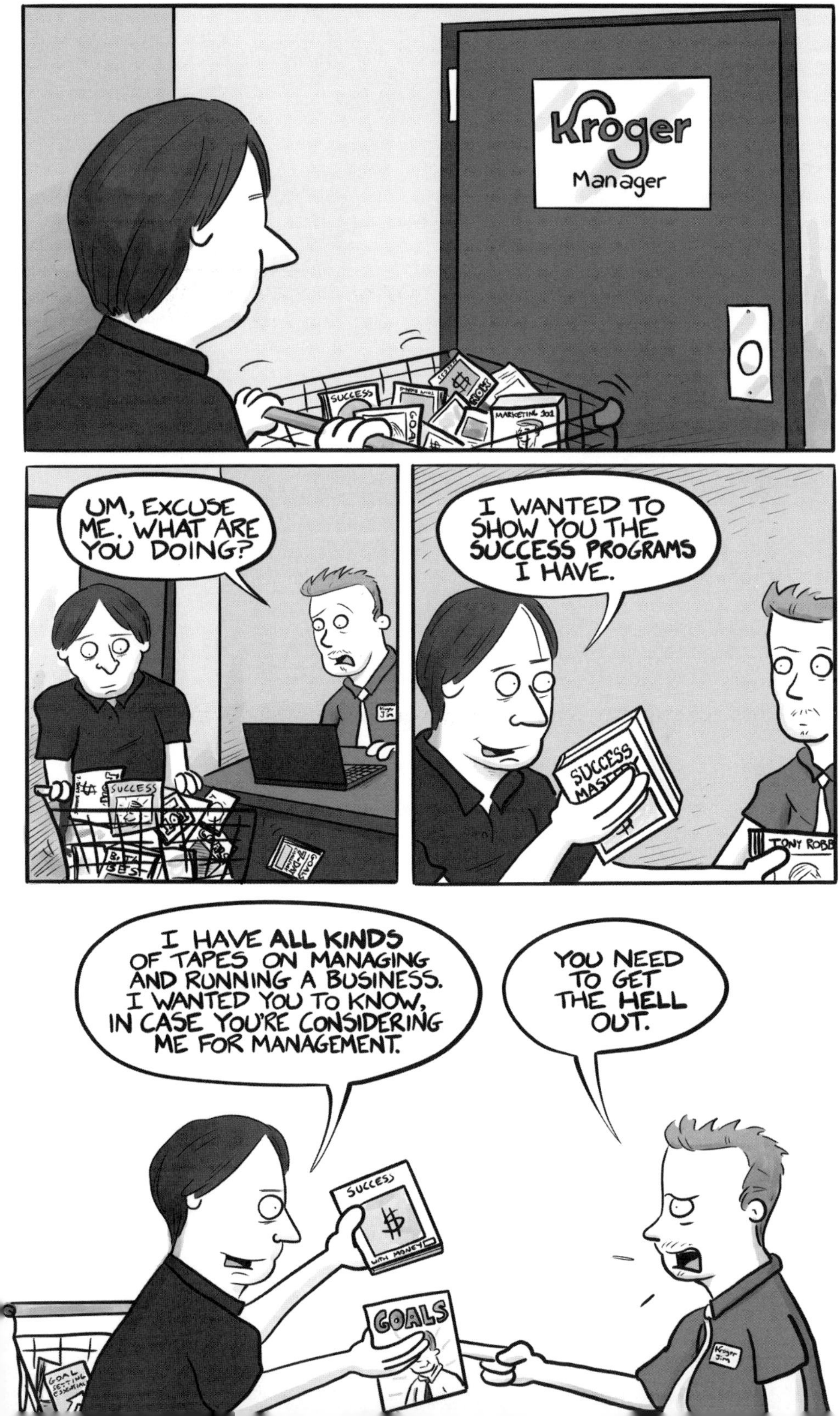
Kroger
Manager
SUCCESS
MARKETING 101
UM, EXCUSE ME. WHAT ARE YOU DOING?
SUCCESS
I WANTED TO SHOW YOU THE SUCCESS PROGRAMS I HAVE.
SUCCESS MASTERY
TONY ROBB
I HAVE ALL KINDS OF TAPES ON MANAGING AND RUNNING A BUSINESS. I WANTED YOU TO KNOW, IN CASE YOU'RE CONSIDERING ME FOR MANAGEMENT.
YOU NEED TO GET THE HELL OUT.
SUCCESS
WITH MONEY
GOALS
GOAL SETTING ESSENTIALS
Kroger Jim

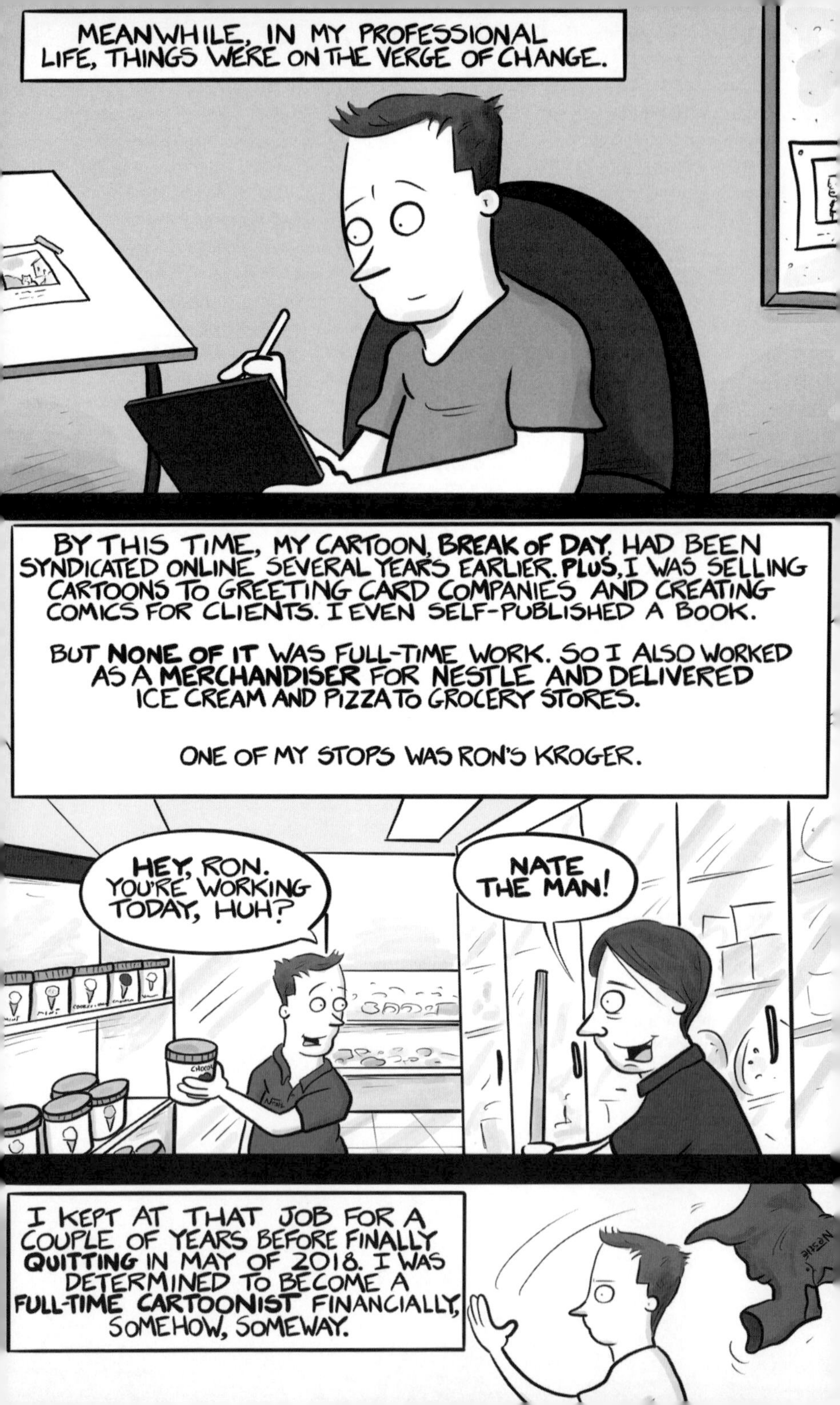
MEANWHILE, IN MY PROFESSIONAL LIFE, THINGS WERE ON THE VERGE OF CHANGE.
BY THIS TIME, MY CARTOON, BREAK OF DAY, HAD BEEN SYNDICATED ONLINE SEVERAL YEARS EARLIER. PLUS, I WAS SELLING CARTOONS TO GREETING CARD COMPANIES AND CREATING COMICS FOR CLIENTS. I EVEN SELF-PUBLISHED A BOOK.
BUT NONE OF IT WAS FULL-TIME WORK. SO I ALSO WORKED AS A MERCHANDISER FOR NESTLE AND DELIVERED ICE CREAM AND PIZZA TO GROCERY STORES.
ONE OF MY STOPS WAS RON'S KROGER.
HEY, RON. YOU'RE WORKING TODAY, HUH?
NATE THE MAN!
I KEPT AT THAT JOB FOR A COUPLE OF YEARS BEFORE FINALLY QUITTING IN MAY OF 2018. I WAS DETERMINED TO BECOME A FULL-TIME CARTOONIST FINANCIALLY, SOMEHOW, SOMEWAY.

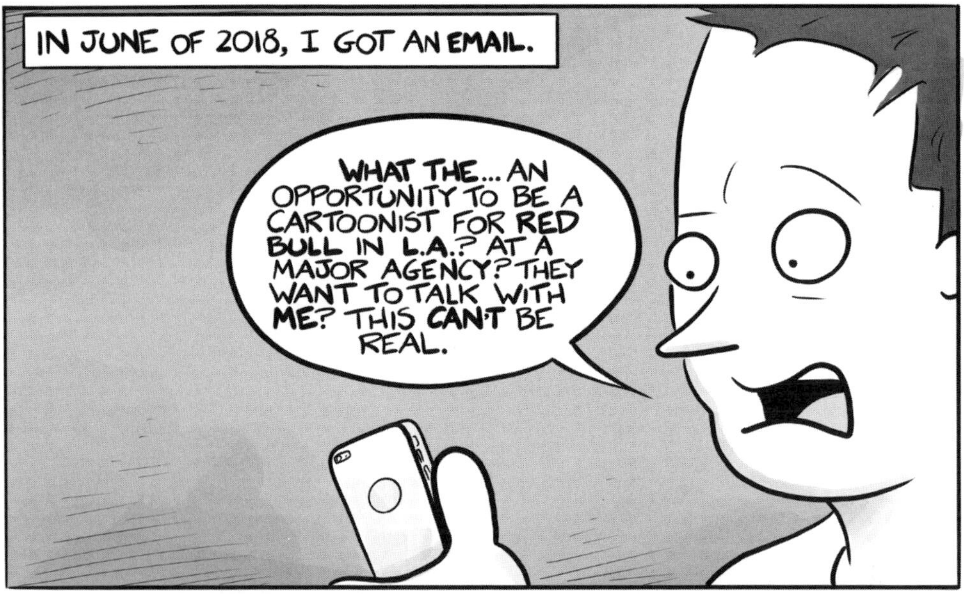
IN JUNE OF 2018, I GOT AN EMAIL.
WHAT THE... AN OPPORTUNITY TO BE A CARTOONIST FOR RED BULL IN L.A.? AT A MAJOR AGENCY? THEY WANT TO TALK WITH ME? THIS CAN'T BE REAL.

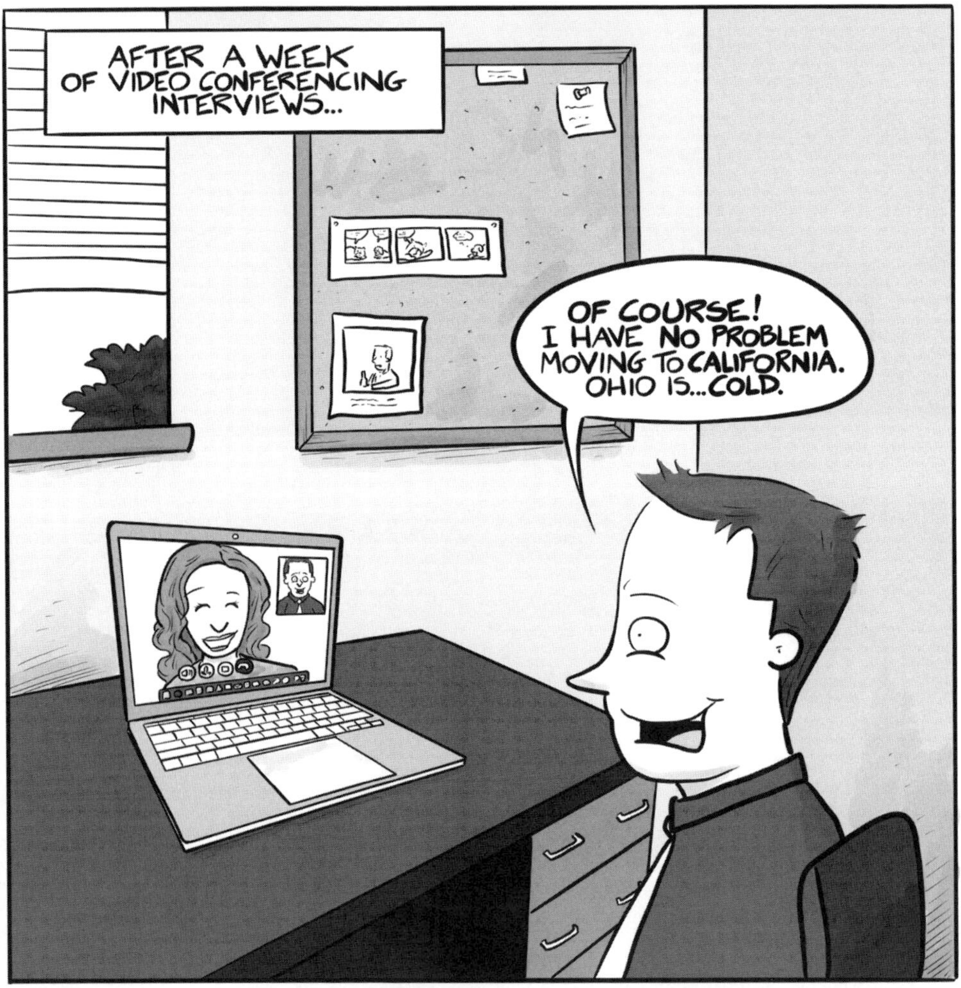
AFTER A WEEK OF VIDEO CONFERENCING INTERVIEWS...
OF COURSE! I HAVE NO PROBLEM MOVING TO CALIFORNIA. OHIO IS...COLD.

...THE JOB CAME.

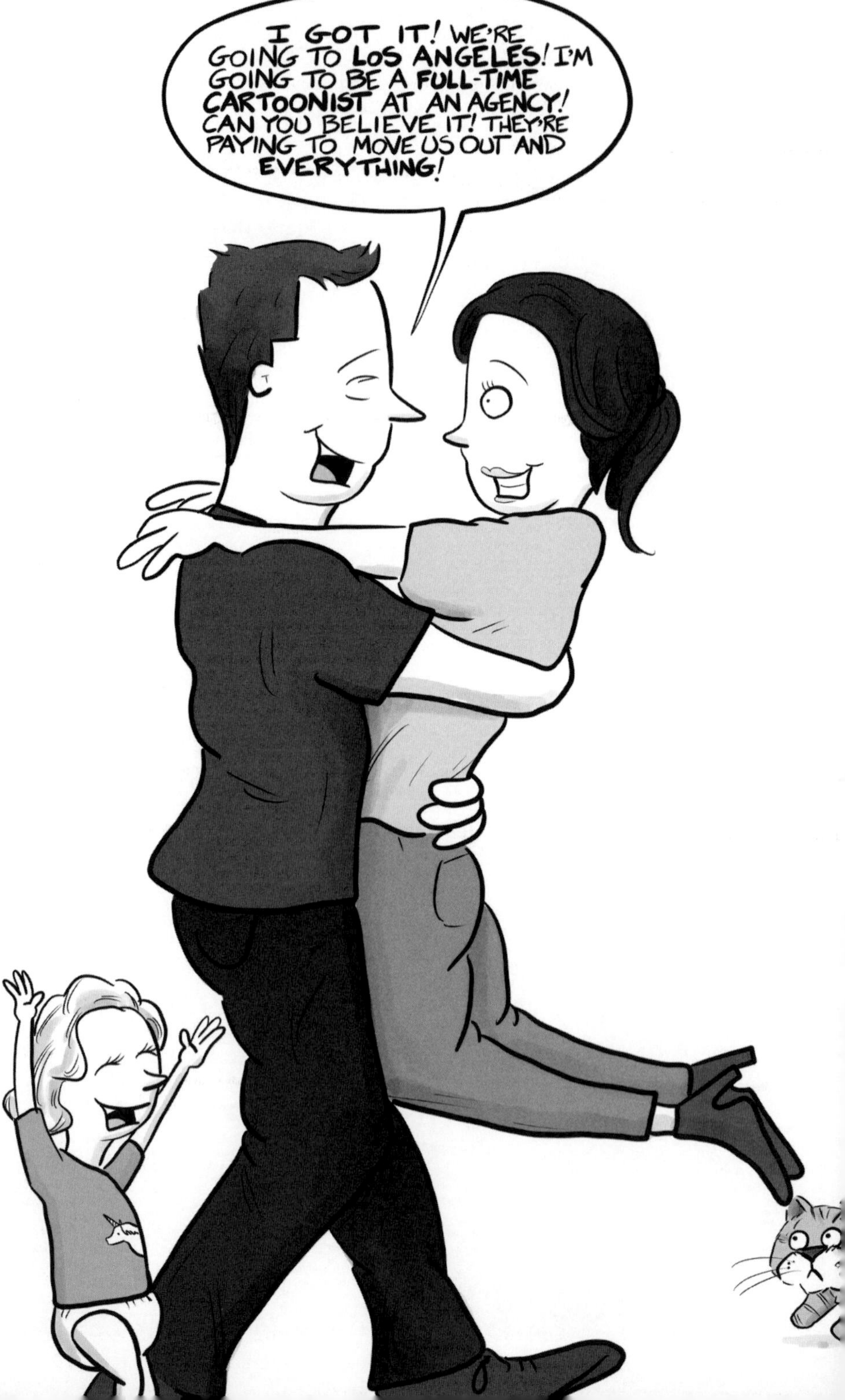
I GOT IT! WE'RE GOING TO LOS ANGELES! I'M GOING TO BE A FULL-TIME CARTOONIST AT AN AGENCY! CAN YOU BELIEVE IT! THEY'RE PAYING TO MOVE US OUT AND EVERYTHING!

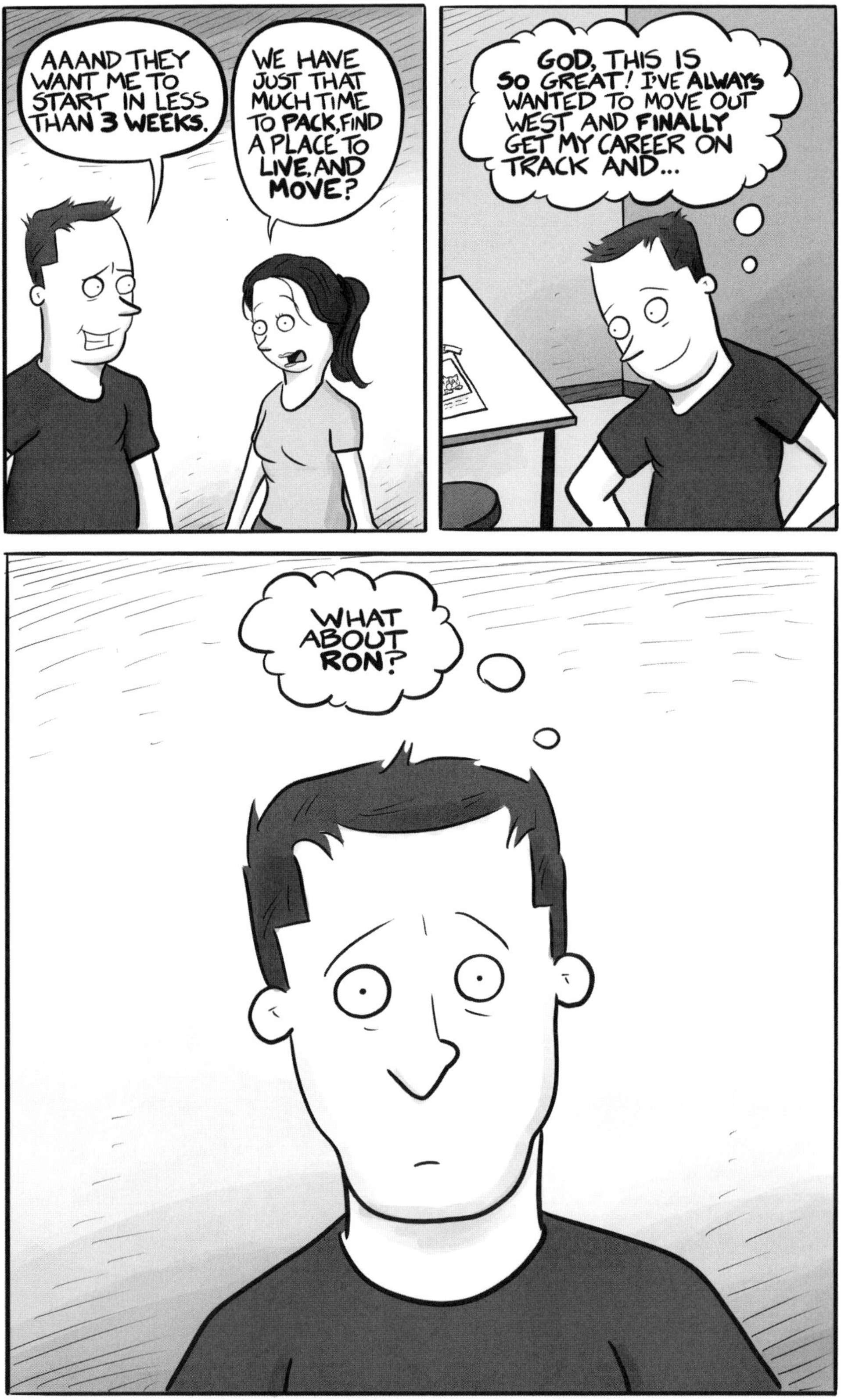
AAAND THEY WANT ME TO START IN LESS THAN 3 WEEKS.
WE HAVE JUST THAT MUCH TIME TO PACK, FIND A PLACE TO LIVE, AND MOVE?
GOD, THIS IS SO GREAT! I'VE ALWAYS WANTED TO MOVE OUT WEST AND FINALLY GET MY CAREER ON TRACK AND...
WHAT ABOUT RON?

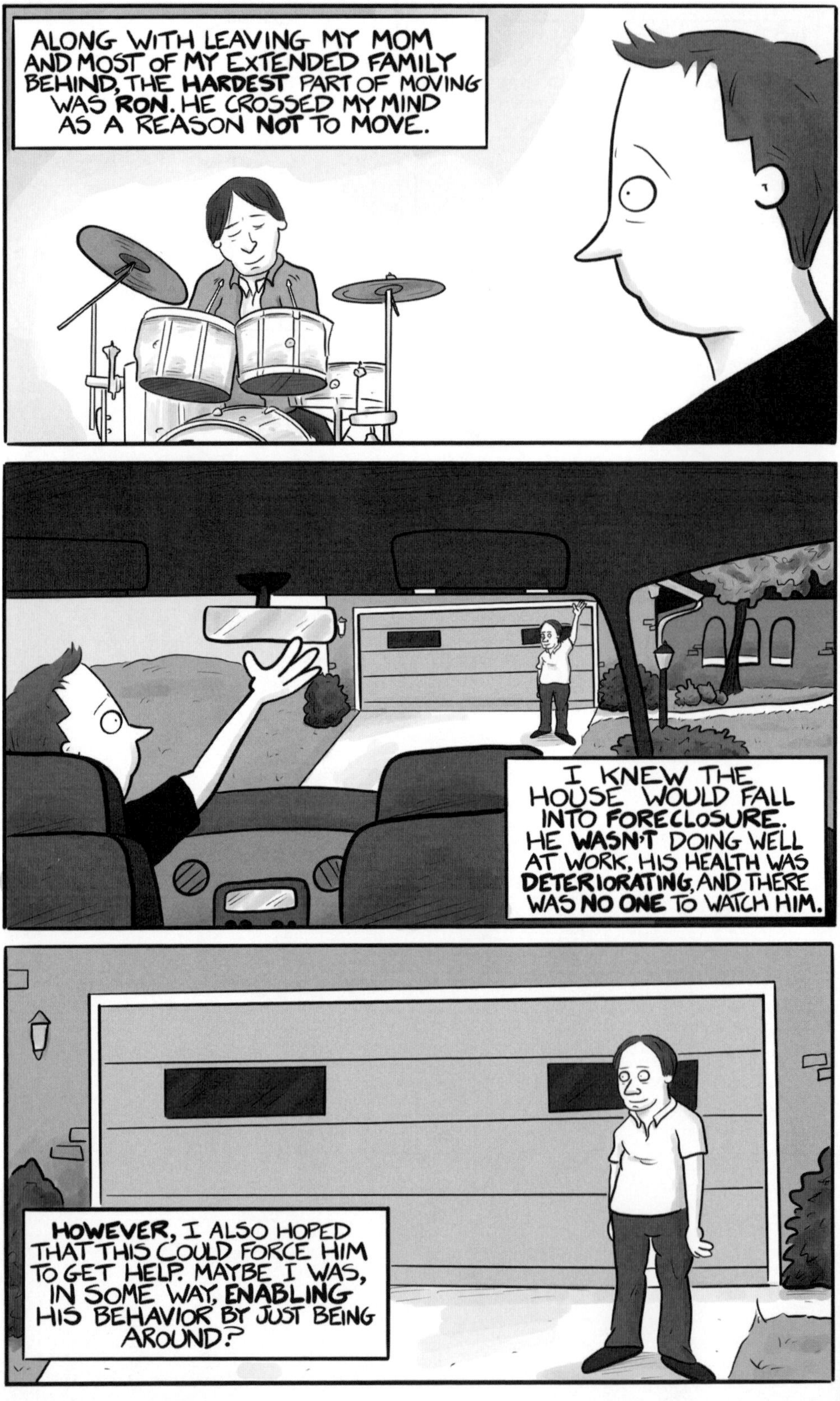
ALONG WITH LEAVING MY MOM AND MOST OF MY EXTENDED FAMILY BEHIND, THE HARDEST PART OF MOVING WAS RON. HE CROSSED MY MIND AS A REASON NOT TO MOVE.
I KNEW THE HOUSE WOULD FALL INTO FORECLOSURE. HE WASN'T DOING WELL AT WORK, HIS HEALTH WAS DETERIORATING, AND THERE WAS NO ONE TO WATCH HIM.
HOWEVER, I ALSO HOPED THAT THIS COULD FORCE HIM TO GET HELP. MAYBE I WAS, IN SOME WAY, ENABLING HIS BEHAVIOR BY JUST BEING AROUND?

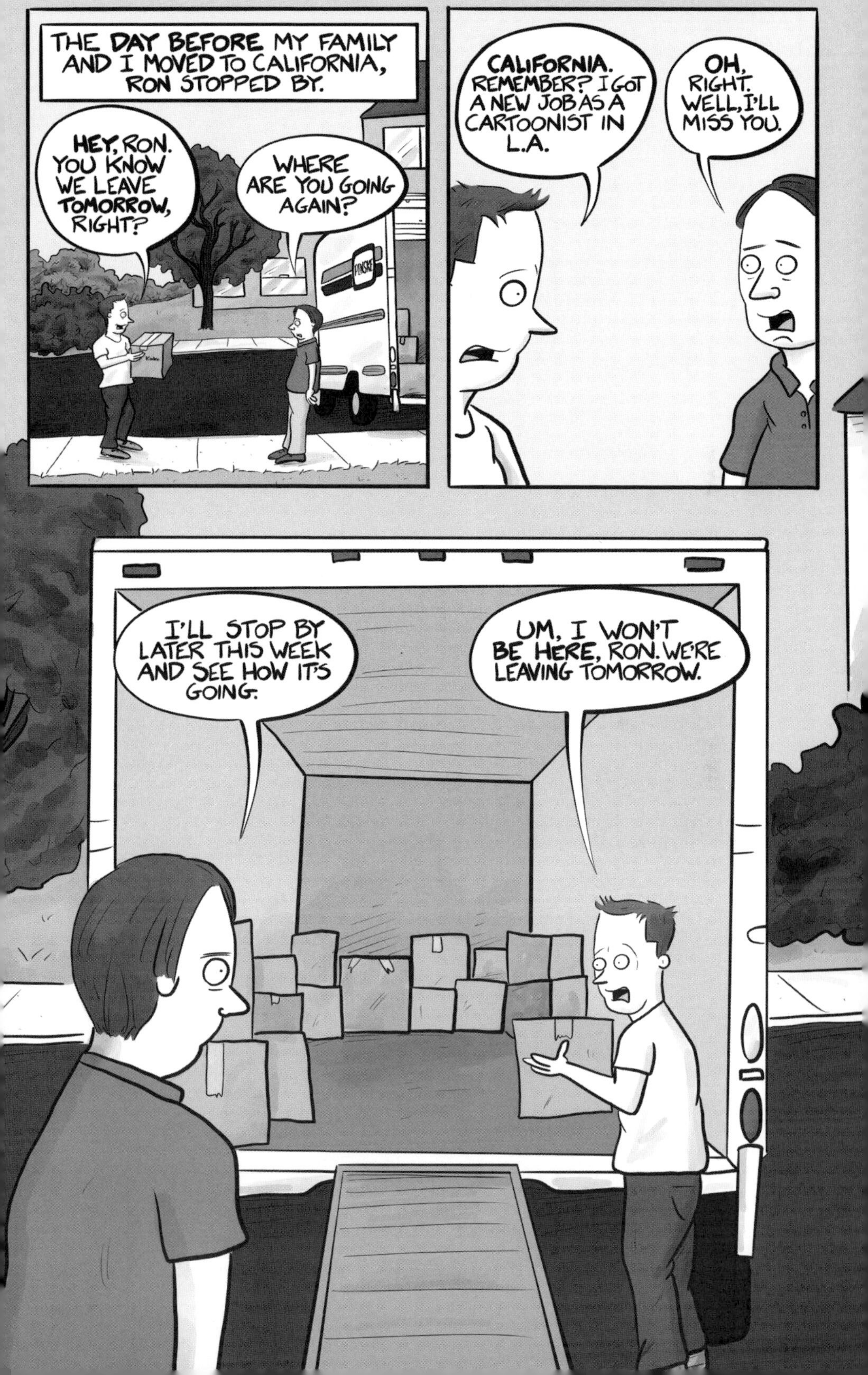
THE DAY BEFORE MY FAMILY AND I MOVED TO CALIFORNIA, RON STOPPED BY.
HEY, RON. YOU KNOW WE LEAVE TOMORROW, RIGHT?
WHERE ARE YOU GOING AGAIN?
CALIFORNIA. REMEMBER? I GOT A NEW JOB AS A CARTOONIST IN L.A.
OH, RIGHT. WELL, I'LL MISS YOU.
I'LL STOP BY LATER THIS WEEK AND SEE HOW IT'S GOING.
UM, I WON'T BE HERE, RON. WE'RE LEAVING TOMORROW.

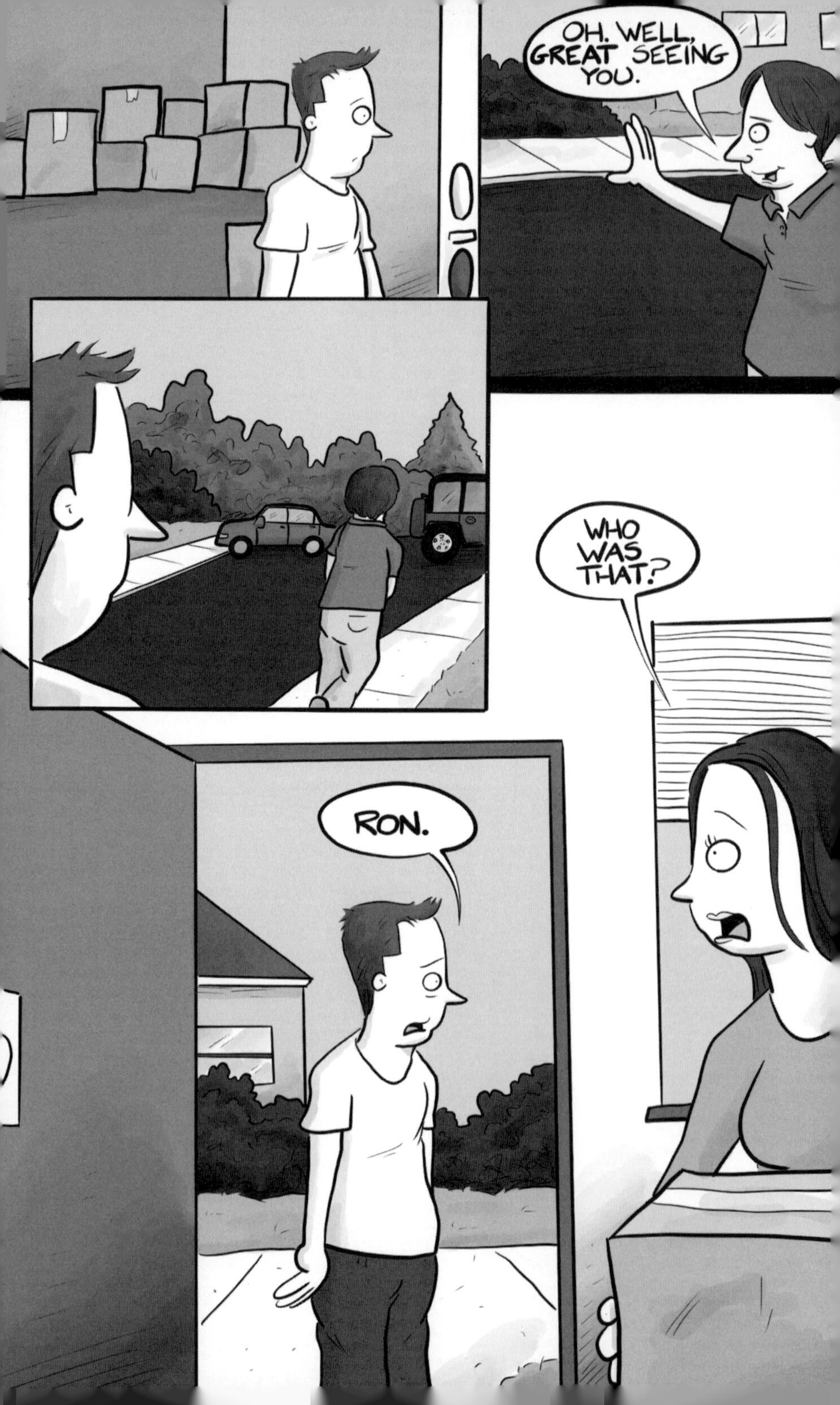
OH. WELL, GREAT SEEING YOU.
WHO WAS THAT?
RON.

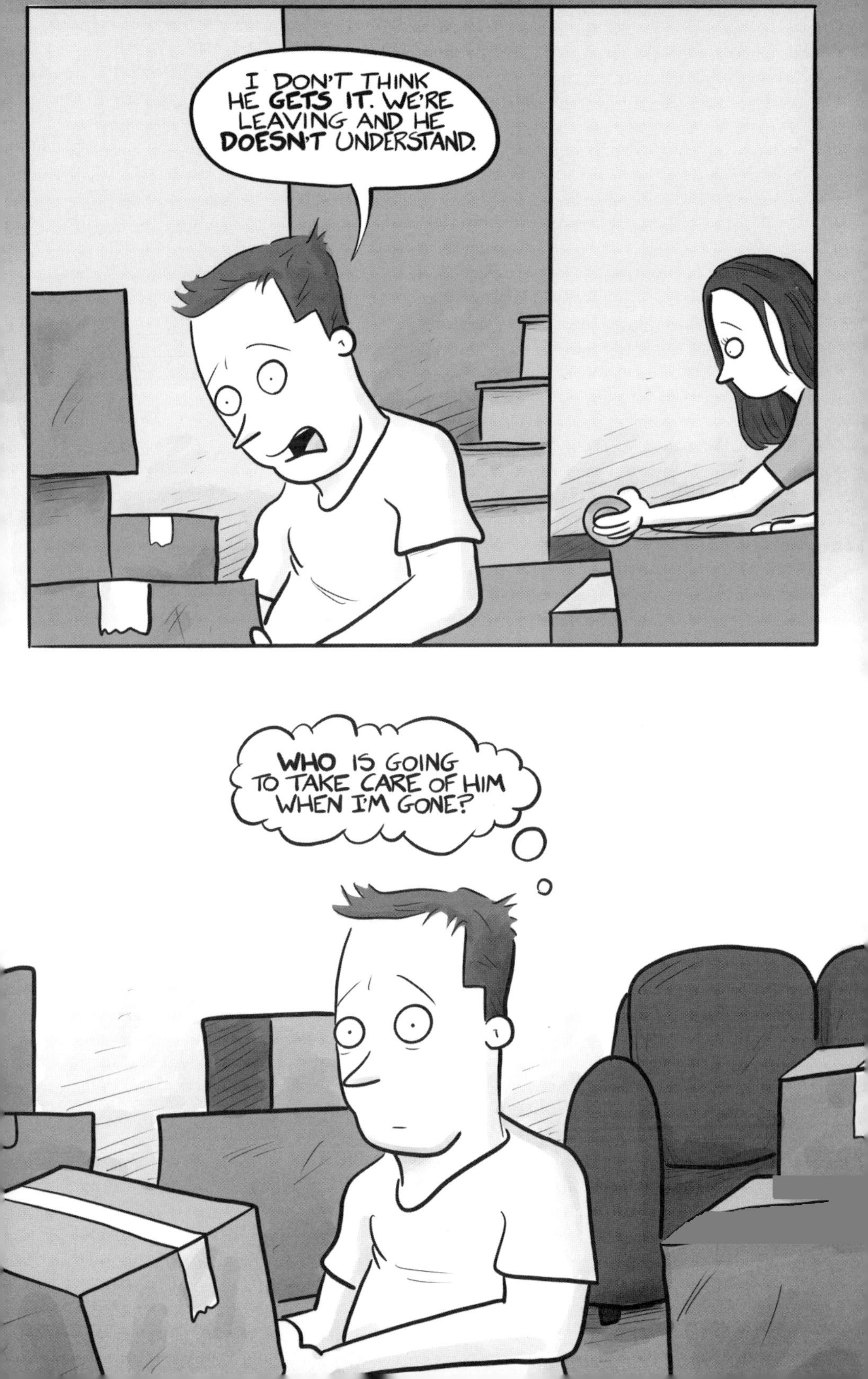
I DON'T THINK HE GETS IT. WE'RE LEAVING AND HE DOESN'T UNDERSTAND.
WHO IS GOING TO TAKE CARE OF HIM WHEN I'M GONE?

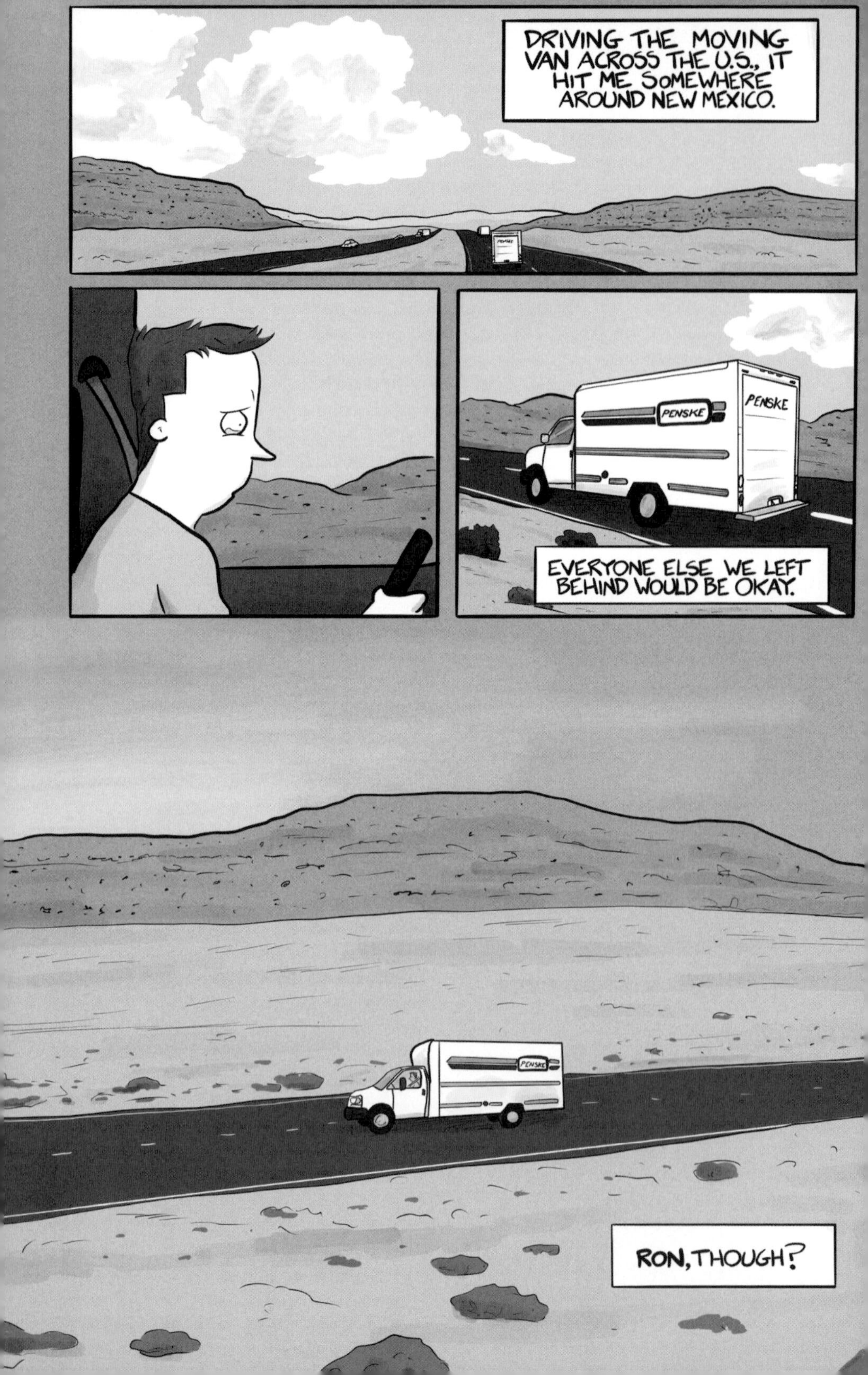
DRIVING THE MOVING VAN ACROSS THE U.S., IT HIT ME SOMEWHERE AROUND NEW MEXICO.
PENSKE
PENSKE
PENSKE
EVERYONE ELSE WE LEFT BEHIND WOULD BE OKAY.
PENSKE
RON, THOUGH?

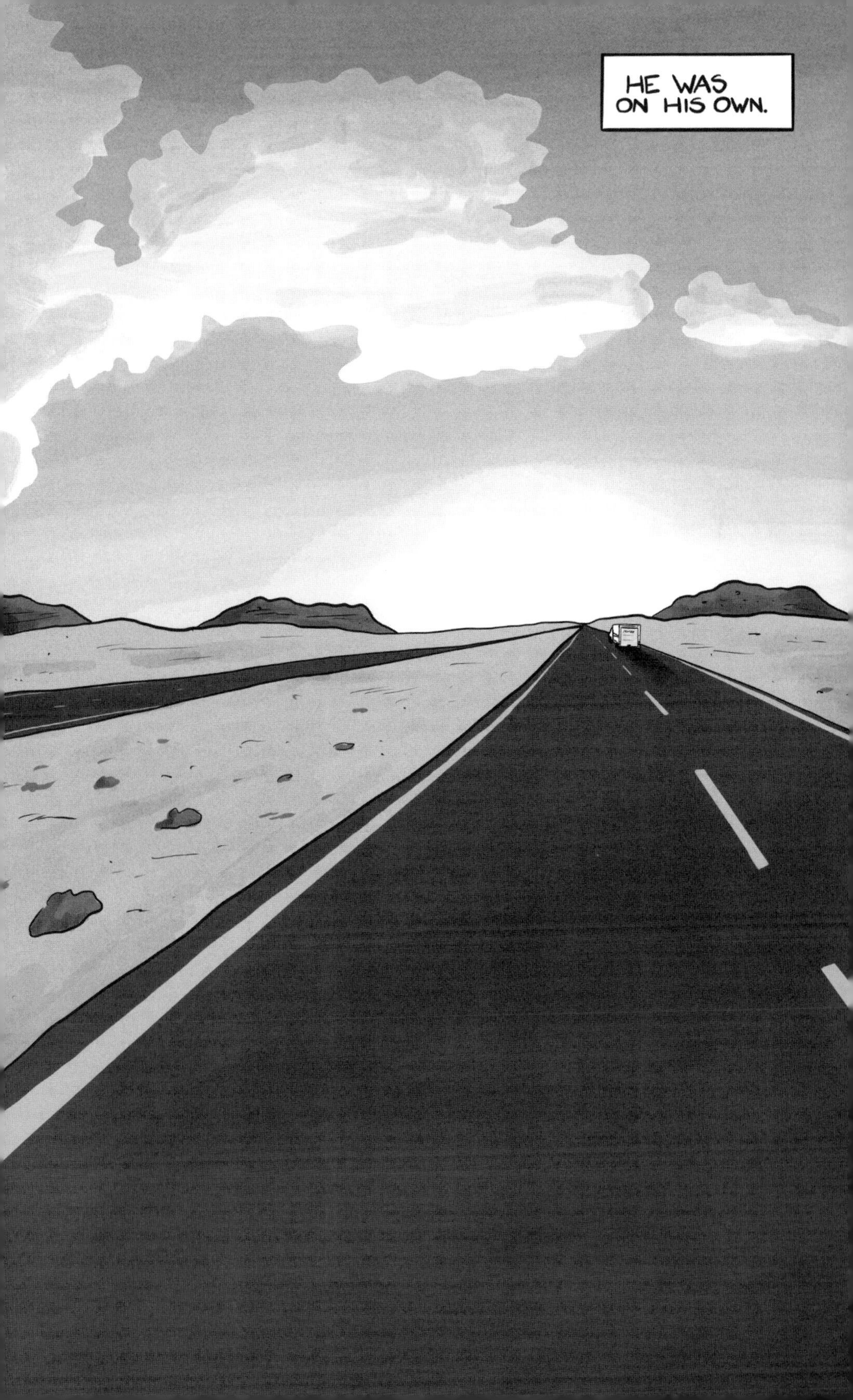
HE WAS ON HIS OWN.

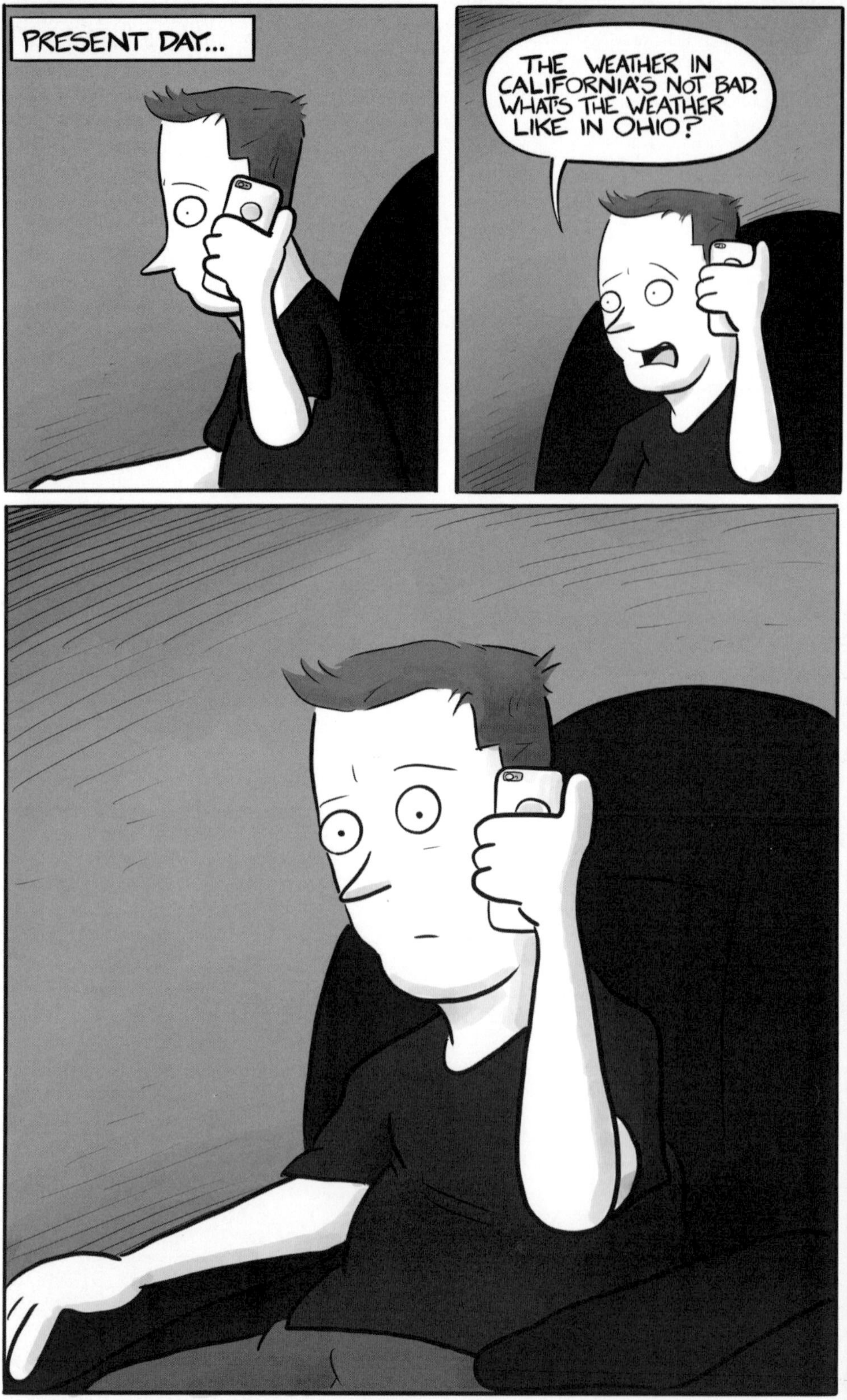
PRESENT DAY...
THE WEATHER IN CALIFORNIA'S NOT BAD. WHAT'S THE WEATHER LIKE IN OHIO?

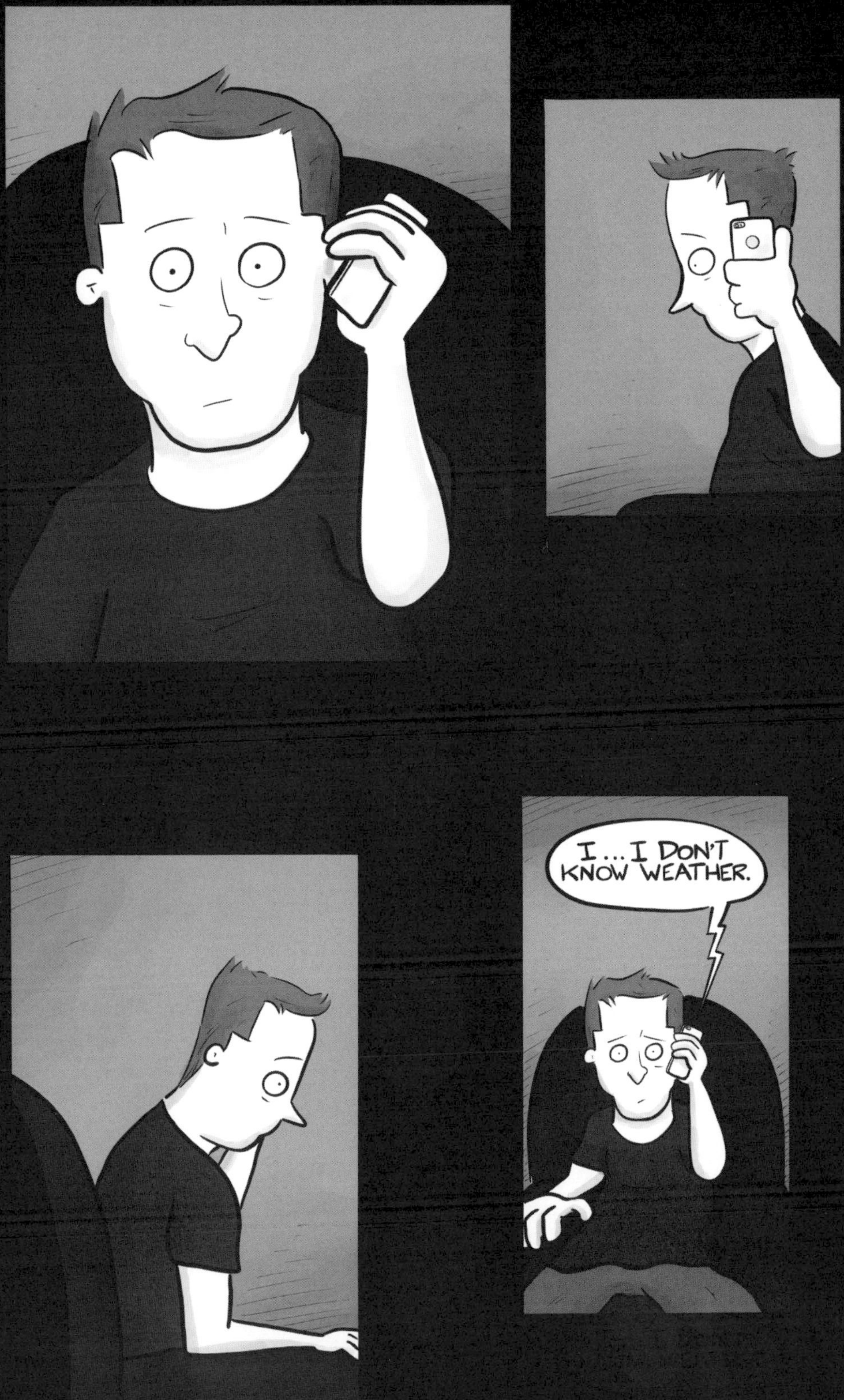
I... I DON'T KNOW WEATHER.

PART FOUR

THE FALL

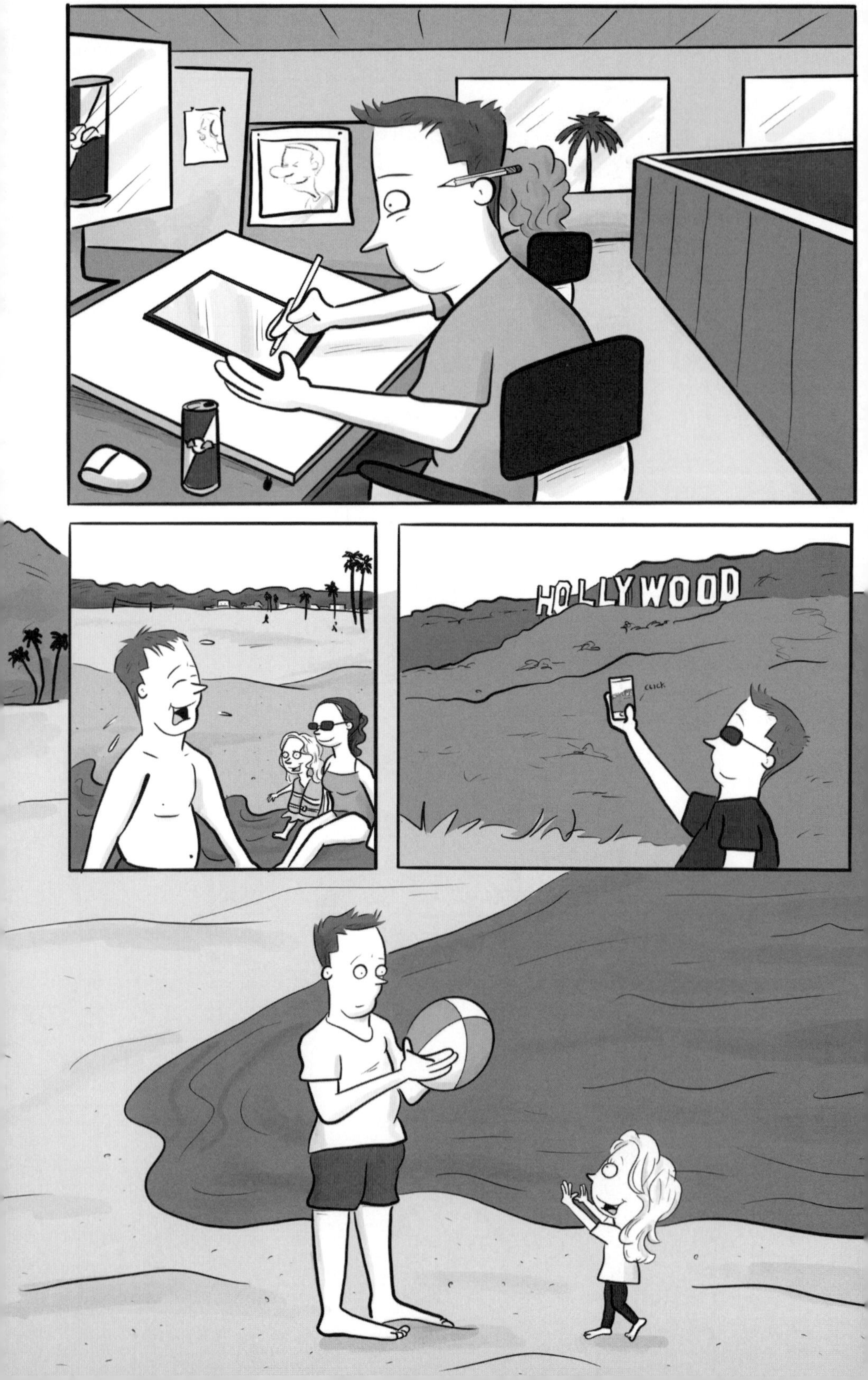
HOLLYWOOD
CLICK

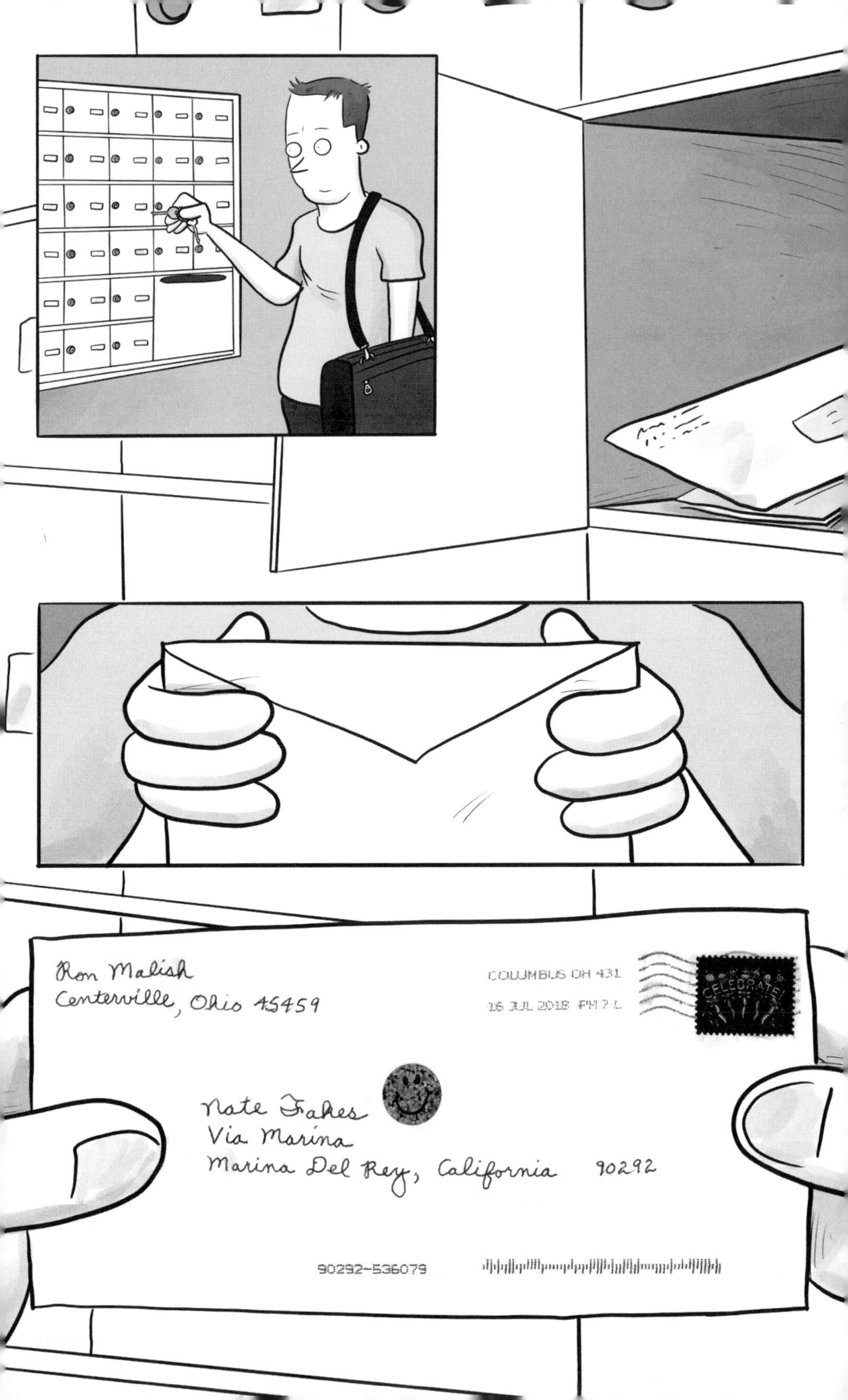

Ron Malish
Centerville, Ohio 45459
COLUMBUS OH 431
16 JUL 2018
CELEBRATE!
Nate Fakes
Via Marina
Marina Del Rey, California 90292
90292-536079

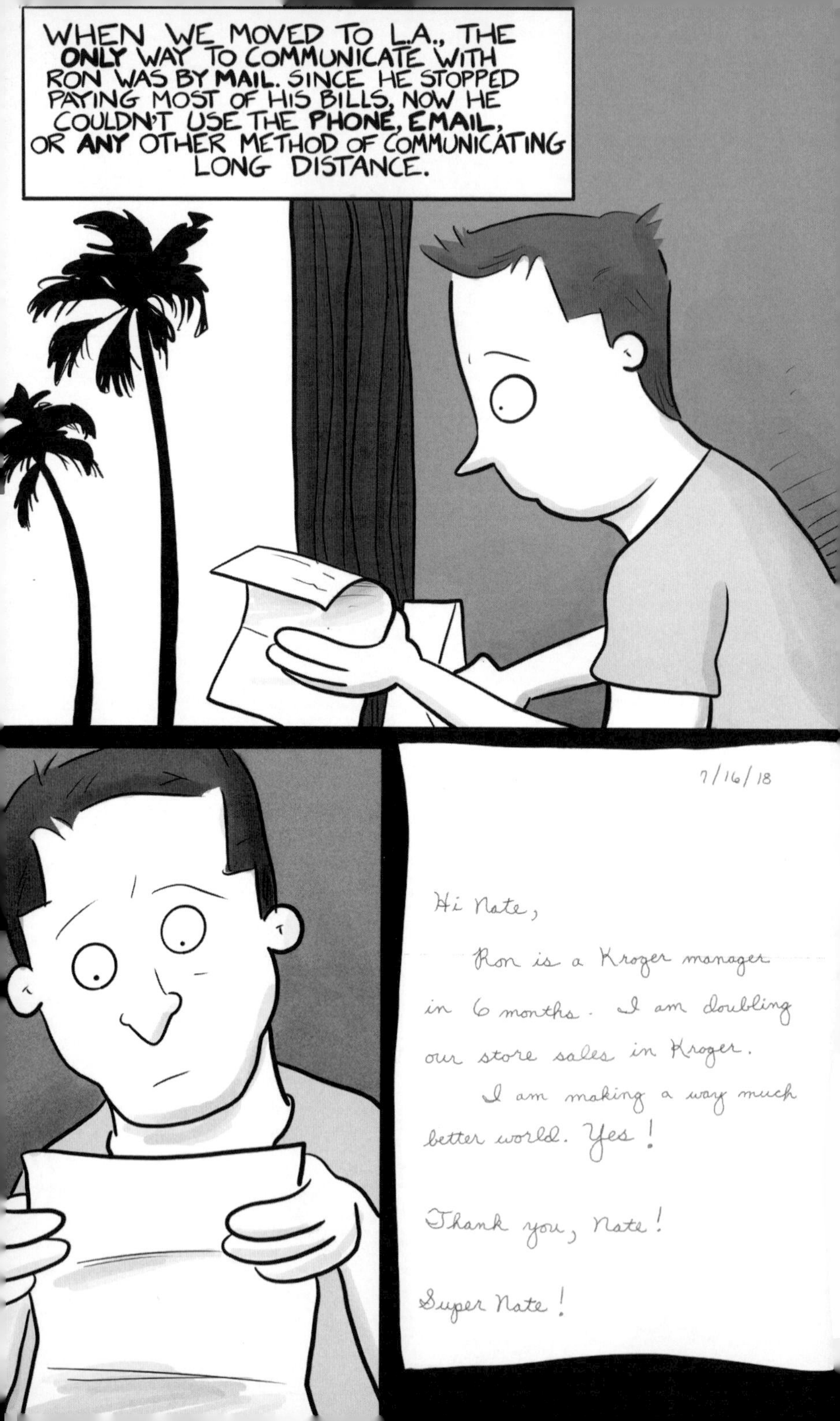
WHEN WE MOVED TO L.A., THE **ONLY** WAY TO COMMUNICATE WITH RON WAS BY **MAIL**. SINCE HE STOPPED PAYING MOST OF HIS BILLS, NOW HE COULDN'T USE THE **PHONE**, **EMAIL**, OR **ANY** OTHER METHOD OF COMMUNICATING LONG DISTANCE.
7/16/18
Hi Nate,
Ron is a Kroger manager in 6 months. I am doubling our store sales in Kroger.
I am making a way much better world. Yes!
Thank you, Nate!
Super Nate!

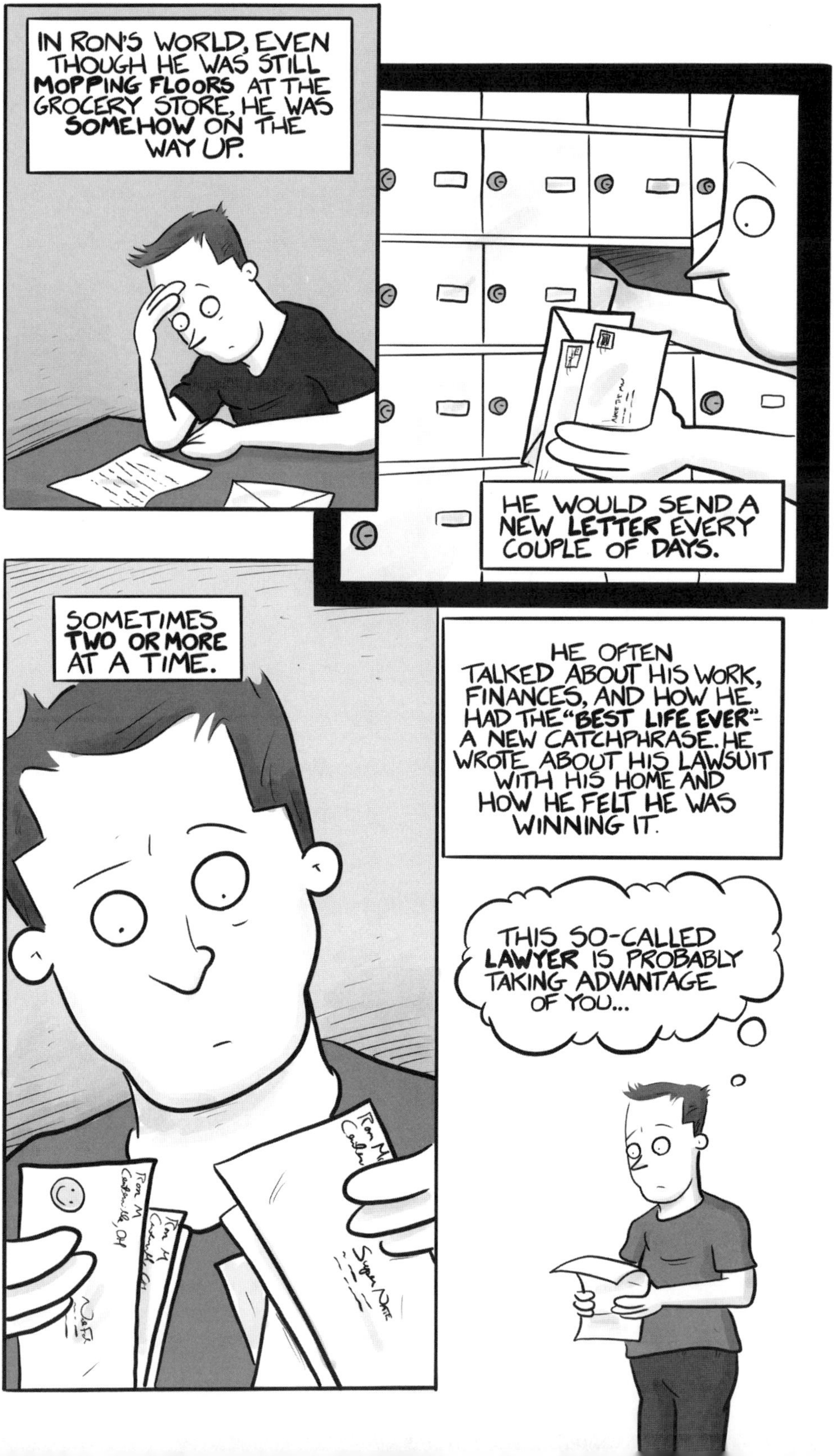
IN RON'S WORLD, EVEN THOUGH HE WAS STILL **MOPPING FLOORS** AT THE GROCERY STORE, HE WAS **SOMEHOW** ON THE WAY UP.
HE WOULD SEND A NEW **LETTER** EVERY COUPLE OF **DAYS.**
SOMETIMES **TWO OR MORE** AT A TIME.
HE OFTEN TALKED ABOUT HIS WORK, FINANCES, AND HOW HE HAD THE "**BEST LIFE EVER**"- A NEW CATCHPHRASE. HE WROTE ABOUT HIS LAWSUIT WITH HIS HOME AND HOW HE FELT HE WAS WINNING IT.
THIS SO-CALLED **LAWYER** IS PROBABLY TAKING ADVANTAGE OF YOU...

RON WAS ALSO TRYING TO SELL A **HEALTH PLAN** AROUND THE CENTERVILLE AND DAYTON AREA. IN HIS LETTERS, HE TOLD ME THAT HE PASSED OUT INFORMATION ABOUT IT AT MALLS, DOOR TO DOOR, AND **ALL OVER THE PLACE.**

OF COURSE, HE SENT IT TO ME AS WELL.

ONE OF THE PERKS OF IT WAS LIVING FOREVER.

Family health is number one.

Ron Malish;

You can have one FREE family health meeting for the very best family health. I am making a much better world starting in Centerville.

Do you want your family to sometimes work on living forever. I kept studying to live forever over 30 years. At my age 57 years old, most all people keep telling me that I am looking younger than 57 years old. I keep feeling like the health of a very healthy kid. I do not need to take any medicines, because of my very excellent foods, distilled water, oxygen and my very best family health plan.

I keep spending thousands of dollars to keep studying health for families to keep living. If you have any questions, you can have a free meeting with me Ronald Kevin Malish ████████ ███ Centerville, Ohio 45459. 9am to 5pm Monday thru Friday. I work in my home to not waste money, I will not be working in an expensive office, for excellent family health meetings.

I have 100% protein, carbohydrates, vitamins, minerals everyday and other most important, too. I would like kids parents to sometimes study to keep working on living forever, for their families. My health books, cd's, tape recorders and online I keep seeing most people not working excellently very well for peoples health. Even when books, cd's, tape recorders also online are very expensive. Once again you can come to my home.████████ ████ in Centerville and have a FREE family health meeting to take a look at my very best family health plan.

Later on some people can give me $25 once a year to keep making our world much better for families health. So I can always keep studying health. I do not need people to give me more than $25 a year. You can keep having free family health meetings all year to keep working on making our world much better for families.

Once again I want to keep making our world better starting in Centerville. You can practice the very best family health plan sometimes for best health numbers.

Ronald Kevin Malish

Ronald Kevin Malish

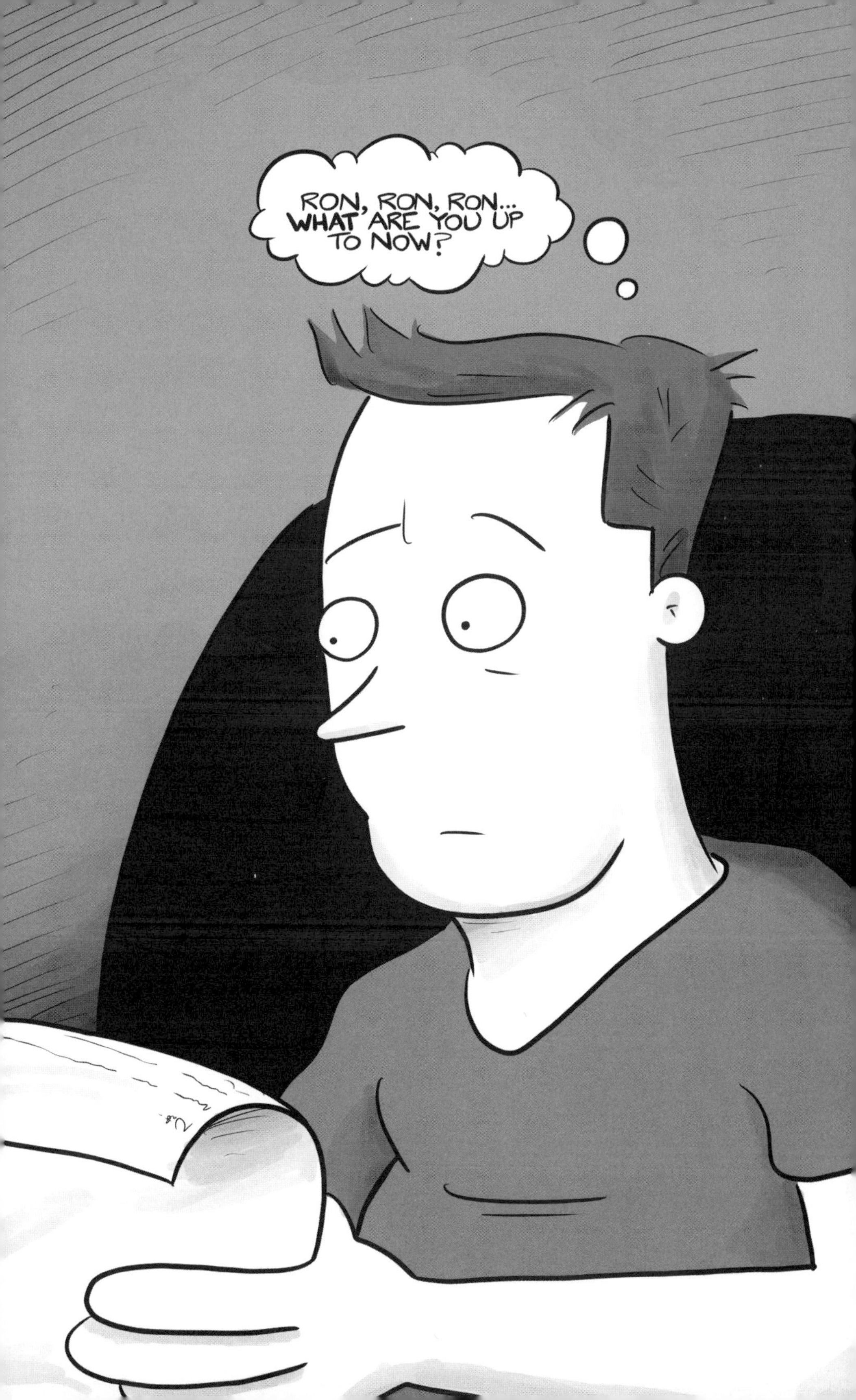
RON, RON, RON... WHAT ARE YOU UP TO NOW?

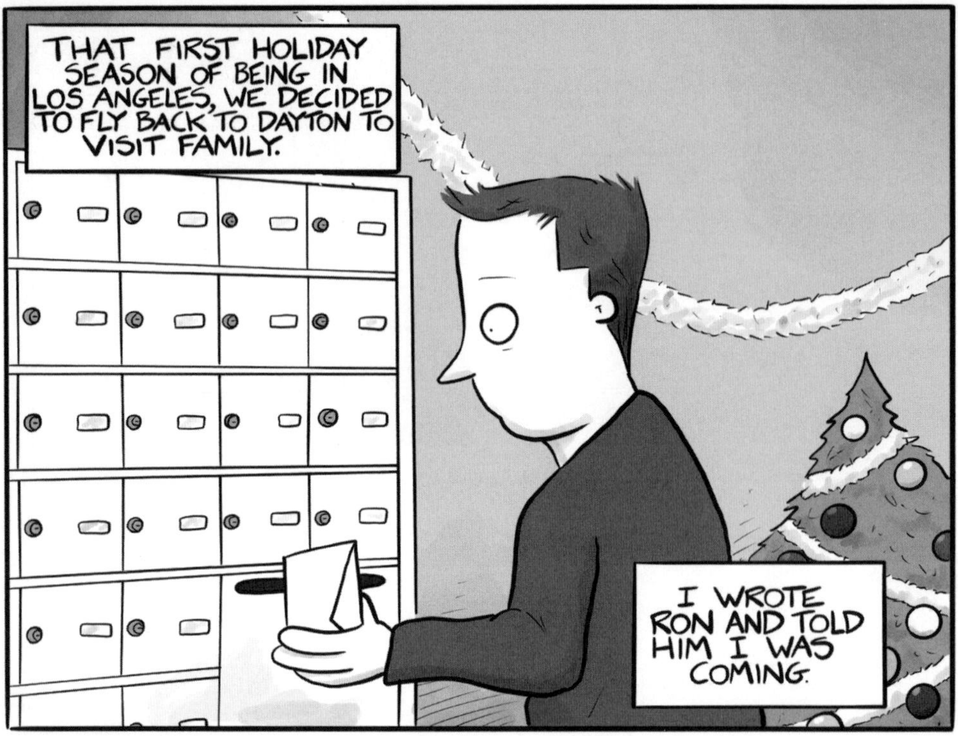
THAT FIRST HOLIDAY SEASON OF BEING IN LOS ANGELES, WE DECIDED TO FLY BACK TO DAYTON TO VISIT FAMILY.
I WROTE RON AND TOLD HIM I WAS COMING.

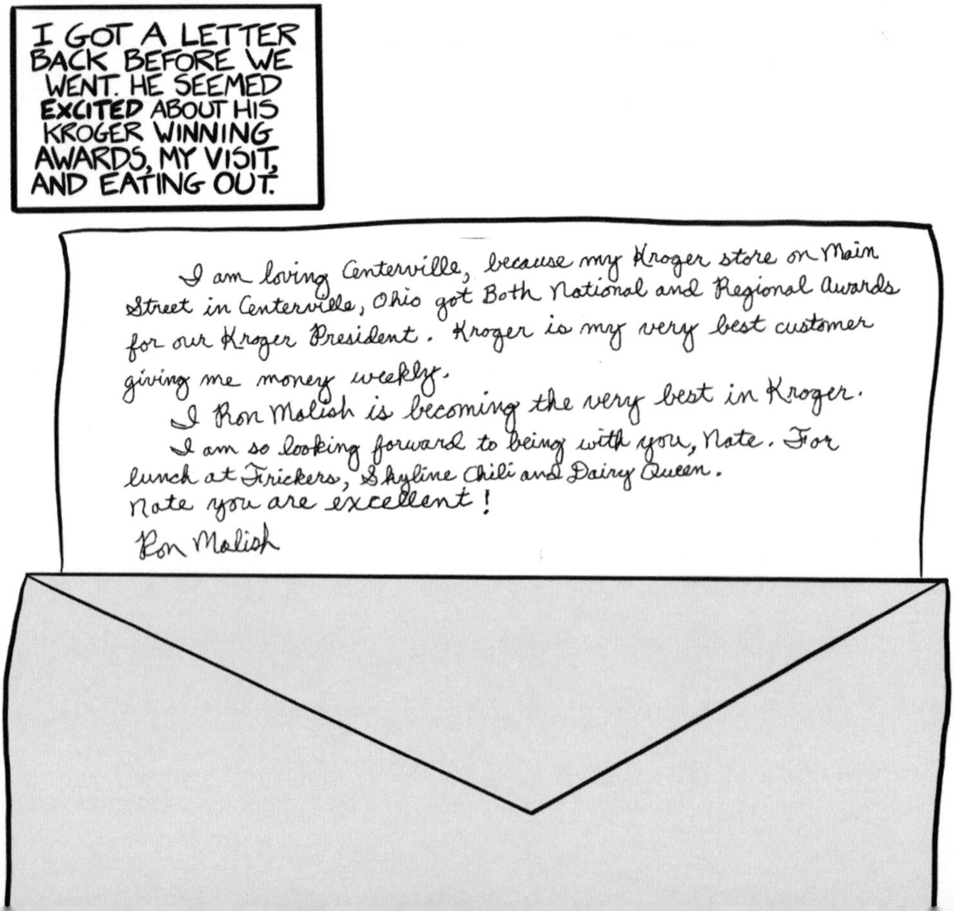
I GOT A LETTER BACK BEFORE WE WENT. HE SEEMED **EXCITED** ABOUT HIS KROGER WINNING AWARDS, MY VISIT, AND EATING OUT.
I am loving Centerville, because my Kroger store on Main Street in Centerville, Ohio got Both National and Regional Awards for our Kroger President. Kroger is my very best customer giving me money weekly.
I Ron Malish is becoming the very best in Kroger.
I am so looking forward to being with you, Nate. For lunch at Frickers, Skyline Chili and Dairy Queen.
Nate you are excellent!
Ron Malish

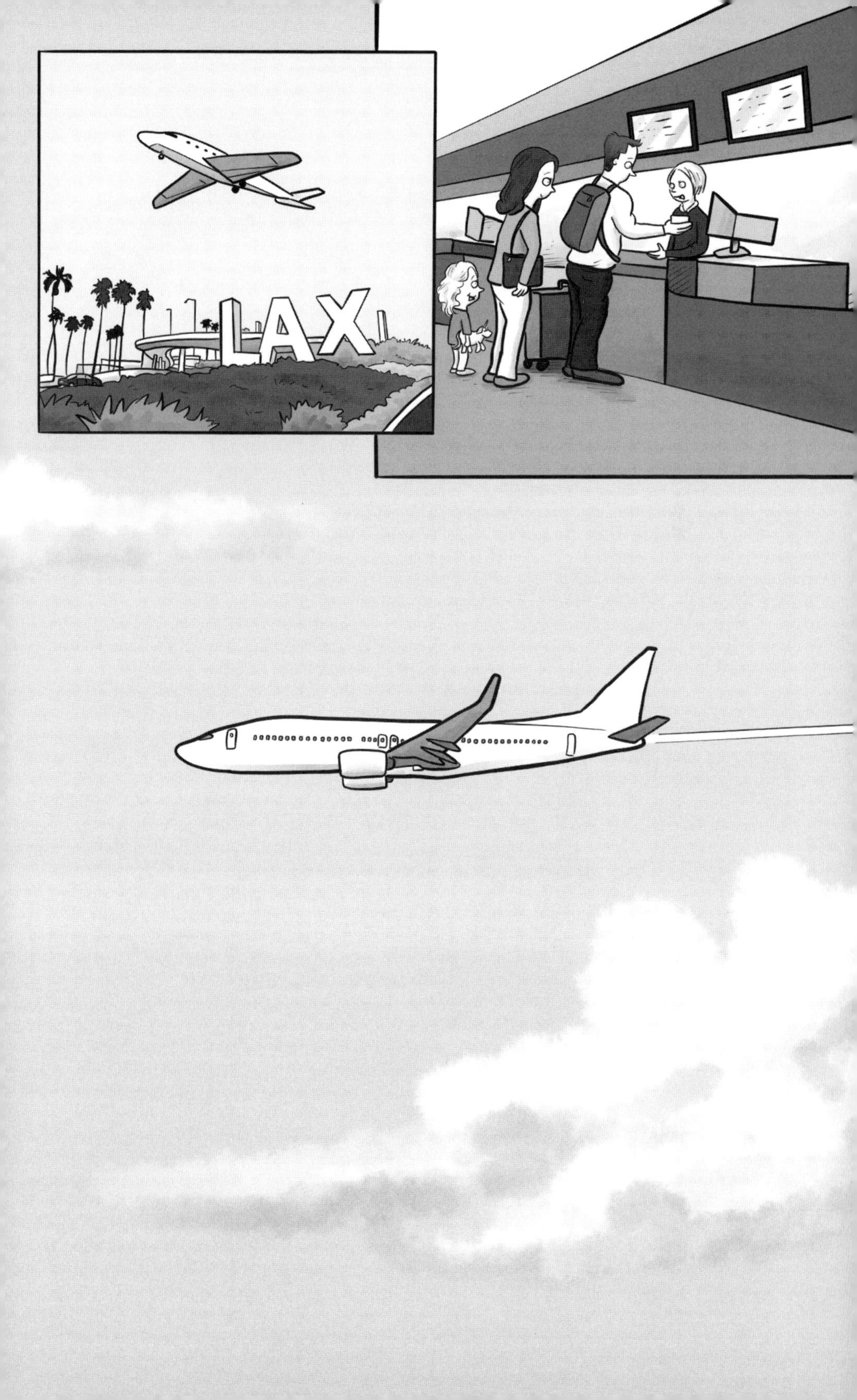
LAX

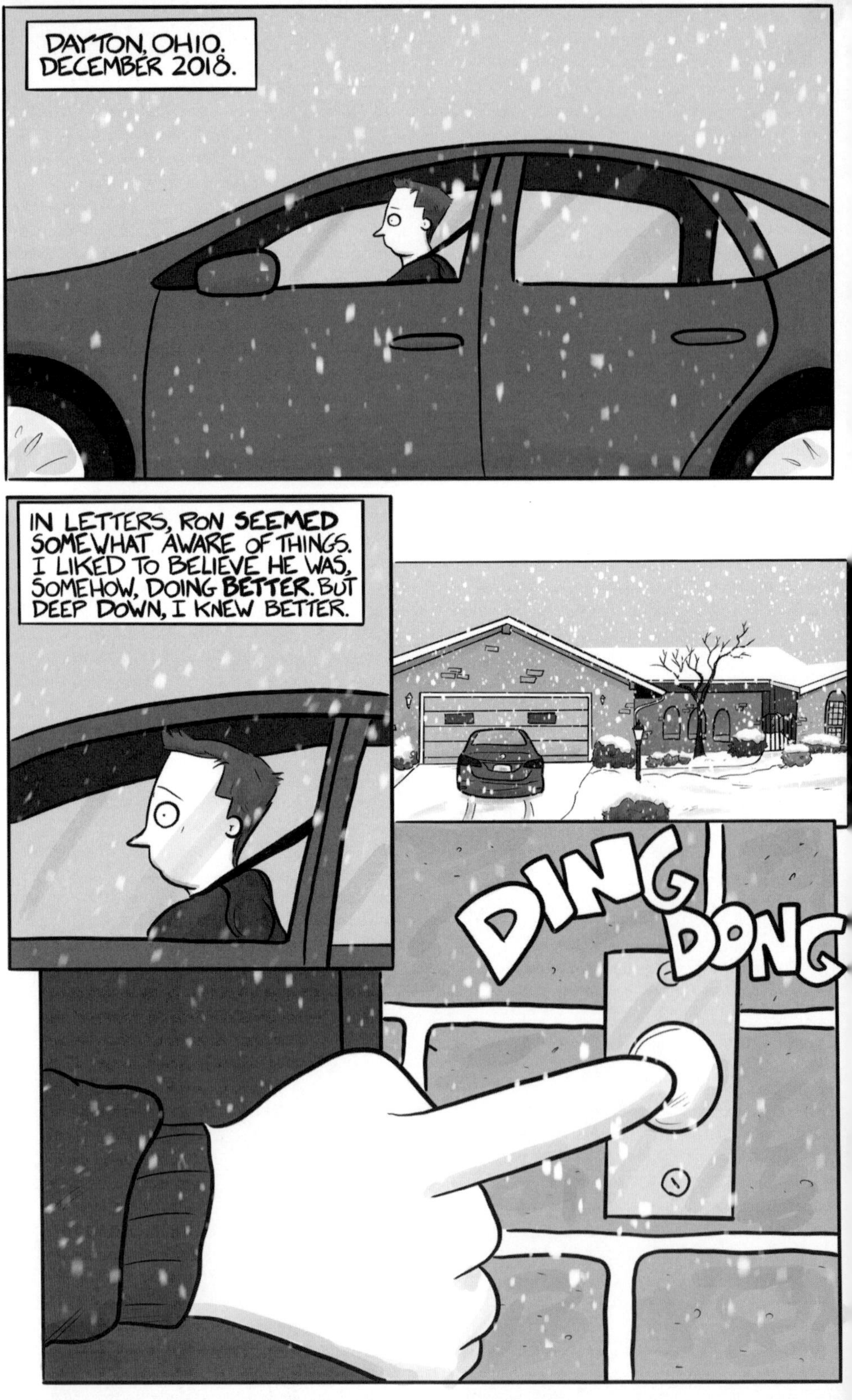
DAYTON, OHIO.
DECEMBER 2018.
IN LETTERS, RON SEEMED SOMEWHAT AWARE OF THINGS. I LIKED TO BELIEVE HE WAS, SOMEHOW, DOING BETTER. BUT DEEP DOWN, I KNEW BETTER.
DING DONG

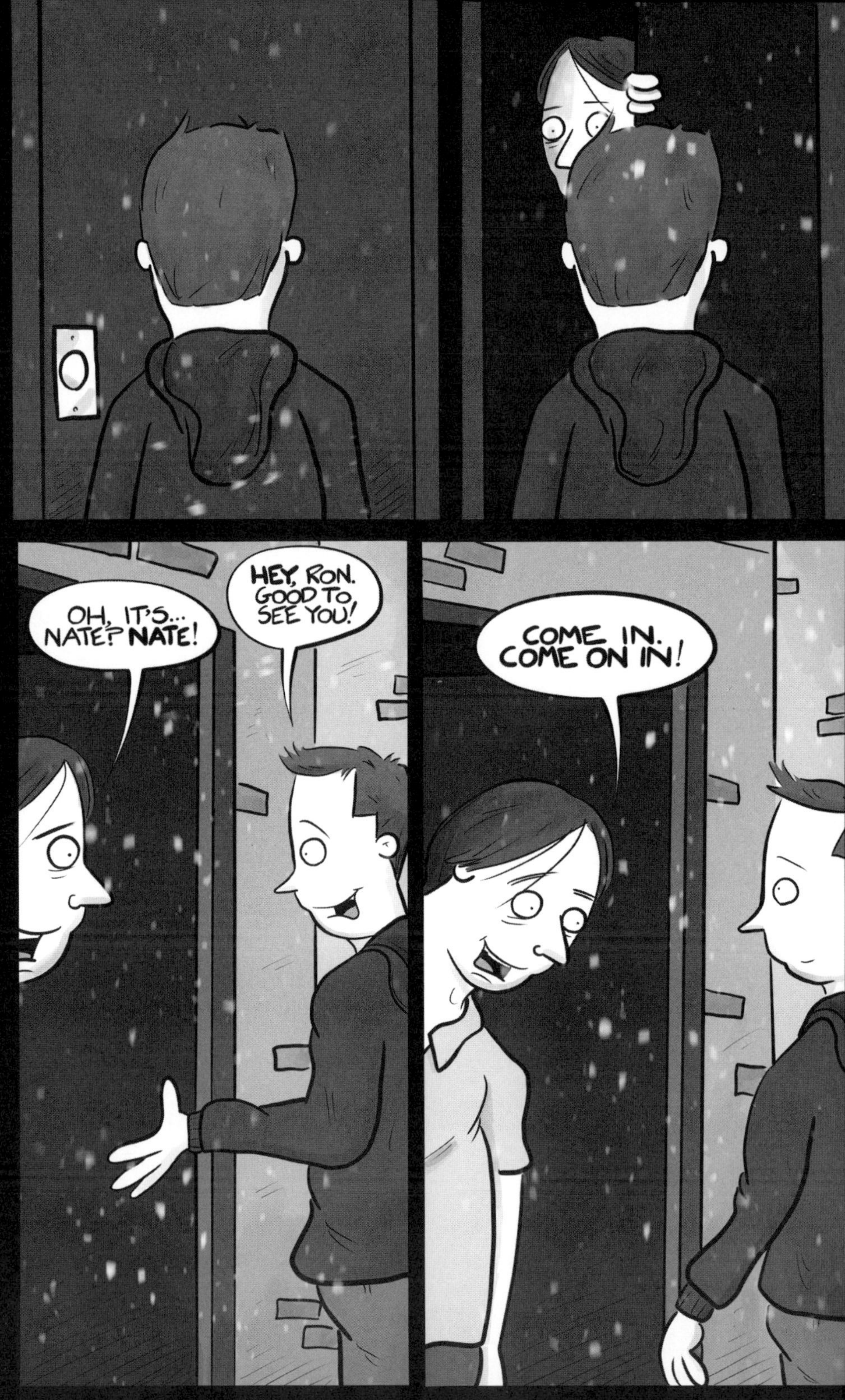
OH, IT'S... NATE? NATE!
HEY, RON. GOOD TO SEE YOU!
COME IN. COME ON IN!

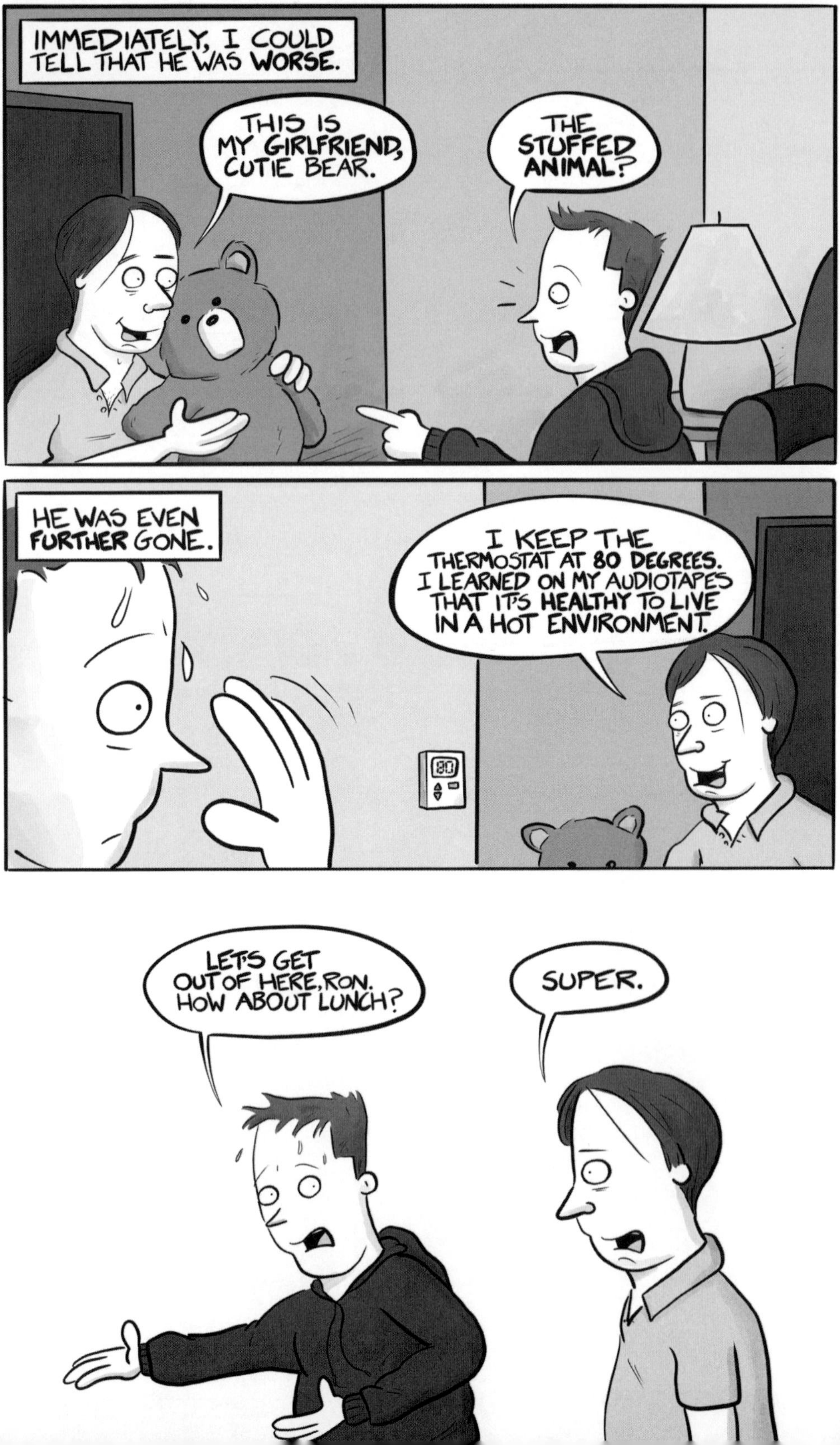
IMMEDIATELY, I COULD TELL THAT HE WAS WORSE.
THIS IS MY GIRLFRIEND, CUTIE BEAR.
THE STUFFED ANIMAL?
HE WAS EVEN FURTHER GONE.
I KEEP THE THERMOSTAT AT 80 DEGREES. I LEARNED ON MY AUDIOTAPES THAT IT'S HEALTHY TO LIVE IN A HOT ENVIRONMENT.
80
LET'S GET OUT OF HERE, RON. HOW ABOUT LUNCH?
SUPER.

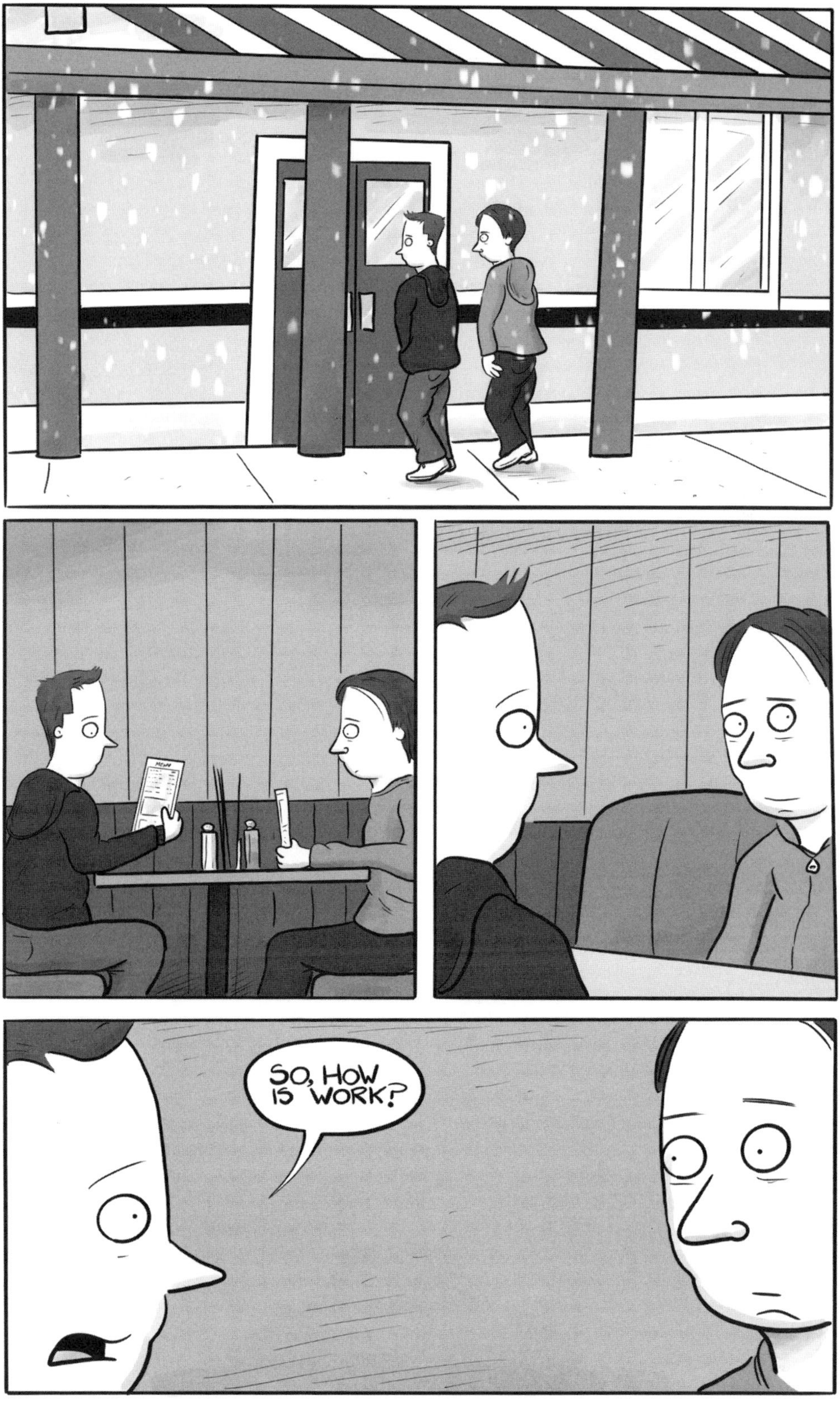
SO, HOW IS WORK?

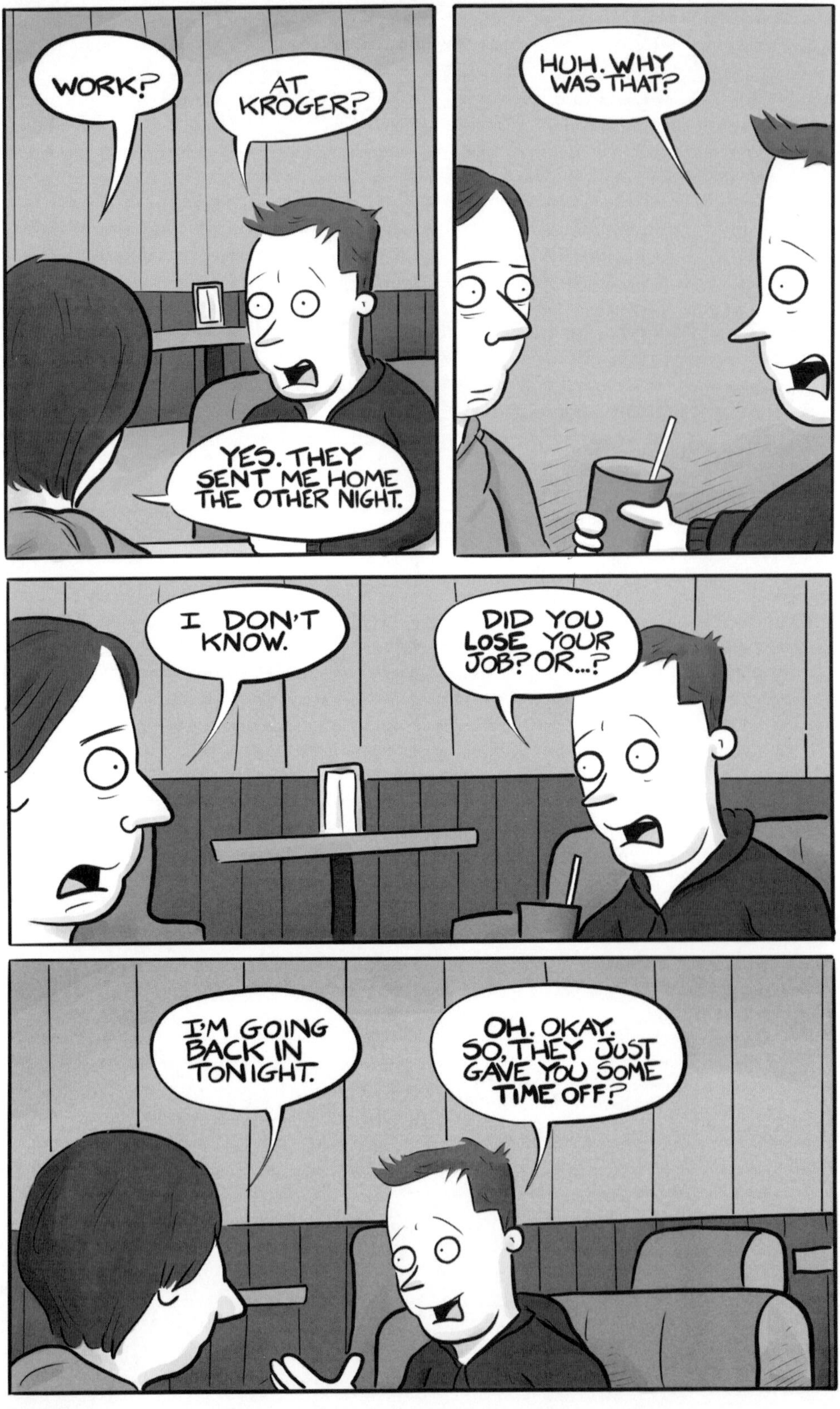
WORK?
AT KROGER?
YES. THEY SENT ME HOME THE OTHER NIGHT.
HUH. WHY WAS THAT?
I DON'T KNOW.
DID YOU LOSE YOUR JOB? OR...?
I'M GOING BACK IN TONIGHT.
OH. OKAY. SO, THEY JUST GAVE YOU SOME TIME OFF?

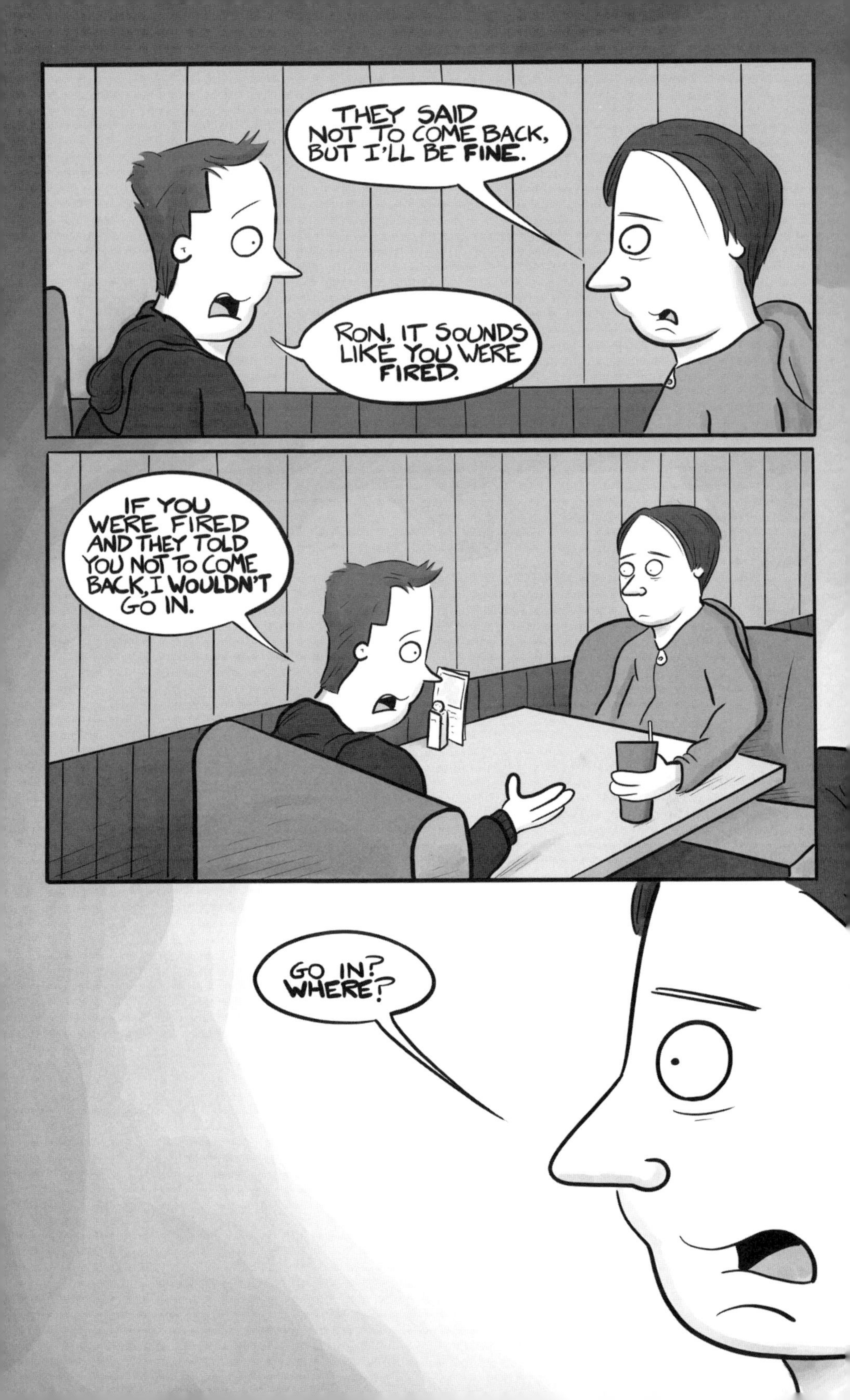
THEY SAID NOT TO COME BACK, BUT I'LL BE **FINE**.
RON, IT SOUNDS LIKE YOU WERE **FIRED**.
IF YOU WERE FIRED AND THEY TOLD YOU NOT TO COME BACK, I **WOULDN'T** GO IN.
GO IN? **WHERE?**

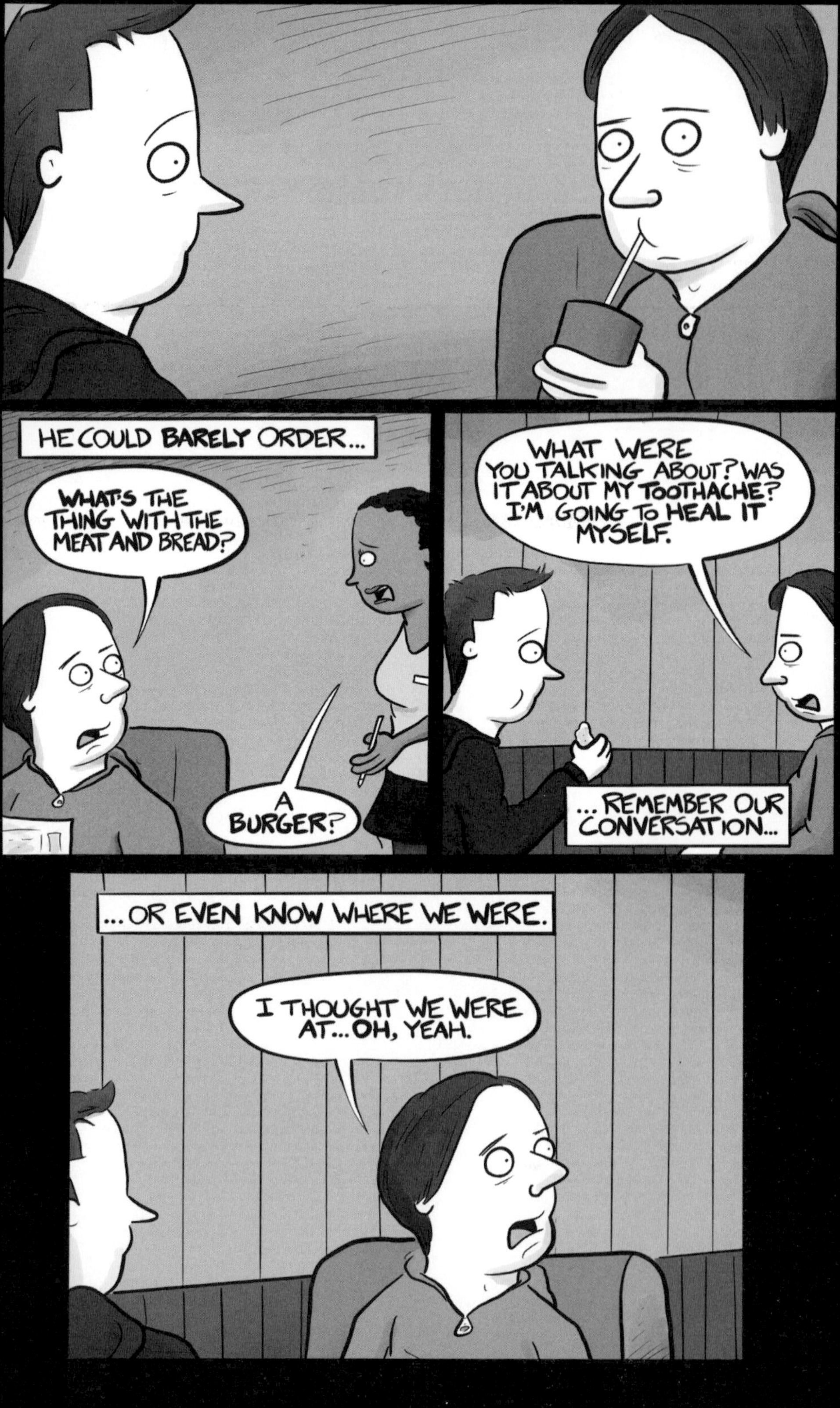
HE COULD BARELY ORDER...
WHAT'S THE THING WITH THE MEAT AND BREAD?
A BURGER?
WHAT WERE YOU TALKING ABOUT? WAS IT ABOUT MY TOOTHACHE? I'M GOING TO HEAL IT MYSELF.
...REMEMBER OUR CONVERSATION...
...OR EVEN KNOW WHERE WE WERE.
I THOUGHT WE WERE AT...OH, YEAH.

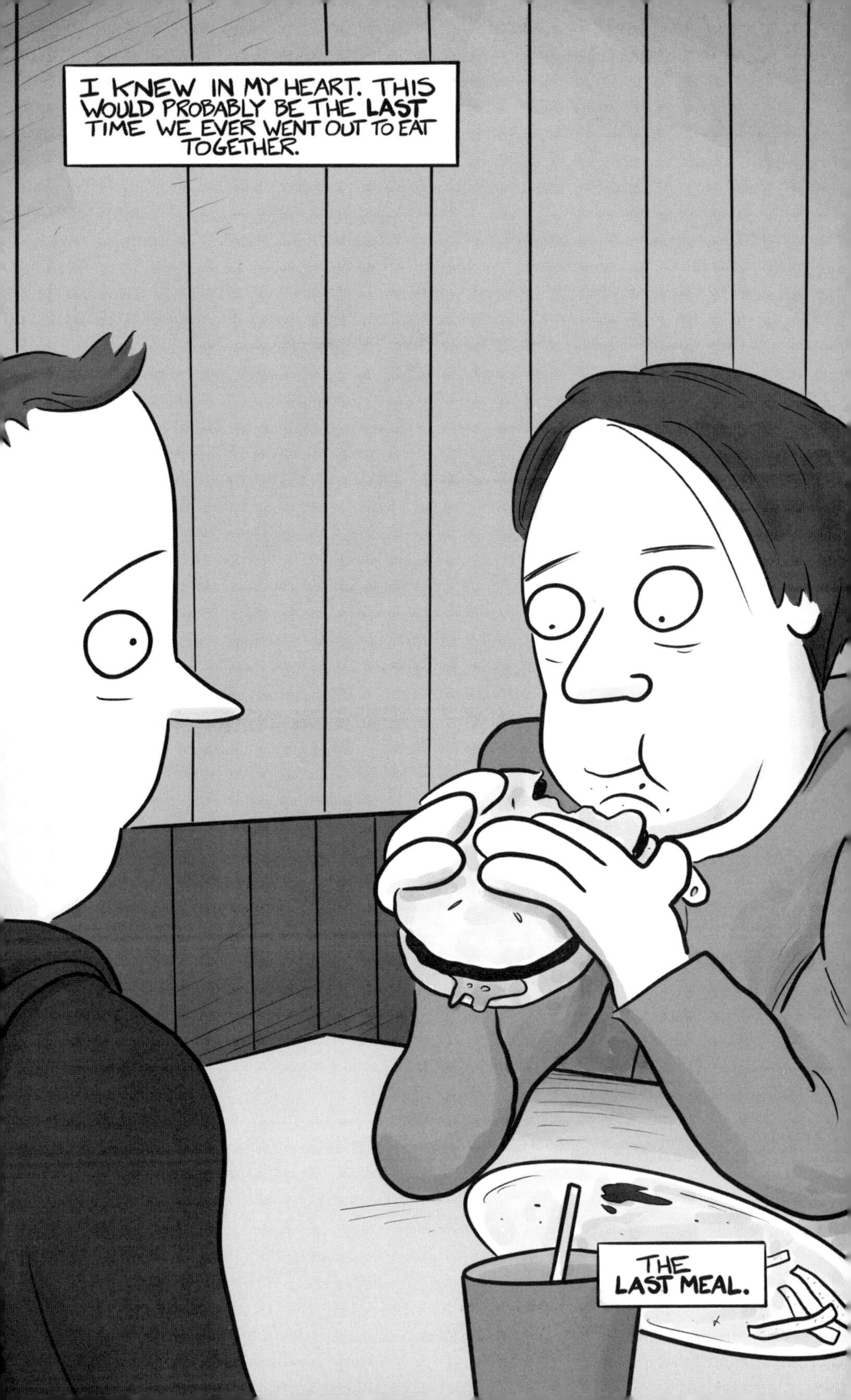
I KNEW IN MY HEART. THIS WOULD PROBABLY BE THE LAST TIME WE EVER WENT OUT TO EAT TOGETHER.
THE LAST MEAL.

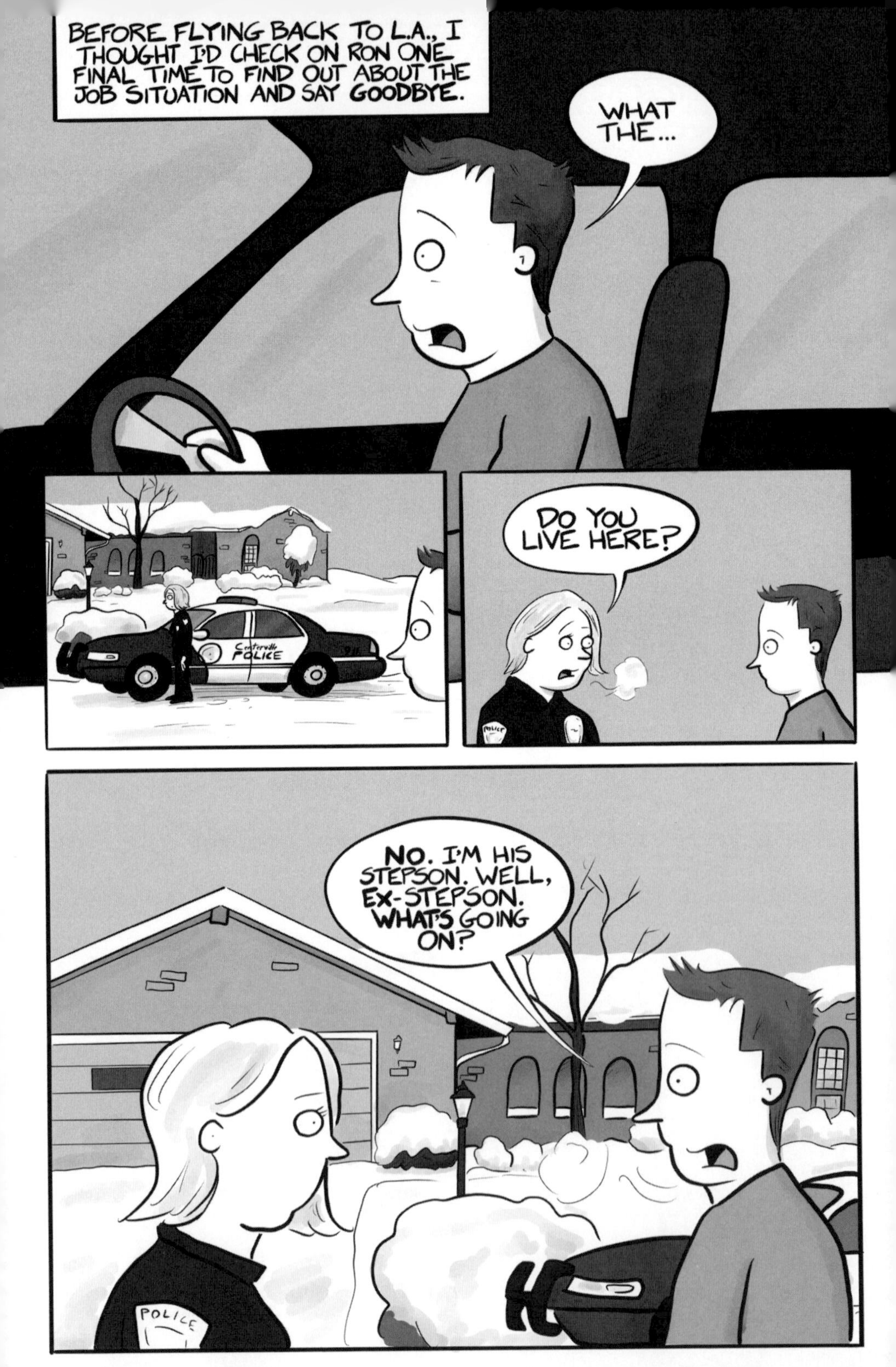
BEFORE FLYING BACK TO L.A., I THOUGHT I'D CHECK ON RON ONE FINAL TIME TO FIND OUT ABOUT THE JOB SITUATION AND SAY GOODBYE.
WHAT THE...
DO YOU LIVE HERE?
NO. I'M HIS STEPSON. WELL, EX-STEPSON. WHAT'S GOING ON?
POLICE

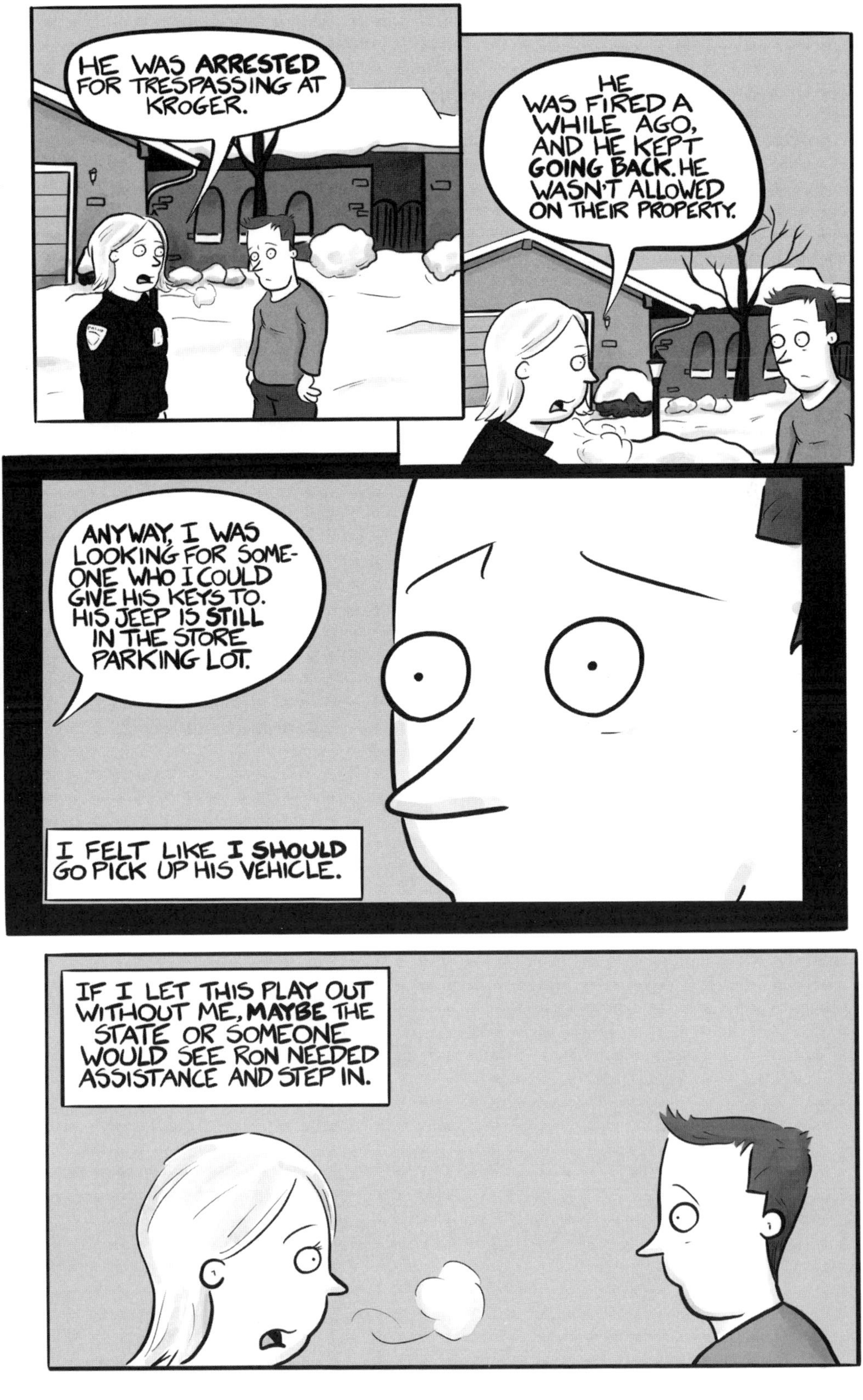
HE WAS ARRESTED FOR TRESPASSING AT KROGER.
HE WAS FIRED A WHILE AGO, AND HE KEPT GOING BACK. HE WASN'T ALLOWED ON THEIR PROPERTY.
ANYWAY, I WAS LOOKING FOR SOME-ONE WHO I COULD GIVE HIS KEYS TO. HIS JEEP IS STILL IN THE STORE PARKING LOT.
I FELT LIKE I SHOULD GO PICK UP HIS VEHICLE.
IF I LET THIS PLAY OUT WITHOUT ME, MAYBE THE STATE OR SOMEONE WOULD SEE RON NEEDED ASSISTANCE AND STEP IN.

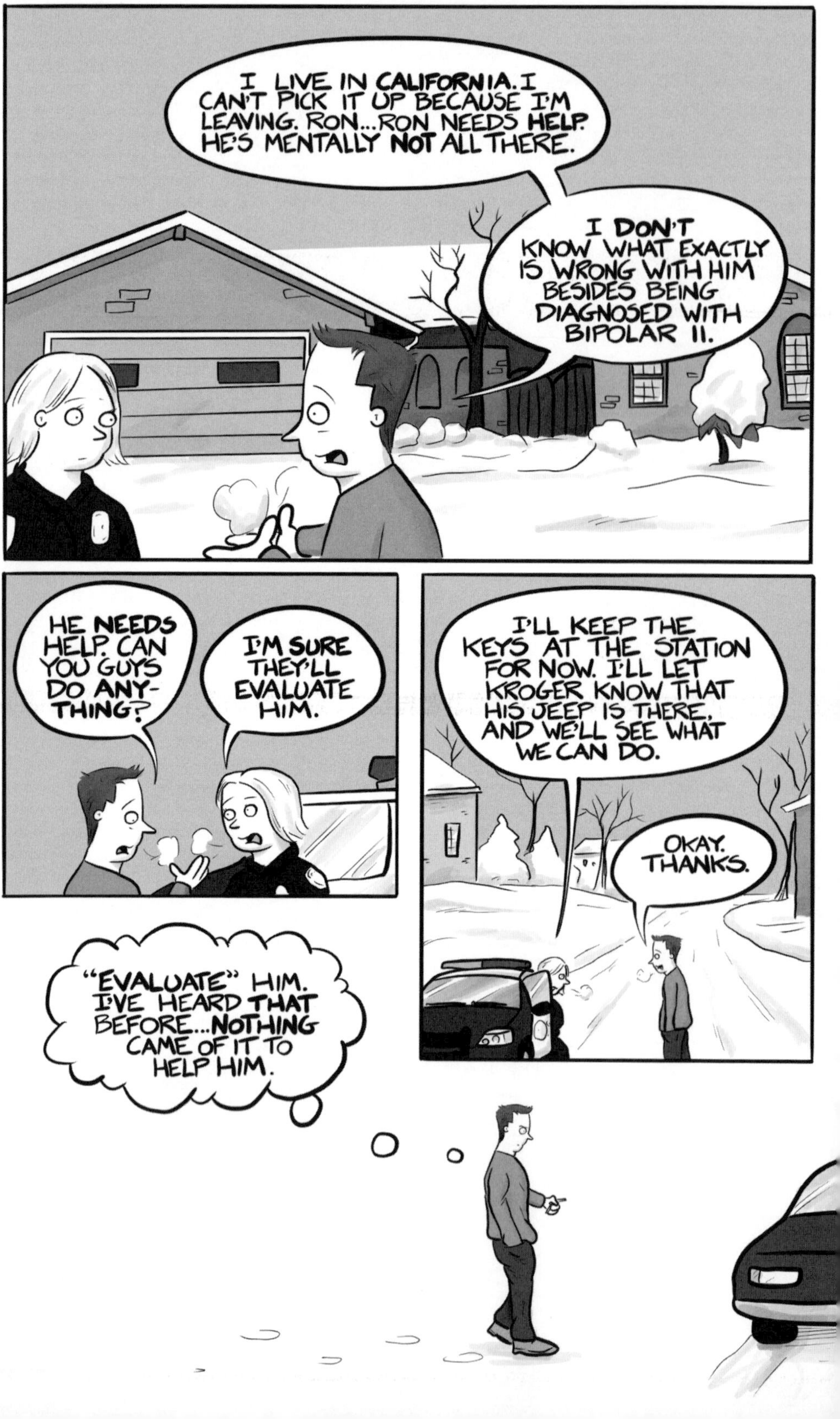
I LIVE IN CALIFORNIA. I CAN'T PICK IT UP BECAUSE I'M LEAVING. RON...RON NEEDS HELP. HE'S MENTALLY NOT ALL THERE.
I DON'T KNOW WHAT EXACTLY IS WRONG WITH HIM BESIDES BEING DIAGNOSED WITH BIPOLAR II.
HE NEEDS HELP. CAN YOU GUYS DO ANY-THING?
I'M SURE THEY'LL EVALUATE HIM.
I'LL KEEP THE KEYS AT THE STATION FOR NOW. I'LL LET KROGER KNOW THAT HIS JEEP IS THERE, AND WE'LL SEE WHAT WE CAN DO.
OKAY. THANKS.
"EVALUATE" HIM. I'VE HEARD THAT BEFORE...NOTHING CAME OF IT TO HELP HIM.

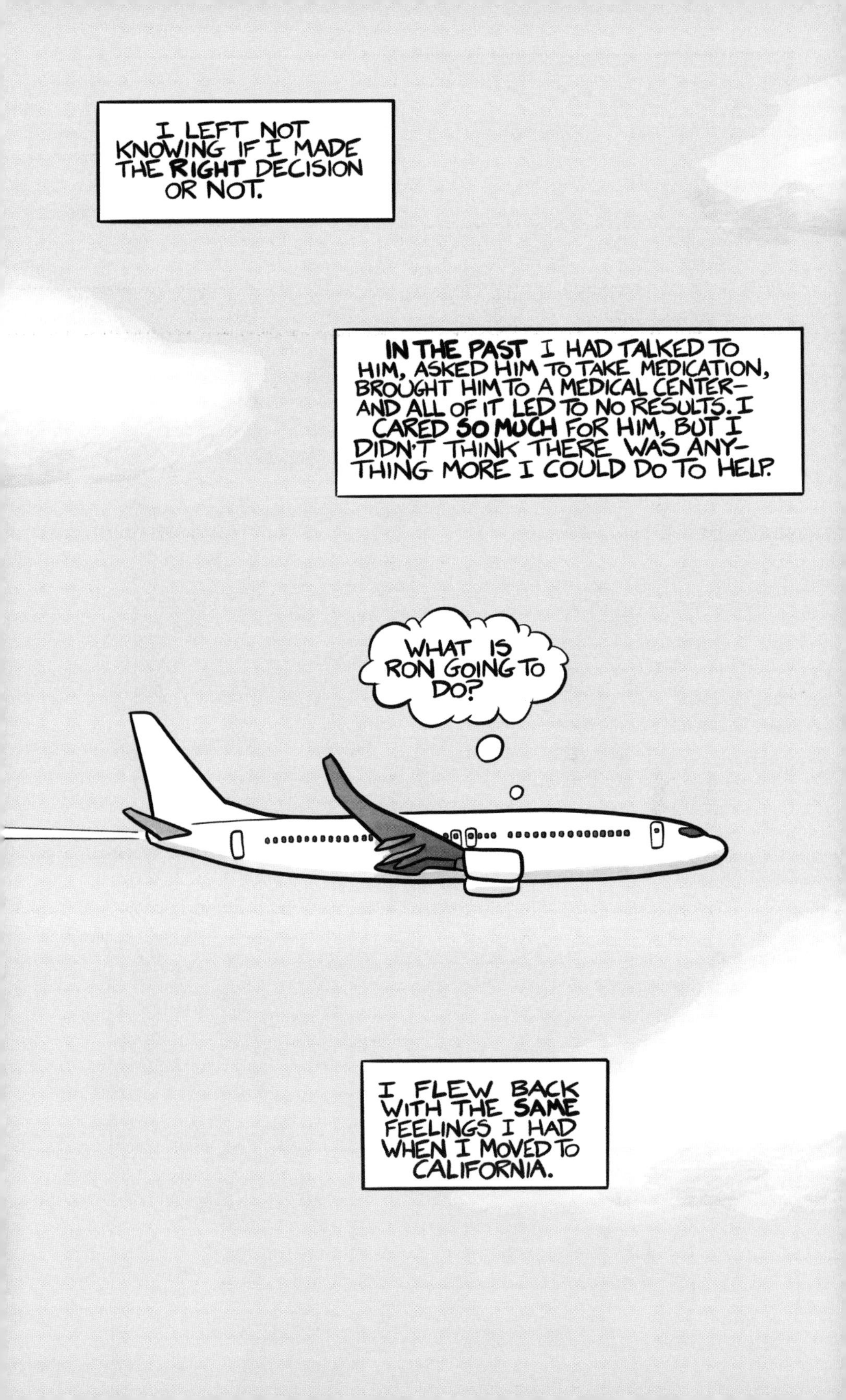
I LEFT NOT KNOWING IF I MADE THE RIGHT DECISION OR NOT.
IN THE PAST I HAD TALKED TO HIM, ASKED HIM TO TAKE MEDICATION, BROUGHT HIM TO A MEDICAL CENTER- AND ALL OF IT LED TO NO RESULTS. I CARED SO MUCH FOR HIM, BUT I DIDN'T THINK THERE WAS ANY-THING MORE I COULD DO TO HELP.
WHAT IS RON GOING TO DO?
I FLEW BACK WITH THE SAME FEELINGS I HAD WHEN I MOVED TO CALIFORNIA.

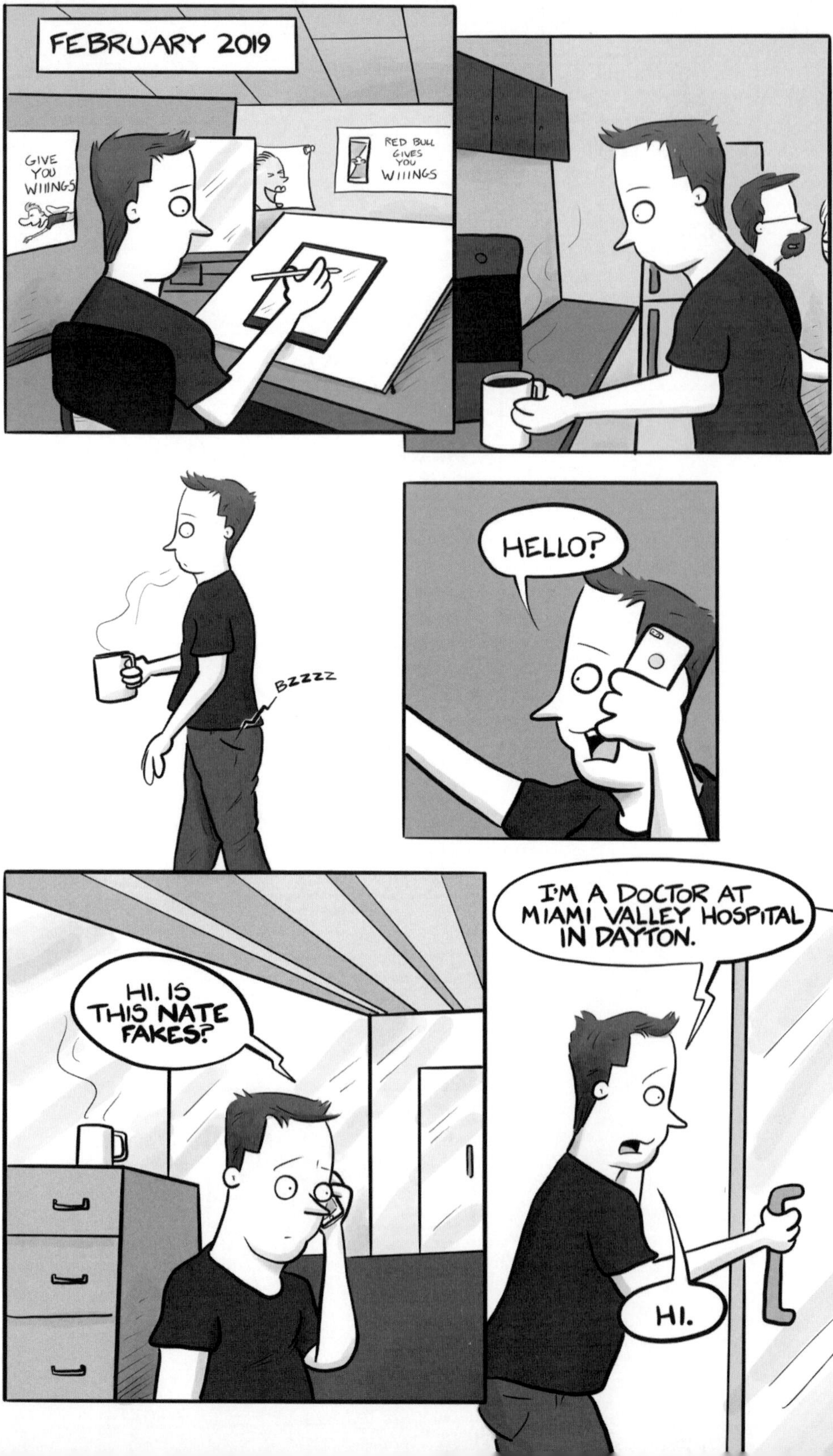

FEBRUARY 2019
GIVE YOU WIIINGS
RED BULL GIVES YOU WIIINGS
BZZZZ
HELLO?
HI. IS THIS NATE FAKES?
I'M A DOCTOR AT MIAMI VALLEY HOSPITAL IN DAYTON.
HI.

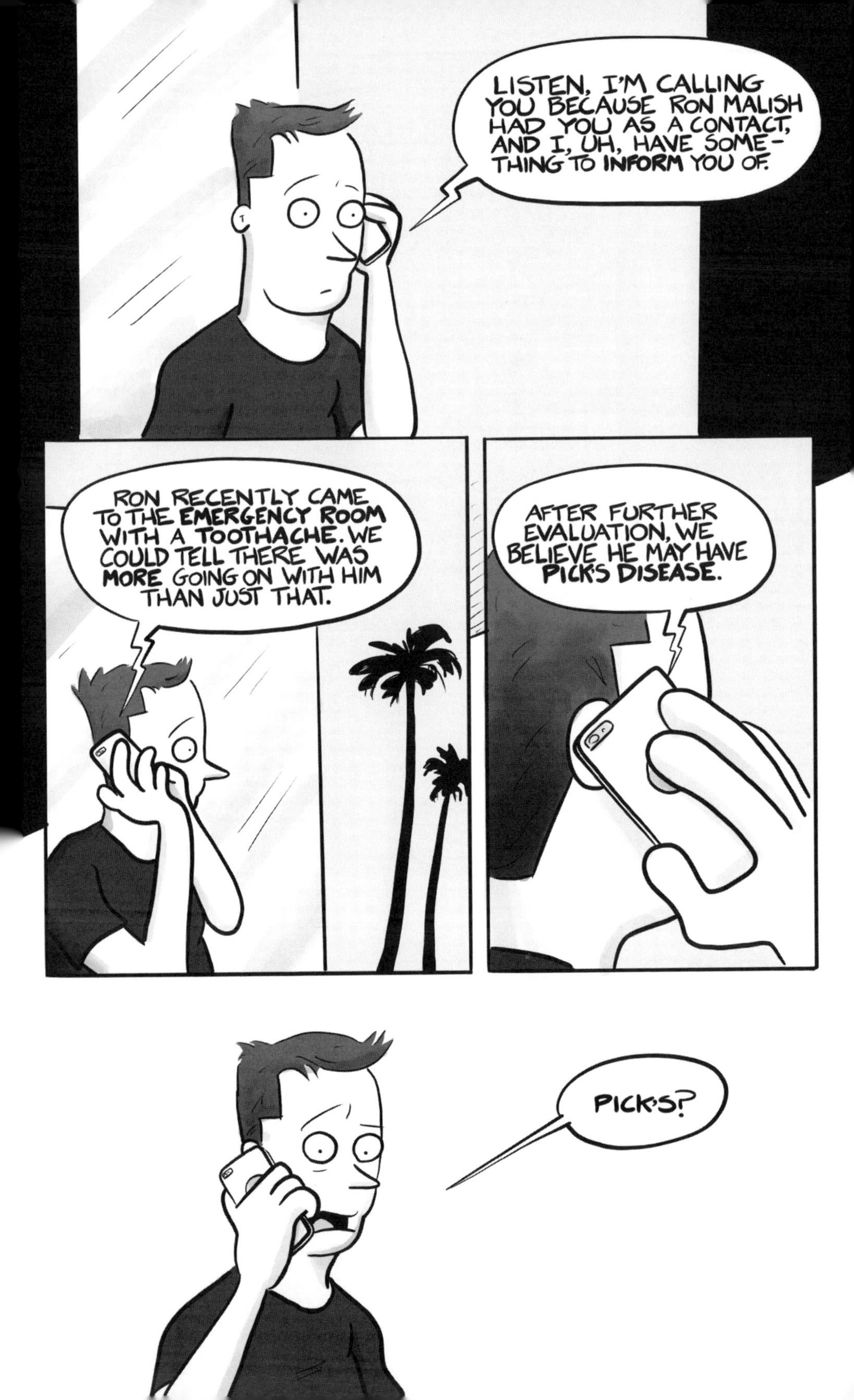
LISTEN, I'M CALLING YOU BECAUSE RON MALISH HAD YOU AS A CONTACT, AND I, UH, HAVE SOME-THING TO **INFORM** YOU OF.
RON RECENTLY CAME TO THE **EMERGENCY ROOM** WITH A **TOOTHACHE**. WE COULD TELL THERE WAS **MORE** GOING ON WITH HIM THAN JUST THAT.
AFTER FURTHER EVALUATION, WE BELIEVE HE MAY HAVE **PICK'S DISEASE**.
PICK'S?

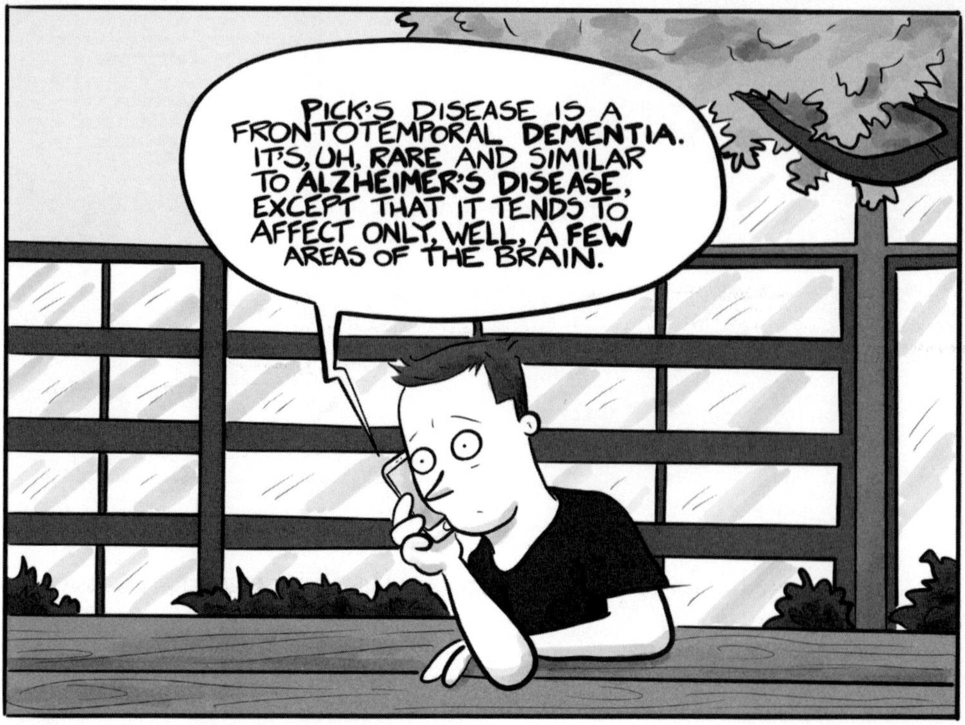
PICK'S DISEASE IS A FRONTOTEMPORAL DEMENTIA. IT'S, UH, RARE AND SIMILAR TO ALZHEIMER'S DISEASE, EXCEPT THAT IT TENDS TO AFFECT ONLY, WELL, A FEW AREAS OF THE BRAIN.

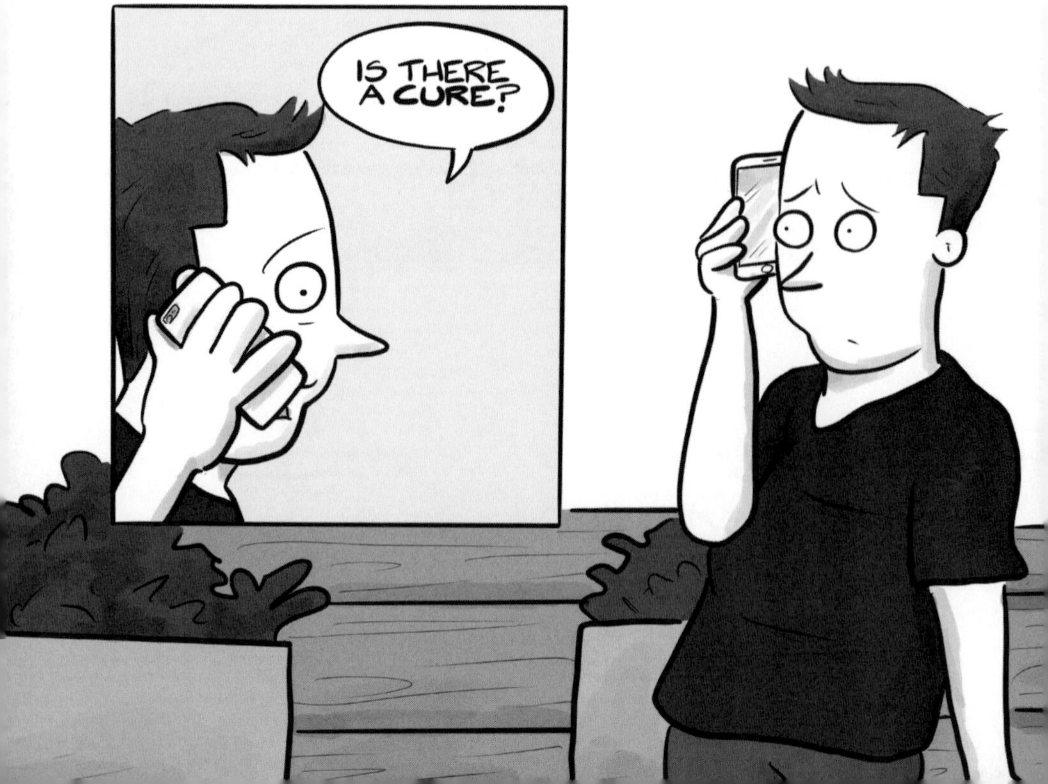
IS THERE A CURE?

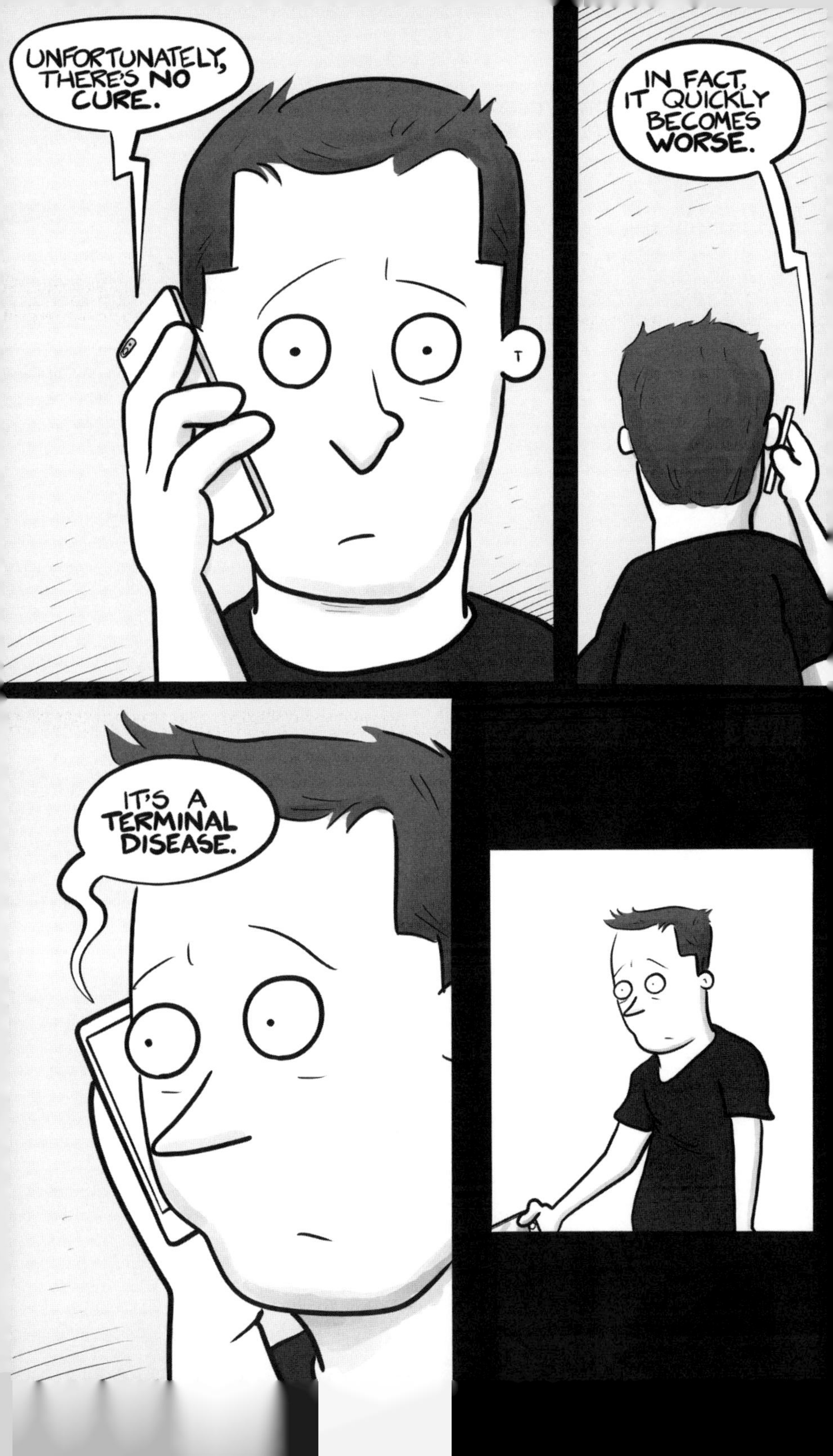
UNFORTUNATELY, THERE'S NO CURE.
IN FACT, IT QUICKLY BECOMES WORSE.
IT'S A TERMINAL DISEASE.

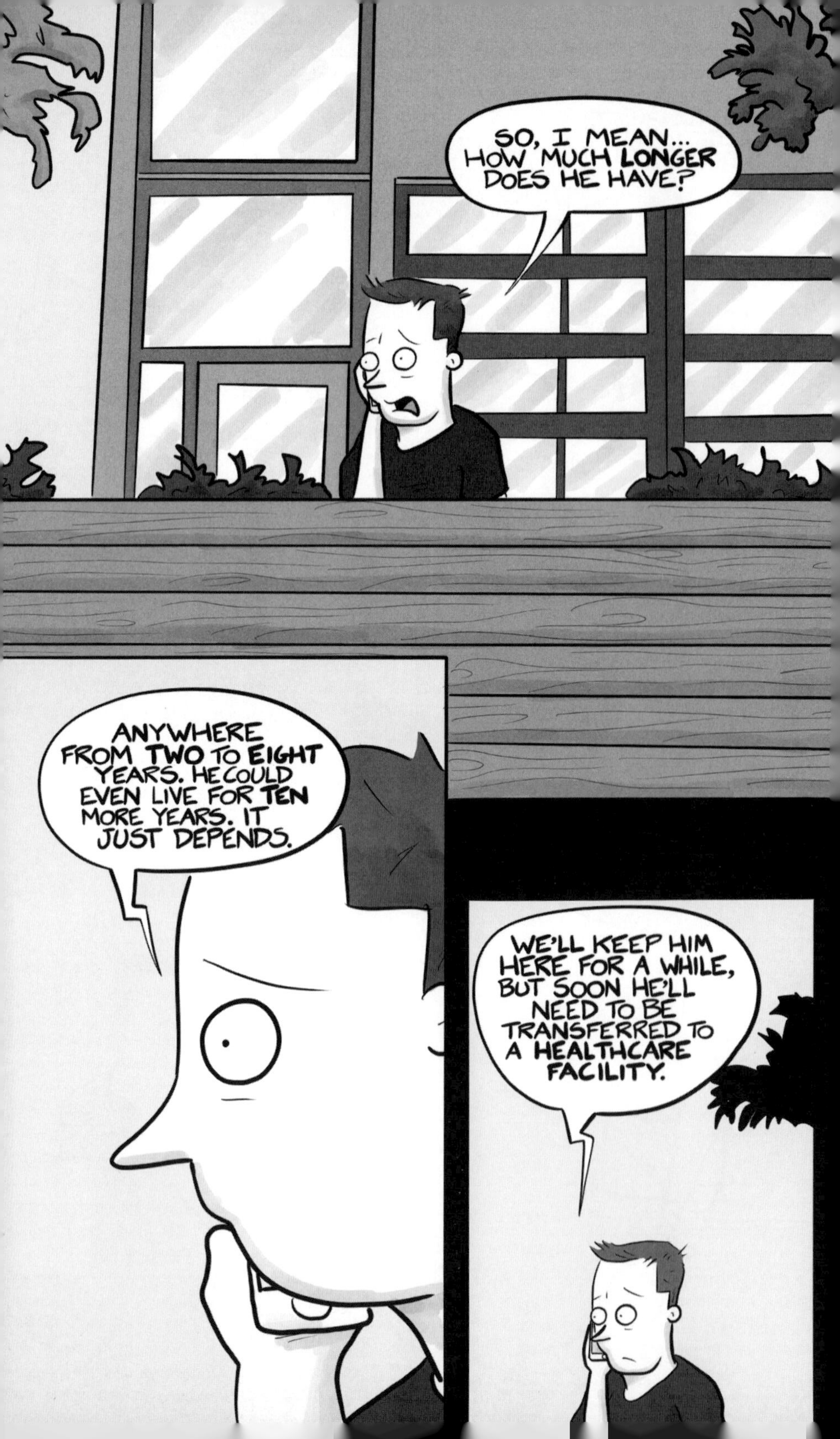
SO, I MEAN... HOW MUCH LONGER DOES HE HAVE?
ANYWHERE FROM TWO TO EIGHT YEARS. HE COULD EVEN LIVE FOR TEN MORE YEARS. IT JUST DEPENDS.
WE'LL KEEP HIM HERE FOR A WHILE, BUT SOON HE'LL NEED TO BE TRANSFERRED TO A HEALTHCARE FACILITY.

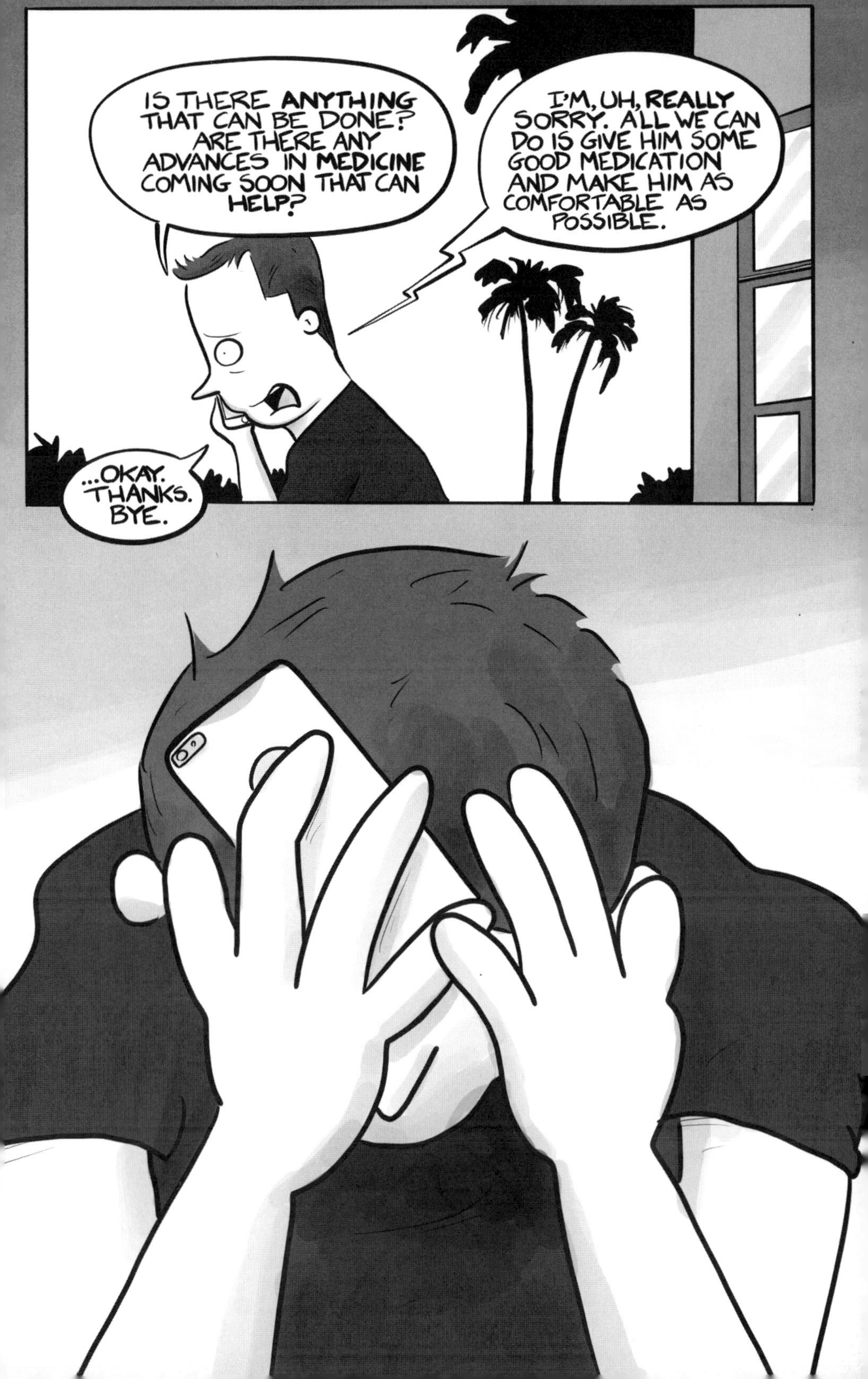
IS THERE ANYTHING THAT CAN BE DONE? ARE THERE ANY ADVANCES IN MEDICINE COMING SOON THAT CAN HELP?
I'M, UH, REALLY SORRY. ALL WE CAN DO IS GIVE HIM SOME GOOD MEDICATION AND MAKE HIM AS COMFORTABLE AS POSSIBLE.
...OKAY. THANKS. BYE.

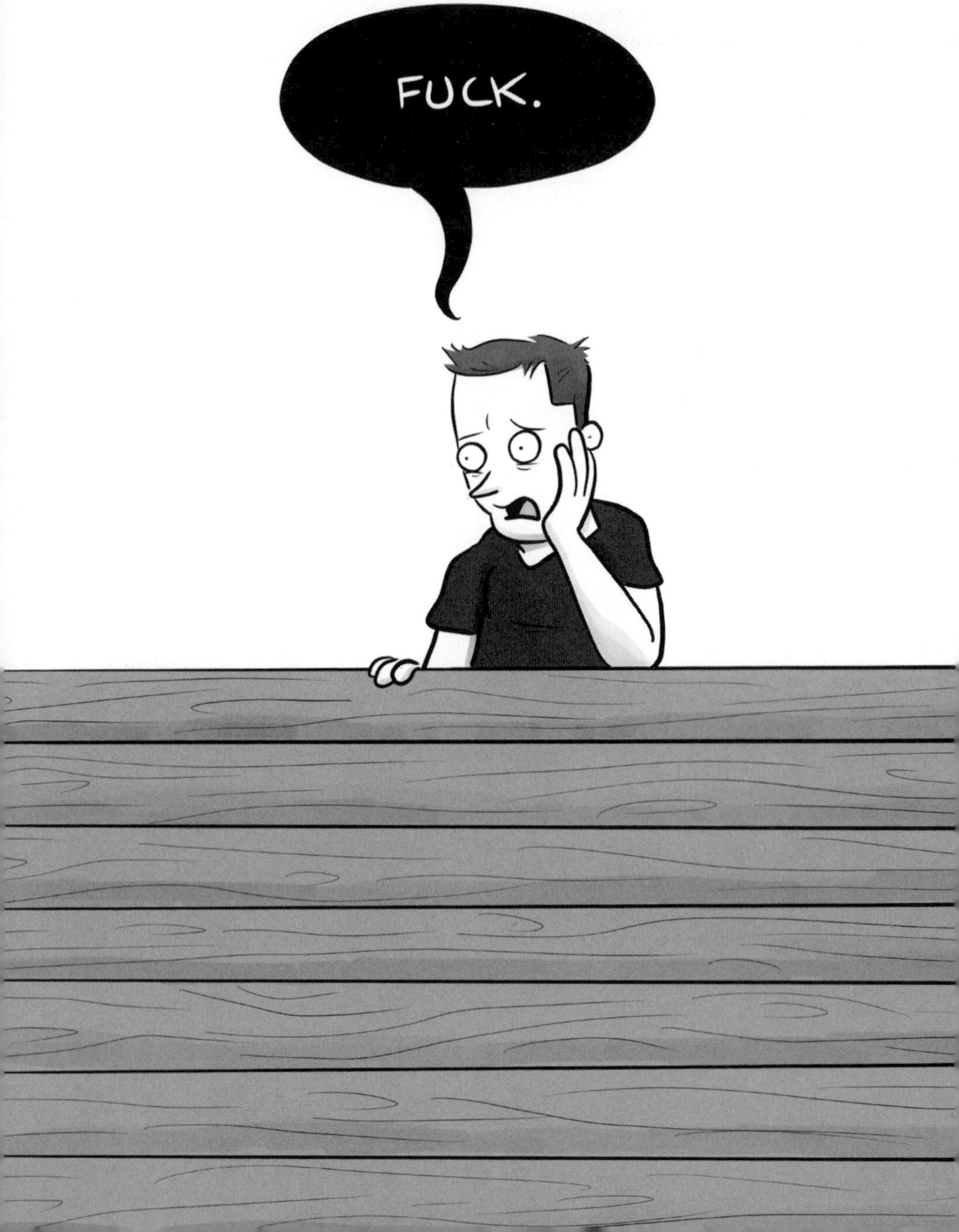
FUCK.

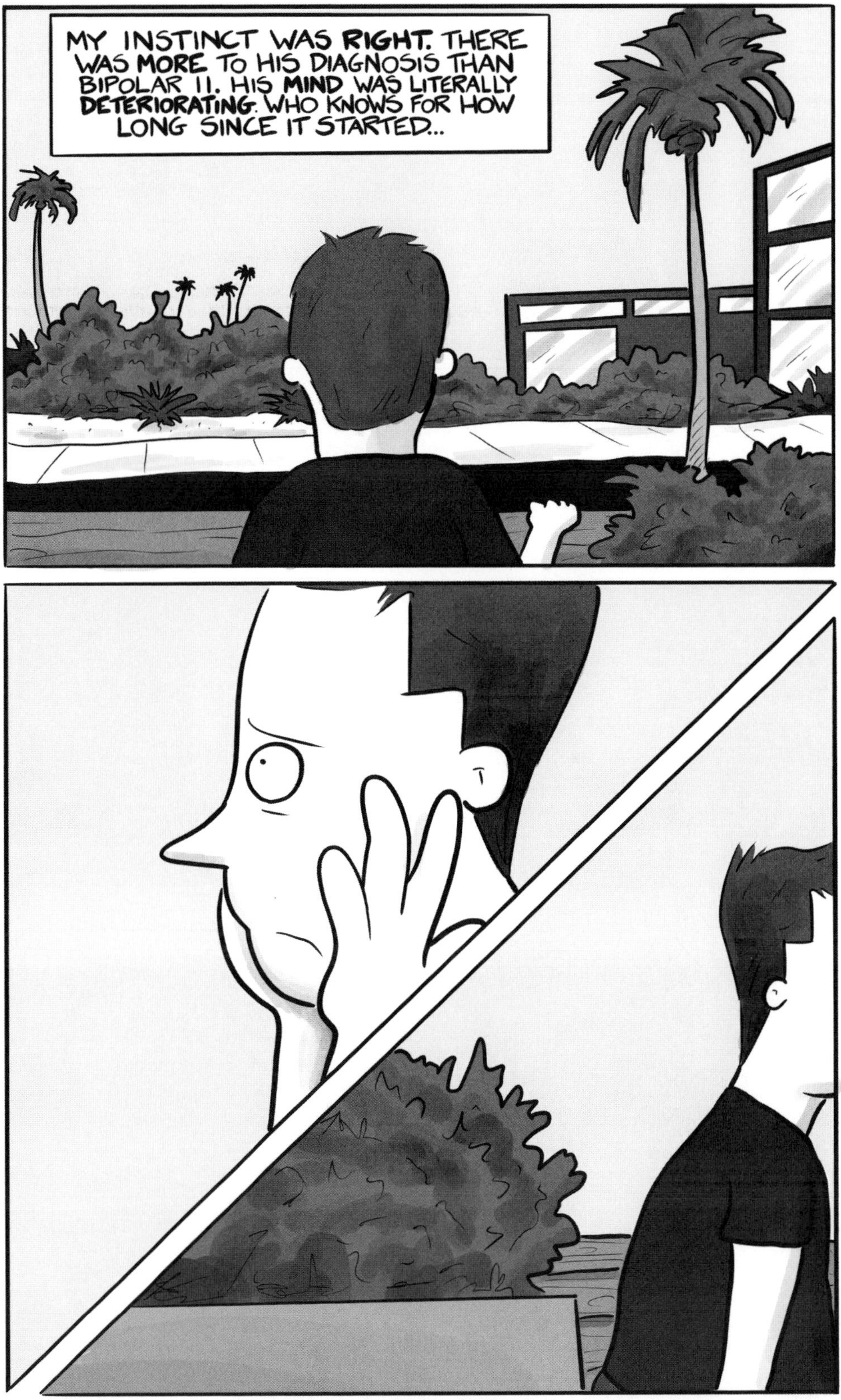
MY INSTINCT WAS RIGHT. THERE WAS MORE TO HIS DIAGNOSIS THAN BIPOLAR II. HIS MIND WAS LITERALLY DETERIORATING. WHO KNOWS FOR HOW LONG SINCE IT STARTED...

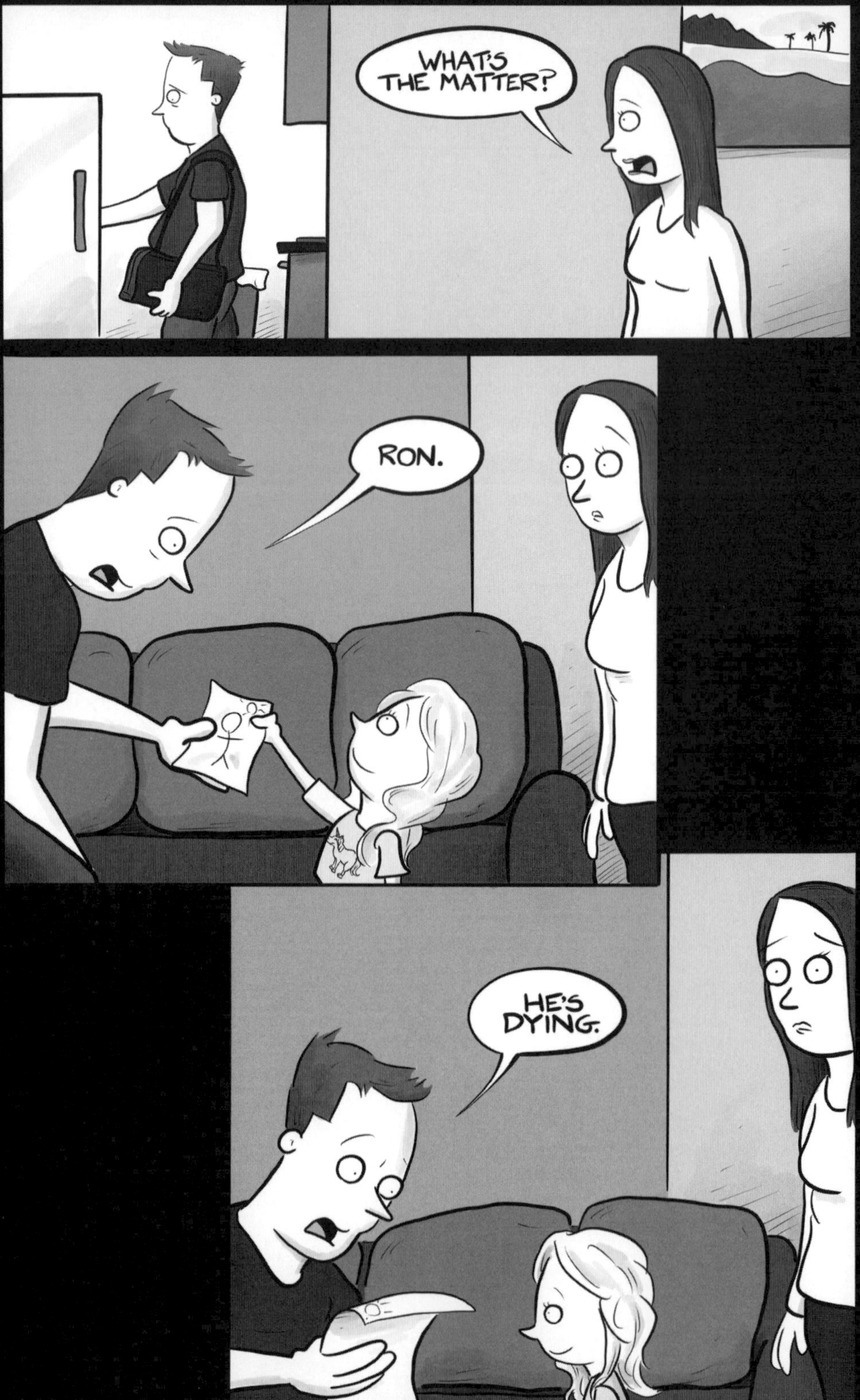
WHAT'S THE MATTER?
RON.
HE'S DYING.

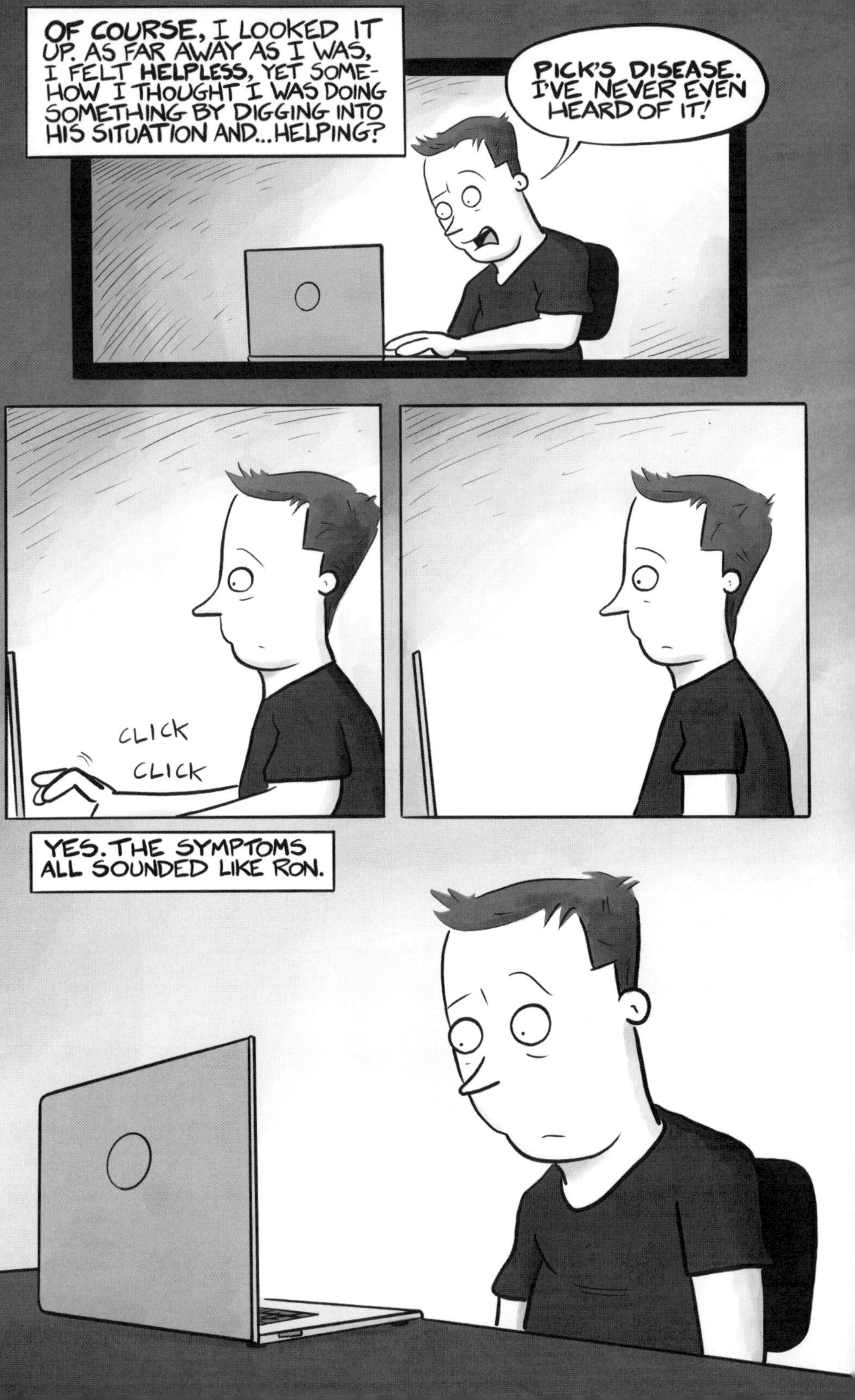
OF COURSE, I LOOKED IT UP. AS FAR AWAY AS I WAS, I FELT HELPLESS, YET SOMEHOW I THOUGHT I WAS DOING SOMETHING BY DIGGING INTO HIS SITUATION AND...HELPING?
PICK'S DISEASE. I'VE NEVER EVEN HEARD OF IT!
CLICK
CLICK
YES. THE SYMPTOMS ALL SOUNDED LIKE RON.

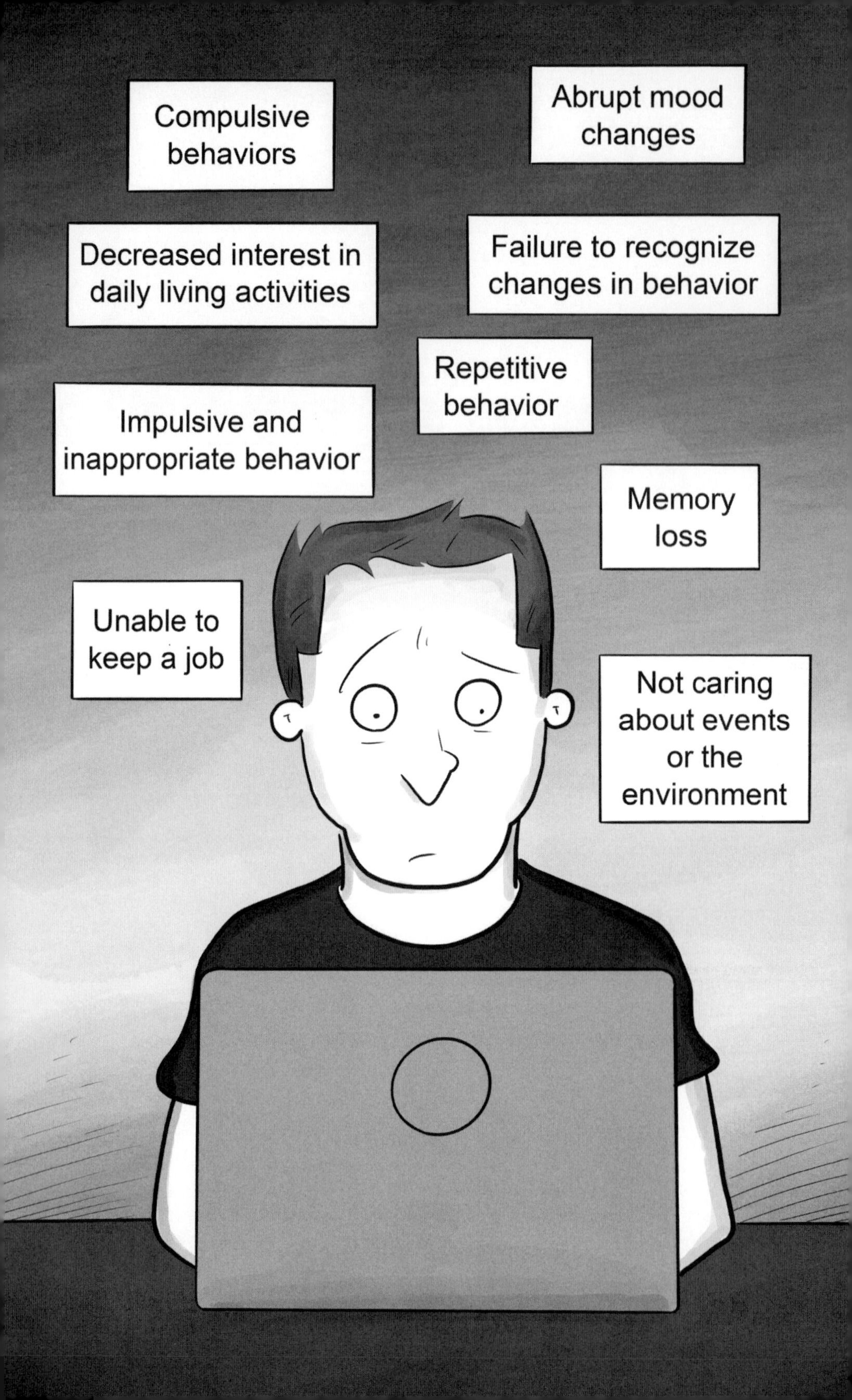
Compulsive behaviors
Abrupt mood changes
Decreased interest in daily living activities
Failure to recognize changes in behavior
Repetitive behavior
Impulsive and inappropriate behavior
Memory loss
Unable to keep a job
Not caring about events or the environment

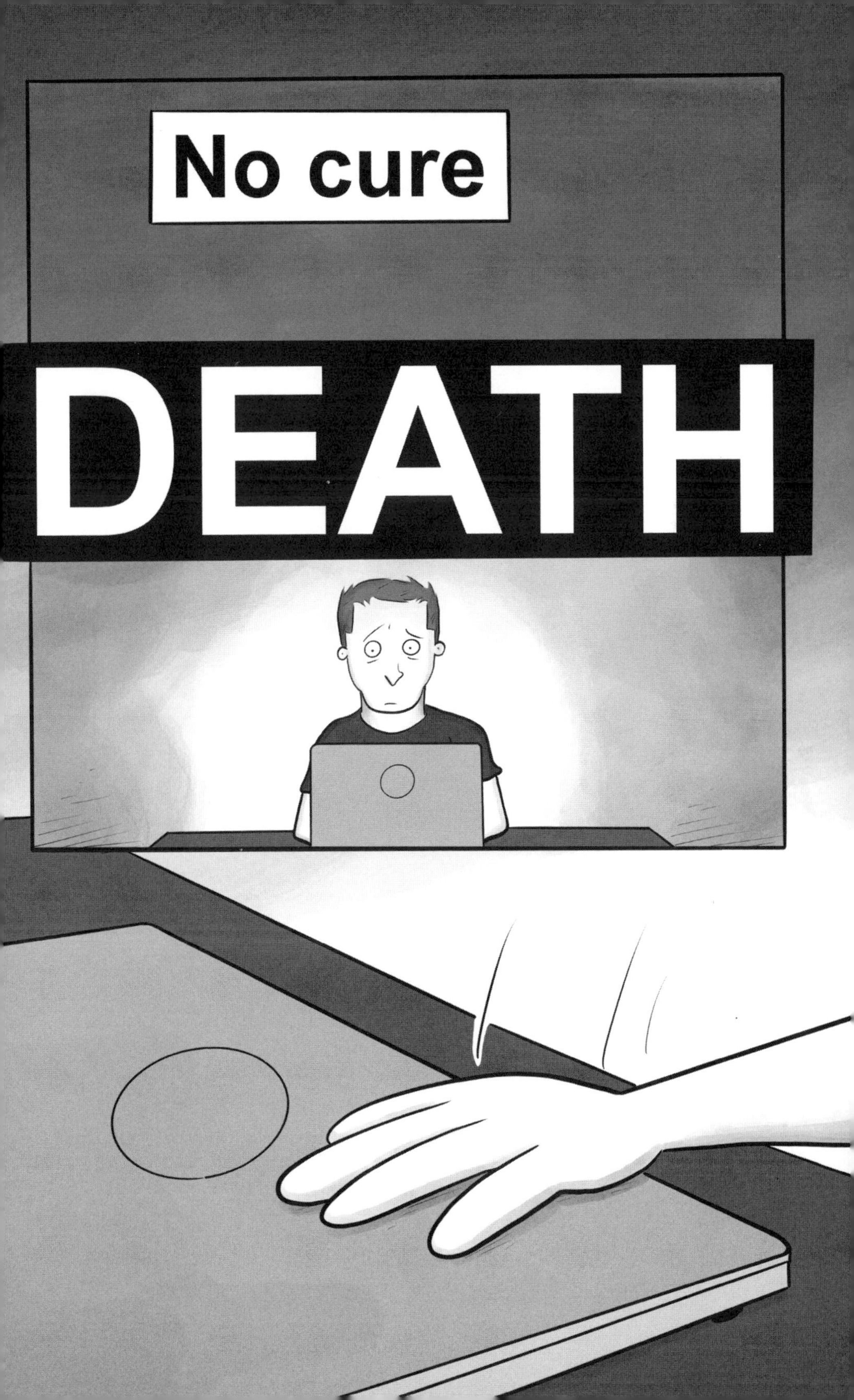
No cure
DEATH

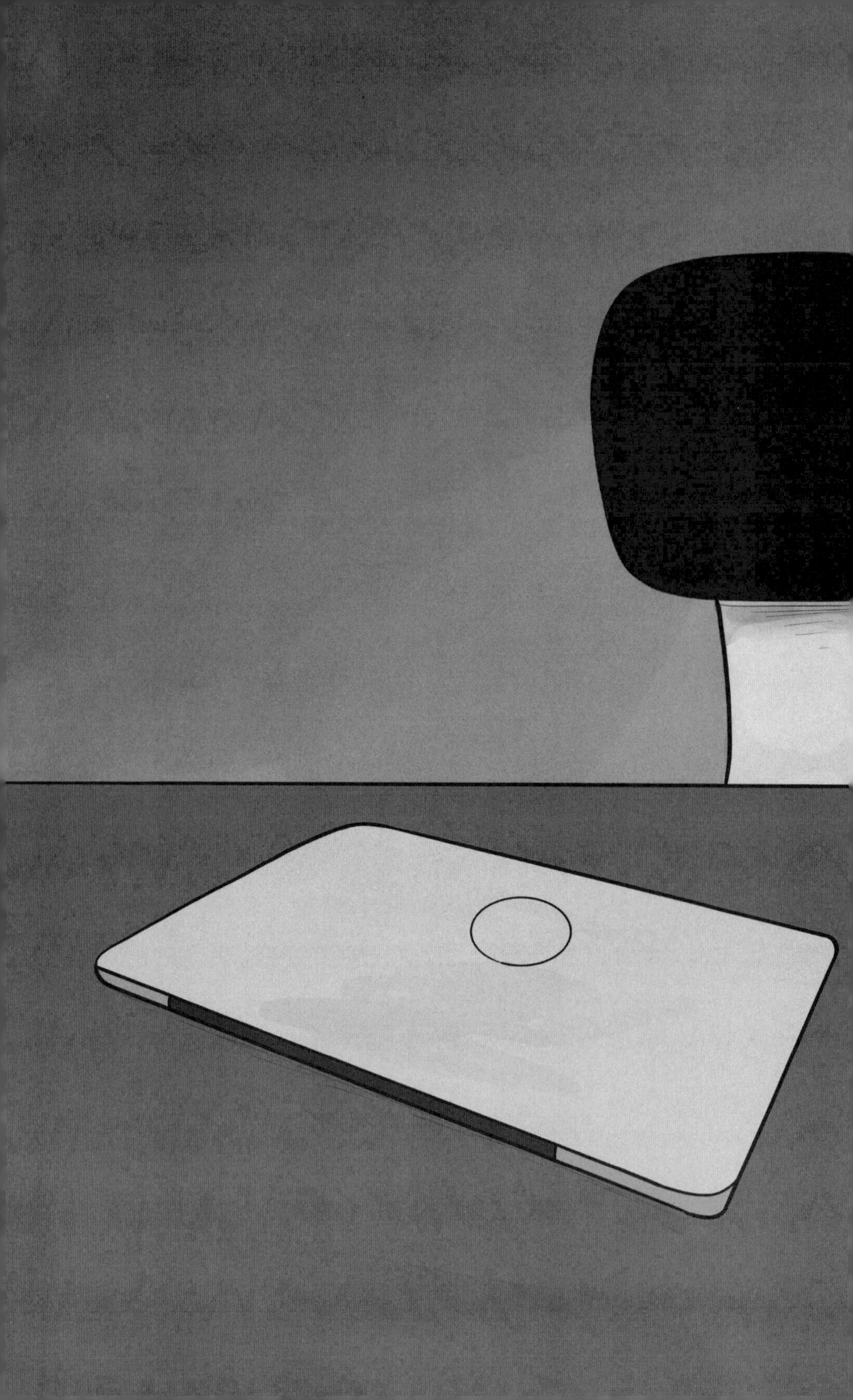

PART FIVE

THE LIGHT DIMS

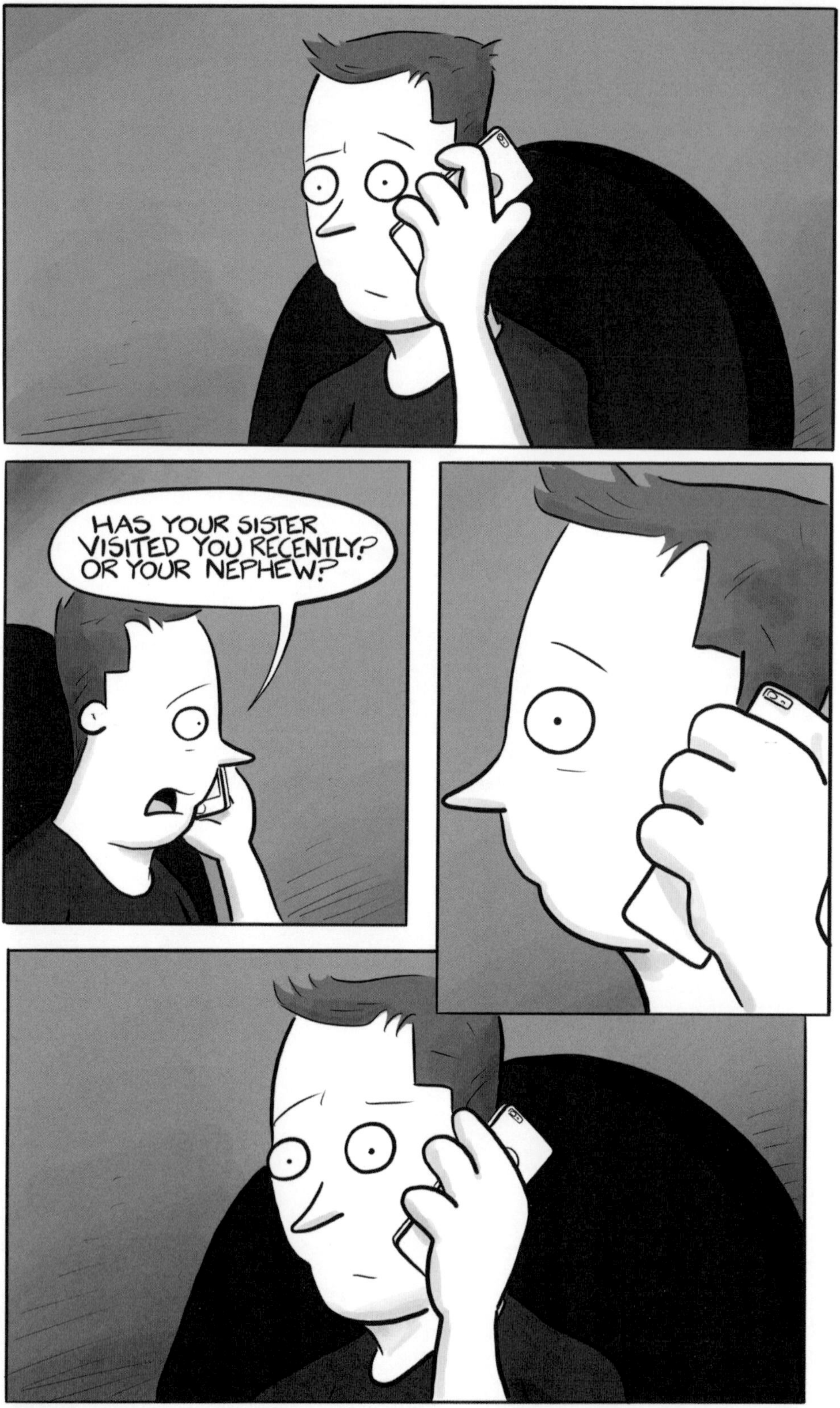
HAS YOUR SISTER VISITED YOU RECENTLY? OR YOUR NEPHEW?

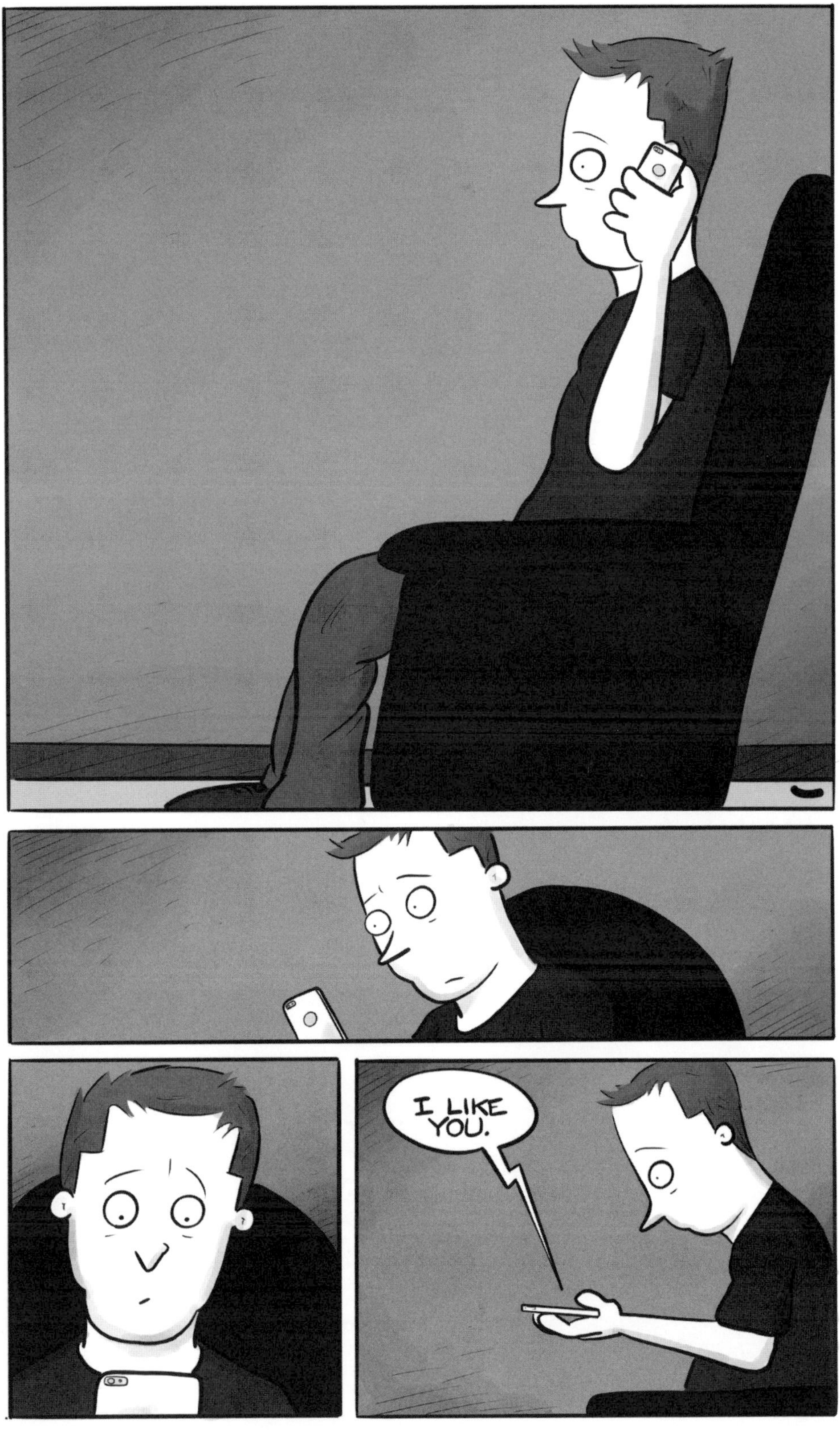
I LIKE YOU.

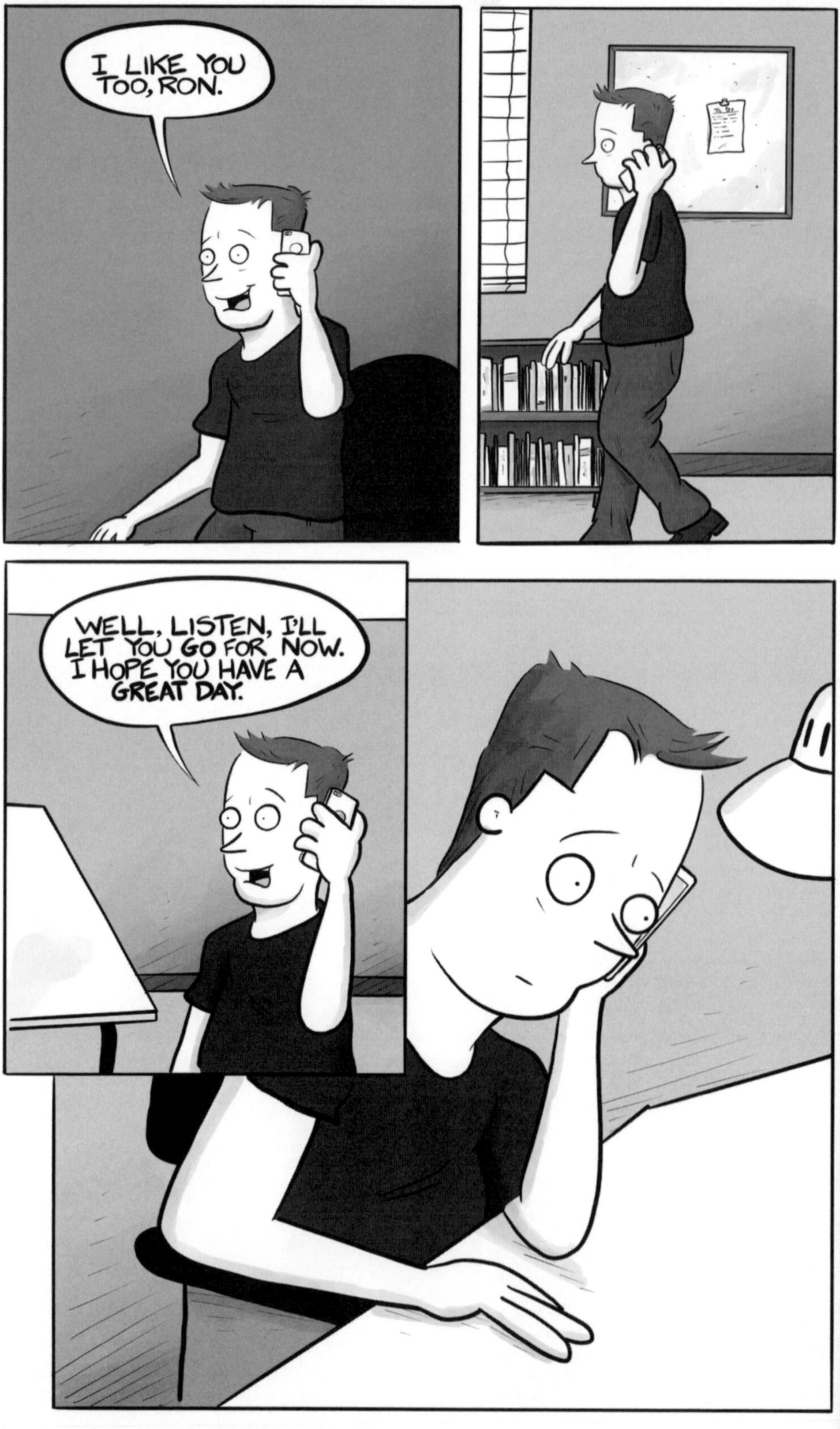
I LIKE YOU TOO, RON.
WELL, LISTEN, I'LL LET YOU GO FOR NOW. I HOPE YOU HAVE A GREAT DAY.

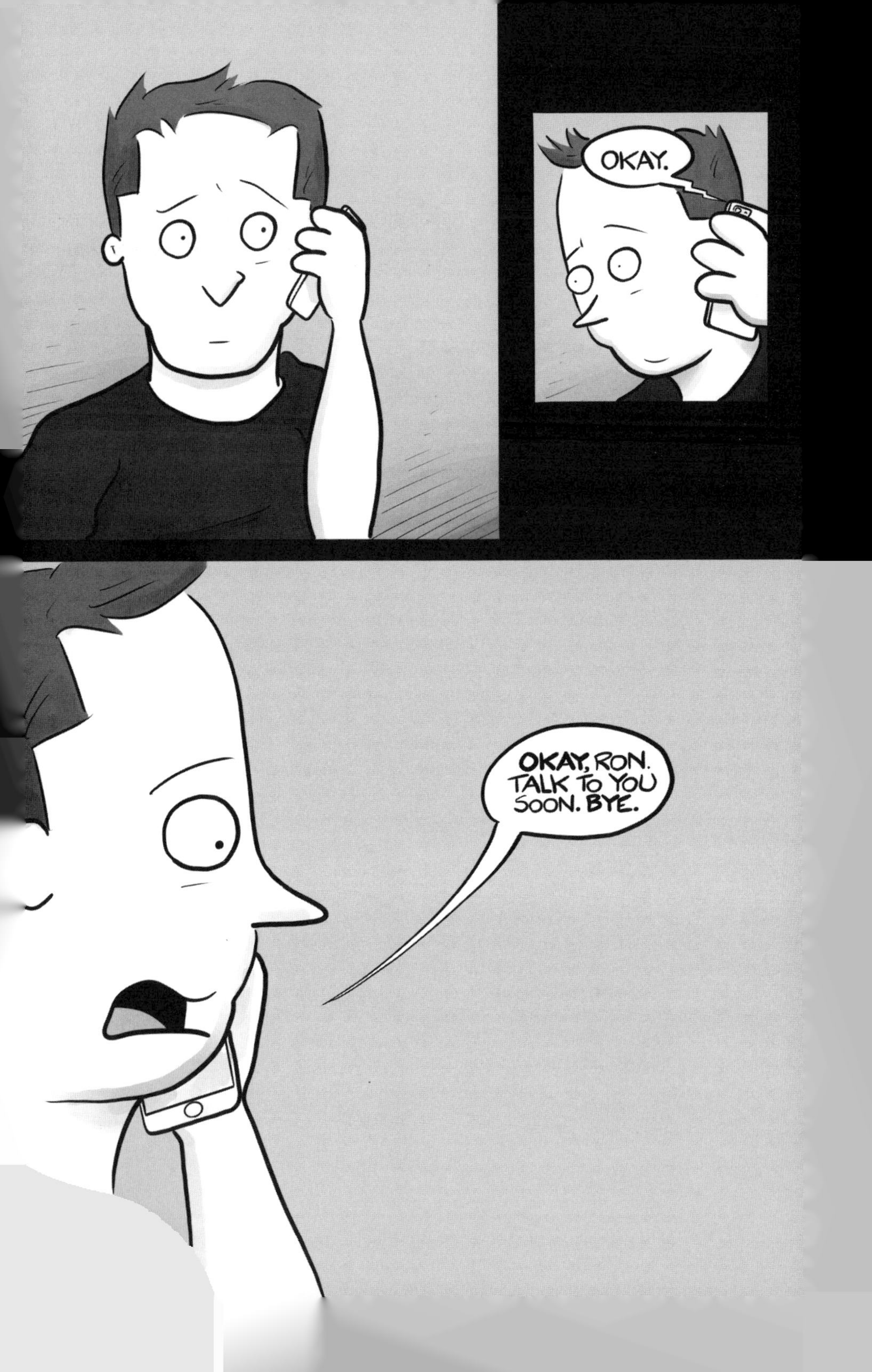
OKAY.
OKAY, RON. TALK TO YOU SOON. BYE.

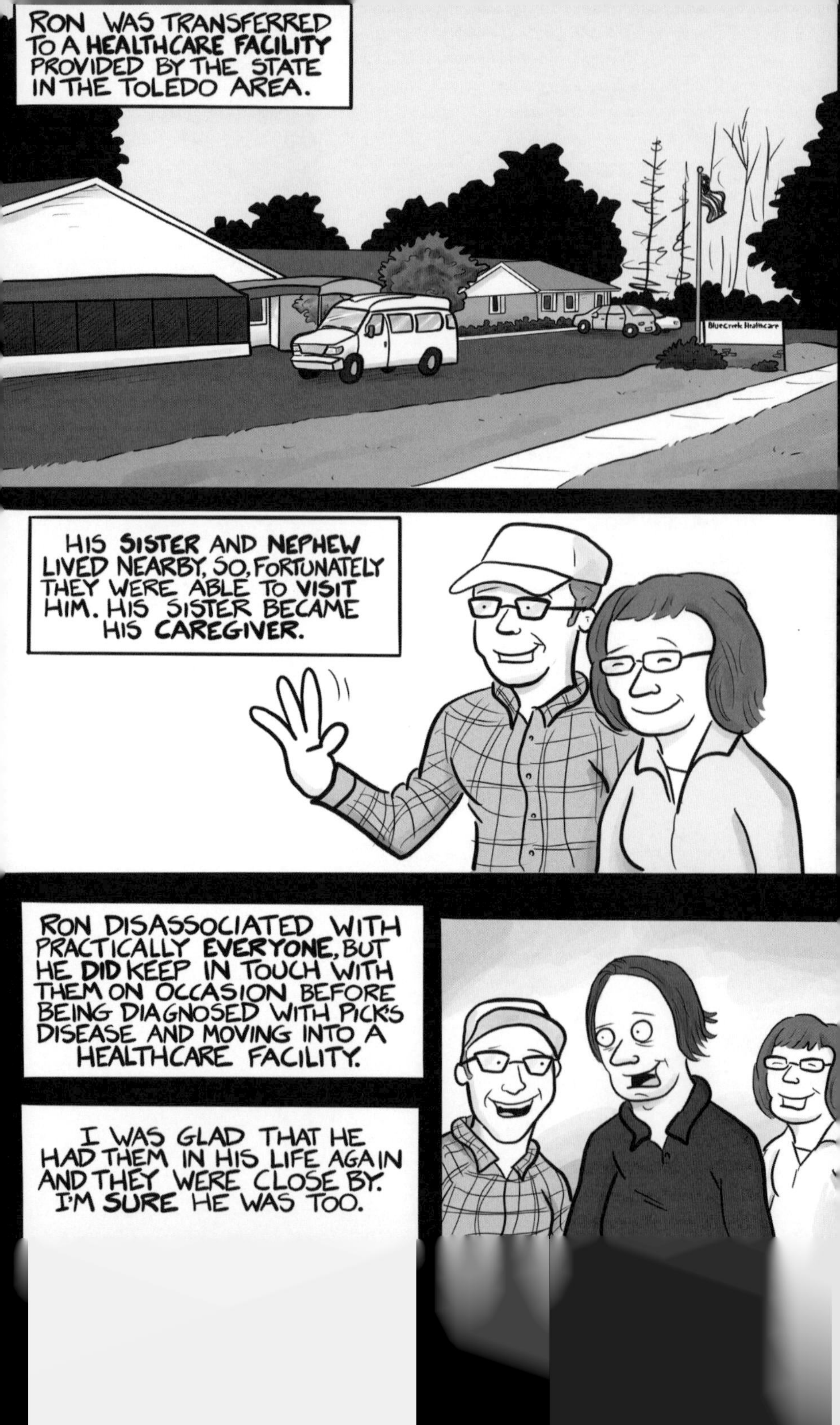
RON WAS TRANSFERRED TO A **HEALTHCARE FACILITY** PROVIDED BY THE STATE IN THE TOLEDO AREA.
Bluecreek Healthcare
HIS **SISTER** AND **NEPHEW** LIVED NEARBY, SO, FORTUNATELY THEY WERE ABLE TO **VISIT** HIM. HIS SISTER BECAME HIS **CAREGIVER.**
RON DISASSOCIATED WITH PRACTICALLY **EVERYONE**, BUT HE **DID** KEEP IN TOUCH WITH THEM ON OCCASION BEFORE BEING DIAGNOSED WITH PICK'S DISEASE AND MOVING INTO A HEALTHCARE FACILITY.
I WAS GLAD THAT HE HAD THEM IN HIS LIFE AGAIN AND THEY WERE CLOSE BY. I'M **SURE** HE WAS TOO.

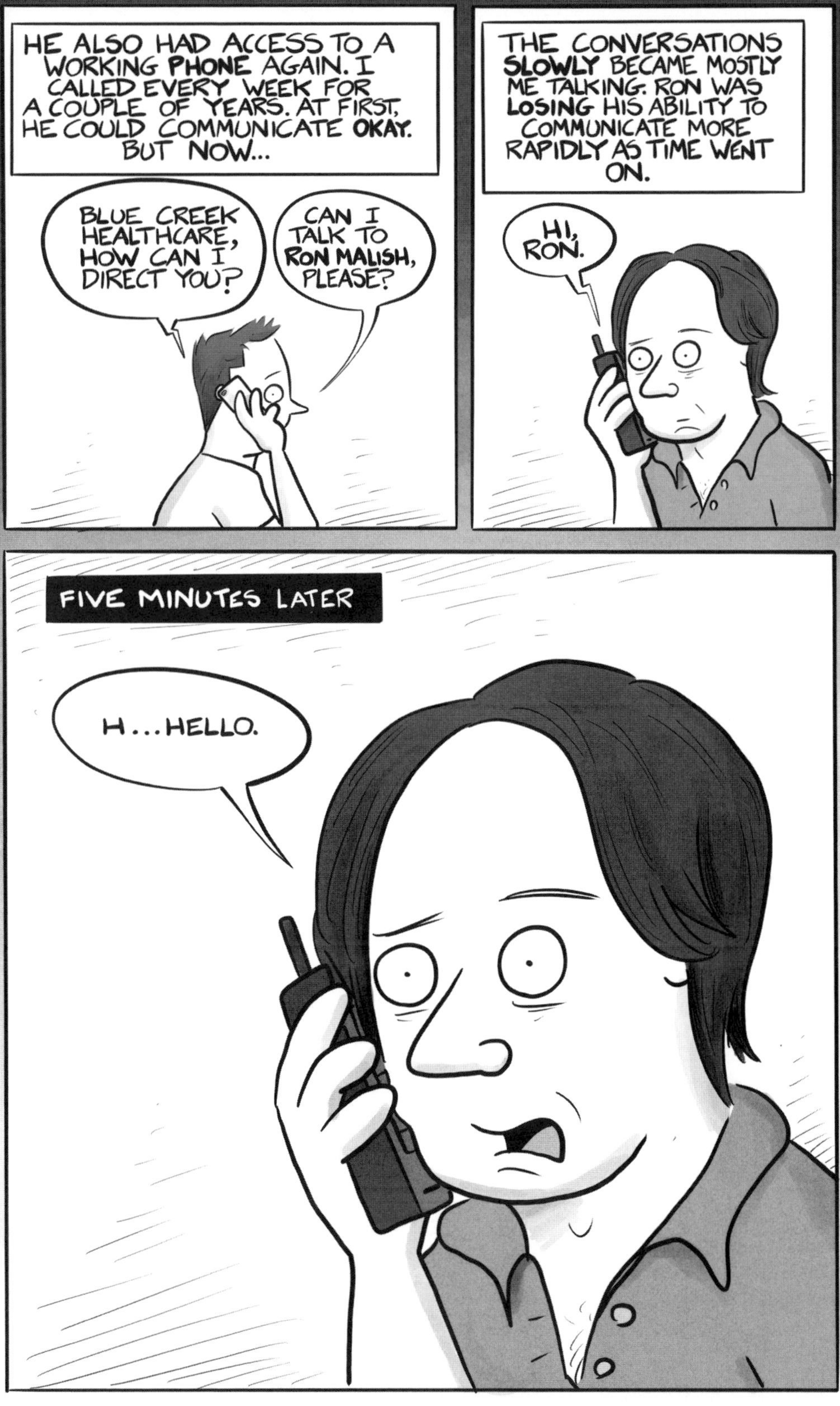
HE ALSO HAD ACCESS TO A WORKING **PHONE** AGAIN. I CALLED EVERY WEEK FOR A COUPLE OF YEARS. AT FIRST, HE COULD COMMUNICATE **OKAY**. BUT NOW...
BLUE CREEK HEALTHCARE, HOW CAN I DIRECT YOU?
CAN I TALK TO **RON MALISH**, PLEASE?
THE CONVERSATIONS **SLOWLY** BECAME MOSTLY ME TALKING. RON WAS **LOSING** HIS ABILITY TO COMMUNICATE MORE RAPIDLY AS TIME WENT ON.
HI, RON.
FIVE MINUTES LATER
H...HELLO.

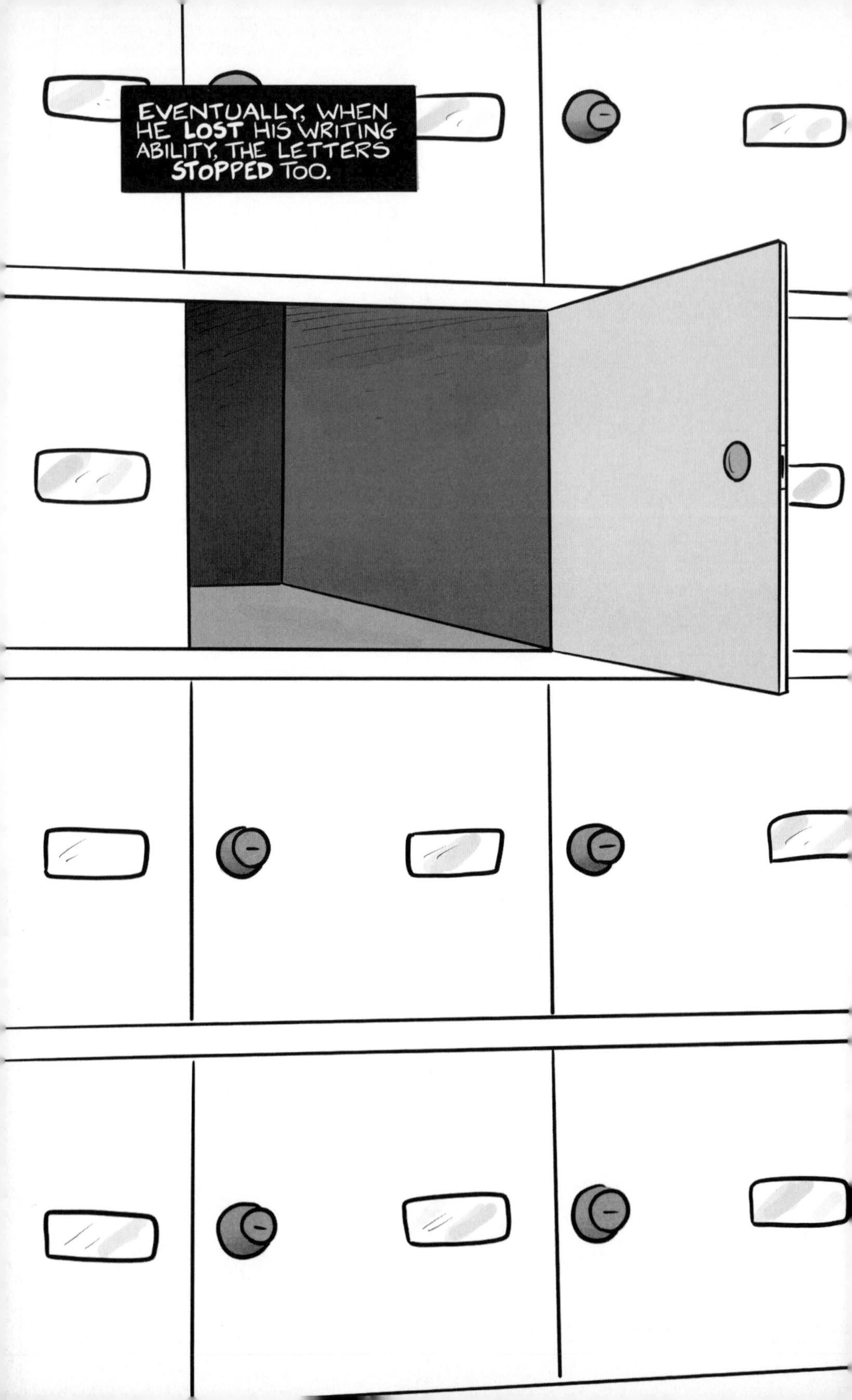
EVENTUALLY, WHEN HE LOST HIS WRITING ABILITY, THE LETTERS STOPPED TOO.

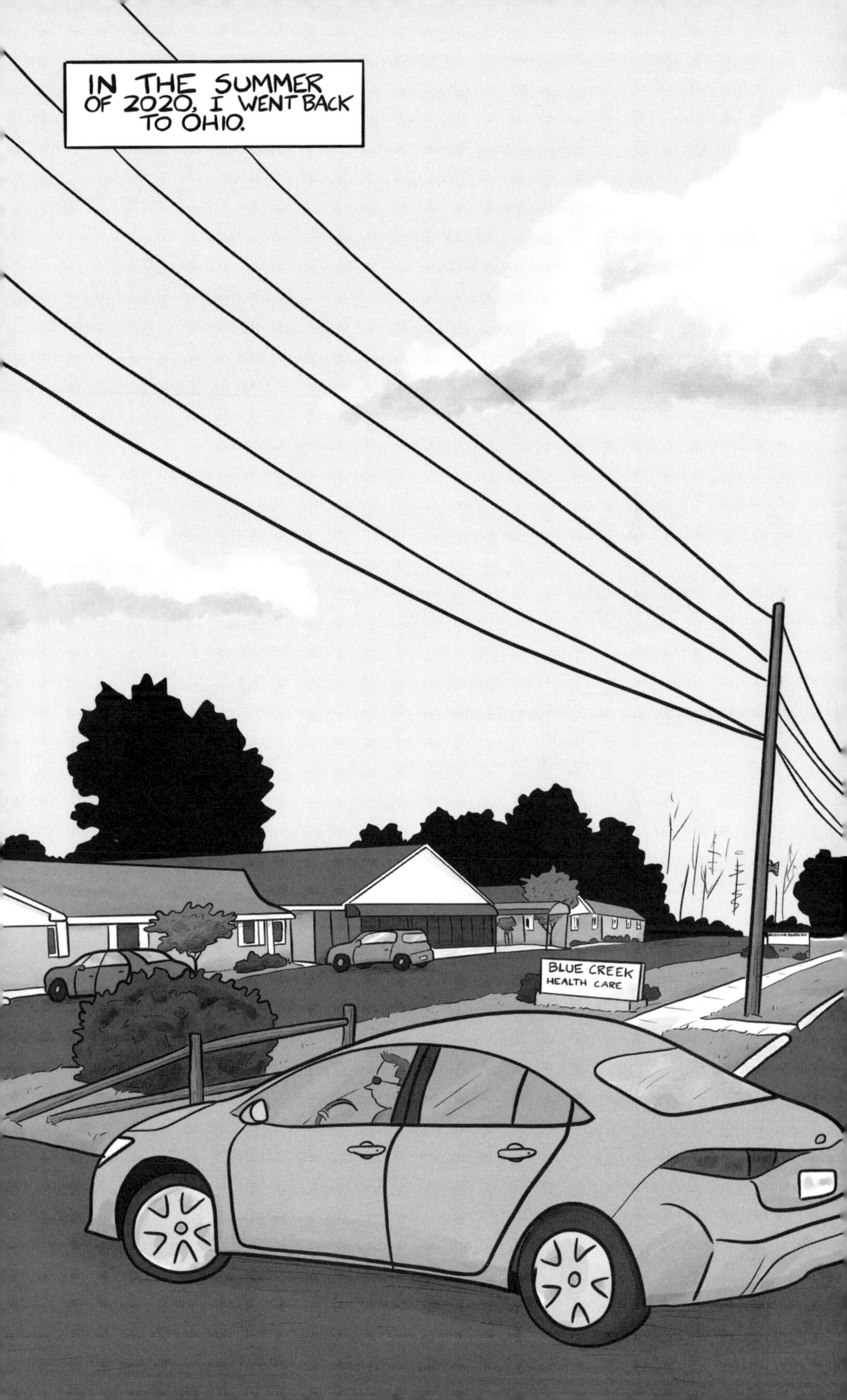
IN THE SUMMER OF 2020, I WENT BACK TO OHIO.
BLUE CREEK HEALTH CARE

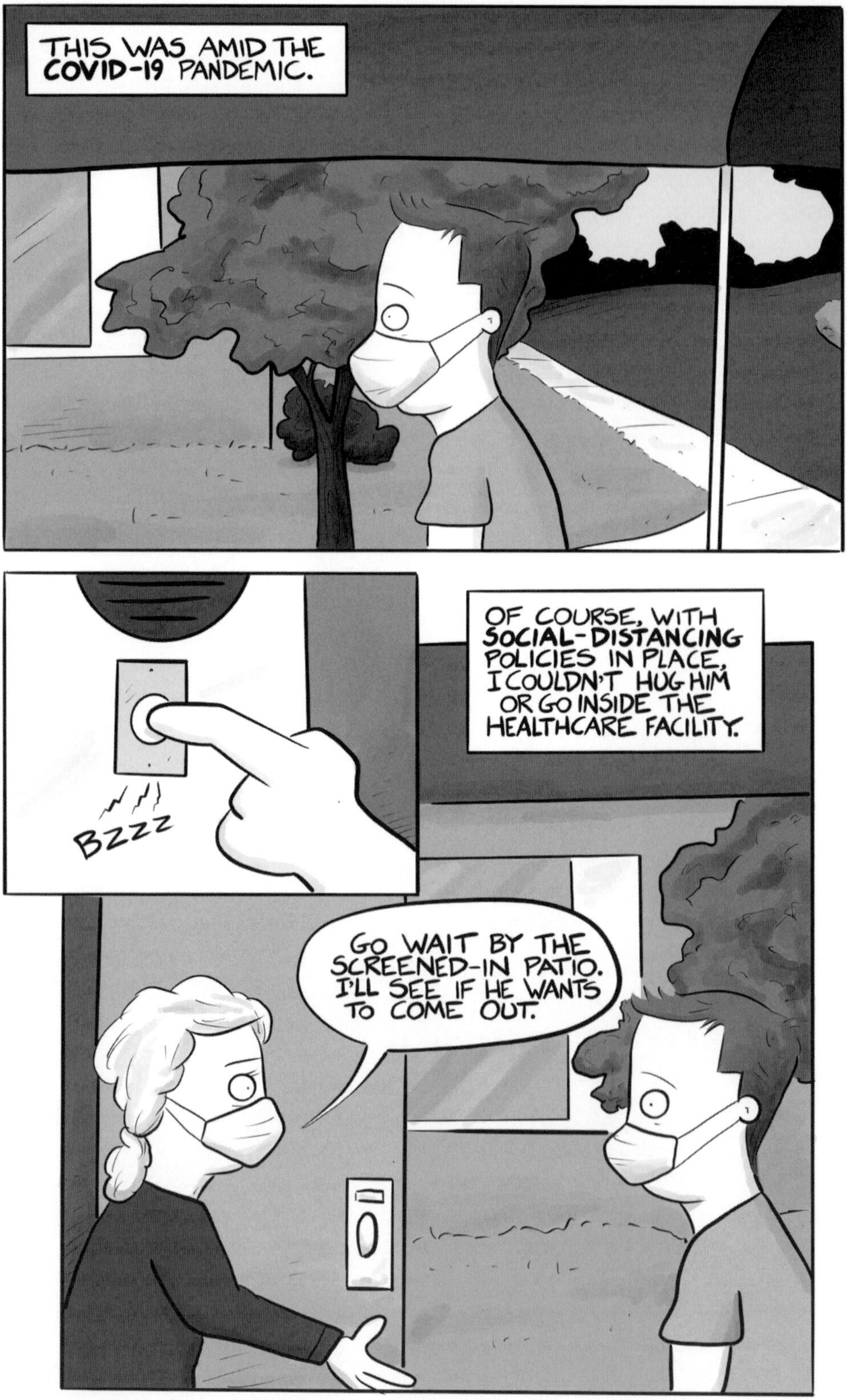
THIS WAS AMID THE COVID-19 PANDEMIC.
BZZZ
OF COURSE, WITH SOCIAL-DISTANCING POLICIES IN PLACE, I COULDN'T HUG HIM OR GO INSIDE THE HEALTHCARE FACILITY.
GO WAIT BY THE SCREENED-IN PATIO. I'LL SEE IF HE WANTS TO COME OUT.

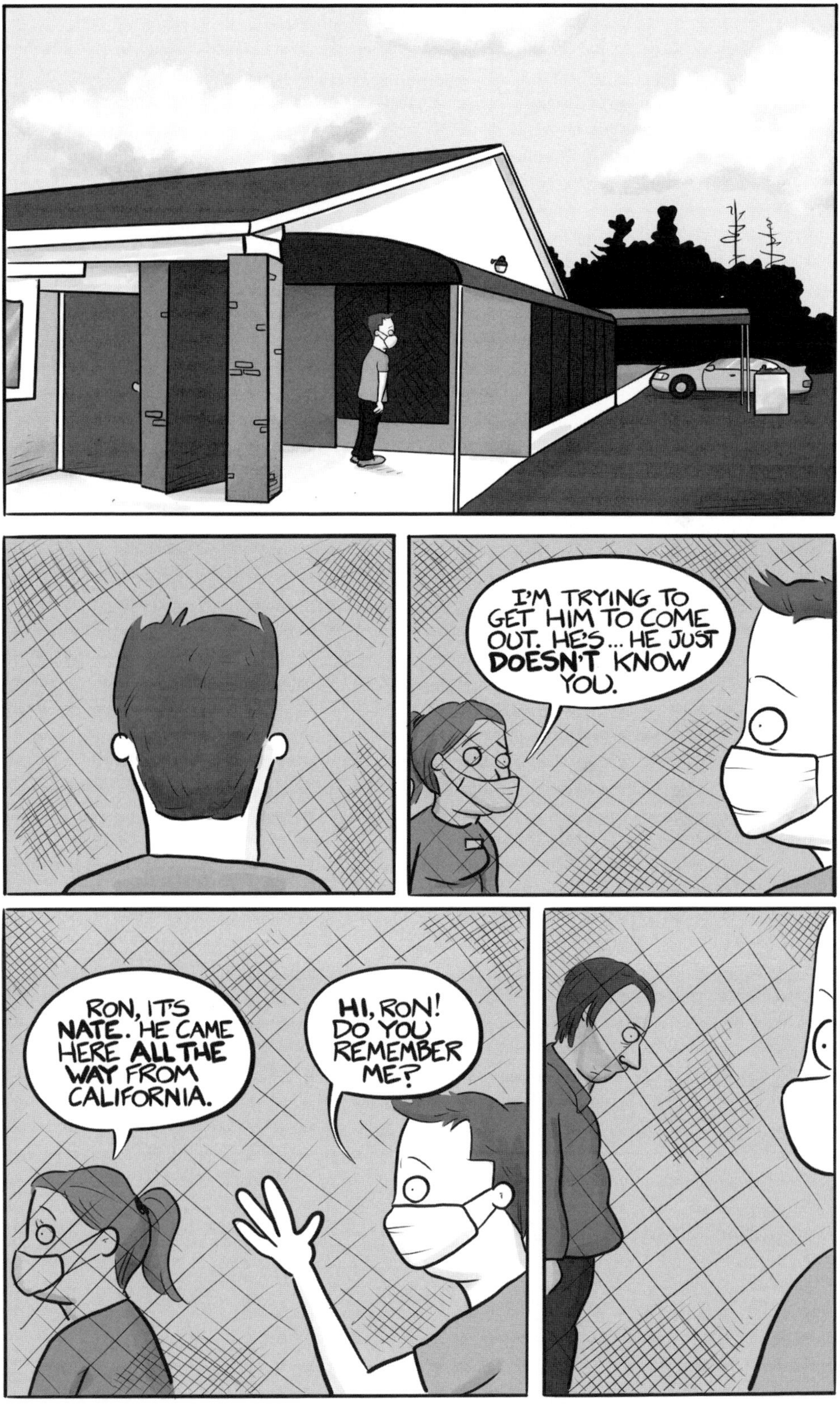
I'M TRYING TO GET HIM TO COME OUT. HE'S... HE JUST **DOESN'T** KNOW YOU.
RON, IT'S **NATE**. HE CAME HERE **ALL THE WAY** FROM CALIFORNIA.
HI, RON! DO YOU REMEMBER ME?

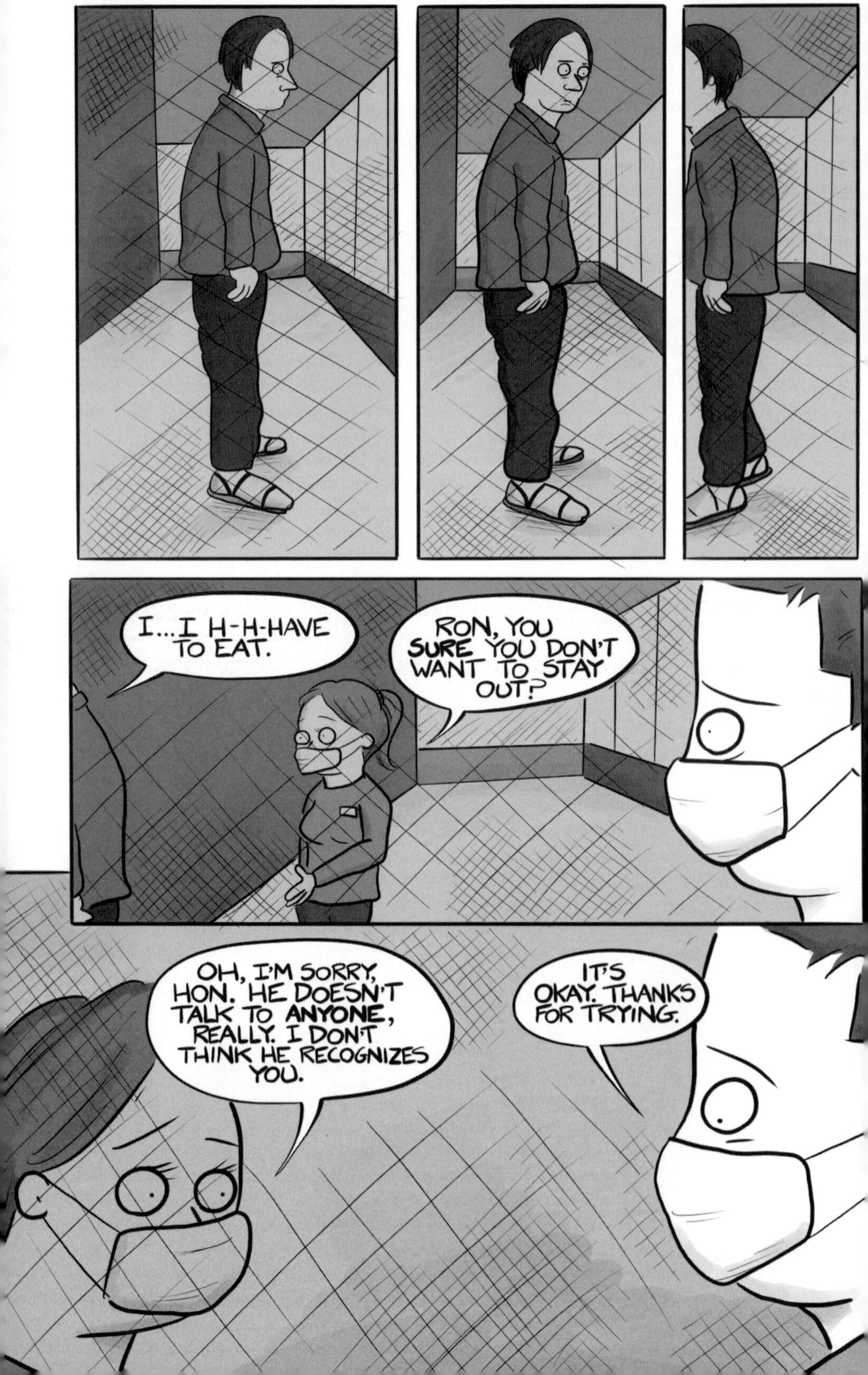

I...I H-H-HAVE TO EAT.
RON, YOU SURE YOU DON'T WANT TO STAY OUT?
OH, I'M SORRY, HON. HE DOESN'T TALK TO ANYONE, REALLY. I DON'T THINK HE RECOGNIZES YOU.
IT'S OKAY. THANKS FOR TRYING.

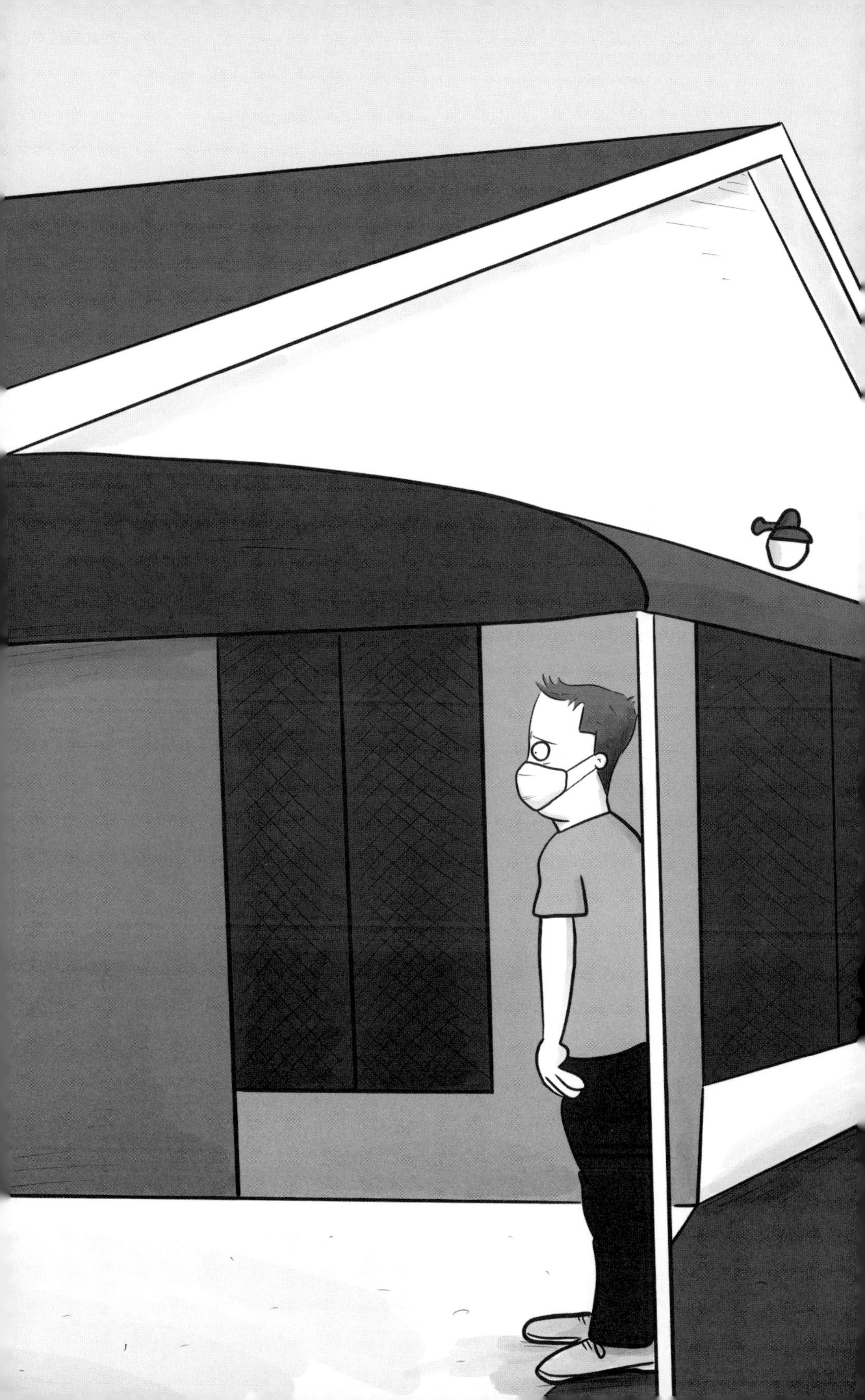

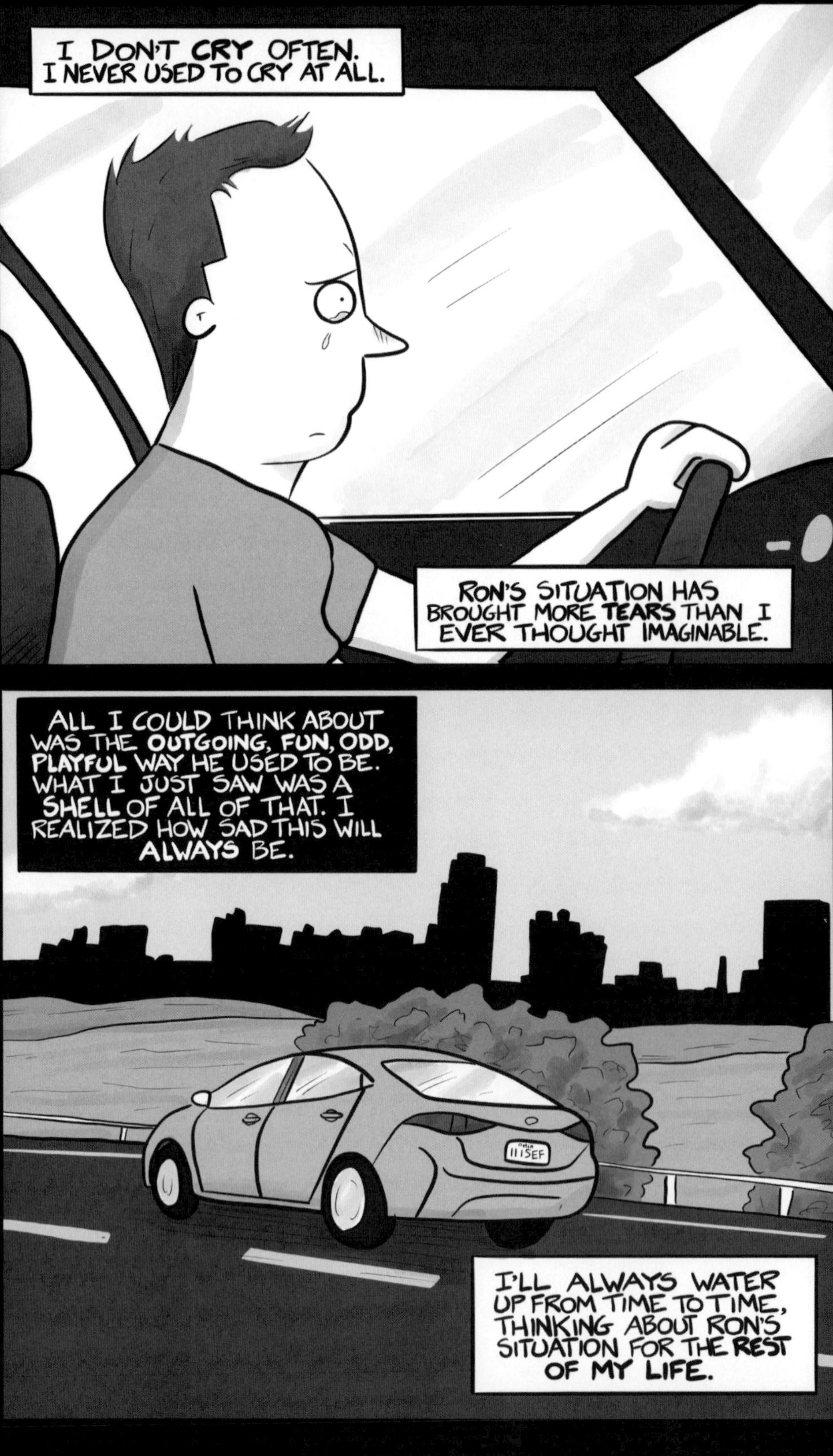
I DON'T **CRY** OFTEN.
I NEVER USED TO CRY AT ALL.
RON'S SITUATION HAS BROUGHT MORE **TEARS** THAN I EVER THOUGHT IMAGINABLE.
ALL I COULD THINK ABOUT WAS THE **OUTGOING**, **FUN**, **ODD**, **PLAYFUL** WAY HE USED TO BE. WHAT I JUST SAW WAS A **SHELL** OF ALL OF THAT. I REALIZED HOW SAD THIS WILL **ALWAYS** BE.
I'LL ALWAYS WATER UP FROM TIME TO TIME, THINKING ABOUT RON'S SITUATION FOR THE **REST** OF **MY LIFE**.

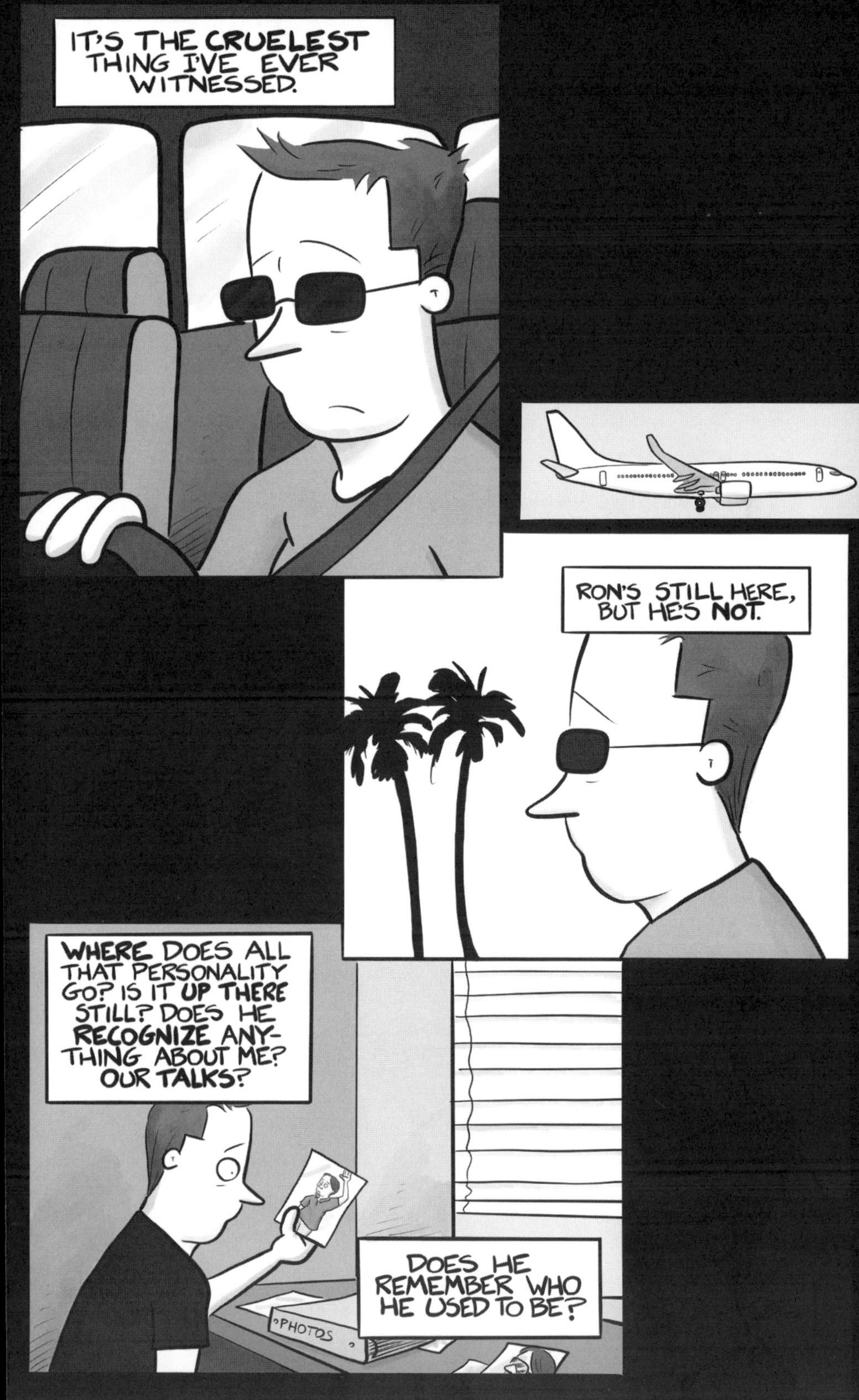
IT'S THE CRUELEST THING I'VE EVER WITNESSED.
RON'S STILL HERE, BUT HE'S NOT.
WHERE DOES ALL THAT PERSONALITY GO? IS IT UP THERE STILL? DOES HE RECOGNIZE ANYTHING ABOUT ME? OUR TALKS?
DOES HE REMEMBER WHO HE USED TO BE?
PHOTOS

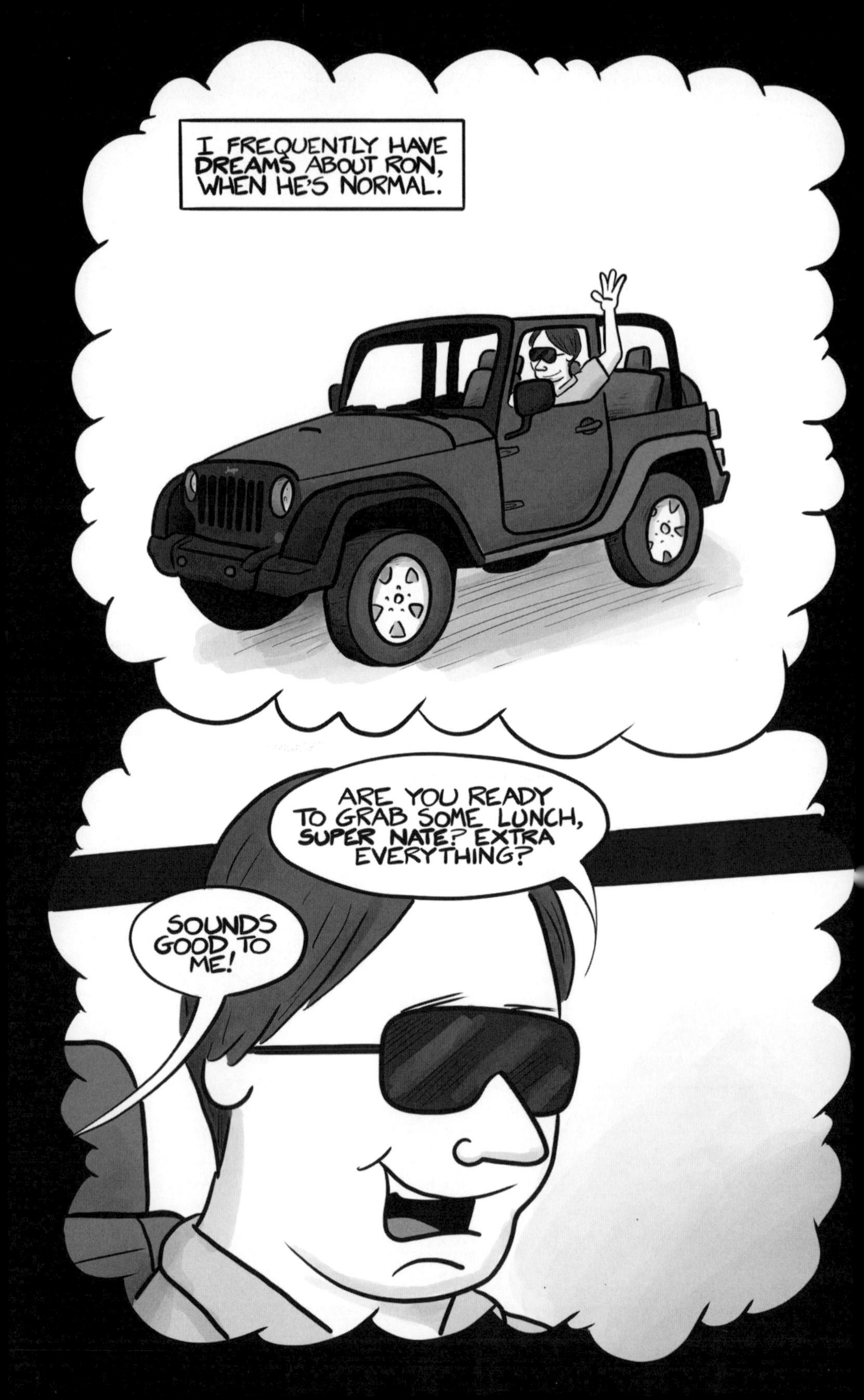
I FREQUENTLY HAVE DREAMS ABOUT RON, WHEN HE'S NORMAL.
ARE YOU READY TO GRAB SOME LUNCH, SUPER NATE? EXTRA EVERYTHING?
SOUNDS GOOD TO ME!

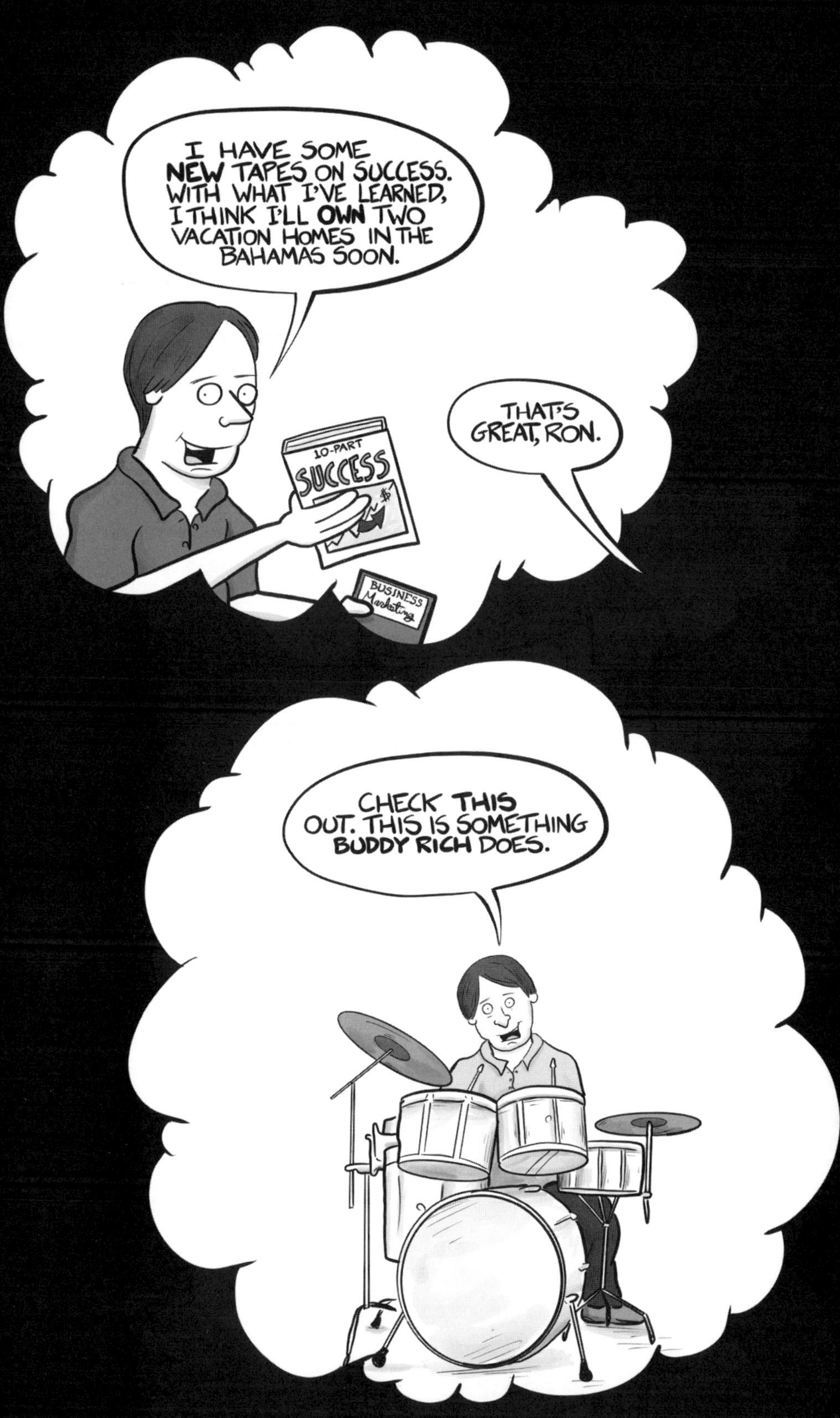
I HAVE SOME NEW TAPES ON SUCCESS. WITH WHAT I'VE LEARNED, I THINK I'LL OWN TWO VACATION HOMES IN THE BAHAMAS SOON.
10-PART SUCCESS
BUSINESS Marketing
THAT'S GREAT, RON.
CHECK THIS OUT. THIS IS SOMETHING BUDDY RICH DOES.

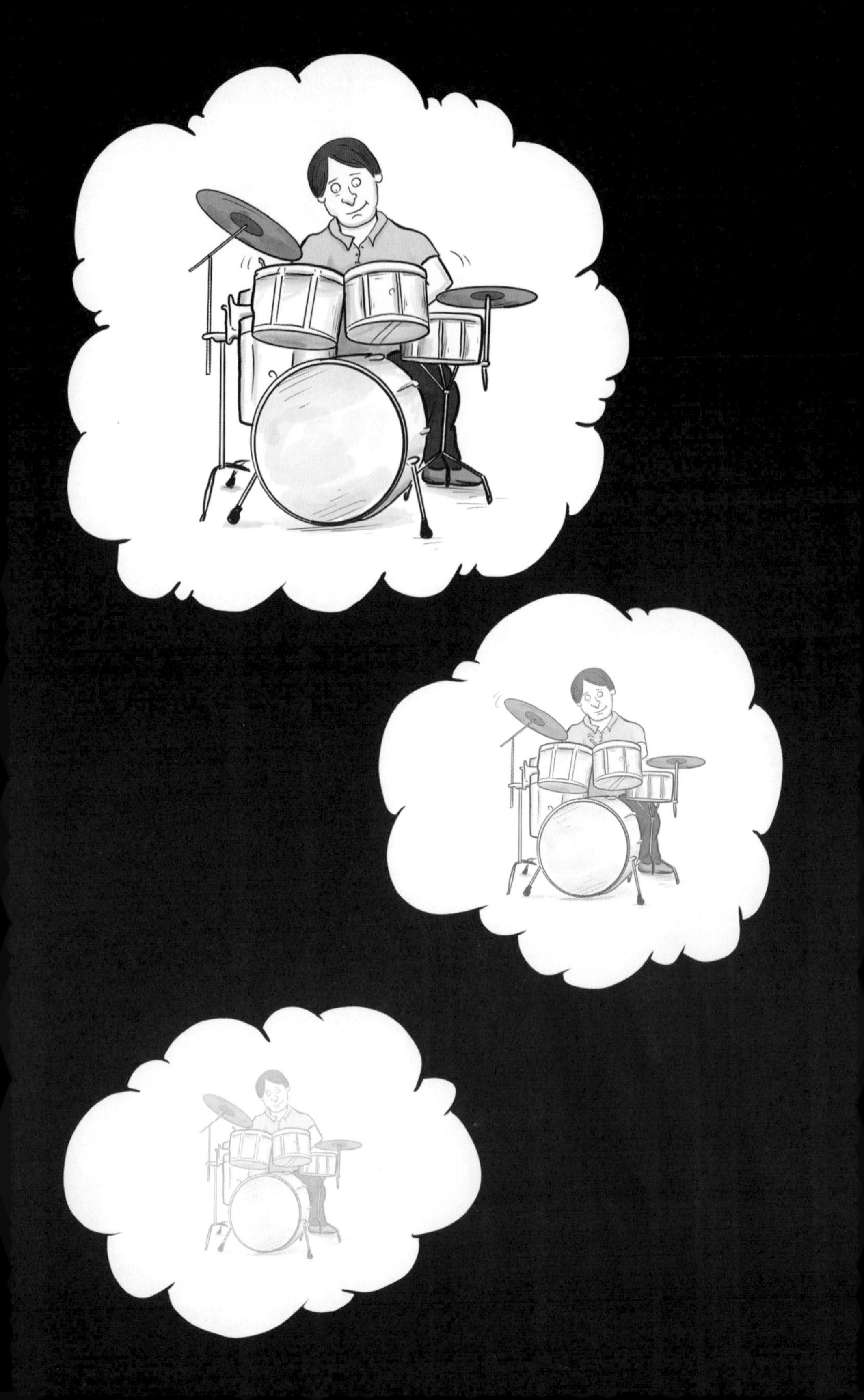

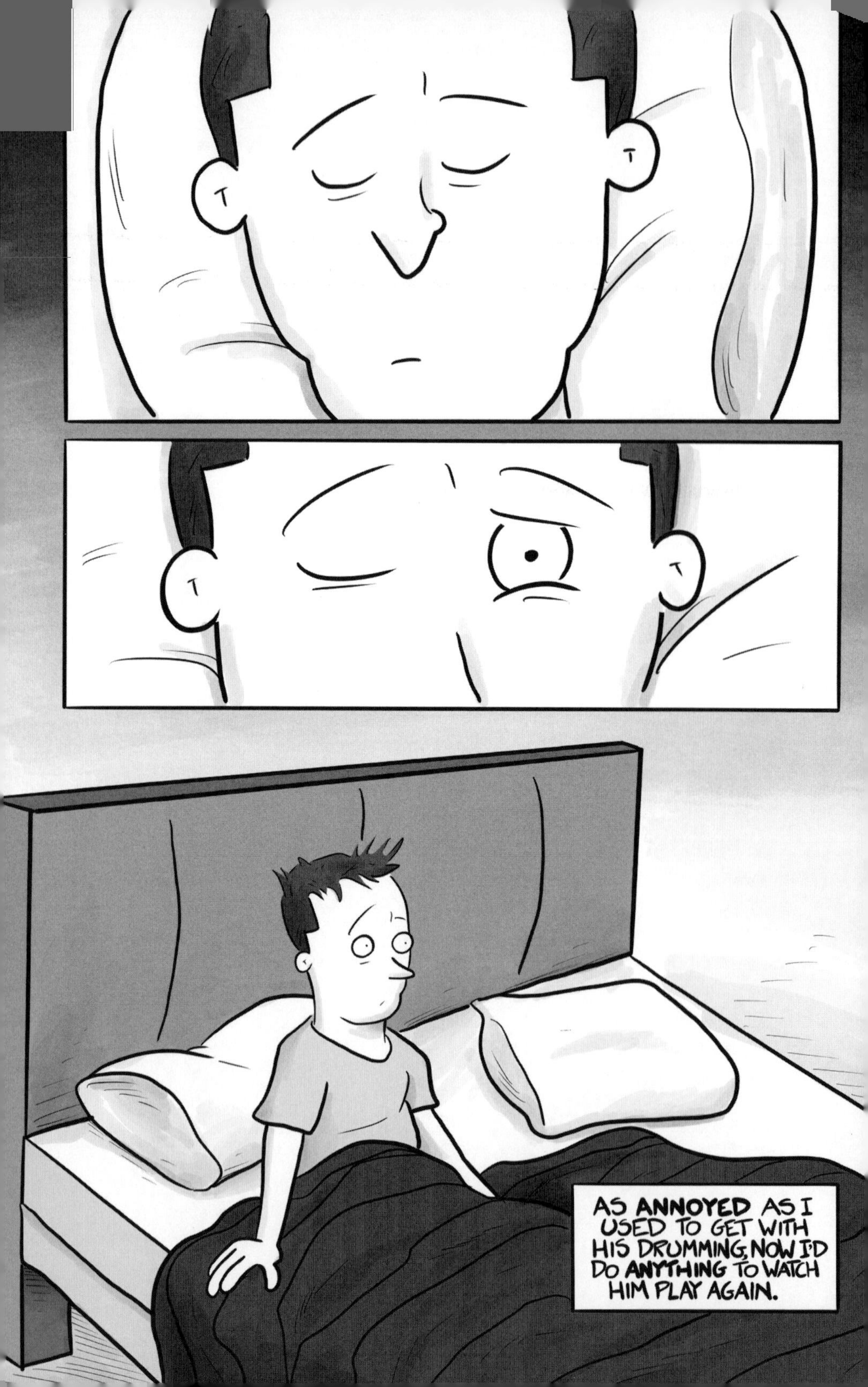
AS ANNOYED AS I USED TO GET WITH HIS DRUMMING, NOW I'D DO ANYTHING TO WATCH HIM PLAY AGAIN.

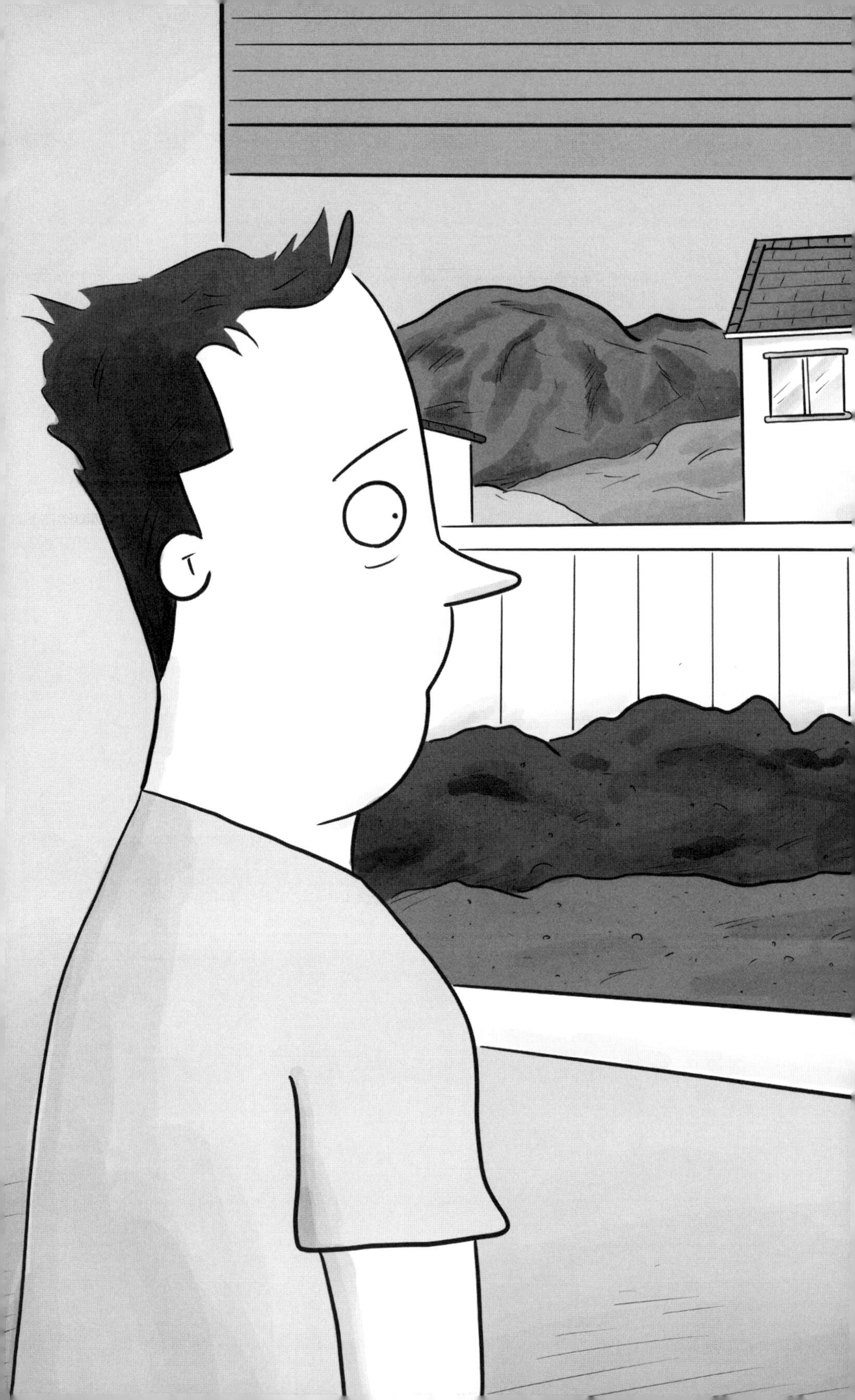

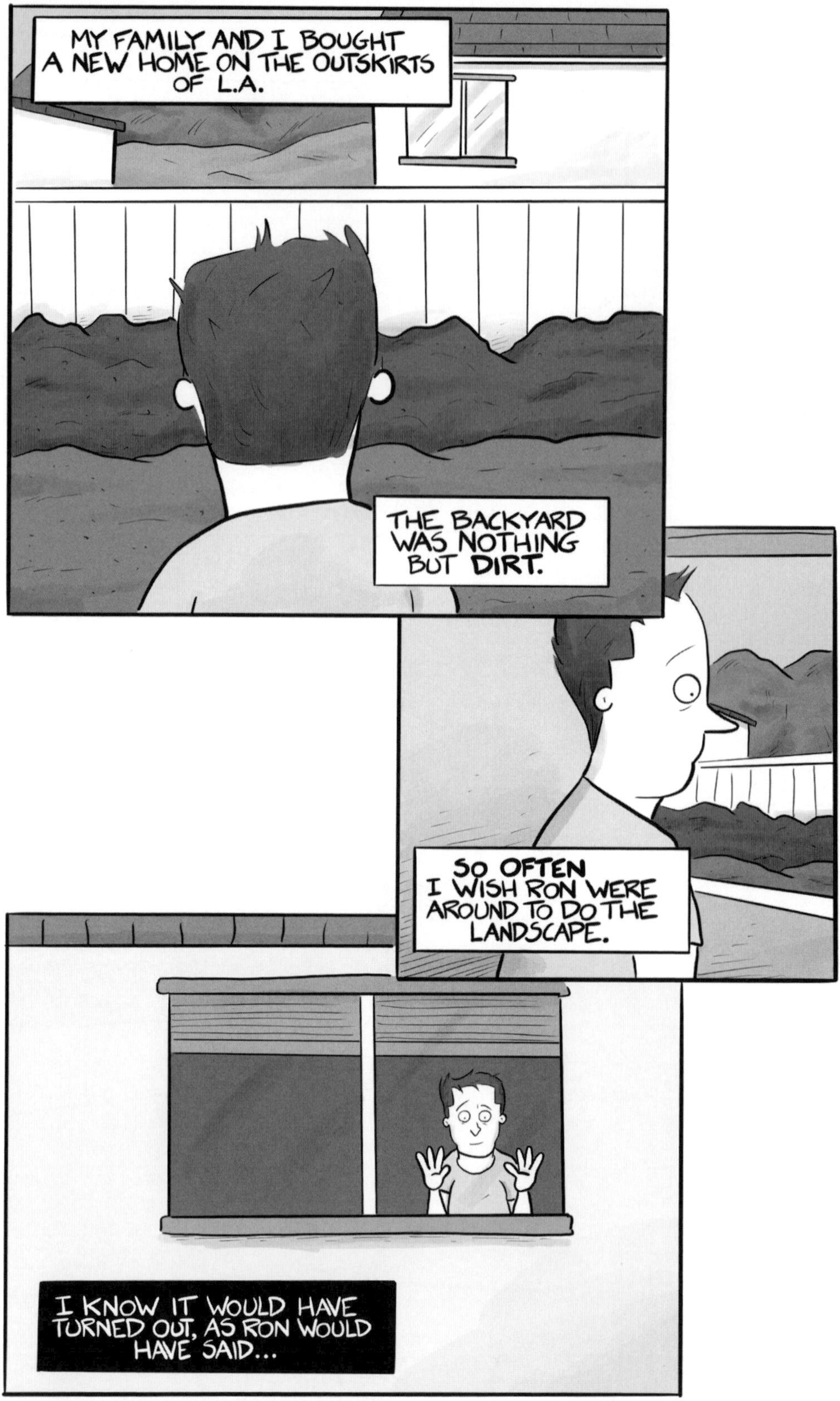
MY FAMILY AND I BOUGHT A NEW HOME ON THE OUTSKIRTS OF L.A.
THE BACKYARD WAS NOTHING BUT DIRT.
SO OFTEN I WISH RON WERE AROUND TO DO THE LANDSCAPE.
I KNOW IT WOULD HAVE TURNED OUT, AS RON WOULD HAVE SAID...

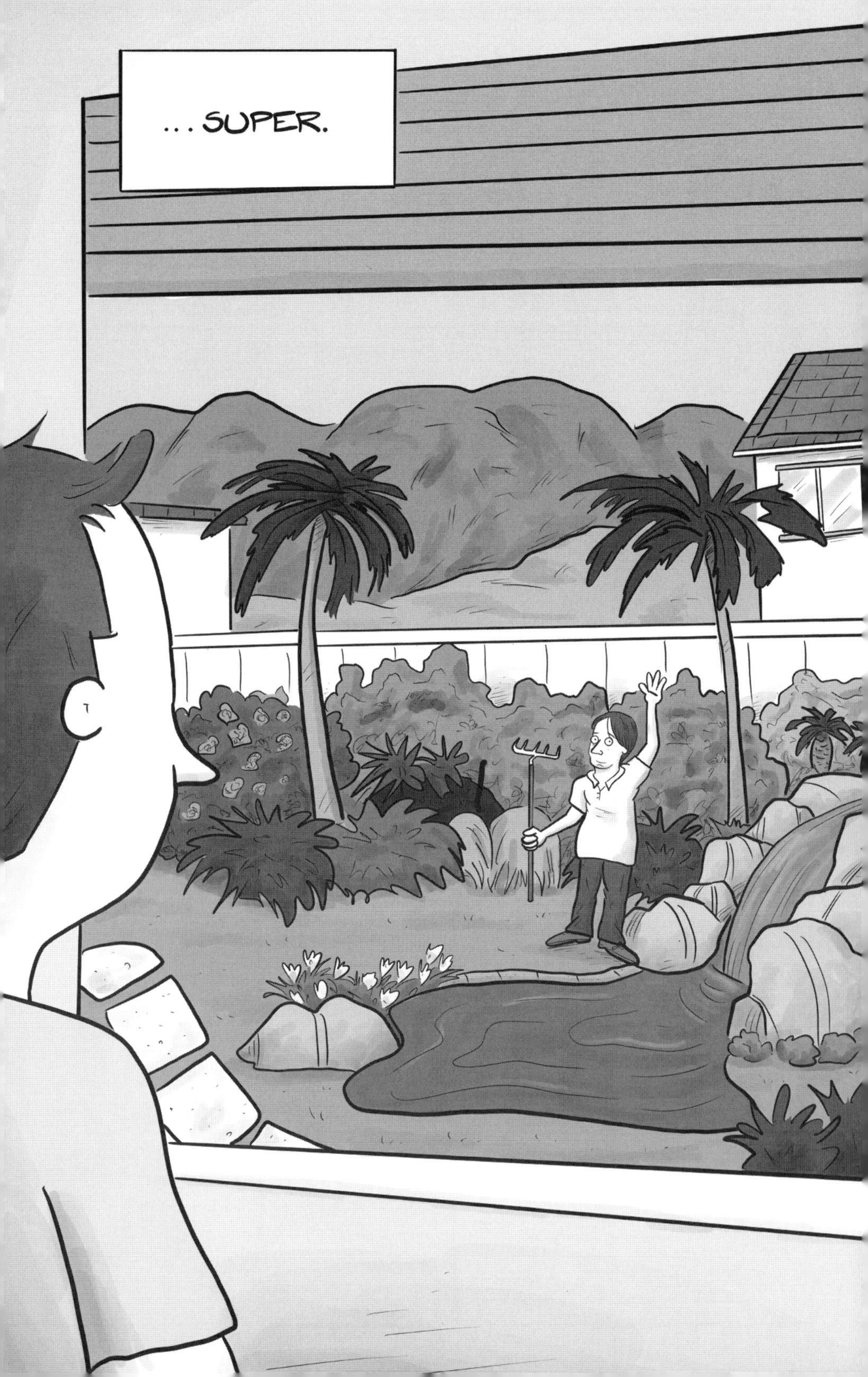
. . . SUPER.

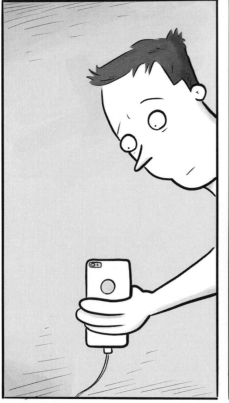

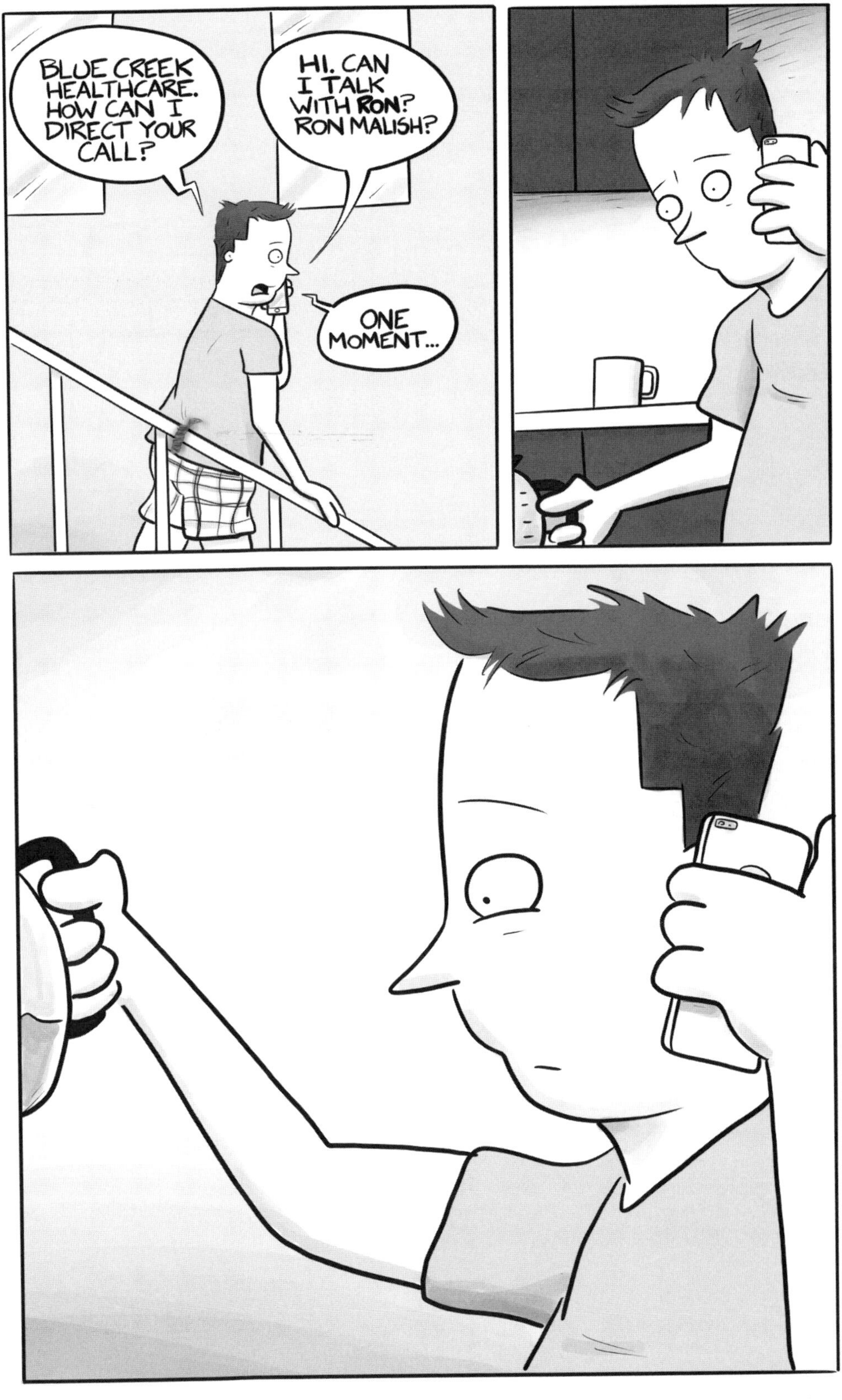

BLUE CREEK HEALTHCARE. HOW CAN I DIRECT YOUR CALL?
HI. CAN I TALK WITH RON? RON MALISH?
ONE MOMENT...

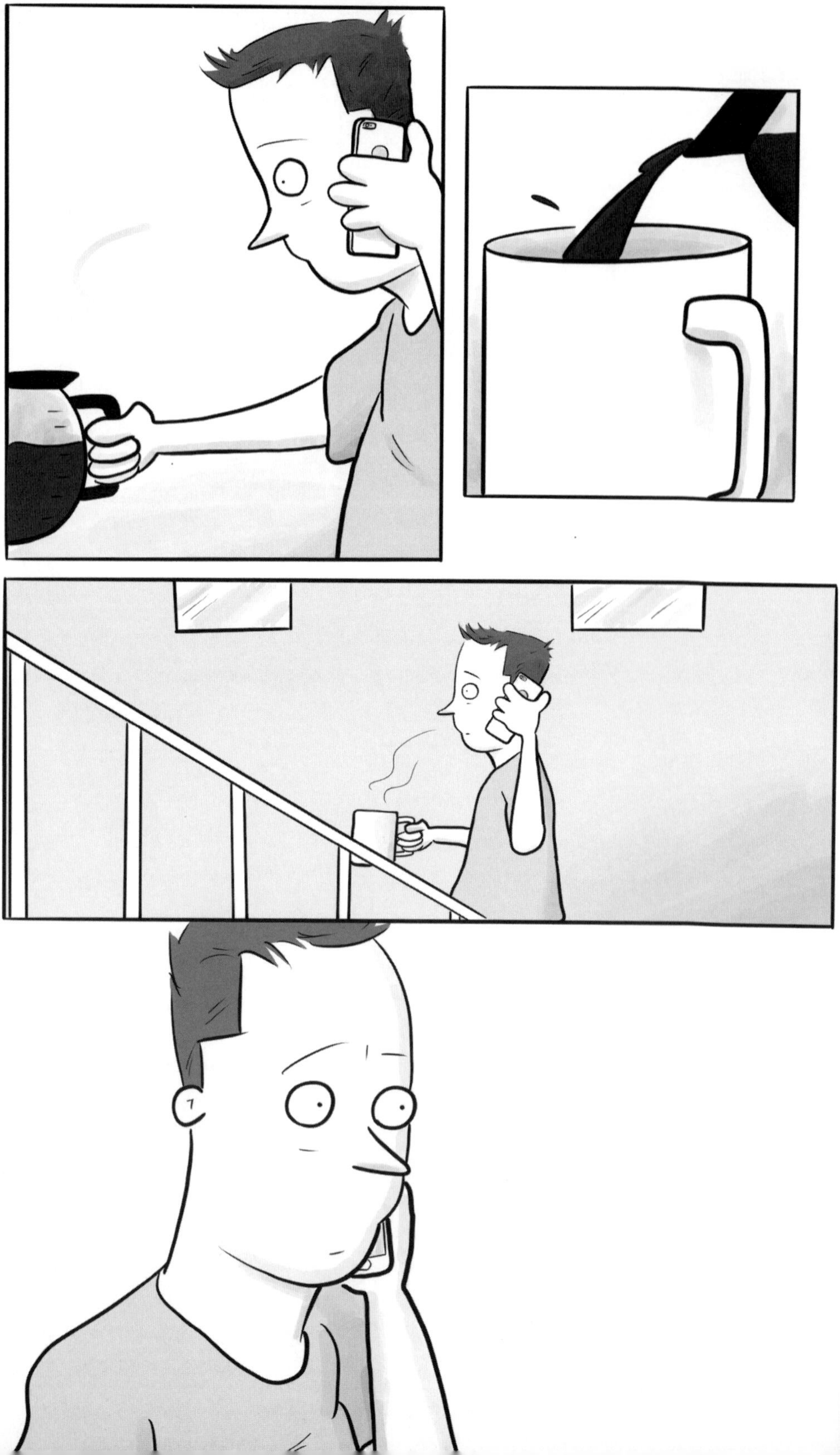

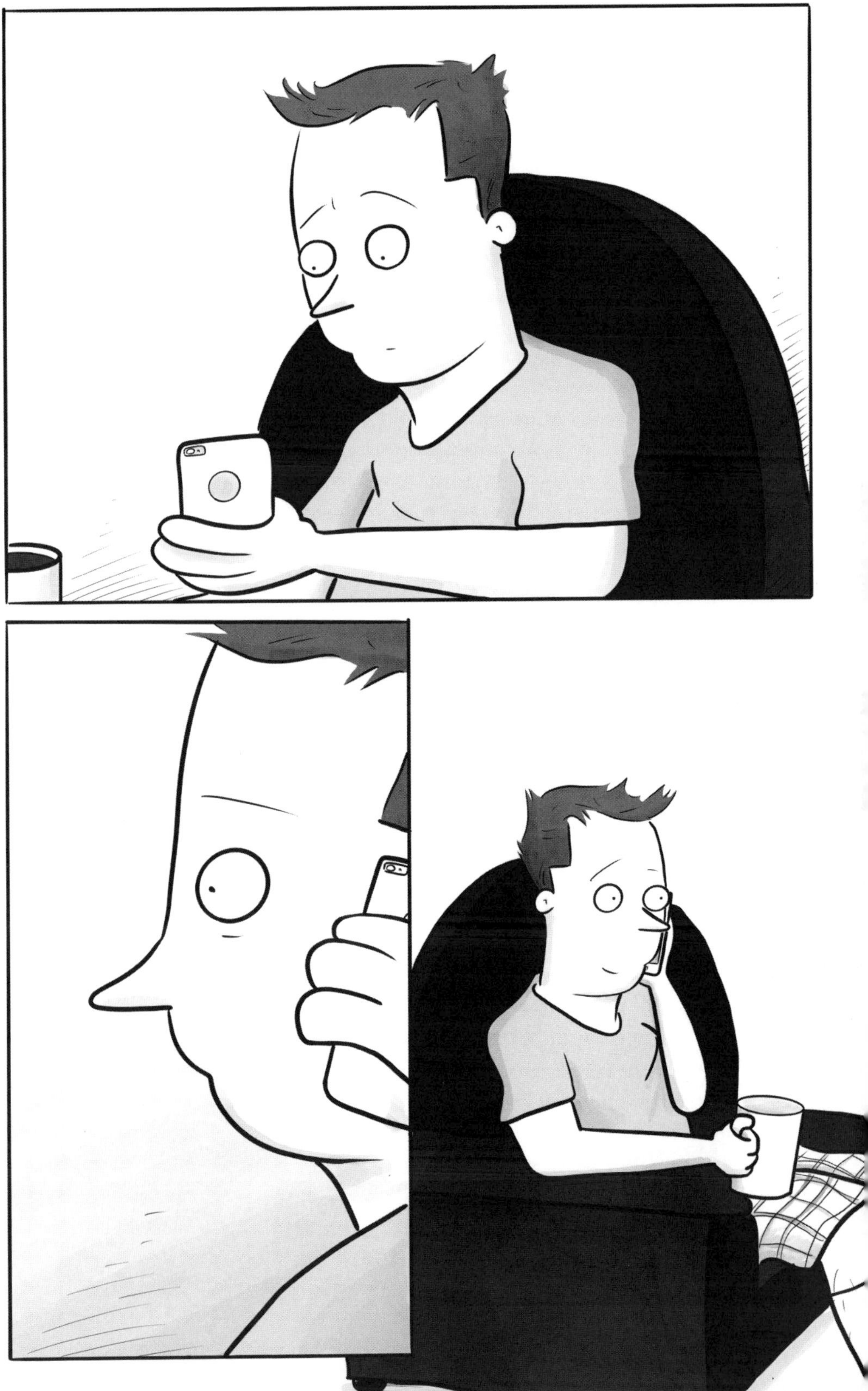

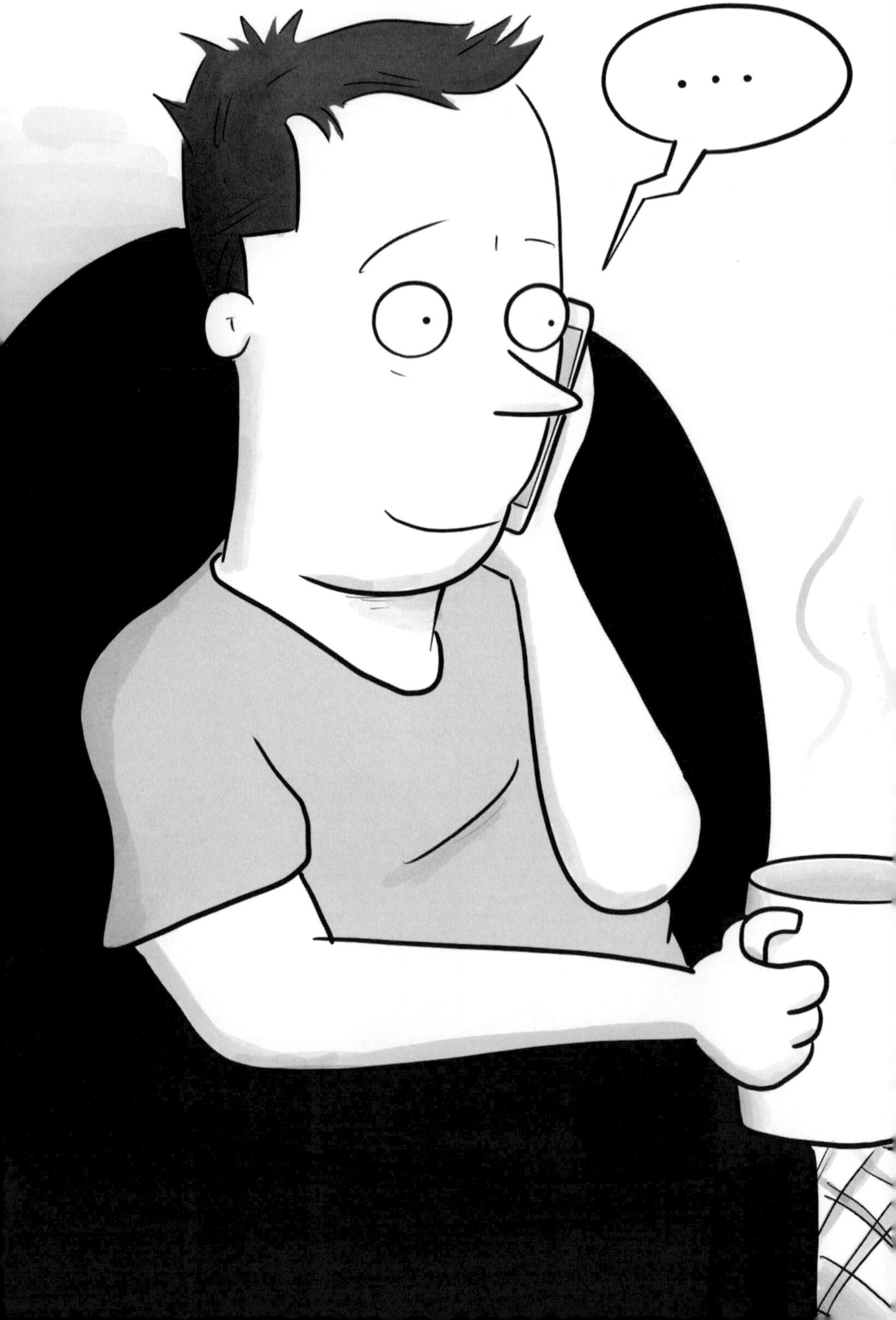
. . .

AT THE TIME
OF WRITING THE CONCLUSION
TO THIS BOOK, RON IS 59
YEARS OLD.

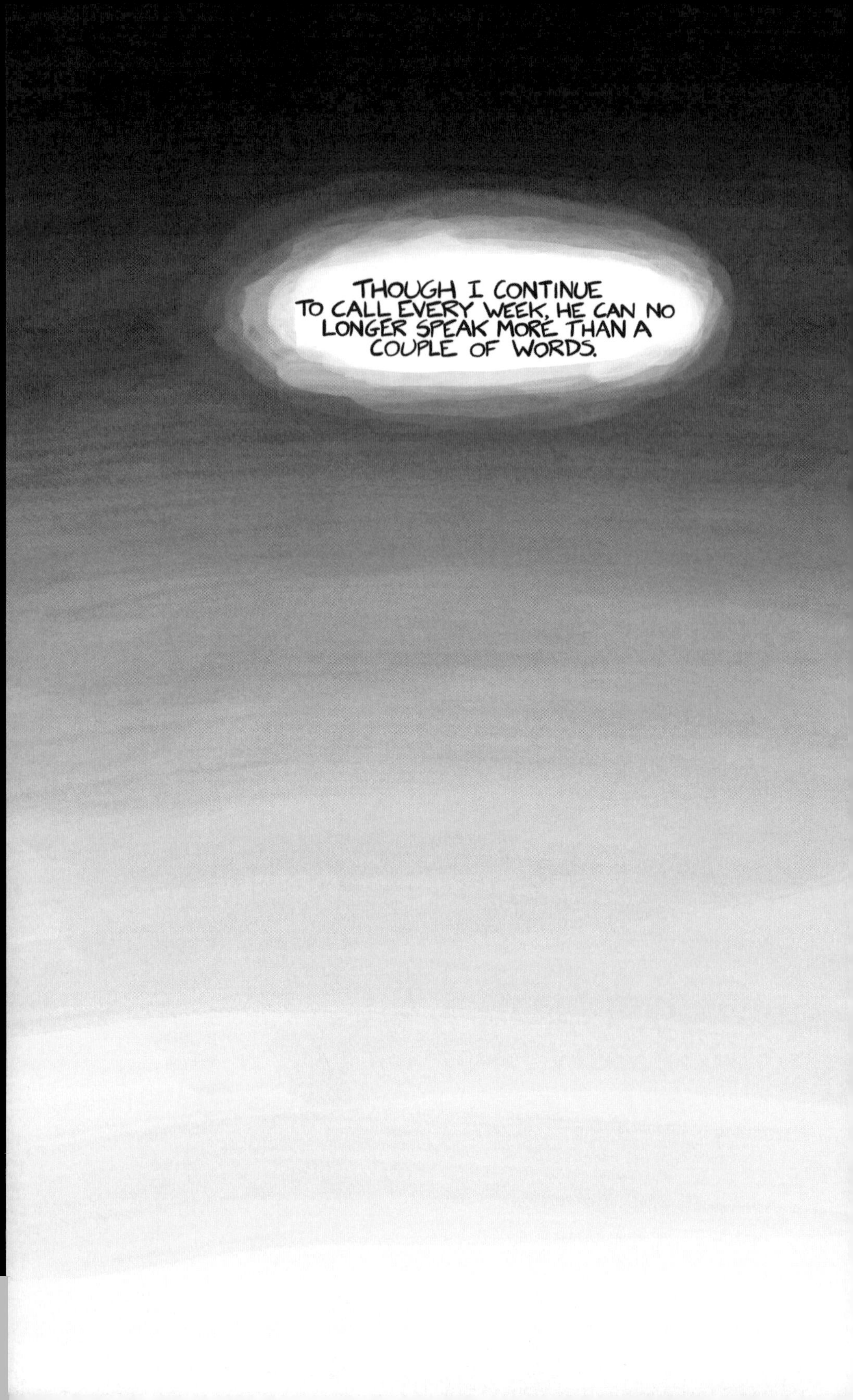
THOUGH I CONTINUE TO CALL EVERY WEEK, HE CAN NO LONGER SPEAK MORE THAN A COUPLE OF WORDS.

ABOUT 50,000 TO 60,000
PEOPLE IN THE UNITED STATES
HAVE PICK'S DISEASE,
ALSO KNOWN AS FRONTOTEMPORAL
DEMENTIA (FTD).

IT AFFECTS
THE PARTS OF THE BRAIN
ASSOCIATED WITH BEHAVIOR,
PERSONALITY, AND LANGUAGE.

PEOPLE WITH
FTD ARE FREQUENTLY
MISDIAGNOSED.

IT CAN TAKE MORE
THAN THREE YEARS TO
GET AN ACCURATE DIAGNOSIS.

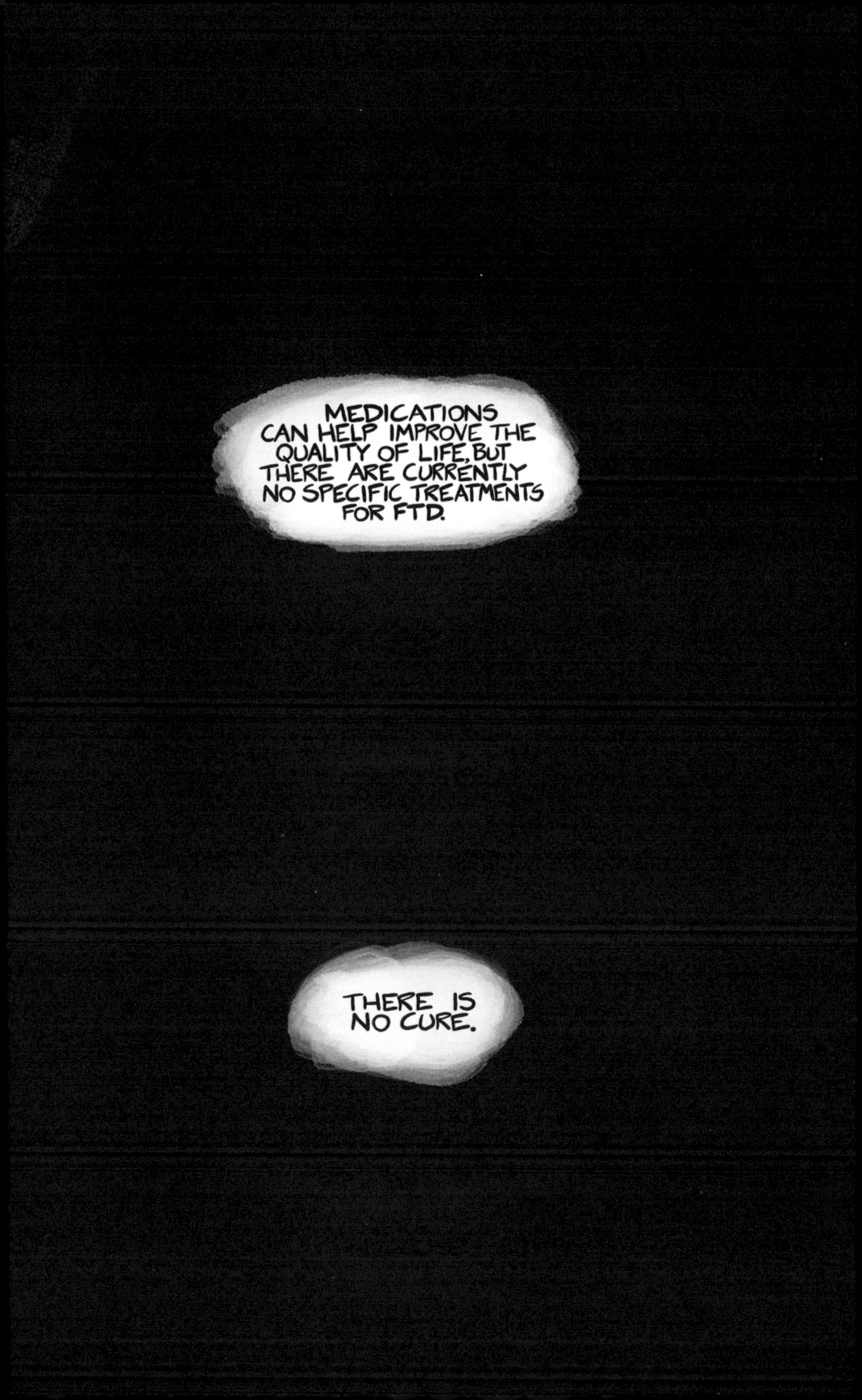
MEDICATIONS CAN HELP IMPROVE THE QUALITY OF LIFE, BUT THERE ARE CURRENTLY NO SPECIFIC TREATMENTS FOR FTD.
THERE IS NO CURE.

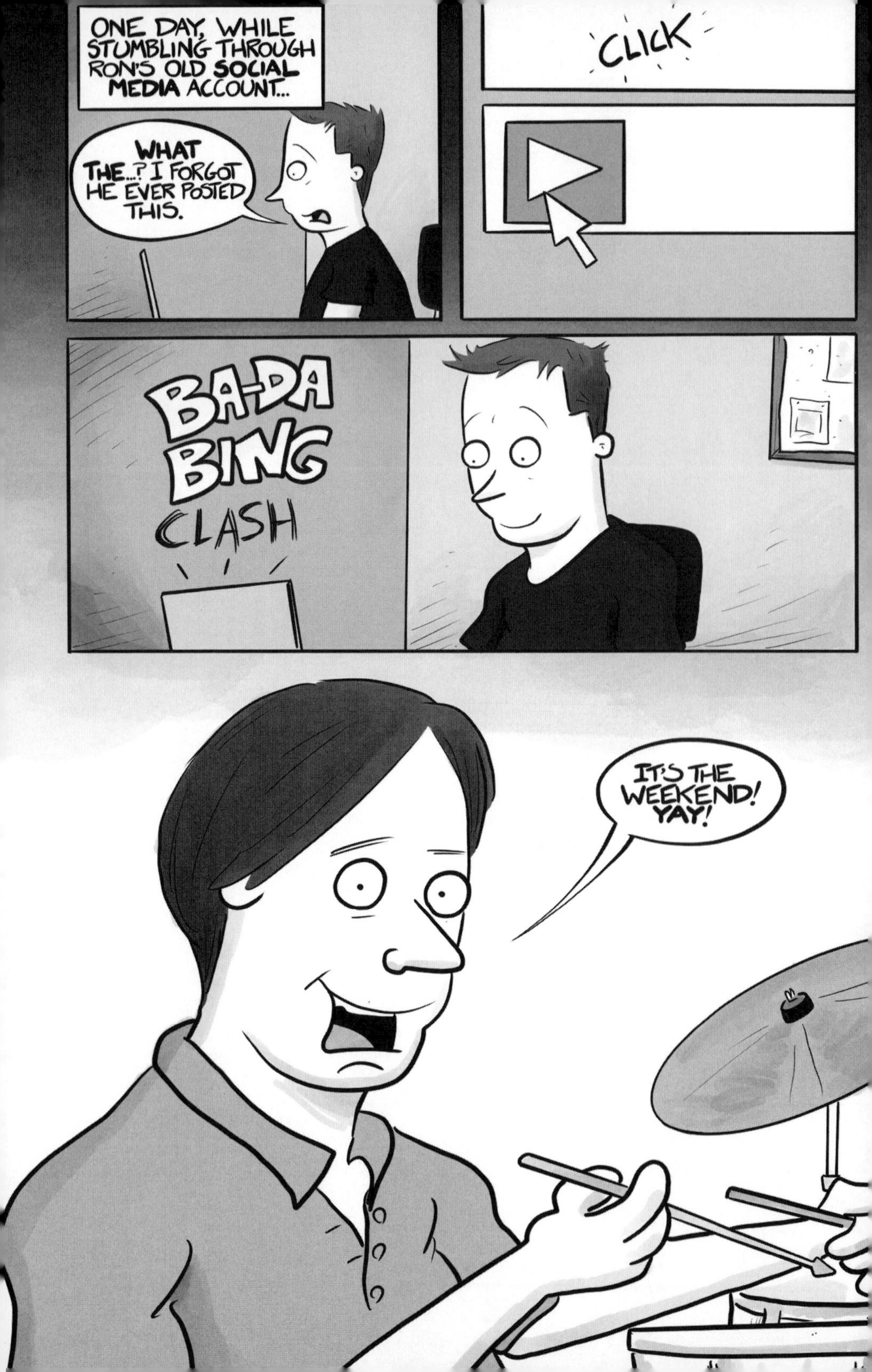
ONE DAY, WHILE STUMBLING THROUGH RON'S OLD SOCIAL MEDIA ACCOUNT...
WHAT THE...? I FORGOT HE EVER POSTED THIS.
CLICK
BA-DA BING
CLASH
IT'S THE WEEKEND! YAY!

GENERAL INFORMATION

LEARN ABOUT FTD, ALZHEIMER'S, AND OTHER TYPES OF DEMENTIA:

ALZHEIMER'S ASSOCIATION: HTTPS://WWW.ALZ.ORG

ASSOCIATION FOR FRONTOTEMPORAL DEGENERATION: HTTPS://WWW.THEAFTD.ORG

DEMENTIA FRIENDLY AMERICA: HTTPS://WWW.DFAMERICA.ORG

NATIONAL ALZHEIMER'S AND DEMENTIA RESOURCE CENTER: HTTPS://NADRC.ACL.GOV

CAREGIVER HELP AND SUPPORT

FOR FAMILY CAREGIVERS, FIND LOCAL SUPPORT GROUPS AND SHARE INFORMATION:

CAREGIVER ACTION NETWORK: HTTPS://CAREGIVERACTION.ORG

NATIONAL ALLIANCE FOR CAREGIVING: HTTPS://WWW.CAREGIVING.ORG

CLINICAL TRIALS

FOR THOSE WHO HAVE OR THINK THEY HAVE DEMENTIA, PARTICIPATE IN SAFE SCIENTIFIC RESEARCH STUDIES WHILE RECEIVING MEDICAL CARE:

ALZHEIMER'S DISEASE RESEARCH CENTER: HTTPS://WWW.NIA.NIH.GOV/HEALTH/ALZHEIMERS-DISEASE-RESEARCH-CENTERS

UCSF MEMORY AND AGING CENTER: HTTPS://MEMORY.UCSF.EDU/RESEARCH-TRIALS/RESEARCH

ACKNOWLEDGMENTS

THIS BOOK COULD NOT HAVE BEEN MADE WITHOUT THE SUPPORT OF MANY PEOPLE.

FIRST OF ALL, HERE AT HOME, MY WIFE, KELSEY FAKES, WHO HELD IN THERE WITH ME THROUGH 12-HOUR DAYS OF WORKING MY REGULAR GIGS, ALL WHILE WRITING AND DRAWING A FADE OF LIGHT. IT TOOK ABOUT TWO YEARS FROM CONCEPTION TO FINISH, AND I THANK HER FOR HER PATIENCE WHILE I PLOWED THROUGH THIS EMOTIONALLY EXHAUSTING WORK. PLUS, MY DAUGHTER, ELLA. SHE'S THE LITTLE CHEERLEADER WHO ALWAYS MAKES ME SMILE— WHICH WAS GREAT FOR THE TIMES WHEN PARTS OF THIS BOOK WERE HARD TO MAKE.

OF COURSE, I HAVE TO MENTION MY FATHER AND MOTHER, DENNIS FAKES AND JANIS FAST. I KNOW THIS BOOK MIGHT BE DIFFICULT FOR BOTH OF YOU IN A FEW WAYS TO READ, SO THANK YOU FOR YOUR SUPPORT AND UNDERSTANDING.

MY BROTHER-IN-LAW AND SISTER, DAVE AND CARA DEVER. YOU GUYS HAVE ALWAYS BEEN INTERESTED IN WHAT I'M UP TO AND HAVE ALWAYS HELPED KEEP ME GOING, JUST WITH YOUR INTEREST ALONE.

ALONG WITH THAT, MY EXTENDED FAMILY ON MY SIDE AND MY WIFE'S, AND MY FRIENDS. THANKS FOR SUPPORTING MY WORK AND FOR ALL OF YOUR INQUIRIES ABOUT HOW THE BOOK WAS COMING ALONG WHILE I WAS WRITING IT.

I COULDN'T ASK FOR A BETTER AGENT, MATT BELFORD, WHO REALLY SPARKED THIS FROM AN IDEA TO PRODUCTION. I PITCHED SEVERAL IDEAS HIS WAY, AND THE STORY OF MY STEPDAD WAS SOMETHING HE FELT WAS WORTH PURSUING, SO I DID. THIS BOOK WOULDN'T HAVE HAPPENED WITHOUT HIM AND HIS HELP. THANKS FOR SEEING MY POTENTIAL IN THIS PROJECT WHEN I WASN'T EVEN SURE OF IT.

YVONNE AND CURTIS KLOTZ. YOUR SHARED MEMORIES AND RECONNECTING WITH YOU HELPED A TON WITH GETTING THIS PUT TOGETHER. THANKS FOR YOUR SUPPORT THROUGH ALL OF THIS.

A BIG SHOUTOUT TO THE TEAM AT WEST MARGIN, ESPECIALLY OLIVIA NGAI, RACHEL METZGER, AND JENNIFER NEWENS—YOU ALL WENT ABOVE AND BEYOND ENSURING THE MANUSCRIPT AND ART WAS PUSHED TO THE BEST THAT IT CAN BE. THANKS FOR TAKING A CHANCE ON THIS STORY.

ADDITIONALLY, ALL THE FRIENDS, COLLEAGUES, AND FAMILY WHO I REACHED OUT TO BE INCLUDED IN PARTS OF THE BOOK. YOU HELPED BRING THIS TO LIFE AS ACCURATELY AS POSSIBLE. I WISH I WAS A BETTER CARICATURE ARTIST, BUT I HOPE YOU CAN APPRECIATE MY EFFORTS IN YOUR LIKENESS.

LAST BUT NOT LEAST, OF COURSE, RON. MY FAVORITE DRUMMER. I HOPE THIS IS A BOOK YOU WOULD'VE GIVEN ME A HIGH-FIVE FOR.

NATE FAKES sold his first cartoon in fifth grade, and throughout middle and high school he drew all day instead of paying attention in class. Now he is a storyboard artist, commercial illustrator, cartoonist, and book author. His work has been published in publications like *MAD Magazine* and the *New York Times*, and in numerous books, greeting cards, and advertisements. He is the author of *Break of Day*, a syndicated comic series that has been read worldwide in print and online. Nate lives near Los Angeles, California. Visit him at nfakes.com and @nate_fakes on Instagram.